# Loring
# A Trustee's Handbook

# Loring
# A Trustee's Handbook

1998 Edition

**Charles E. Rounds, Jr.**

*Professor of Law*
*Suffolk University Law School*

*Member*
*Massachusetts Bar*

*Fellow*
*American College of Trust*
*and Estate Counsel*

with

**Eric P. Hayes**

*Vice President and*
*Senior Trust Counsel*
*State Street Global Advisors*
*Member, Massachusetts Bar*

*Formerly published by*
*Little, Brown and Company*

A Panel Publication
Aspen Publishers, Inc.

Permissions
Panel Publishers
A Division of Aspen Publishers, Inc.
1185 Avenue of the Americas
New York, NY 10036

Printed in the United States of America

Library of Congress Catalog Card No. 96-78933

ISBN 1-56706-596-1

# About Panel

Panel Publishers — comprising the former Prentice Hall Law & Business, Little, Brown and Company's Professional Division, and Wiley Law Publications — is a leading publisher of authoritative and timely treatises, practice manuals, information services, and journals written by specialists to assist attorneys, financial and tax advisors, and other business professionals. Our mission is to provide practical, solution based how-to information keyed to the latest legislative, judicial, and regulatory developments.

We offer publications in the areas of compensation and benefits, pensions, employment, civil rights, taxation, estate planning, and elder law.

Other Panel products treating trust and estate issues include:

Estate Planning
Estate and Retirement Planning Answer Book
Estate and Retirement Planning Answer Book: Forms and Checklists
Federal Income Taxation of Estates, Trusts, and Beneficiaries

Income Taxation of Fiduciaries and Beneficiaries
Multistate and Multinational Estate Planning
Price on Contemporary Estate Planning
Scott on Trusts

**PANEL PUBLISHERS**
**A Division of Aspen Publishers, Inc.**
**A Wolters Kluwer Company**
**Practical Solutions for Legal and Business Professionals**

## SUBSCRIPTION NOTICE

This Panel product is updated on a periodic basis with supplements to reflect important changes in the subject matter. If you purchased this product directly from Panel, we have already recorded your subscription for the update service.

If, however, you purchased this product from a bookstore and wish to receive future updates and revised or related volumes billed separately with a 30-day examination review, please contact our Customer Service Department at 1-800-234-1660, or send your name, company name (if applicable), address, and the title of the product to:


**PANEL PUBLISHERS**
**A Division of Aspen Publishers, Inc.**
**7201 McKinney Circle**
**Frederick, MD 21701**

# Summary of Contents

# Contents

# Foreword to the Centennial Edition (1998 Edition)

The first edition of *A Trustee's Handbook,* by Augustus Peabody Loring, appeared in 1898. Mr. Loring, who saw his brainchild through its fourth edition, was a practicing lawyer and a Boston trustee. In the 40 years that passed before his death, his small, compact Handbook played an important role in the dramatic growth of trust administration in this country. It quickly became the trustee's text of first resort. In 1940 Professor Scott wrote that for more than three decades the Handbook had been on his desk or near at hand. Mayo Adams Shattuck, Esq. and James F. Farr, Esq. prepared the Handbook's fifth (1940) and sixth (1962) revisions respectively.

In 1994 the Handbook was given a new lease on life with the publication of the Seventh Edition in hardcover. That was followed by the 1996 Edition in softcover, and then the 1997 Edition also in softcover. The 1998 Edition in hardcover marks the passing of the publishing baton from Little, Brown & Company to Aspen Law & Business. 1998 also marks the 100th anniversary of the Handbook's existence.

I was fortunate to be Professor Rounds' chief student research assistant when he took on the challenge in 1992 of preparing the

Seventh Edition. Times had changed since 1962. The state was now dispensing many more entitlements and regulating commercial activity far more intensely than had been the case thirty years earlier. In the late 1960s — perhaps in response to these developments — law schools had set about the process of downgrading courses in the law of trusts from required to elective status, so that by the early 1990's, while almost all law schools had made courses on state regulation mandatory, only a few (most notably Suffolk University Law School in Boston) were continuing to afford the law of trusts the status it had enjoyed in Mr. Loring's time. In most law schools, the law of trusts had become an afterthought, buried somewhere in an elective course on estate planning. Professor Rounds and I, therefore, could not assume — as Mr. Loring could and surely did — that the young lawyers who would read the Seventh Edition had had any formal instruction in the law of trusts.

Moreover, much had happened in the field of trusts since 1962. The years since then had seen major developments in the area of creditors' rights, spousal rights, and Medicaid eligibility and recoupment. ERISA would not arrive on the scene until 1974. There was no such thing as an IRA or Keogh plan. RICO, CERCLA, and the consumer protection statutes had yet to be enacted. It would be many years before the social investment movement would come into its own. These are just some of the developments that had to be worked into the Seventh Edition.

The challenge of revamping and updating the Handbook proved a daunting task. Working off a table of contents that he had redesigned, Professor Rounds would compose the text, footnotes, and end matter on his word processor. As each chapter was completed, I would parcel various sections of it out to the other research assistants. They would then get to work tying up loose ends and cite checking. Processing and keeping track of the myriad drafts was perhaps the most rewarding of all the support tasks as I was the only one, besides Professor Rounds, who had a sense of the big picture. It was exciting to watch the Seventh Edition inexorably congeal. Professor Rounds set the pace for all of us by working nights, weekends, and holidays for months on end. He wanted the final product to be something of which we all could be proud. His energy, enthusiasm, and intellectual rigor were contagious.

The Seventh Edition was not to be a treatise. We wanted it to be a handy, ready reference: a gateway, as it were, to the treatises, restatements, law review articles, uniform statutes, and seminal cases. In 1898, Mr. Loring had succeeded in producing just such a book. Through the Seventh Edition we were endeavoring to revive and carry on the Loring tradition. In my opinion, we accomplished what we had set out to do.

Now comes the 1998 Edition. Though it is much enhanced from earlier editions, Professor Rounds would be the first to admit that it stands on the shoulders of others. Much, of course, is owed to those who appear in the Acknowledgments. But much also is owed to those who participated in the Loring Project during the Loring, Shattuck and Farr eras: Nathaniel Thayer, Herman Weisman, Frederick W. Doring, Samuel Vaughan, Arthur Drinkwater, Frank L. Wiegand, Jr., Stuart MacMillan, William M. Prest, Harold S. Davis, B. Devereux Barker, Levon Kasarjian, Jr., and Roger B. Hunt.

*George J. McElroy, Jr.*

April 8, 1998

# Preface to the Centennial Edition (1998 Edition)

**New features and enhancements.** The last edition contained only a few paragraphs on the *federal income taxation of trusts.* The Centennial Edition has an entire chapter, Chapter 10, devoted to the subject. It includes an introduction to the federal fiduciary income tax; sections on income, deductions, and tax and payments; the 1998 tax rate schedule for trusts; and material devoted to practical information on when and how to file. A copy of the Form 1041 and its accompanying schedules is reprinted in Appendix III.

The Handbook's coverage of the *federal estate and generation-skipping tax* has been substantially enhanced as well. There are now sections on tax-sensitive powers, tax apportionment within trusts, the Charitable Remainder Unitrust (CRUT), the Charitable Remainder Annuity Trust (CRAT), the IRS-approved Charitable Lead Trust, the Qualified Domestic Trust (QDOT), and the Qualified Personal Residence Trust (QPRT). There are also materials on the interaction of the estate and generation-skipping tax and on those situations when a trustee must prepare and file the estate tax returns of a deceased settlor, beneficiary, or power-holder. The implications of recent domestic asset protection legislation for the federal estate tax (and the implications of recent initiatives to abolish the Rule Against Perpetuities for the generation-skipping tax) are also discussed.

**Important developments in the law of trusts since April 1998.** *Regulation 9 was revised,* effective January 29, 1997. There is now a separate section on the revision, which is reprinted in Appendix II. All references to the regulation throughout the text and footnotes have been inventoried and revised to accommodate the many changes brought about by the revision.

Fortunately, the *Taxpayer Relief Act of 1997* was enacted into law before press time. Accordingly, the Handbook charts the incremental *increase in the unified credit* culminating in $1 million for the year 2006 and thereafter. The legislation also substantially does away with the *throwback rules* for domestic trusts. This long overdue simplification of the federal tax code is flagged in Chapter 10.

The Centennial Edition contains a section on the initiatives of Alaska and Delaware to become *domestic asset protection havens.* Elsewhere, text and footnotes — including, as mentioned, the tax sections — have been revised to accommodate this development. There is a section on the *initiatives of at least 5 states to abolish in whole or in part the Rule Against Perpetuities* and what the implications of all of this may be for the institution of the trust. This edition flags the recent approval by the National Commissioners on Uniform State Laws of the *1997 Update of the Uniform Principal and Income Act.* Text has been revised to accommodate those *recent changes to CERCLA* that are designed to ameliorate the lot of the fiduciary title-holder and to accommodate those changes in the U.S. tax laws that relate to the filing of reports on the establishment of, and receipt of income from, *foreign trusts.* Our region by region mathematical analysis of *standard charge schedules* of corporate trustees has been updated to June 1997. There is now a section on the *non-charitable unitrust movement,* a response to the widespread acceptance of the "total return" approach to investing. A pre-existing section on spousal rights has been enhanced with a discussion of *divorce settlements* that involve equitable interests. Finally, material on the progress of the *evolution of the trust relationship into an "entity"* has been woven into the text and footnotes.

**Miscellaneous topics.** Other topics that have found their way into the Handbook with the Centennial Edition are: *statutory* *trusts; insurance for bank trust departments;* the *condominium trustee; loans of trust assets to current beneficiaries and remaindermen;* the *Common Fund Doctrine;* trust *reformation to remedy faulty tax planning;* the *charitable trust and the doctrine of separation of powers;* and a *bank account (or debt) is not a trust.* There are expanded discussions of *virtual representation,* the *Doctrine of Capture,* the *Massachusetts Rule of Allocation,* and when a trustee may invoke the *attorney-client privilege.*

**Statistics.** The enhanced text is tight, sparse, and efficient in the Loring tradition. At the same time it is rich in new and useful information. In fact, a substantial portion of the Centennial Edition is new. There are more than 100 pages of new text. Besides the new chapter on the income taxation of trust, the Handbook contains 31 new sections or subsections and 189 new footnotes. The Table of Cases contains 51 new entries. 370 items have been added to the already extensive index, which is perhaps the Handbook's most valuable feature. The number of scholarly articles cited in the text and footnotes has increased by 55. Hundreds of footnotes have been revised to conform and integrate cross-references to accommodate the new chapter and the new sections and subsections. And, of course, myriad dated references have been made current.

*Charles E. Rounds, Jr.*

April 8, 1998

# Acknowledgments

I wish to acknowledge the assistance of my current research assistants from Suffolk University Law School: Adam R. Bemporad, John L. Dolan, Jennifer A. Fazzi, Cherie L. Fineberg, Lisa M. Glanvill, Nicholas S. Gray, Brian Howard Kudish, and Kurt Steinkrauss. My thanks again go to John J. Yered, Esq. for continuing to do the mathematics that makes possible the §8.4 region by region analysis of standard charge schedules and to Thomas R. Barker for keeping me current as the Taxpayer Relief Act of 1997 made its way through Congress.

My colleagues: Prof. Joseph Franco, who teaches the law of securities regulation; Prof. Bernard V. Keenan; who teaches the law of property; Prof. Joseph D. Cronin, who teaches constitutional law; Prof. Marc G. Perlin, who specializes in litigation practice and procedure; and Prof. Malcolm M. Donahue, a private trustee, offered valuable suggestions for those portions of the Handbook that touch on their areas of expertise. I am grateful to Dean E. Miller, Esq., recently retired from the Office of the Comptroller of the Currency, for briefing me on the changes to Regulation 9, effective January 29, 1997, and the thinking behind those changes. My thanks also go to Natalie B. Choate, Esq. for sharing with me her in-depth knowledge of the taxation of retirement benefits; to Roland Gray, III, Esq., for sharing with me his in-depth knowledge of structured settlement trusts; and to Donald J. Danilek, Esq. for teaching me the secrets of the off-shore asset protection haven. I again wish to recognize Sanborn Vincent, Esq., Trust Counsel (retired) and to Harrison Gardner, Esq. for sharing with me his practical knowledge of non-charitable unitrusts. The First National Bank of Boston, who introduced me to the world of trusts and endeavored to furnish me with the skills needed to confront its challenges. I acknowledge, as well, Hanson S. Reynolds, Esq. for the invaluable advice and counsel he generously has rendered to me over the years on the scope and direction of the Loring Project. Congratulations to Hanson on his elevation to the post of President-Elect of the American College of Trust and Estate Counsel.

To complete the record, I note in alphabetical order my able past research assistants who are alumni/ae of the Loring Project: Christopher J. Akeley, Linda E. Alsalihi, Nina Bartush, Jennifer M. Callahan, Diana J. Cally, Jessica E. Coccoli, John Condon, Phong T. Dinh, Suzanne Goldberg, Thomas Gormley III, Ann Graglia-Kostos, Ernst Guerrier, Michael F. Hogan, W. Todd Huston, Celia M. Ketley, Cynthia A. Korhonen, John P. Larochelle, Emanuel J. Markis, George J. McElroy, Jr., Colleen J. McHugh, James A. Miller, Salina Millora, Paul J. Moura, Suzanne Marie Murray, Robert S. Nedder, Jr., Melanie Ann Petenaude, Michael J. Riley, Randall Pratt, Gwendolyn Ann Rotter, Anthony Sciaraffa, Mark L. Seiden, John D. Tuerck, and James Patrick Winston.

Finally, thanks as always go to my wife, Alicia, and my sons, Chad and Mark, for cheerfully working their schedules around the seasonal time demands of the Loring Project.

April 8, 1998 *Charles E. Rounds, Jr.*

# Special Notice

The citations to the following books are thus abbreviated:

A. W. Scott & W. F. Fratcher, Scott on Trusts (4th ed. 1987), is cited as "Scott on Trusts."

G. G. Bogert & G. T. Bogert, The Law of Trusts and Trustees (2d ed., Revised, 1984), is cited as "Bogert, Trusts and Trustees."

# Loring
# A Trustee's Handbook

CHAPTER *1*

# Introduction

A trustee holds title to property for the benefit of another. That is the essence of the trust, whose development from century to century is, in the opinion of Professor Maitland, the greatest achievement of English jurisprudence[1] and the largest and most important of equity's exploits.[2] Title is the key to unlocking the secret of the trust. To the person who does not know this, the trust is a vague, elusive, somewhat mysterious concept. Title is what makes the trust work. Title is what gives the trust its utility.

Let us take, for example, the matter of probate avoidance. As title is not in the beneficiary per se, the beneficiary's incapacity or death usually will not interrupt the continuity of the trust's administration. Thus a single trust can substitute for the durable power of attorney, the property guardianship, and the will.

To the lawyer, the trust is a "fiduciary relationship with respect to property, subjecting the person by whom the title to the property is held to equitable duties to deal with the property for

[1]Maitland, Selected Essays 129 (1936), *quoted in* 1 Scott on Trusts §1.
[2]Maitland, Equity 23 (1936), *quoted in* 1 Scott on Trusts §1.

the benefit of another person, which arises as a result of a manifestation of an intention to create it."[3] It is likely that the layman thinks of the trust in quite different terms, as some kind of basket or receptacle. How property gets into the basket and what role the trustee is supposed to play in the matter is never made entirely clear to most laymen.

This is a practical handbook that addresses the rights, duties, and obligations of the parties once the trustee takes title to the trust property, that is, once the property is in the basket. The focus is on "personal" trusts — trusts created by human beings for human beings. Some attention is paid as well to trusts created by corporations for their employees. It should also be noted that trusts are everywhere. Mutual funds are essentially trusts.[4] Much commercial real estate is held in trust. The trust is not merely an estate planning tool.

In this handbook, the term *settlor* encompasses any person who creates a trust, whether by lifetime transfer, by declaring himself trustee (i.e., by *declaration*), or by will. The reader should bear in mind, however, that the usual term for the creator of a testamentary trust is *testator.* A trust created by transfer pursuant to the terms of a will is referred to as a *testamentary* trust. A trust created by lifetime transfer or declaration is referred to as an *inter vivos trust.* The terms *inter vivos trust* and *living trust* are synonymous.

In this handbook, unless otherwise specified, the term *beneficiary* encompasses not only the person who during the life of the trust has some right to the income from — or use of — the trust property but also the remainderman. This interest of the beneficiary of an ongoing trust is known as an *equitable* or *beneficial* interest and is itself a property right.[5]

The trust is a complex legal organism that survives on private property. Its earlier forms predate even the Norman con-

[3]Restatement (Second) of Trusts §2 (1959).

[4]At the end of April 1998, the aggregate value of participations in U.S. mutual funds was $5,048, 317,700,000. *See* R. McGough, Bull Milestone: Mutual Funds Cross the $5 Trillion Mark, Wall St. J., May 28, 1998, pg. C1, col. 3.

[5]Restatement of Property Introductory Note (1936); *See* In re Catherwood's Trust, 173 A.2d 86, 91 (1961) ("A gift of an equitable life estate in income or of a remainder does constitute a grant of a vested property right of which the recipients cannot be divested by legislative action.").

quest.[6] The trust as we know it today is the product of centuries of evolution. It is "an 'institute' of great elasticity and generality; as elastic, as general as contract."[7] It provides enlightened property owners and their lawyers with a mechanism for seeing to the needs of the young, the disabled, and the elderly far more efficiently, far more cost-effectively, far more creatively, far more flexibly, far more expeditiously, and with far more dignity than the state could ever do. In this regard, even a charitable trust is no match for the private personal trust. Only one's imagination limits the purposes for which such trusts may be created. To be sure, the institution of the private personal trust can never accommodate the needs of everyone, but each person in need of assistance who is properly cared for pursuant to its terms is one less person who has to encounter — and be a burden to — the welfare bureaucracy.

For the institution of the trust to flourish, however, there must be a bench and bar that understand the concept of the trust and appreciate its myriad possibilities; and there must be a corps of incorruptible and conscientious trustees. Thus the law has demanded — and must continue to demand — that the trustee be absolutely loyal to the trust, that the trustee act solely in the interest of the beneficiary, and that any behavior on the trustee's part which compromises the trust be subject to judicial sanction.

As a general rule, for a trust to arise, there needs to be *property,*[8] an *intention* to impress a trust on the property,[9] *beneficiaries* that are ascertained or ascertainable within the period of the Rule Against Perpetuities,[10] *title* in the trustee,[11] and an *absence of*

[6]*See* W. F. Fratcher, Trusts *in* VI Intl. Encyclopedia of Comp. Law, ch. 11, pp. 3, 8-20 (Frederick H. Lawson ed. 1973). *See also,* Avini, The Origins of the Modern Trust Revisited, 70 Tulane L-R-1139 (1996) (Suggesting the trust has its origins in Islamic Law). *See generally* §8.12 (Where the Trust is Recognized Outside the United States) and §8.15.1 (Statute of Uses).

[7]Maitland, *supra* note 2.

[8]*See* Chapter 2.

[9]*See generally* I Scott on Trusts §23 (Requirement of Manifestation of Intention).

[10]*See* Chapter 5 (The Beneficiary), §8.2.1 (The Rule Against Perpetuities).

[11]*See* §3.5.1 (Nature and Extent of the Trustee's Estate).

*merger.*[12] There are always exceptions, however. In some jurisdictions, for example, an inter vivos trust with an associated pour over will need not be token funded during the lifetime of the settlor.[13] A statutory trust may exist without the element of intent.[14] Charitable trusts cannot have ascertained beneficiaries.[15]

The fountainhead of the trustee's powers is the trust instrument. The settlor has the right to include in the trust instrument any provision relating to management of property or to the duties and powers of the trustee, provided it is not contrary to public policy or in derogation of the concept of the trust. These provisions, unless varied by the court, are binding upon the trustee and will supersede the default law applicable to trustees that is threaded throughout this handbook. Accordingly, the trustee has no authority to enter into a contract that would have the effect of altering the terms of the trust, absent the consent of *all* the beneficiaries (and perhaps the settlor) or a court order (e.g., a *cy pres* action).[16] Thus, in the words of Mr. Loring, ". . . THE FIRST AND MOST IMPORTANT DUTY OF THE TRUSTEE IS TO STUDY AND BECOME THOROUGHLY FAMILIAR WITH THE PROVISIONS OF THE TRUST INSTRUMENT, AND THEREAFTER TO FOLLOW THEM OUT IMPLICITLY."[17]

[12] *See* §8.7 (Merger).

[13] *See* §2.2.1 (The Pour-over Statute).

[14] *See* §9.16 (Statutory Trusts); *see also,* §3.3 (Involuntary Trustees).

[15] *See* §9.4 (The Charitable Trust).

[16] *See generally* Bogert, Trusts and Trustees §713. The *cy pres* doctrine is discussed in §9.4.3.

[17] *See generally* Easterbrook and Fischel, Contract and Fiduciary Duty, 36 J.L. & Econ., 425, 429 (1993) (Nothing illustrates the contractual character of fiduciary law better than one of the cornerstones of trust law: An express provision in the trust instrument governs over the duty of loyalty in the event of conflict.); *see* Ritchie, Reviewing Wills and Trust Agreements by Trust Legal Counsel, 121 Trusts and Estates 35 (Nov. 1982).

CHAPTER 2

# The Property Requirement



## §2.1 The Property Requirement

As a general rule, a trust cannot exist without property.[1] Any transferable property interest, legal or equitable, may be the subject of a trust. Usually, legal title to the property is in the trustee.[2]

**§2.1** [1]*See generally* 1A Scott on Trusts §74. *But see* §2.2.1, noting that the Uniform Testamentary Additions to Trusts Act has been interpreted as allowing an inter vivos trust to arise without property when there is an associated "pour over" will.

[2]When a trustee holds the beneficial interest in another trust, however, title to the underlying property is in the trustee of the other trust.

### *§2.1.1 The Inter Vivos Trust*

A will is a *testamentary* intrument (*i.e.*, it speaks only at death). An inter vivos trust is not a testamentary instrument. Under the common law, an inter vivos trust arises when title to some interest in property passes to the trustee *during the lifetime of the settlor.*[3] Because a will is *ambulatory* (*i.e.*, it speaks only at death), the mere execution of a will that names a trustee as legatee or devisee under a so-called *pour-over provision* will not alone give rise to an inter vivos trust. This is because no property interest passes at the time of the will's execution. A will may be employed to add property postmortem to a trust already established through an inter vivos property transfer[4] and, of course, to impress a testamentary trust upon probate property. The trustee should be aware, however, that some states have enacted statutes that have somewhat eroded this common law property requirement.[5]

In the context of postmortem additions to a trust in existence prior to the execution of the will, an *agency* is to be contrasted with a *will.* An agency terminates upon the death of the principal.[6] Thus an agent of the settlor acting under a Durable Power of

[3] *See generally* Comment Note — Creation of express trust in property to be acquired in the future, 3 A.L.R. 3d 1416 (1965); Restatement (second) of Trusts §75 (1959).

[4] As a general rule, under the common law the inter vivos trust must be in existence prior to the execution of the pour-over will. *See* Clark v. Citizens Natl. Bank of Collingswood, 38 N.J. Super. 69, 118 A.2d 108 (1955). *But see* Bogert, Trusts and Trustees §106 (suggesting that under the common law a pour-over provision may be effective even though the inter vivos trust comes into existence after the will is executed). *See also* Uniform Probate Code §2-511 comment, 8 U.L.A 156 (1998); *see generally* §8.15.9 (Doctrine of Independent Legal Significance).

[5] *See* §2.2.1.

[6] *But see* Uniform Probate Code §5-504 comment, 8 U.L.A. 423 (1998) which states:

> The death of a principal who has executed a written power of attorney, durable or otherwise, does not revoke or terminate the agency as to the attorney in fact or other person, who, without actual knowledge of the death of the principal, acts in good faith under the power. Any action so taken, unless otherwise invalid or unenforceable, binds successors in interest of the principal.

Attorney may not make postmortem additions of the settlor's property to a trust. To effect such a transfer there must be compliance with the Statute of Wills.

Any transferable interest may be used to establish an inter vivos trust.[7] All a settlor need do, for example, in order to make the settlor's 50 shares of stock the subject of a trust is to have the shares re-registered in the name of the trustee. A simple phone call to a broker should set the re-registration process in motion. Rights under an insurance contract may be transferred during the insured's lifetime to a trust by assigning the policy itself to the trustee or by merely filling out a form designating the trustee as recipient of the insurance proceeds. For a more detailed discussion of funding procedures, see How to Fund a Revocable Living Trust Correctly.[8]

A transferable interest in one trust (perhaps an interest in a realty trust) may be held in another trust (perhaps a revocable inter vivos trust), except if an effective spendthrift provision prevents a beneficiary from making such a transfer.[9]

The antialienation provisions of ERISA should not extend to preventing an employee from making a present revocable transfer of any employee's remainder interest in a qualified employee benefit plan to the trustee of an inter vivos personal trust.[10] Such a transfer could be accomplished merely by the employee's filling out a beneficiary designation form supplied by the employer's human resources office.

One's contractual rights to the personal services of another are probably nontransferable under the terms of the contract and therefore cannot be the subject of a trust.[11] As a matter of public policy, an unlitigated personal injury claim probably cannot be assigned to an inter vivos trustee,[12] although there would seem to

[7] *See generally* 1A Scott on Trusts §74.1.

[8] Schmidt, How to Fund a Revocable Living Trust Correctly, 20 Est. Plan. 67 (No. 2-1993).

[9] *See generally* 2A Scott on Trusts §152.4.

[10] Treas. Reg. §1.401-1(b)(4) (as amended in 1976).

[11] *See generally* S. Williston, Contracts §421 (W. Jaeger ed., 3d ed. 1960).

[12] A claim to unliquidated damages for tortious injury to person or reputation is generally nonassignable, but once such a claim is reduced to judgment it

be no public policy reason why such a claim should not be assignable for probate avoidance purposes to the trustee of a revocable inter vivos trust.

Transferable partial interests may be presently assigned to an inter vivos trustee. Thus, one's interest in property as a tenant in common may be so transferred.[13] Could an inter vivos trust be funded through a joint tenancy with right of survivorship, that is, could a nontrustee settlor hold property jointly with a trustee? Such an arrangement is probably not a viable way of effecting the funding of an inter vivos trust, not because there is no inter vivos transfer of a property interest associated with the creation of a joint interest — there is — but because there may not be a joint tenancy under such circumstances. The interests of the individual and the trustee, while perhaps concurrent, would not be *equal*,[14] for unlike the lifetime of an individual, that of the modern trust tends to be either fixed or perpetual, and not tied to the lifespan of the trustee.[15]

One cannot extinguish one's obligation as a debtor by transferring away the obligation to a trustee.[16] Presumably the right to extinguish the obligation (if any) is lodged with the creditor or his transferee — the one who has the property interest in the debt. Although some commentators disagree on the grounds that one

---

becomes a money debt which *is* assignable. *See generally* 4 A. Corbin, Contracts §857 (1951); 1A Scott on Trusts §79.

[13]In a tenancy in common, each cotenant owns an interest, separate and distinct, that may be transferred at different times (independently of other cotenants). C. Moynihan, Introduction to the Law of Real Property 213-214 (2d ed. 1988).

[14]In a joint tenancy, cotenants have exactly the same rights in their individual proportional interests as the other cotenants have in theirs. Id. at 207.

[15]Under the common law, a corporation and an individual or two corporations could not hold property as joint tenants, but only as tenants in common. This is because a corporation might have a life of unlimited duration that would defeat the individual's right to survivorship. *See generally* 2 Scott on Trusts §103.1 n.1 and accompanying text. By analogy, this principle ought to apply to the trust as well as the corporation. *But see* 2 Scott on Trusts §103.1 on the related issue of whether an individual and a corporation may serve jointly as cotrustees.

[16]An individual must have an interest in property to make a present disposition. An obligor has no property interest in that obligation that is capable of being transferred. 1A Scott on Trusts §§74, 87.

cannot be indebted to oneself,[17] a debtor — at the direction of the creditor — ought to be able to hold the debt in trust for the benefit of another without causing the trust to fail as to that property. This is because in equity the debtor essentially is indebted not to himself but to himself in a fiduciary capacity — to the office of trustee as it were.[18] It should be noted that when a bank trust department invests trust assets in the bank's commercial deposit accounts, the bank is acting as a trustee of its own obligations.[19]

### §2.1.2 *The Testamentary Trust*

The provisions of a testamentary trust are set forth in a will. A testamentary trust arises when title to a portion or all of the decedent's probate estate is transferred from the executor or personal representative to the testamentary trustee. Thus a testamentary trust cannot arise until after the testator dies. Only then does the probate property come into existence, because only then does the will speak. The term *pour-over* is generally not used in connection with a testamentary trust.[20] It refers to the transfer of probate assets to the trustee of an inter vivos trust.[21]

## §2.2 Funding Issues

In recent years, the revocable trust, the life insurance contract, and the employee benefit plan (including the Individual

[17] A "person cannot have a legal claim against himself, whether for his own benefit or for the benefit of another." 1A Scott on Trusts §87. Where a debtor is indebted to himself there is no longer an enforceable debt. Id. at §87.4 (1987). *See also* Bogert, Trusts and Trustees §115.

[18] *See generally* Restatement (Third) of Trusts, Tent. Draft No. 1 (April 5, 1996), Reporter's Notes on §2, comment *i*.

[19] *See generally* 2A Scott on Trusts §170.18; Bogert, Trusts and Trustees §598.

[20] *See generally* Polasky, "Pour-Over" Wills and the Statutory Blessing, 98 Trusts & Estates 949 (1959).

[21] *See generally* 1A Scott on Trusts §54.3.

Retirement Account) have been transferring postmortem as much property as the will, and perhaps more.[1] These flexible, ambulatory, will-like devices have come to be known as *will substitutes,* and their proliferation has raised some trust-related funding issues.

### *§2.2.1 The Pour-over Statute*

No property is passed at the time a will is executed. At common law, therefore, the execution of a will with a pour-over provision could not serve as the initial funding vehicle for an inter vivos trust. Something more was needed.

Thus the practice evolved of funding inter vivos trusts with nominal amounts of property (*token funding*). It can be argued that if there is no inter vivos transfer of property, there is no inter vivos trust; if there is no inter vivos trust, the will's pour-over provision will lapse or fail. Many states have adopted in one form or another the Uniform Testamentary Additions to Trusts Act,[2] which some courts have interpreted as essentially allowing an inter vivos trust to arise without property, provided the trustee is named a beneficiary of a portion of the settlor's probate estate pursuant to a pour-over provision in the settlor's will.[3] Yet to be

**§2.2** [1] *See generally* Langbein, The Nonprobate Revolution and the Future of the Law of Succession, 97 Harv. L. Rev. 1108 (1984); Langbein, The Twentieth Century Revolution in Family Wealth Transmission, 86 Mich. L. Rev. 722 (1988).

[2] The Uniform Testamentary Additions to Trusts Act is a freestanding model statute, promulgated in 1960 and revised in 1991, to track §2-511 of the Uniform Probate Code, which was promulgated in 1969 and revised in 1990. Of course it is the prerogative of each state wishing to adopt such a statute to adopt either model, with or without modification. *See* 1A Scott on Trusts §54.3 for a list of states adopting the Uniform Testamentary Additions to Trusts Act. *See also* Uniform Probate Code §2-511, 8 U.L.A. 156 (1998); 1991 Uniform Testamentary Additions to Trusts Act, 8B U.L.A. 451 (1993).

[3] Earlier forms of the Uniform Testamentary Additions to Trusts Act and the Uniform Probate Code were somewhat ambiguous on the issue whether funding of an inter vivos trust was necessary during the lifetime of the settlor, provided there was a pour-over clause in the will. *See* Clymer v. Mayo, 393 Mass. 754, 473 N.E.2d 1084 (1985), involving a pour-over to an inter vivos trust that the court termed *unfunded.* The court suggested that the inter vivos trust was *unfunded* notwithstanding the fact that the trustee was a designated beneficiary of a life insurance policy. While it interpreted the Massachusetts Uniform Testamentary Additions to Trusts Act as not requiring that the inter vivos trust be funded at the

clarified is whether the inter vivos trust would come into existence at the time the will is executed or at the time the testator dies. As to the common law Doctrine of Independent Legal Significance as it applies to testamentary pour-overs to amendable inter vivos trusts, *see* §8.15.9.

### §2.2.2 *Life Insurance Beneficiary Designations*

It is a popular misconception that the revocable inter vivos designation of a trustee as a beneficiary of future life insurance proceeds is, alone, not enough to fund an inter vivos trust.[4] It is believed that something more is required, such as the present transfer of title to the contract itself or token funding. Some incorrectly refer to such trusts as *unfunded.*[5] It is settled law, however, that even the revocable designation of a trustee as the recipient of life insurance proceeds upon the future death of the insured constitutes the present transfer of property to the trustee.[6] The inter vivos trustee is the third-party beneficiary of a contract under which there has been an inter vivos exchange of consideration between the insured and the insurance company, that is, the insured having transferred inter vivos a premium and the company having transferred inter vivos a promise to pay proceeds upon the death of the insured. The trustee has an enforceable claim against the insurance company in the event the designation remains unrevoked at the death of the in-

---

time the will is executed, the court erred in characterizing the trust at issue as *unfunded.* The trust was in fact funded because the trustee had been designated the beneficiary of life insurance policies and beneficiary of the employee benefit plan and thus contained property in the form of contractual rights. *See* §2.2.2. In response to this confusion surrounding the term *unfunded,* the Uniform Probate Code and the Uniform Testamentary Additions to Trusts Act were revised to unequivocally provide that an inter vivos "trust" need not be funded during the lifetime of the settlor, provided there is an associated pour-over will. *See* Uniform Probate Code §2-511, 8 U.L.A. 156 comment (1998). *See also* 1991 Uniform Testamentary Additions to Trusts Act, 8B U.L.A. 451 (1993).

[4] *See generally* 1A Scott on Trusts §57.3.

[5] Id. *See also* U.P.C. §2-511, *supra* note 3.

[6] *See generally* 1A Scott on Trusts §57.3.

sured.[7] The revocable life insurance beneficiary designation differs from a pour-over provision in a will in that under the common law there has been no inter vivos transfer of a property interest to anyone pursuant to the terms of the will at the time the will is executed, whereas there *is* such a transfer at the time the insurance beneficiary designation is filled out.

### §2.2.3 *The Custodial IRA*

A taxpayer's Individual Retirement Account may be administered pursuant to what amounts under state law to an investment management agency agreement, known as a *custodial IRA*.[8] Because an agency terminates at the death of the principal, many jurisdictions have enacted statutes that provide that an IRA custodian may honor the postmortem dispositive provisions of the beneficiary designation form notwithstanding the requirements of the Statute of Wills.[9] In essence these statutes extend the life of these IRA agency arrangements beyond the death of the taxpayer-principal. If such a statute has been enacted in the trustee's jurisdiction, do its terms provide that the designation of the trustee of an inter vivos trust as postmortem beneficiary of the taxpayer's custodial IRA constitutes an actual or constructive transfer of property that will cause the inter vivos trust to arise? If not, then something more may be needed, such as a token funding or the execution of a will with provisions that conform to the jurisdiction's pour-over statute.

[7] *See* Gordon v Portland Trust Bank, 271 P. 2d 653, 656 (Ore. 1954) (". . . the beneficiary is the owner of a promise to pay the proceeds at the death of the insured, subject to insured's right of revocation.").

[8] I.R.C. §408(h) (1974) (effective for tax years beginning after December 31, 1974).

[9] *See, e.g.*, Mich. Comp. Laws Ann. §700.257 (West 1995); Mass. Gen. L. ch. 167D, §30 (1983); N.Y. Est. Powers & Trusts Law §13-3.2 (McKinney 1992); Conn. Gen. Stat. Ann. §45a-347 (West 1991); Tex. Prop. Code Ann. §121.052 (West 1995); *see generally* Bogert, Trusts and Trustees §255 n.11 and accompanying text (second note 11).

## §2.3 Wrongful Defunding

If trust property is wrongfully removed from a trust through the actions of a trustee or another, the trust ought not to be extinguished for want of trust property.[1] A reasonable argument can be made that the absent trust property has merely been transformed into another type of property, namely the personal equitable obligation of the wrongdoer.[2]

**§2.3** [1] *But see generally* 1A Scott on Trusts §74.2.

[2] Id.; *see generally* Restatement (Third) of Trusts, Tent. Draft No. 1 (April 5, 1996) §2 comment *i* at 29-30, and Reporter's Notes on §2, comment *i*, 39, 40.

CHAPTER 3

# The Trustee's Office



## §3.1 Who Can Be a Trustee?

Legal capacity to receive, hold, and manage property in trust is one thing; fitness to serve as trustee is another. One with legal capacity to take title or hold property for oneself, may do so as trustee. A minor has the capacity to hold title to property either in his or her own right or as trustee,[1] but because a minor's contracts are voidable, a minor is unfit to administer a trust.[2] Likewise, a

**§3.1** [1] *See generally* 2 Scott on Trusts §91.
[2] Id.

trust estate may vest in an insane person, but such an individual is unfit to administer a trust and will be removed.[3] A trust ordinarily does not fail because the individual or corporation named fails for whatever reason to serve or to continue to serve as trustee. The court will appoint another trustee to serve in his place, unless to do so would contravene the intentions of the settlor.[4] Thus the transfer of property in trust to a minor or an insane person ordinarily will not prevent the trust from coming into being.[5]

A nonresident individual generally may receive and administer trust property.[6] Many states require that nonresident testamentary trustees appoint resident agents for the purpose of accepting service of process.[7] The capacity of an alien to act as trustee may be limited in states where there are remnants of common law restrictions upon the capacity of an alien to hold property.[8]

The United States, a state of the United States, or a municipality may be a trustee, although principles of sovereign immunity may make the trust unenforceable absent a statute to the contrary.[9] A partnership can act as trustee if under state law it has the capacity to hold the legal title to property.[10]

At early common law, a corporation could not serve as trustee.[11] This is no longer the case.[12] A corporation may act as trustee in furtherance of and as an adjunct to its corporate purpose.[13] As a general rule, however, a corporation now needs statutory authority to have as its purpose the administration of trusts.[14] Thus, absent trust powers conferred by statute, an automobile

[3]Id. at §92.

[4]*See* Restatement (Second) of Trusts §2 comment *i* (1959).

[5]Id.

[6]*See generally* 2 Scott on Trusts §§94 (nonresident individuals), 96.6 (nonresident corporations); Bogert, Trusts and Trustees §132.

[7]Bogert, Trust and Trustees §132.

[8]2 Scott on Trusts §93.

[9]*See generally* id. §§95, 96.4; Hughes, Can the Trustee Be Sued for Its Breach: The Sad Saga of United States v. Mitchell, 26 S.D. L. Rev. 447 (1981) (discussing the fate of a breach of trust claim against the United States).

[10]*See generally* 2 Scott on Trusts §98.

[11]*See* id. §96.

[12]Id.

[13]*See generally* id. §96.3; Restatement (Second) of Trusts §96 (1959).

[14]*See generally* 2 Scott on Trusts §96.3.

manufacturing company, for example, may act as trustee of its own employee benefit plan but not as trustee of the plans of other companies.[15] Legislatures have traditionally conferred trust powers upon trust companies and banks, although the culture of the lender is to some extent incompatible with that of the trust fiduciary.[16] It is not uncommon for state *X*, by statute, to prohibit a bank or trust company from another state from qualifying as a testamentary trustee, unless the other state allows state *X*'s institutions to qualify within its borders; those states that place no restriction on the qualification rights of out-of-state institutions, however, will generally require the appointment of a local official as agent to accept service of process.[17]

A corporation acting as trustee without express statutory authority would be well advised to have in its file a legal opinion that it has the authority to so act. For example, a corporation in the business of transacting in real estate should have such a letter to the extent it utilizes trusts in the conduct of its business. The same also could be said for the charitable corporation administering a trust with a noncharitable component (perhaps a provision for the benefit of a benefactor's spouse).[18] A corporation acting as trustee under a statutory grant of authority — most often this will be a bank — should know the limits of its authority and the regulatory framework within which it must operate.[19] A national bank may be in danger that its commercial personnel may not be operating in compliance with "Regulation 9," the collection of federal regulations governing national bank fiduciary activities.[20] This could hap-

[15]Id.

[16]*See generally* id. §§96.5, 170.23A.

[17]*See generally* 5A Scott on Trusts §558 (containing in footnote 1 a catalog of state statutes that deal with the right of out-of-state banks and trust companies to serve as testamentary trustee); Bogert, Trusts and Trustees §132.

[18]*See generally* 2 Scott on Trusts §96.3.

[19]National banks must operate within the guidelines set out in Comptroller of the Currency Regulations, 12 C.F.R. Part 9 (as revised effective Jan. 29, 1997) (known as "Regulation 9") and are subject to the laws of the state in which they operate unless such laws conflict with federal laws or interfere with their purposes as defined by Congress. *See generally* 10 Am. Jur. 2d Banks §§15, 305 (1963); 2 Scott on Trusts §96.5.

[20]12 C.F.R. Part 9, as revised, effective January 29, 1997 (Reprinted in full in Appendix II of this handbook). Revised Reg. 9, in part, defines "fiduciary capacity"

pen, for example, in the context of the marketing of trusteed IRAs, and investment management agency services.[21] This could also happen when a bank enters into certain types of commercial relationships with a trust beneficiary or with the asset of one of its trusts.[22]

One's capacity to be a trustee is not affected by the fact that one is also a beneficiary of the trust. A person, however, may not be sole trustee and the sole beneficiary, because if there is a merger of the legal and equitable interests there is no trust.[23] A man may be trustee for himself and others, or with others be trustee for himself alone, and of course, may be trustee for himself for life with remainder for others or for others for life with remainder to himself. In each of these situations the trustee-beneficiary does not possess the *entire* legal and *entire* beneficial interest.

## §3.2 Who Is Fit to Be a Trustee?

Trust administration is not for every personality and every ethic. It is not for the wheeler-dealer and the dabbler. A trust is a legally complicated relationship requiring sustained attention, often over a period of many years, to a myriad of details of which some are clerical in nature (*e.g.*, keeping track of dividends) and some are not (*e.g.*, making discretionary distributions). Stewardship of another's property in and of itself is serious business, and yet it is only one of the trustee's many nondelegable functions.

---

as "any capacity in which the bank possesses investment discretion on behalf of another." 12 C.F.R. §9.2(e). *See generally* §8.18 (Regulation 9 Revised). *See generally* 2A Scott on Trusts §172.1.

[21] Id.

[22] *See* §6.1.3. Duty to be Loyal to the Trust); *see also* 12 C.F.R. §9.5 (Revised Reg. 9) (Requiring that a national bank exercising fiduciary powers adopt and follow written policies and procedures that address methods for preventing self-dealing and conflicts of interest.).

[23] *See generally* Bogert, Trusts and Trustees §129; 2 Scott on Trusts §99. *See also* §8.7 (Merger).

Above all the trustee must act solely in the interest of the beneficiaries.[1] The trustee may not transact with the trust property for personal benefit, absent authority from the settlor, the court, or from all the beneficiaries. One of the hallmarks of the trust relationship is the trustee's duty of absolute loyalty to the trust. One should not accept the office of trustee if there are any doubts about one's ability to carry out the duty of loyalty.[2]

This does not mean that trust administration should be something other than a business. It *is* a business, and it should be. Compensation provides a trustee with the incentive to keep trust matters high on his list of priorities. But trusteeship should not degrade to a state where it is merely an adjunct to other businesses such as brokerage, law, accounting, banking, or financial planning. Trust administration is a worthy profession in and of itself; it is a profession that thrives on regular attention over the long term, stability of personnel, the tried and true, and slow incremental changes for the better.

The court may appoint a trustee, or the governing trust instrument may empower an individual to appoint one.[3] In appointing a trustee the court will have due regard for the wishes of the settlor but will decline to appoint an unfit person. Thus, if someone authorized by the governing trust instrument selects an unfit or incapable person as trustee, the court may review the appointment. Ordinarily, one should not appoint oneself as trustee. The responsible individual should, giving due regard to the intentions of the settlor, consult the beneficiaries and appoint someone agreeable to them; this is what a court is expected to do.

Courts are reluctant to appoint nonresidents but as a practical matter they often do, particularly where some or all of the beneficiaries or property are out of state, and especially if nominated by the testator.[4] In some states the court may appoint a cotrustee to serve with a nonresident trustee.[5]

**§3.2** [1]Restatement (Third) of Trusts §170(1) (1992).

[2]*See* §6.1.3 (Duty to be Loyal to the Trust).

[3]*See generally* 2 Scott on Trusts §108.2 (appointment by the court), §108.3 (noncourt appointments).

[4]*See generally* Bogert, Trusts and Trustees §132.

[5]*See, e.g.*, 20 Pa. Cons. Stat. Ann. §7103 (Purdon 1972).

A substance abuser[6] or person of dishonest or bad character will not be appointed since the property would not be in safe hands.[7] The entire matter of appointment lies in the reasonable discretion of the court with due deference being given to reasonable provisions in the governing instrument.[8]

### *§3.2.1 The Professional Trustee and Single-Purpose Trust Company*

In an ideal world, only single-purpose trust companies and individuals engaged full-time in the business of trust administration would serve as trustees. Experience in and knowledge of trust matters would be broad and deep. Attention to the welfare of the trust would be exclusive, focused, and sustained. Goods and services would be contracted for at arm's length on behalf of the trust.

Economic realities, however, are such that only a small percentage of the population has the wherewithal to purchase the services of trustees so single-mindedly committed. Moreover, there are those who feel that the professional trustee, no matter how competent, is unacceptable because of its inability to offer the personal attention that a family member ostensibly provides. In a less than ideal world, persons in other lines of work are called upon to serve as trustees. While their involvement is not per se undesirable, each category raises its own collection of red flags.

### *§3.2.2 The Lawyer*

The advantage of having a lawyer serve as trustee is that lawyers understand the equitable rights and obligations of the

[6] *See, e.g.*, Ohio Rev. Code Ann. §2109.24 (Anderson 1953) (intoxication grounds for removing a trustee). The Pennsylvania fiduciary removal statute, however, has been amended to eliminate a reference to intoxication. 20 Pa. Cons. Stat. Ann. §3182 (Purdon 1992).

[7] *See generally* 2 Scott on Trusts §107; Bogert, Trusts and Trustees §519 (the court's power to remove trustee).

[8] *See generally* 2 Scott on Trusts §108.2.

parties. The disadvantage is that the lawyer who renders legal services to the trust for compensation over and above his or her reasonable trustees fees brushes with a conflict of interest.[9] The lawyer-trustee is after all transacting with the trust "for his own account." It is not always clear when one is acting as trustee and when one is acting as counsel, nor is it clear what portion of the compensation is attributable to actions as trustee and what portion is attributable to the rendering of legal services. But perhaps the fundamental problem is the loss to the trust of the independent perspective, of the checks and balances that operate when the functions are assumed by different entities.[10] It is a loss to the beneficiaries that cannot be mitigated or rationalized away by compensation adjustment. When functions are separated, the trustee to some extent monitors the lawyer and vice versa. When the functions coalesce in one person, there arises the danger that the lawyer as a practical matter is unaccountable as to performance and compensation.[11]

### *§3.2.3 The Stockbroker*

The trustee, under a duty to act solely in the interests of the beneficiaries, faces a built-in, structural incentive to violate that duty

[9] *See* Blake v. Pegram, 109 Mass. 541, 553 (1872) (charges to the trust of legal fees by the lawyer/trustee are "open to serious question, because of the liability to abuse, or, at least, to the suspicion of abuse," this because the lawyer/trustee "is his own client."); *see also* Kentucky Natl. Bank v. Stone, 93 Ky. 623, 20 S.W. 1040 (1893); Estate of Lankershim, 6 Cal. 2d 568, 58 P.2d 1282 (1936); Ontjes v. MacNider, 234 Iowa 208, 12 N.W.2d 284 (1942); Florida Bar v. Della-Donna, 583 So. 2d 307 (Fla. 1989); First Natl. Bank of Boston v. Brink, 372 Mass. 257, 268, 361 N.E.2d 406, 412 (1977) (Liacos, J., concurring in part and dissenting in part) (commenting on the perceived or actual conflicts of interest that can arise when an attorney and fiduciary are one in the same); *see generally* Kindregan, Conflicts of Interest and the Lawyer in Civil Practice, 10 Val. U. L. Rev. 423, 431 (1976); Krier, The Attorney as Personal Representative or Trustee, 65 Fla. B.J. 69 (1991).

[10] *Supra* note 9.

[11] *See generally,* Gibbs v. Breed, Abbott and Morgan, 649 N.Y.S. 2d 974 (N.Y. 1996) (Unacceptable stress is placed on a lawyer-executor's duty of undivided Loyalty when his law firm requires that he remit to the firm (out of fiduciary commissions) any shortfall in his legal fees).

when he or she also serves as the trust's commissioned stockbroker. By selling when it is in the interest of the beneficiaries to hold and by buying when it is in the interests of the beneficiaries not to buy, the trustee-stockbroker personally benefits when the portfolio is "churned."[12]

One solution is for the trustee-stockbroker to place trades with another firm. This avoids the conflict inherent in placing trades with the trustee-stockbroker's firm, but it will not eliminate the indirect personal benefit — in good will and implied IOU's — that inevitably accrues to someone who parcels out business. Of course, this conflict is not confined to brokers of stock. It would also apply to brokers of insurance and real estate. If the trustee intends to operate the trust out of a brokerage facility, at the very least the facility's infrastructure should be capable of accommodating the trust's specialized operational requirements.

### *§3.2.4 The Bank*

A full-service bank is said to have two sides: the commercial side and the trust side. The trust side operates in the fiduciary's labor-intensive world, where beneficiaries are entitled to full disclosure, deference, and a degree of intimacy, while the commercial side operates in the world of the marketplace and by its rules. If a loan to a commercial customer goes bad, generally the lender is not bound by fiduciary ties and can take necessary steps to protect its interest. The bank in its role as creditor is different from the bank acting as trustee since as trustee the bank is the legal owner of the property and as trustee has a fiduciary duty to place the interest of the beneficiaries ahead of its own interests.

The cultures, too, are very different. If commercial officers run the full-service bank, they must strive to understand and adequately fund the trust function — a function that operates in a world that values, among other things, continuity of management and a smooth-running operational and administrative infrastructure.

[12] *See, e.g.*, Armstrong v. McAlpin, 699 F.2d 79 (2d Cir. 1983).

### §3.2.5 The Family Member

The seeds of family disharmony are too often sown when a beneficiary is appointed trustee. Particularly in the case where siblings and their issue are permissible beneficiaries of a discretionary trust, the appointment of one sibling can be a prescription for disaster.[13] The sibling-trustee is tempted either to bend over backwards to the economic detriment of the sibling or the sibling's issue in order to avoid even the appearance of impropriety and conflict of interest (thus perhaps thwarting the settlor's wishes that all siblings and their issue be treated fairly) or the sibling is tempted to take unfair advantage of the office in furtherance of the sibling's economic interests to the exclusions of the interests of the other beneficiaries. On the other hand, it can be a prescription for gridlock and deadlock if all the siblings are serving as cotrustees. Moreover the matter of trustee compensation can become a sensitive issue when the trustee is also a beneficiary.

The appointment of a beneficiary's near relation brings with it its own set of problems, although in the United States relations are more often appointed than strangers. Laxness of management, the overweening influence of beneficiaries, and condonations of misconduct too often are the price of these family arrangements.

There is no rule against making the spouse of a beneficiary trustee. However, the risk does exist that the marriage will end in divorce before the trust terminates. In addition, it would be a tragedy if the spouse's appointment itself were to have a destabilizing effect on a marriage which till then had been solid.

### §3.2.6 Considerations in the Selection of a Trustee

The expected duration of the trust, the complexity of its assets, the needs of the beneficiaries, the level of administrative and investment expertise required and the fees a professional

[13] *See, e.g.*, Fletcher v. Fletcher, 480 S.E.2d 488 (Va. 1997) (Involving an unsuccessful attempt on the part of the sibling trustee to deny a sibling beneficiary access to the entire trust document).

trustee will charge must be considered in the selection of a trustee. The settlor should take the long view. A trust for a retarded child or an orphaned grandchild, for example, could extend 50, 60, or 70 years beyond the settlor's lifetime, long after the settlor's close friends and relatives have died. In other words, the trust needs a spine. This could take the form of an institution in the first instance, an institution as a cotrustee, or an institution as a fallback in default of named individuals.

The settlor should not confuse the function of a *guardian* of the person with the function of a *trustee.* The loving grandfather may be the perfect guardian of the orphaned grandchild's person, but he may be totally unsuited because of his age to act as trustee. Moreover, if both positions are held by different people, the guardian benefits from the trustee's independent perspective and the child benefits from the checks and balances inherent in a separation of these responsibilities. A separation of responsibilities is also preferable if the settlor intends that the guardian of the person receive generous discretionary distributions of income and principal for domestic help, the construction of an addition on the guardian's house, or such other purposes as will lessen the financial burden of the guardianship. It is always awkward for trustees, even though duly authorized, to make discretionary distributions to themselves.

The settlor ought not to measure one's suitability to be a trustee solely by his or her investment successes. There is much more to a trusteeship than merely investing.

If the settlor intends to name himself as trustee in the first instance, he should make sure that matters of trustee succession are adequately addressed in the governing instrument. It is very important that the matter of the settlor's incapacity be addressed.

Finally, the settlor should be reminded that the selection is not an either/or choice between the bank or the lawyer or the family member. Many permutations and combinations of cotrusteeships and orders of succession can exploit strengths and mitigate weaknesses. The governing instrument might provide for the appointment of a third party to "advise" the trustee.[14] For the settlor wishing to build in a measure of nonjudicial oversight,

[14] *See,* J.R. Kemper L.L.B, Annot., Construction and operation of will or trust provision appointing advisors to trustee or executor, 56 A.L.R. 3d 1249 (1974).

there are provisions for trustee removal and appointment that need not create tax problems if properly drafted.[15]

## §3.3 Involuntary Trustees

With the following exceptions, one cannot be forced to serve as a trustee:

(1) Once a trusteeship is voluntarily accepted, the law may require the trustee to remain in office until a qualified successor is in place.[1] Thus a trustee who at some point wants to resign may end up serving a portion of the trusteeship involuntarily. This is yet one more reason why the decision to serve as a trustee is not to be taken lightly.

(2) If the trustee dies and there is no provision for a successor, the trustee's personal representatives or those having an interest in the trustee's personal estate may find themselves de facto successor trustees until such time as qualified successors are in place.[2]

(3) *The constructive trust.* This is an equitable remedy employed by the courts to avoid unjust enrichment. It is a device more often employed to remedy breaches of contract than breaches of trust, and works as follows: If a person comes into possession of property as a result of fraud, undue influence, or some other such intentional wrong (with a few minor exceptions), he will hold the property not for himself or the perpetrator of the wrong but as a constructive trustee for the person who, but for the wrong, would have received the property.[3] The con-

[15] *See generally* Estate of Wall v. Commissioner, 101 T.C. 300 (1993); Rev. Rul. 95-58, 1995-36 I.R.B. 16; *see also,* Berall, New Ruling Provides More Flexibility in Removal of Trustees, 23 Est. Planning 99 (March/April 1996)..

**§3.3** [1] *See generally* Bogert, Trusts and Trustees §§511-512; 2 Scott on Trusts §106.1.

[2] *See generally* Bogert, Trusts and Trustees §529.

[3] *See, e.g.,* Lackey v. Lackey, 691 So. 2d 990 (Miss. 1997) (trust beneficiary entitled to have constructive trust imposed on proceeds of life insurnace policy purchased with property embezzled from trust).

structive trustee's primary responsibility is to get title and possession safely into the hands of the rightful owner.[3]

(4) *The purchase money resulting trust.*[4] A purchase money resulting trust[5] may arise where property is purchased and the purchase price is paid by one person and at his direction the seller transfers the property to another person.[6] If there is no intent that the transferee take the beneficial interest, the titleholder (*i.e.,* the resulting trustee) must turn the property over to the person who paid the consideration. A purchase money resulting trust does not arise automatically. For example, when there is an intent on the part of the person who paid the consideration to make a gift to the transferee, no purchase money resulting trust will arise.

(5) It has long been the practice of federal, state, and local governments, in lieu of taking property for just compensation, to place restrictions on how certain types of properties may be used by their owners.[7] These restric-

[3]A constructive trust, unlike an express trust, is not a fiduciary relation. Restatement of Restitution §160 comment *a* (1937). *See also* 5 Scott on Trusts §462.1. Although the constructive trust is technically a legal mechanism for transferring title, the prudent constructive trustee will act as a short-term fiduciary with respect to the property until title is transferred.

[4]*See generally* 5 Scott on Trusts §440.

[5]*See generally* id. §440.1. If *A* purchases land and puts the legal title in *B*'s name, or *A* gives *B* money to purchase land on *A*'s behalf, and if there is no intention by *A* to make a gift to *B*, a *purchase money resulting trust* will arise.

[6]Id.

[7]*See, e.g.,* Penn Central Transp. Co. v. City of New York, 438 U.S. 104 (1978); Nollan v. California Coastal Commn., 483 U.S. 825 (1987); Dolan v. Tigard, 512 U.S. 374 (1994); Kmiec, At Last the Supreme Court Solves the Takings Puzzle, 19 Harv. J.L. & Pub. Poly. 147 (1995). A point is reached, however, when a body of restrictions so circumscribes how an owner may use his property that he becomes a de facto trustee of the property for the benefit of the public. While the matter of restraints on coastal development has received considerable publicity because of the de facto takings cases, and while the spotted owl and the snail darter have brought public attention to matters of wildlife conservation, efforts to regulate the use of Native-American burial sites discovered on private property or the interiors of historic homes in private hands perhaps show the trusteeship by restriction at its most intrusive. *See also* Rounds, Protections Afforded to Massachusetts' Ancient Burial Grounds, 73 Mass. L. Rev. 176 (1988). The better approach, both for the property owner and the public, is for the state to take a

tions are intended to further certain state interests, such as land and wildlife conservation, historic preservation, and residential zoning. In times when public treasuries are strapped for funds, trusteeships by restriction have a certain superficial appeal: They appear to be effective, cost-free mechanisms for limiting the use of property on behalf of the public. But one has to question the long-term effectiveness of such involuntary arrangements that require de facto trustees to serve without compensation and without reimbursement for expenses.

In the case of state-imposed restrictions on archaeological sites and the interiors of homes, there can be no credible enforcement of such trusts over the long-term without massive state expenditure and intrusion. Another problem is that the trusteeship by restriction is essentially a passive arrangement that neither makes provision for the perpetual maintenance of assets nor protects an asset in the event it is constructively abandoned (*e.g.*, due to the property owner's impoverishment).

## §3.4 Avoiding, Assuming, and Vacating the Office

A trust arises as a result of the settlor's general intention to create it. The transfer of title to the trustee is a legal consequence of that intention. A trust, however, will not fail for want of a trustee. Thus, if property is transferred to one who cannot act, or if the one nominated disclaims, or if the trustee has died or is unable to act, the property will be held by the person in possession until a proper

particular asset by eminent domain for just compensation and then irrevocably transfer it into a common law charitable trust, together with sufficient funds for its perpetual maintenance and for the adequate compensation of willing competent trustees.

trustee can be appointed. The power to appoint a trustee will arise whenever the circumstances make it necessary, either (1) in the nature of things (as in the case of the death of the trustee), (2) whenever the provisions of the trust instrument prescribe it, (3) when the number of trustees sinks below the prescribed number, or (4) when the safety of the property or the proper administration of the trust requires an additional trustee.

### *§3.4.1 Appointment*

The appointment of the trustee under a declaration of trust (i.e., when the settlor and trustee are one and the same) requires no action by the court and no act of property transfer.[1] The declarant becomes trustee simply by intending to impress a trust upon his property. However, the segregation of the property and the re-registration of securities and other such items of intangible personal property are advisable in order to generate factual evidence of the intent to impress a trust upon the property.

A trust created by inter vivos transfer from *A* to *B* also requires no judicial act of appointment.[2] A completed transfer of the trust property must occur before the appointment is effective.[3] When the property is land, delivery of a deed completes the transfer; when the property is intangible personal property (*e.g.*, stocks and bonds), re-registration in the name of the trustee completes the transfer. But what if the securities remain in the name of the original owner who, in lieu of re-registration, places them in the hands of the trustee with the intention that they be held in trust? Has the appointment of a trustee been consummated? The better view is that it has. It is settled law, for example, that notice to an insurance company is not a requirement for impressing a trust

**§3.4** [1] *See* 1 Scott on Trusts §17.1; *see, e.g.,* Taliaferro v. Taliaferro, 9521 P.2d 803, 809 (Kan. 1996) (". . . there is no requirement that a settlor who also serves as trustee of a trust established by declaration must transfer legal title to the trust property.").

[2] 5A Scott on Trusts §557.

[3] *See* 1 Scott on Trusts §§32.1-32.2.

in equity upon rights under an insurance contract.[4] Nor is notice to a bank required to impress a trust upon a bank account.[5] Likewise no notice to a transfer agent is required to impress a trust in equity upon a block of securities.[6] Thus it logically follows that the trustee's appointment can be effected in equity by the transfer of physical possession in lieu of re-registration, provided the act is coupled with the appropriate intent.

Of course no rational person would purposely forgo re-registration, settling only for a transfer of physical possession. The absence of a paper trail would hamper efforts to defend the trust against those who would attack the transfer. But what if the securities are physically inaccessible and their precise descriptions not readily ascertainable? Could an appointment be effected if the settlor executes and delivers a general unspecific assignment of all the securities he owns to the trustee? In this case there is no re-registration *and* no physical transfer of the underlying paper. It is suggested that in cases of emergency (*e.g.*, the imminent death of the settlor), the transfer is sufficiently complete in equity to effect an appointment, because the owner has done all that can be done under the circumstances to place the property in the hands of a trustee.

Whether an agent acting under a Durable Power of Attorney can effect the appointment of a trustee for the principal's property remains somewhat unsettled.[7] In some jurisdictions, the issue has been resolved by legislation.[8] However, if a particular appointment is in the interest of the principal and within the scope of the agent's express authority, it ought to be upheld in equity.

In the case of testamentary trusts the common requirement is that the trustee nominated must obtain appointment by the

[4] *See generally* 1A Scott on Trusts §57.3.

[5] *See generally* id. §§58-58.6.

[6] *See generally* 2A Scott on Trusts §179.3.

[7] *See generally* Collin, Gift Giving Under Durable Powers of Attorney, 20 Tax Mgmt., Est., Gifts & Tr. 63 (1995); Van Dolson & Whitaker, Gifts by Agents Under Durable Powers of Attorney, 9 Prob. & Prop. 33, 38 (1995); McGovern, Trusts, Custodianships, and Durable Powers of Attorney, 27 Real Prop. Prob. & Tr. J. 1 (Spring 1992); 11 Institute on Estate Planning §305.2 (P. E. Heckerling, ed. 1977).

[8] *See generally* Restatement (Third) of Trusts, Tent. Draft No. 1 (April 5, 1996), Reporter's Notes on §11, pp. 228-252.

court.[9] Some authorities describe this procedure as a mere confirmation of the appointment made by the will inasmuch as it is conceded that the trustee's powers, after appointment, mainly flow from the trust instrument and not from the court. However, the trustee's powers also arise partly from the general body of the law, and it is at least certain that no valid exercise of any testamentary trust power may be made by the trustee prior to his court appointment and qualification.[10]

Trustees who are appointed by decree of court may be required to give bond to the court for the faithful performance of their trust.[11] In testamentary trusts the trustee's bond ordinarily is required to be with sureties unless the testator expressly has excused the trustee from furnishing them or unless all persons beneficially interested join in requesting the exemption.[12] In many jurisdictions corporate fiduciaries are exempt from providing sureties on their bonds.[13]

Probate courts (usually by virtue of statute) and courts acting under statute or under their general equity jurisdiction have broad powers with regard to the appointment of trustees.[14] The court's power to appoint a trustee is exercised wherever circumstances make it necessary.[15] In case of need, such as the death of a sole trustee, the court will appoint a temporary trustee or receiver. In New York, apparently the court will undertake to administer the trust itself.[16] The cardinal principle is that a trust will not be allowed to fail for lack of a trustee.[17]

The trust instrument, testamentary or inter vivos, may specify a manner of appointment of a successor trustee. If so, the pre-

[9] *See generally* 5A Scott on Trusts §557; *see also* §3.5.4.3 (Bond and Sureties).
[10] Id.
[11] *See generally* Bogert, Trusts and Trustees §151; *see also* §3.5.4.3.
[12] Id.
[13] Id.
[14] *See generally* 2 Scott on Trusts §§108.2, 556; Bogert, Trusts and Trustees §151.
[15] 2 Scott on Trusts §108; Bogert, Trusts and Trustees §151.
[16] *See generally* Bogert, Trusts and Trustees §529 n.13 and accompanying text.
[17] *See* Restatement (Second) of Trusts §101 (1959). *But see* 2 Scott on Trusts §101.1 (discussing failure of the trust when the named trustee was deemed essential to the creation, purpose, and maintenance of the trust).

scribed method should be followed strictly whether or not the matter is before the court.[18] If the instrument does not provide for a successor trustee, when a vacancy occurs only the court may appoint a successor.[19] Some instruments bestow on trustees the power to appoint their own co-trustees and successor trustees.[20]

The carefully drawn trust instrument provides for the contingency of vacancy and succession in the office of trustee and commonly states that upon appointment the new trustee shall have title to the trust property. This sort of provision, if accurately followed, has been held sufficient to pass title.[21] Similarly, in cases where the new or successor trustee was appointed by the court, the decree has operated to vest title in him.[22] In many states today, doubt as to the vesting of title in the successor trustee pursuant to court appointment has been removed by statute.[23] In any case, where the court appoints a new trustee it is good practice to incorporate an order for conveyance in the decree.

### *§3.4.2 Acceptance and Disclaimer*

Acceptance of the duties of the trustee may be shown by words or by conduct.[24] In the case of testamentary trusts, the intent to accept is ordinarily demonstrated by the filing of a petition of appointment, usually in the probate court.[25] In the case of declarations of trust, the existence of intent to accept is

[18] *See however,* W.E. Shipley, J.D., Annot., Court's power to appoint additional trustees over number specified in trust instrument, 59 A.L.R. 3d 1129 (1974).

[19] *See generally* 2 Scott on Trusts §108; Bogert, Trusts and Trustees §532 n.8 and accompanying text (suggesting that no power to appoint exists by implication in anyone other than the court).

[20] *See* Annot., Trustee's appointment of associate or successor trustee under powers of trust instrument, 57 A.L.R. 2d 887 (1958).

[21] *See* 2 Scott on Trusts §110.

[22] *See* id. §109.

[23] *See* id. §109 nn.2-3 and accompanying text.

[24] *See* Restatement (Second) of Trusts §102 (1959); *see generally* 2 Scott on Trusts §102.1.

[25] *See, e.g.,* Uniform Probate Code §3-601, 8 U.L.A. 111 (1998) (a personal representative shall qualify by filing with the appointing court any required bond and a statement of acceptance of the duties of the office).

obvious, since the owner declares himself trustee. In the case of inter vivos transfers in trust, receipt of the property coupled with the transferee's failure to disclaim within a reasonable time will amount to an acceptance of the office.[26] In order to avoid a period of uncertainty it is good practice to require a nontestamentary trustee to immediately and formally accept either by signing the trust instrument or an instrument of acceptance.[27] An instrument of acceptance need not be in any particular form; a letter will be sufficient.

As a general rule, no one need be a trustee involuntarily.[28] Usually the trustee nominated has the alternative of acceptance or disclaimer. No particular form of disclaimer is necessary; it may be by words or by conduct.[29] A trustee who wishes to disclaim obviously will desire to be certain of complete lack of responsibility from the outset. It is good practice to make certain that the disclaimer is in writing and is affirmative and unequivocal in nature. It can be recorded in the place where the trust instrument is recorded, or delivered to the person having custody of the instrument. It is also good practice to serve notice on cotrustees, if any, current beneficiaries, if any are known to the nominee, as well as to other parties having an equitable interest in the trust property, if known. If the trust instrument is a will, a disclaimer filed in the probate court is appropriate and a printed form generally is used. As many states have enacted statutes establishing procedures and timeframes for the filing of disclaimers, a person contemplating the disclaimer of a trusteeship would be well advised to search the annotated laws for any statutes that may apply.[30]

[26] *See generally* Bogert, Trusts and Trustees §150.

[27] Many instruments will specify procedures for acceptance, and it is good practice to follow these procedures to the letter. However, acceptance may be construed even in the absence of compliance with procedures set forth in the governing instrument. Thus, the nominee should not assume that mere noncompliance will suffice as a disclaimer. If a nominee wishes not to assume fiduciary responsibilities, he should take positive steps to disclaim. Id.

[28] *See generally* Restatement (Second) of Trusts §102 (1959); 2 Scott on Trusts §102. *See* §3.3 (Involuntary Trustees) for a few exceptions.

[29] *See generally* 2 Scott on Trusts §102.1; Restatement (Second) of Trusts §102, comment *b* (1959).

[30] For a list of statutes expressly providing that a person named as trustee may disclaim, *see* 2 Scott on Trusts §102 n.4.

Disclaimer is not allowable after acceptance of the office has taken place; resignation then becomes the only available option if a trustee no longer wishes to serve as such.[31] Thus, since acceptance may be shown by actions as well as by words, it will be important for the nominee to make up his mind one way or the other speedily and unequivocally.

If the nominee decides upon disclaimer, meticulous care should be taken to avoid any assumption of authority or voluntary interference with or control of the trust property, as such action may be construed as an acceptance. Of course, one's actions are always open to reasonable explanation,[32] but it is easier to avoid the burden of such explanation.[33]

The effect of a disclaimer of one of several trustees is to vest the entire title in those who accept,[34] and it is said that in the case of a sole trustee who disclaims, the title is temporarily revested in the settlor or the settlor's successors as of the time of the transfer.[35] It is certain that the disclaiming trustee is relieved ab initio of any liability.[36] This does not mean destruction of the trust, however, since equity will not allow the trust to fail because of the failure of the individual trustee, except in the rare case where a particular trustee is deemed essential to the whole trust purpose.[37] If for some reason the settlor has expressed an intent that the person nominated is to be the only trustee qualified, it can be said that the

[31] *See* §3.4.3 (Death and Resignation).

[32] If a person proceeds to administer the trust property as would a trustee, such action may be construed as an acceptance. *See* Carter v. Carter, 321 Pa. 391, 184 A. 78 (1936) (acceptance indicated by collecting insurance proceeds due the trust); Lentz v. Lentz, 5 N.C. App. 309, 168 S.E.2d 437 (1969) (acceptance indicated by executing assignment of option to purchase real estate). However, if the nominee is merely protecting the property temporarily until a trustee is appointed, such action ought not to be construed as acceptance. *See generally* Bogert, Trusts and Trustees §150.

[33] Disclaimer has been implied under the following circumstances: lack of interest and inconsistent conduct; lack of acceptance; failure to give bond and to qualify as trustee; failure to act for a prolonged period. *See* 2 Scott on Trusts §102.2.

[34] *See* Bogert, Trusts and Trustees §150.

[35] *See* Restatement (Second) of Trusts §102 comment *g* (1959); 2 Scott on Trusts §102.3.

[36] *See generally* 2 Scott on Trusts §102.3.

[37] *See generally* id. §101.1.

nominee's acceptance is necessary to the creation of the trust.[38] Once one has disclaimed, one cannot thereafter withdraw it except with the permission of the court.[39]

### *§3.4.3 Death and Resignation*

Trustees (where there is more than one) take a joint estate that is not subject to partition.[40] A conveyance out of the trust from one cotrustee acting alone is void.[41] This means that a contract that relates to the trust property between one of the cotrustees and a third party with notice of the trust is ineffective absent a statute to the contrary.[42] Of course, the trust instrument may permit action by fewer than all of the trustees.

When one trustee dies the whole estate vests in the survivors.[43] Even in states in which there is a statutory presumption that multiple parties take title to property as tenants in common, cotrustees generally take as joint tenants.[44] If the trust instrument specifies a definite number of trustees and the death of one or more of them reduces the number below the required amount, the whole estate will still vest in the surviving trustees and will remain there until a successor or successors assumes responsibility for the trust property whether pursuant to court order or the terms of the governing instrument.[45] In certain situations where the trustees and the beneficiaries are one and the same, the fact that the trustees hold the legal title jointly with right of survivorship and the beneficiaries hold the equitable interest as tenants in

[38] *See generally* Bogert, Trusts and Trustees §150 n.22 and accompanying text.

[39] *See* 2 Scott on Trusts §102.3.

[40] The joint tenancy of trustees does not share all of the characteristics of the classic joint tenancy. The parties to a classic joint tenancy are entitled to convert the interest into a tenancy in common (a *petition to partition*). Cotrustees, however, have no power to partition the trust or extinguish the trust by a conveyance or other action. Their powers are confined to joining with their cotrustees in conveying the whole estate or a part of it. *See generally* Bogert, Trusts and Trustees §145.

[41] Id. *See also* 3 Scott on Trusts §194.

[42] *See generally* 3 Scott on Trusts §194.

[43] *See* Restatement (Second) of Trusts §103 (1959).

[44] *See* id. §103 comment *a.*

[45] *See* §3.4.4.3 (Successor Trustees).

common may prevent the destruction of the trust through merger.[46]

At common law, if a sole trustee died without leaving a will, the title to the trust property passed to the trustee's heirs, in the case of real estate, or to the trustee's personal representative in the case of personal property. The heirs or personal representatives were not permitted to administer the trust unless authorized to do so by the terms of the trust.[47] If a sole trustee died leaving a will, title to the trust property passed at common law to the general takers under the trustee's will unless it happened that the testator-trustee expressed an intention to confine the testamentary disposition to that in which the testator-trustee had a beneficial interest.[48] Fortunately, in many jurisdictions statutes have been enacted to address the issue.[49]

Some statutes provide that both title and the office of trusteeship pass to the takers under the will; others provide that the title and right to possession vest in a court and that the court is to appoint a successor trustee; still others provide that the title and right to possession vest in the successor trustee.[50] In general a clear distinction is made between the deceased trustee's own property and the property that is held in trust. Thus the surviving spouse of the deceased trustee does not take an interest in the trust property as statutory heir or by dower or curtesy.[51]

One may not be relieved of one's obligations as trustee by mere transfer and abandonment.[52] Essentially the trustee will be held to have improperly delegated to the transferee — or the world at large in case of abandonment — responsibility for administering the trust.[53] The trustee may resign either upon permission of the court or in accordance with the terms of the trust instrument or with the consent of all of the beneficiaries, including the

[46] *See generally* 2 Scott on Trusts §99.5; First Alabama Bank of Tuscaloosa v. Webb, 373 So. 2d 631 (Ala. 1979). *See* §8.7 (Merger).

[47] *See generally* Bogert, Trusts and Trustees §529; 2 Scott on Trusts §104.

[48] Id.

[49] *See generally* Bogert, Trusts and Trustees §529.

[50] Id.

[51] *See generally* 2 Scott on Trusts §104 n.6 and accompanying text.

[52] *See generally* Bogert, Trusts and Trustees §§511, 512.

[53] *See generally* Bogert, Trusts and Trustees §512.

remaindermen, be their interests vested or contingent.[54] The consent of the beneficiaries will not be a complete protection to the trustee, of course, unless every one of them is of full capacity and has joined in the consent.[55] More often than not, consent will not be a viable option as there are likely to be unborn and unascertained individuals with beneficial interests under the trust. Statutes in most states govern the resignation of trustees.[56]

The mere resignation and acceptance thereof may not, in the absence of statute or appropriate language in the governing instrument, operate to transfer the title to a successor trustee. Thus the resigning trustee may need to execute suitable conveyances of the trust property to the successor in office.[57] The outgoing trustee will want to in any case so as to put others on notice of the succession.

The resignation of a testamentary trustee will likely require court involvement. In inter vivos trust instruments, a nonjudicial method of resignation always should be provided. Absent an express provision, it is likely the trustee of an inter vivos trust will need judicial approval to resign.[58] If the trust expressly provides a method for the trustee's resignation, then the trustee must follow these requirements.[59] Many trusts provide that upon written notice to the beneficiary or beneficiaries then entitled to receive income, the trustee may resign.[60] Often the instrument specifies that the resignation becomes effective after a period of time from the date notice is mailed. In the interim, the resigning trustee remains responsible for the administration of the trust. Written notice should be sent by certified mail to ensure receipt by the beneficiary, and regardless of what the instrument may say, the prudent trustee should assume that he is not discharged until the trust property has been transferred to a qualified successor.[61]

[54]*See* 2 Scott on Trusts §106.

[55]Id. *See also* §5.5 (Loss of the Beneficiary's Rights).

[56]*See* id. §106 n.4 (a list of statutes governing the resignation of trustees).

[57]Restatement (Second) of Trusts §106 comment *b* (1959).

[58]*See generally* 2 Scott on Trusts §106.1.

[59]*See* 2 Scott on Trusts §106.2; *see also* Croslow v. Croslow, 38 Ill. App. 3d 373, 347 N.E.2d 800 (1976) (holding ineffective a resignation not in accordance with the terms of the trust).

[60]*See* Bogert, Trusts and Trustees §1293, for examples of trustee resignation provisions.

[61]*See* §3.3 note 1 (involuntary trustees).

## *§3.4.4 Exercise and Devolution of Powers*

Upon acceptance of the trusteeship, the trustee acquires the panoply of express and implied powers needed to carry out the terms of the trust.[62] If a power is not confined to the doing of a single act or restricted in point of time, it remains available throughout the trust and may be executed in part or in whole at any time.

### §3.4.4.1 Multiple Trustees

Where there are several trustees, the powers, like the title, vest jointly.[63] Thus, with possible exception of the charitable trust, trust powers can only be executed by the joint action of all trustees; an action by fewer than all, even though a majority, is void unless permitted by the instrument or by statute.[64] A theoretical result of this principle would be that refusal to concur on the part of one of several trustees would block all action. It has long been settled, however, that if a trustee unreasonably refuses to concur in the joint exercise of a power, the court may remove the trustee.[65] It has also been held that, in an emergency, one trustee may exercise joint powers without the concurrence of the others.[66]

All of several trustees must join or be joined in any suit, or to the settlement or compromise thereof, because trustees are joint tenants. For the same reason it is always safer to insist that receipts and other papers be signed by all of the trustees, for, although payment received by one of them may amount to a good discharge at law, the validity of the receipt may well remain open to question in equity.

[62] *See* §3.5.3, which discusses the nature and scope of these powers.

[63] *See* Restatement (Second) of Trusts §194 (1959).

[64] Id. *See also* 3 Scott on Trusts §194 (containing at footnotes 21 & 22 a catalog of statutes authorizing action by a majority of a trust's cotrustees).

[65] *See generally* 3 Scott on Trusts §194. *See also* Restatement (Second) of Trusts §107(a) comment *b* (1959).

[66] *See* 3 Scott on Trusts §194.

#### §3.4.4.2 Surviving Trustees

When for any reason one of several trustees ceases to hold his office, the trust powers ordinarily remain in the surviving trustees.[67] This may be the case even when a delay in filling vacancies occurs.[68] Only in cases where there are special reasons for believing that the settlor intended to limit discretion to all the trustees originally named, or to those times when all vacancies are filled, will the court conclude that the powers do not vest in the survivors.[69] This is in contrast to what was once the rule, namely that transfers in trust to two or more individuals specified by name implied an intention that neither could exercise discretionary powers alone.[70]

#### §3.4.4.3 Successor Trustees

It is an equitable maxim that a trust shall not fail for want of a trustee. Furthermore the settlor is presumed to intend that the trust shall continue until its purposes are accomplished. This leads to the general rule that all express and implied powers vested in the original trustee shall pass to the successor trustees, unless the settlor expresses a contrary intention.[71]

The cardinal principle, however, is that *the intention of the settlor as expressed in the trust instrument is controlling.*[72] A well-drawn trust will specify that successor trustees shall have all powers granted the original trustees. In the absence of such specific language, however, the settlor's intentions on the matter must be inferred from the general terms of the instrument.[73] It has been said that the settlor who names a corporate trustee intends that

[67] *See* Restatement (Second) of Trusts §195 (1959); *see generally* 3 Scott on Trusts §195.

[68] *See* 3 Scott on Trusts §195 n.6 and accompanying text.

[69] *See generally* 3 Scott on Trusts §195.

[70] *See, e.g.*, Weeks v. Frankel, 128 A.D. 223, 112 N.Y. Supp. 562 (N.Y. App. Div. 1908).

[71] *See* Restatement (Second) of Trusts §196 (1959).

[72] *See* id.

[73] *See generally* 3 Scott on Trusts §196.

discretionary powers will pass to the successor trustees.[74] On the other hand, the fact that discretionary powers are conferred on a named individual may be a slight indication that the powers were not intended to be exercised by anyone except the individual named.[75] The modern trend however is to disregard this distinction. In the great bulk of cases all powers, express and implied, have been found to be transmitted.[76] For the releated issue of what happens when a bank trustee merges or consolidates, *see* §8.19.

## §3.5 Trustee's Relationship to the Trust Estate

Professor Fratcher notes that the trust — in contrast to the corporation — is not a legal entity; rather it is "an aggregation of property," where the rights and duties associated with its ownership "are divided between the trustee and the beneficiary." Thus "the trust, as such, is incapable of owning property, acquiring claims or incurring liabilities."[1] Because the trust is not an entity, it is more legally accurate to say that "a trust has been impressed on Blackacre" or "Blackacre has been transferred to a trustee" than it is to say that "Blackacre has been put into a trust."

[74] *See* Restatement (Second) of Trusts §196, comment *f* (1959).
[75] Id. comment *a*.
[76] Id. comment *a*.
**§3.5** [1] W. F. Fratcher, Trust §95, *in* VI Intl. Encyclopedia of Comp. Law ch. 11 (F. H. Lawson, ed., 1973) (hereinafter "Fratcher"); *but see* Restatement (Third) of Trusts, Tent. Draft No. 1 (April 5, 1996), Reporter's Notes on §2, comment *i*, at p. 39 (Note the tendency of modern law to treat trusts as distinct legal entities by distinguishing the trustee individually from the trustee in a fiduciary capacity, such as for purposes of the trustee's liability to third parties for trust obligations.); *see also,* Curtis, The transmogrificaton of the American Trust, 31 Real Prop. Prob. and Tr. J. 251 (no. 2 1996) (suggesting that the "corporate paradigm" is not completely analagous to trusts.).

## *§3.5.1 Nature and Extent of the Trustee's Estate*

In every trust there are two estates: the trustee's *legal* estate and the beneficiary's *equitable* estate.[2] Though these two estates are separate, they are bound together and tend to travel on parallel lines.[3] Legal title to the trust property is held by the trustee, unless one of the following exceptions applies: it is a passive trust involving real estate;[4] the subject of the trust is an equitable interest; or the settlor expresses a contrary intent.[5] Thus it is said that the trustee owns the property.

To the nonlawyer this splitting of interests is as mysterious as the Trinity. How can it be that the trustee and the beneficiaries both own the property? Perhaps it would be helpful to look at it this way: The trustee has all rights to the trust property except the right to its benefit. That right is given to the beneficiary. Of course it is the prerogative of the settlor to withhold from the trustee other rights, such as the right to sell the trust property.[6] In England in earlier times the beneficiary would look to the ecclesiastical courts for help in protecting his beneficial interest. Today the beneficiary looks to the secular courts in the exercise of their equitable powers.[7]

What then is the practical difference between a trust and a contract, or between a trust and an agency such as a power of attorney, when it comes to the property that is the subject of these arrangements? By way of illustrating how the trust fits into the framework of fundamental common law legal relationships, let us take the village inn. Assume that one evening the building inspector is about in the village, and he notices that the fire escapes have fallen off the building. Whom then does he cite for an infraction of

[2]The *legal estate* is the whole estate, and the holder of the legal title is the sole owner. When the title is held for the benefit of another, as in a trust, the beneficial interest thus created is called an *equitable estate*. *See generally* C. Moynihan, Introduction to the Law of Real Property §173 (2d ed. 1988).

[3]*See generally* 2 Scott on Trusts §130.1; Bogert, Trusts and Trustees §181.

[4]*See generally* 1A Scott on Trusts §88 and §8.15.1 (Statute of Uses).

[5]*See generally* id. §88.1.

[6]*See generally* 3 Scott on Trusts §190. *See also* §3.5.3.1(a) (The Power to Sell).

[7]*See generally* id. §197.

the building code? Certainly not the guests. The innkeeper is cited because he owns the inn. Now the guests may well find themselves out in the cold that evening. Their recourse however is a *legal* one against the innkeeper with whom they have a contractual relationship.[8] In earlier times this would have been a legal matter for the secular courts. That is still the case today.

Let us now assume that the innkeeper is trustee of the inn and that the guests are beneficiaries, not parties to a contract with the innkeeper. Whom does the building inspector now cite? Again the innkeeper is cited because, as far as the inspector is concerned, the innkeeper legally owns the inn. Any complaint the guests may have with the innkeeper is not the inspector's problem. In earlier times, the beneficiary, not being in a contractual relationship with his trustee, would have had recourse against the innkeeper only to the ecclesiastical courts for any breach of trust; today the beneficiary must invoke the *equitable* powers of the secular courts. It always should be kept in mind that even though the innkeeper receives the citation as legal owner of the trust property, the equitable or beneficial interests of the guests are very much interests in property as well.[9] A beneficiary's equitable right of enjoyment, for example, may not be seized by the *trustee's* personal creditors or by the *trustee's* spouse.[10]

It is out of more than mere historical interest that we ponder the nature of the trustee's estate. As one can see, rights are affected. For example, what about the ironmonger who improperly installed the fire escapes? Who pursues him, the trustee or the beneficiaries? Under the common law, the trustee is the plaintiff because, as owner of the property, the trustee is in a contractual relationship with the ironmonger.[11] What if the fire escape fell on a passerby? Is the trustee personally liable above and beyond the

[8]A breach of contract gives the injured party a right to damages (usually a sum of money based on an expectation interest) against the party in breach. Restatement (Second) of Contracts §§346-347 (1979).

[9]*See* 1 Restatement of Property at 3 (1936) (introductory note to chapter 1); *see also* In re Catherwood's Trust, 173 A.2d 86, 91 (1961) ("A gift of an equitable life estate in income or of a remainder does constitute a grant of a vested property right of which the recipients cannot be divested by legislative action").

[10]*See generally* Bogert, Trusts and Trustees §146 (creditor) and §146 (spouse).

[11]*See generally* 4 Scott on Trusts §280.2.

value of the trust property for any negligent harm caused? Under the common law the trustee's liability probably would not be limited to the value of the trust estate.[12] What if the trustee sells the inn in violation of the terms of the trust to someone who has no notice of the trust? Under the common law the sale is probably good with the result that the beneficiaries have no recourse against the purchaser.[13] When the trust terminates, must the trustee convey the property to the remaindermen or do the remaindermen take automatically? Under the common law a conveyance would be required, with the possible exception of certain trusts involving real estate.[14]

The trustee's ownership interest in the trust estate is subtle and complex and thus the rights, duties, and obligations of those who come in contact with the trust estate are entangled. As the trustee may be exposed to potential personal liability to third parties as an incident of the "ownership" interest in the trust estate, the potential trustee should seek the advice of counsel and purchase appropriate liability insurance before venturing into this strange world of bifurcated interests. With respect to a given situation, the trustee should also understand the extent to which these common law duties and obligations may be altered by statute, by decision, and by the terms of a particular governing instrument.

Finally, what about the agency? What if the guests own the inn and the innkeeper is operating the inn under a power of attorney? In that case the innkeeper is their agent and he receives the citation on their behalf, as they possess both the legal estate and the equitable estate.

### §3.5.2 *Rights of the Trustee*

In the tangle of legal relationships that is the trust, the trustee as well as the beneficiary has certain rights. The trustee's rights are incident to holding the *title* (*e.g.*, the right of possession and alien-

[12] *See generally* id. §264.
[13] *See generally* id. §284; *see also* §8.3.2 (Purchasers for Value of Trust Property).
[14] *See generally* 1A Scott on Trusts §88; §18.15.1 (Statute of Uses).

ation) and the *office* (*e.g.*, the right of reasonable compensation and reimbursement).

### §3.5.2.1 Right at Law to Possession

In the absence of statute, decision, or the settlor's contrary intention, the trustee, as holder of the legal title, is entitled to the possession of the real property; thus the trustee may eject the beneficiary.[15] With the same qualifications the trustee is entitled also to the possession of the personal property.

### §3.5.2.2 Right at Law to Transfer Title

The trustee, being the legal owner, may make conveyance, and the transferee will stand at law entitled in place of the trustee.[16] But if the settlor bestowed on the trustee no power to convey, any transferee with notice of the restriction takes the property subject to the trust, receiving no larger title than the trustee is authorized to convey.[17] Under these circumstances, the sale is voidable at the option of the beneficiary.[18]

Because of the trustee's right to transfer title, it is said that the trust is not a restraint on the alienability of property.[19] This is because "if the trustee makes a transfer under powers conferred by law or the terms of the trust, the transferee acquires the whole title, free of trust; if he makes a transfer in breach of trust to a bona fide purchaser, the transferee also acquires the whole title, free of trust; [e]ven a transfer in breach of trust to a donee, or to a purchaser with notice of the breach, carries the title, subject to the trust, which is all the trustee ever owned."[20]

[15] *See generally* 2A Scott on Trusts §175; *but see generally,* V. Woerner, Annot., Right of appeal from order on application for removal of personal representative, guardian, or trustee, 37 A.L.R. 2d 751 (1954).

[16] *See generally* 4 Scott on Trusts §283.

[17] *See generally* id. §284.

[18] *See generally* id. §291.

[19] *See generally* Broadway Natl. Bank v. Adams, 133 Mass. 170 (1882).

[20] Fratcher, *supra* note 1, §108 at 89.

### §3.5.2.3 Right in Equity to Exoneration and Reimbursement

Inasmuch as there is a rigid restriction against personal participation by the trustee in any of the profits and gains resulting from the administration of the trust estate, equity takes pains to hold the trustee harmless from personal liability for obligations properly incurred.[21]

Inherent in the right of exoneration is the trustee's right to pay directly from the estate all of the expenses properly incurred as owner, including taxes, repairs, insurance, and other legitimate expenses of management, traveling expenses, the cost of justifiable litigation including attorneys' fees, and expenses of consulting counsel when there is reasonable cause.[22] This right of exoneration is coupled with a right of reimbursement for sums paid from the trustee's own pocket for expenses properly incurred.[23]

### §3.5.2.4 Right in Equity to Compensation

The English rule is that the trustee is not entitled to compensation unless the instrument expressly provides for it.[24] In the United States and some parts of the British Commonwealth, however, the trustee is entitled in equity to reasonable compensation, even when the instrument is silent upon the subject.[25] In some jurisdictions, a trustee's compensation is set by statute.[26]

[21] *See generally* Bogert, Trusts and Trustees §718.

[22] Id.; *see generally* 3 Scott on Trusts §188; *see generally,* Lee R. Russ, J.D., Annot., Award of attorneys' fees out of trust estate in action by trustee against co-trustee, 24 A.L.R. 4th 624 (1983); *see also* F.M. English, Annot., Right of coexecutor or trustee to retain independent legal counsel, 66 A.L.R. 2d 1169 (1959); *but see* Barber v. Barber, 915 P.2d 1204 (Alaska 1996) (Trustee who brought complaint for instructions is a neutral party, not a "prevailing" party and therefore *not* entitled to legal fees.); *see also* Malachowski v. Bank One, Indianapolis, 682 N.E. 2d 530 (Ind. 1997) (Though trustee prevailed, not awarded trustee fees because litigation not reasonably necessary).

[23] *See generally* Bogert, Trusts and Trustees §718.

[24] *See generally* 3A Scott on Trusts §242.

[25] Id; *see also* §8.4 (The Trustee's Compensation).

[26] *See generally* Bogert, Trusts and Trustees §975.

### *§3.5.3 The Powers of the Trustee in Equity to Manage the Trust Estate*

A trustee, being the absolute legal owner of the property, has all the rights of an absolute owner, subject however to the paramount equitable rights of the beneficiary.[27] Thus, for example, a direction in the governing instrument to the trustee to employ a particular person as attorney is generally unenforceable.[28] On the other hand, the courts of equity will restrain the trustee from exercising any power inconsistent with the beneficiary's rights.[29] As a rule of thumb the trustee has only the powers — and all the powers — needed to carry out the terms of the trust and to protect the trust corpus.[30] When the two goals are in conflict or when the terms of the trust or the law is ambiguous, the trustee is entitled to petition the court for guidance.[31]

Ascertaining the limits of the trustee's equitable authority (in other words, the limits of the trustee's powers) is more an art than a science. The panoply of powers with respect to a given trust are drawn from long-established customs and practice, the common law, statute, the express language of the governing instrument, and by implication from the general purposes of the trust. The trustee's general powers incidental to the office are numerous; to name just a few, they include: the power to sell,[32] lease,[33] sue and defend,[34] contract and incur expense,[35] and to vote stock proxies.[36] In short, the trustee has all the powers needed to carry out the duties of a trustee.

When it comes to trust powers, however, things are not always as they seem. Trustees should be cautious in exercising an express power that expands the common law authority of a

[27] *See generally* id. §146.
[28] 2 Scott on Trusts §126.3.
[29] *See* 3 Scott on Trusts §199.
[30] *See* id. §186.
[31] Restatement (second) Trusts §259 (1959).
[32] *See* §3.5.3.1(a) (The power to sell).
[33] *See* §3.5.3.1(b) (The power to lease).
[34] *See* §3.5.3.1(c) (The power to sue and defend).
[35] *See* §3.5.3.1(d) (The power to bind the trust in contract).
[36] *See* §3.5.3.1(e) (The power to vote proxies).

trustee. For example, one would be ill advised to rely on an expansive general power in the governing instrument "to do all things which the settlor could have done with his own property." Courts are unlikely to interpret such language as a license to speculate or self-deal or otherwise engage in acts that are inconsistent with the concept of a trust.[37] Even a tightly drafted specific power to retain a particular investment remains outstanding only so long as the investment furthers the general purposes and economic well-being of the trust.[38] If, for example, the investment is in an industry whose products are becoming obsolete and thus unmarketable, the trustee may have a duty to sell the investment notwithstanding the express retention authority.[39] The trustee who mechanically relies on powers expressly bestowed in the governing instrument does so at his peril. (On the other hand, when the law is ambiguous as to whether the trustee has an implied power in a given situation, the trustee is entitled and advised to seek judicial guidance.)

### §3.5.3.1 Implied General Powers

Implied powers are granted to the trustee by operation of law, because without them it would be impossible to carry out the trustee's fiduciary responsibilities. They need not be expressly granted in the governing instrument. The power to sell intangible personal property, lease, sue and defend, bind the trust in contract, and vote proxies are some of the more important powers that the trustee possesses incidental to his office. Thus they are powers that the trustee possesses unless the settlor expressly or by implication denies them to the trustee.

**(a) The power to sell.** Absent statutory authority or authority in the governing instrument, does the trustee have an implied

[37] *See* Restatement (Second) of Trusts §186 comment *f* (1959).

[38] *See* id. §167 comments *g* & *h*; Restatement (Third) of Trusts §229 comment *d*.

[39] *See, e.g.*, Mueller v. Mueller, 28 Wis. 2d 26, 135 N.W.2d 854 (1965); Restatement (Third) of Trusts §229 comment *d*.

power on behalf of the trust to sell the trust property to a third party for reasonable consideration? At early common law the answer was "no" when it came to land.[40] This was appropriate for a time when a family would derive its very identity from a specific parcel of land.[41] In the United States today courts will generally find a power of sale unless it appears from the language of the trust instrument, interpreted in light of the circumstances, that the settlor intended that the land should be retained by the trust.[42] Such a presumption is appropriate for a society that has come to look upon real estate as just one form of investment. Moreover, unless there is an indication of a contrary intention on the part of the settlor, the trustee has had the implied or inherent authority to sell intangible personal property (*e.g.*, stocks and bonds) since the concept of the *Prudent Man Rule* took root.[43]

With the express or implied duty to invest comes the power to buy and sell.[44] In many jurisdictions the trustee is given by statute the power to sell personal property, unless the terms of the trust indicate a contrary intention.[45] The Restatement of Trusts provides that a trustee has an implied power of sale unless the terms of the trust indicate a contrary intent.[46]

A power of sale does not necessarily include the power to sell the trust property on credit.[47] Whether a sale on credit is allowed depends in large part on whether the receipt of notes in lieu of cash would put the trust at unnecessary risk.[48] If the buyer has a good credit rating, the sale may be proper, particularly if the sale is desirable and cannot otherwise be made.[49] A trustee would

[40] *See generally* 3 Scott on Trusts §186.

[41] *See generally* id. §190.

[42] Id.

[43] *See generally* Restatement (Third) of Trusts at 3 (1992) (introduction to Topic 5); Harvard College v. Amory, 26 Mass. (9 Pick.) 446 (1830).

[44] See Restatement (Third) of Trusts §190 comments *b* & *d* (1992).

[45] See 3 Scott on Trusts §190 n.10 & §190.4 n.10 for statutes governing the sale of trust property. *See also* Uniform Trustee's Powers Act, §§3(c)(7), 12 (a trustee has power "to acquire or dispose of an asset, for cash or on credit, at public or private sale").

[46] Restatement (Third) of Trusts §190 (1992).

[47] *See generally* 3 Scott on Trusts §190.7.

[48] Id.

[49] *See* Restatement (Third) of Trusts §190 comment *j* (1992).

have the implied power to sell on credit, that is, in exchange for an unsecured promissory note, provided the promissory note is an appropriate trust investment. Likewise, a power of sale does not automatically bring with it a power in the trustee to grant an option.[50] It depends upon whether to do so is in the best interests of the trust, taking into account all the facts and circumstances.[51]

A general power of sale or investment would allow the trustee to exchange trust property for property other than cash, provided the property received is a proper trust investment.[52]

It appears to be the current state of the law that a power of sale, in and of itself, will not bring with it the power to incorporate the trust property.[53] Let us assume, for example, that a portion of the trust estate comprises an unincorporated business enterprise. The trustee may wish to exchange the assets of the enterprise for shares in an incorporated entity in order to insulate the other trust assets from the risks of the business.[54] Some commentators have suggested that court approval may be needed to effect such an incorporation, absent express authority in the governing instrument.[55] It would seem, however, that any concerns regarding incorporating the trust property have more to do with issues of improper delegation than issues of the abuse of the power of sale.

It should be emphasized that a general express or implied power of sale does not contemplate sales to third parties for less than reasonable consideration.[56] Nor does it contemplate sales to the trustee himself.

**(b) The power to lease.** Associated with the trustee's duty to make the trust property productive is the power in the trustee to

[50] *See* 3 Scott on Trusts §190.8.

[51] *See* id. §190.8 n.3 and accompanying text.

[52] *See* Restatement (Third) of Trusts §190 comment *m* (1992). *See also* 3 Scott on Trusts §190.9 n.2 and accompanying text. The trustee should be aware that, under certain circumstances, like-kind exchanges may offer income tax advantages for the trust. *See* I.R.C. §1031.

[53] *See generally* 3 Scott on Trusts §190.9A; *see generally,* D.E. Ytreberg, Annot., Trustee's power to exchange trust property for share of corporation organized to hold the property, 20 A.L.R. 3d 841 (1968).

[54] Id.

[55] Id.

[56] *See* Restatement (Third) of Trusts §190 comment *i* (1992).

lease the real estate, unless to do so would violate the express or implied intentions of the settlor.[57] However, because the remaindermen are entitled to the entire interest upon termination, the lease may not extend beyond the period of the trust.[58] A lease that extends beyond the reasonably anticipated duration of the trust may not be binding on the remaindermen, but such a lease will be valid for the duration of the trust.[59] Thus the trustee should take care to limit his lease to a reasonable or customary term.

What *is* a "reasonable and customary duration" may depend upon facts peculiar to each case. Thus, long-term leases have been approved when necessary to preserve the trust property.[60] If the trustee enters into a lease where the lessee undertakes to make improvements to the property in partial or total satisfaction of the lessee's rental obligation, the trustee should understand that such an arrangement could have the effect of shifting beneficial interests from the income beneficiary to the remaindermen.[61] Therefore, absent express or implied authority in the governing instrument, the trustee should refrain from entering into such a lease unless a way can be found to compensate the income account for the portion of the lessee's rental obligation that has taken the form of capital improvements.

**(c) The power to sue and defend.** The trustee has the duty of gathering in and protecting the trust property,[62] hence the implied power to sue for it or for any damage to it; to defend suits against the trust; and to employ counsel and incur all necessary costs at the expense of the trust fund, whether successful or not in the litigation, unless the trustee has been imprudent.[63] These expenses are allowed, not only in cases directly affecting the property, but also where the trustee has acted reasonably and in good

[57] *See generally* Restatement (Second) of Trusts §189 (1959).

[58] Id. comment *c* (1959).

[59] Id.

[60] *See generally* 3 Scott on Trusts §189.2.

[61] *See generally* id. §189.5.

[62] *See* §6.2.1 (Duty to Take Active Control of Trust Property) and §6.2.6 (Duty to Defend Trust Against Attack; Duty Not to Attack Trust).

[63] *See* Restatement (Second) of Trusts §188 comment *b* (1959); *see generally* 3 Scott on Trusts §188.4.

faith in attempting to protect the beneficiary (*e.g.*, where the trustee has attempted, though unsuccessfully, to have a guardian appointed for the beneficiary).

**(d) The power to bind the trust in contract.** If there is a fiduciary duty, the trustee has the power to enter into contracts, binding on the trust, for goods and services that are reasonably needed by him to carry out that duty.[64] This would include the costs of judicial proceedings and the expenses of managing, repairing, and improving the trust property.[65] The trustee has the inherent power to hire at trust expense agents such as attorneys and brokers, provided their services are needed for the proper administration of the trust.[66] The trustee, however, has no implied power to hire an agent for the purpose of performing services that the trustee ought personally to perform.[67] The trustee, for example, could not hire at trust expense an agent to decide who among a class of beneficiaries is entitled to discretionary distributions of principal.[68]

**(e) The power to vote proxies.** One of the duties of the trustee is to actively manage and protect the trust estate.[69] Thus with respect to shares of stock the trustee has the power to exercise all of the ordinary rights of a stockholder, including the right to vote on corporate matters.[70] It is the duty of the trustee in voting shares of stock to act solely in the economic interest of the beneficiary in light of the manifested intentions of the settlor.[71] One has no power as trustee to indulge one's own social and political predilections with

[64] *See generally* 3 Scott on Trusts §188; Restatement (Second) of Trusts §271 (1959).

[65] *See generally* 3 Scott on Trusts §188.4 (judicial proceedings), §188.2 (repairs and improvements).

[66] *See* id. §188.3.

[67] *See* §6.1.4 (Duty to Give Personal Attention).

[68] Id.

[69] *See* §6.2.1 (Duties to Take Active Control of, Segregate, Earmark, and Protect Trust Property).

[70] *See generally* 3 Scott on Trusts §193.

[71] *See* id. §193.1.

the stockholder franchise.[72] The lodestars must always be the economic well-being of the trust and the intentions of the settlor.

If a minority interest in a corporation comprises a portion of the trust estate, the trustee probably has the implied power to vote the shares by proxy, provided the trustee is acquainted with the questions to be voted upon, has used due care in selecting the proxy, and has given suitable instructions with regard to the vote.[73] If the trust's interest in the corporation is a controlling one, the trustee has no power to give a general proxy.[74]

### §3.5.3.2 Powers to Engage in Acts That Might Otherwise Be Breaches of Trust

Sometimes it is in the interest of the trust — and the proper execution of its purposes — for the trustee to engage in acts that, at least technically, are breaches of trust. Thus most trust instruments bestow powers that the trustee might not otherwise possess under the common law. Courts will construe such provisions narrowly. The following is a catalog of some standard powers that fall into this category.[75]

**(a) The power to make discretionary applications of income and principal.** Most trust instruments give the trustee the power to pay income to or for the benefit of the beneficiary. However, if the instrument simply requires the trustee to pay the trust's income to the beneficiary, the common law would require that payment be made directly to the beneficiary at reasonable intervals less expenses allocable to income.[76] The trustee would not have the power to choose the alternative of expenditure for the benefit of

[72] *See* §6.1.3 (Duty to Be Loyal to the Trust).

[73] *See* 3 Scott on Trusts §193.3. For a list of statutes providing that fiduciaries may vote by proxy, *see* id., §193.3 nn.2-3.

[74] *See* id. §193.3.

[75] Sample language may be found in Bogert, Trusts and Trustees §§1281-1308.

[76] *See generally* 2A Scott on Trusts §182.

the beneficiary.[77] Thus if the beneficiary is incapacitated a guardian would have to be appointed by the court to receive the income payments on behalf of the beneficiary — an expensive, time-consuming, and inconvenient process.[78] Statutes have now been enacted in some jurisdictions allowing trustees to make payments to or for the benefit of an incapacitated beneficiary absent express authority in the governing instrument.[79]

Under a basic common law trust — *A* (the settlor) to *B* (the trustee) for *C* (the current beneficiary) for life, then to *D* (the remainder beneficiary) — *C* receives all net income accrued to the date of death, and upon *C*'s death, *D* receives the principal outright and free of trust. Because of the duty of impartiality, the trustee has no power to withhold income from *C* or take principal from *D* and give it to *C*.[80] To do so would be a breach of trust.[81] Moreover if there are multiple *C*'s, the trustee has a common law duty to be impartial as among them.[82] Thus each *C* would receive an equal portion of the income stream.

It is now common practice for settlors to bestow on trustees, in derogation of the common law duty of impartiality, the authority to favor the income beneficiary over the remainderman and vice versa, and to discriminate between and among members of a class of income beneficiaries. These discretionary powers to sprinkle, spray, accumulate income, and to invade principal are governed by standards set forth in the governing instrument.[83] A standard can be broadly drafted (*e.g.*, the power to invade principal for *C*'s "benefit") or narrowly drafted, (*e.g.*, the power to invade principal to pay *C*'s "medical bills"). A typical standard found in many trusts permits payment for the "maintenance and support" of the beneficiary. This standard falls somewhere between the underwriting of utility bills and the underwriting of a world cruise. Precisely

[77] Id.
[78] Id. §182.1, n.1 and accompanying text.
[79] Id.
[80] *See* §6.2.5 (Duty of Impartiality).
[81] Id.
[82] Id.
[83] *See generally* 2 Scott on Trusts §§128.3, 128.7; *see also,* Dobris, New Forms of Private Trusts for the Twenty-First Century — Principal and Income, 31 Real Prop. Prob. & Tr. J. 1 (Spring, 1996).

*where* is not always easy to determine. Much may depend on the beneficiary's station in life at the time the inter vivos trust was established, or in the case of a testamentary trust, during the testator's lifetime.[84] The menu of standards available to the settlor is limited only by one's imagination.

The permissible income beneficiaries and the presumptive remaindermen have standing to bring an action against the trustee for abuse of discretion. As a general rule, however, courts will not second guess the trustee's exercise of discretionary powers unless there has been clear abuse.[85] The trustee must be aware that the exercise of a discretionary power to pay income or distribute principal affects the property rights of the beneficiaries. Thus, discretionary decisions should be well documented: A trustee is well advised to keep accurate records of all requests, granted and denied.

The common law offers little useful guidance when it comes to whether the trustee shall take into account assets available to the beneficiary outside of the trust (*e.g.*, a portfolio of securities) or take into account the beneficiary's collateral sources of support (*e.g.*, welfare entitlements or a wealthy spouse). The issue most often arises when the standard is "maintenance" or "support." The Restatement of Trusts takes the position that in trusts for support the inference is that the trustee does not need to take into account other resources available to the beneficiary.[86] This position is followed by many, though not all jurisdictions.[87]

In any case, a court asked to rule on the issue will ground its ruling in the presumed intentions of the settlor as extracted from the particular language at issue.[88] The prudent prospective trustee

[84] *See generally* Halbach, Problems of Discretion in Discretionary Trusts, 61 Colum. L. Rev. 1425 (1961); *see also* IRC §2041(b)(1)(A) (providing that a power holder's right to invade principal for his own "maintenance or support" is *not* treated as a general power for federal estate tax purposes); *see* 2 Scott on Trusts §128.4 (suggesting that "support" encompasses support of a beneficiary's spouse and minor children).

[85] *See generally* 3 Scott on Trusts §187.

[86] *See* Restatement (Second) of Trusts §128(e) (1959).

[87] *See generally* 2 Scott on Trusts §128.4. (For a catalog of jurisdictions where the inference is that trustees do *not* have to consider collateral sources of support, *see* 2 Scott on Trusts §128.4, n.3.)

[88] Id.

will thus attempt to avoid the problem by insisting that the governing instrument reflect clearly whether the trustee shall take into account the beneficiary's other resources.

If the trust instrument grants the trustee the discretionary power to pay income or distribute principal to the beneficiary for the beneficiary's maintenance and support, the trustee may well be under an affirmative duty to determine if the beneficiary needs funds. Some recent cases seem to suggest this.[89]

If authorized to pay income and principal to or for the benefit of a beneficiary, may the trustee pay the beneficiary's funeral bills? Absent express authority to do so, probably not. This is because the equitable property interest is now in someone other than the beneficiary's estate.[90]

Inherent in a trustee's right to make discretionary distributions is the lesser right, in lieu thereof, to make loans. As a practical matter, however, the trustee may not wish to get into the business of administering loans to beneficiaries. Moreover, what if the beneficiary defaults? Should the trustee seek to collect on behalf of the trust or should discretion be exercised and the original transaction treated as an outright distribution? Absent special circumstances, the trustee should keep things as clean and simple as possible. Note, a loan to a beneficiary is an investment and should be carried as such on the books of the trust.

If there are competing requests for discretionary distributions it is up to the trustee, not counsel to the trust, to determine the proper allocation. In making discretionary payments among a group of several beneficiaries, the trustee has reasonable latitude in favoring one beneficiary over the other, since in the absence of abuse the trustee's discretion is final.[91] Under no circumstances, however, should the trustee make any discretionary distribution without a full understanding of the generation-skipping tax consequences.

[89] *See, e.g.,* Marsman v. Nasca, 30 Mass. App. 789, 573 N.E.2d 1025 (1991); Old Colony Trust Co. v. Rodd, 356 Mass. 584, 254 N.E.2d 886 (1970). *See generally* Hayes & Wall, Fiduciary Discretion — Where Is the Better Part of Valor, 132 Trusts & Estates 8 (1993) (discussing the practical considerations of making and documenting discretionary distributions).

[90] *But see* 2 Scott on Trusts §128.4.

[91] *See* 2A Scott on Trusts §183.

**(b) the power to lease beyond the term of the trust.** Under certain circumstances, it may be in the economic interest of the trust for the trustee to enter into a lease that extends beyond the term of the trust.[92] It is good practice, therefore, to provide express language in the governing instrument authorizing such leases. Otherwise the trustee might be held liable for failing to turn over to the remainderman the entire interest in the trust property.

**(c) The power to borrow on behalf of the trust or to pledge or mortgage the trust property.** Whether the trustee has the power to borrow money on behalf of the trust and whether he or she has the right to pledge or mortgage the trust property as security for the loan are separate questions.[93] The trustee, for example, may have a power to borrow money on the general credit of the trust for a particular trust purpose without any authority to pledge or mortgage a specific part of the trust property.[94]

Because the trustee has a common law duty to exercise direct continuing control over the trust property, there is no inherent power to borrow on behalf of the trust absent express statutory authority or express authority in the governing instrument.[95] It follows from this that the trustee would have no implied general power to pledge or mortgage the trust property. However, under limited circumstances (*e.g.*, an emergency threatening the economic well-being of the trust), the powers to borrow and to encumber the trust property may be implied.[96]

Some courts have construed certain expressed powers of management as including the power to borrow.[97] What about the power to borrow for investment purposes? Is that implied in the direction "to invest and reinvest?" Probably not, because such a

[92] *See generally* 3 Scott on Trusts §189.2; L.S. Tellier, Annot., Power of trustee and Court as regards term of lease of trust property, 67 A.L.R. 2d 978 (1959).

[93] *See* 2A Scott on Trusts §191.3.

[94] *See* id.

[95] *See* Restatement (Second) of Trusts §175 (1959). For a list of statutes enlarging the power of trustees to mortgage or pledge trust property, *see* 2A Scott on Trusts §191 n.17.

[96] Id. §167.

[97] *See generally* 3 Scott on Trusts §191.3.

power is tantamount to a power to speculate.[98] The mere power of sale would not carry with it a power to pledge or mortgage.[99]

If the trust expressly permits the trustee to borrow on behalf of the trust, may the trustee become the lender? This question usually arises in the context of a corporate fiduciary that has general banking powers. While there is no absolute prohibition against the trustee lending funds to the trust, if at all possible the practice should be avoided. Any loans that *are* made must be at competitive rates and terms. The issue of conflict of interest is always present whenever the trustee enters into transactions involving the trust estate for the trustee's own account.

It should be noted that the recently revised Restatement of Trusts now grants the trustee an implied power to borrow, pledge, or otherwise encumber trust property for trust purposes, unless prohibited from doing so by statute or the terms of the trust.[100]

**(d) The power to invest in mutual funds, common trust funds, and common funds.** In a jurisdiction where the investment of trust property in a mutual fund is considered a breach of the common law duty not to delegate investment discretion, the trustee will need express authority in the governing instrument.[101] To invest in a common trust fund, the trustee will need statutory authority or express authority in the trust instrument;[102] otherwise the trustee runs afoul of the common law duty not to commingle the assets of the trust with the assets of other trusts.[103]

Nowadays many trusts fracture into separate trust shares upon the happening of a contingency. It may be in the economic interest of all concerned, however, to keep the assets of the separate trusts

[98] *See* id. §227.6.

[99] *See generally* 2A Scott on Trusts §191.

[100] *See* Restatement (Third) of Trusts §191 (1992).

[101] *See* §6.1.4 (Duty to Give Personal Atttention (Not to Delegate)); *See generally* Langbein & Posner, Market Funds and Trust-Investment Law, 1976 Am. B. Found. Res. J. 1, 22 (1976); Shattuck, The Legal Propriety of Investment by American Fiduciaries in the Shares of Boston-Type Open-End Investment Trusts, 25 B.U. L. Rev. 1 (1945).

[102] *See* Restatement (Third) of Trusts §227 comment *m* (1992). *See generally* Bogert, Trusts and Trustees §677.

[103] *See* §6.2.1 (Duties to Take Active Control of, Segregate, Earmark, and Protect Trust Property).

together in a common fund for investment purposes. Because of the common law prohibition against commingling, the trustee will need express authority in the governing instrument to do so.[104]

**(e) The power to hold the trust property in the name of a third party or in the trustee's own name without disclosing the fiduciary relationship.** The trustee has a common law duty to earmark the trust property as the property of the trust.[105] On the other hand, the trustee may, for legitimate reasons, prefer not to disclose the fiduciary relationship. The process of security transfer, for example, is less complicated when securities are registered in the name of someone other than the trustee (there being no need to prove authority to brokers and transfer agents). Any power in the trustee not to disclose the fiduciary relationship must be set forth expressly in the governing instrument or in a statute.[106]

When trust securities are registered in the name of a third party, the level of risk will vary depending upon the type of intermediary. If, for example, trust securities are registered in the name of a partnership established under the auspices of a bank trust department (a nominee),[107] the securities are segregated from the general assets of the bank. In the event of the bank's insolvency, property subject to trust would promptly be transferred to another institution with little or no interruption in asset administration.[108]

When trust securities are registered in the name of a brokerage house (*street name*),[109] however, segregation will be less than

[104]*See generally* 2A Scott on Trusts §179.2.

[105]*See* id. §179.3. *See* §6.2.1.2 (Duty to Segregate and Earmark Trust Property).

[106]*See generally* Bogert, Trusts and Trustees §596.

[107]Id. *See generally* §6.2.1.2 (Duty to Segregate and Earmark Trust Property).

[108]*See* Mooney, Beyond Negotiability: A New Model for Transfer and Pledge of Interests in Securities Controlled by Intermediaries, 12 Cardozo L. Rev. 305, 361 n. 200 (1990) (hereinafter, Mooney, Beyond Negotiability).

[109]"Street Name" generally refers to a security intermediary's practice of holding a fungible bulk of securities in its own name or in that of its nominees, even though the securities may be beneficially owned by its customers. Mooney, Beyond Negotiability, 12 Cardozo L.R. 305, n.4 (1990); *see generally* 5 Scott on Trusts §521.6 n.9 and accompanying text; In re Bevill, Bresler & Schulman, Inc., 59 B.R. 353, 374 (1986); and §6.2.1.2 (Duty to Segregate and Earmark Trust Property).

absolute. The securities are not evidenced by identifiable certificates. Instead, they are held in a fungible bulk that is made up of the securities of all the broker-dealer's customers.[110] In the event of the broker-dealer's insolvency, special rules under the Bankruptcy Code and the Securities Investor Protection Act (SIPA) come into play.[111] These rules could prevent the trustee from exercising immediate control over the trust property. They could also result in the trust taking a pro rata share of the fungible bulk, a share that could be less than what would be owed to it. Should there be a shortfall, recourse could then be had against the assets of the Securities Investor Protection Corporation (SIPIC). The settlor and the trustee will want to give careful consideration to whether SIPIC insurance adequately mitigates the risks of holding securities in street name with a broker-dealer.

**(f) The power to compromise, arbitrate, and abandon claims.** A trustee has the duty to collect that which is owed the trust.[112] On the other hand there is a duty not to squander trust assets in litigating claims that should be dealt with in some other way.[113] Thus the trustee has the inherent common law power to compromise, arbitrate, and abandon claims to the extent it is in the economic interest of the trust to do so.[114] Because of the tension between the two duties, the cautious trustee will seek judicial approval before compromising, arbitrating, or abandoning substantial claims, unless there is clear statutory authority to do so or the matter is expressly addressed in the governing instrument.

**(g) The power to resolve questions as to what is income and what is principal.** Absent authority in the governing instrument,

[110] Mooney, Beyond Negotiability at 331-42.

[111] Id at 351-61. *See also* Don & Wang, Stockbroker Liquidations under the Securities Investor Protection Act and Their Impact on Securities Transfers, 12 Cardozo L. Rev. 509, 540-547 (1990).

[112] *See* Restatement (Second) of Trusts §177 (1959).

[113] Id. comment *c*; 3 Scott on Trusts §192.

[114] Id; *see* C.C. Marvel, Annot., Trustee's power to compromise and settle claims and actions by or against trust estate, 35 A.L.R. 2d 967 (1954).

the trustee has no inherent power to deviate from generally accepted practices of fiduciary accounting when determining what is income and what is principal for purposes of crediting receipts or charging disbursements.[115] Nor would most settlors want to bestow on the trustee such a power, for to do so would permit the trustee to shift beneficial interests arbitrarily between the income beneficiary and the remaindermen.[116] On the other hand, when the law provides no clear guidance on how to characterize a particular item, the trustee ought to have the power to decide such questions without resort to the courts. Thus the settlor should give the trustee the power in doubtful cases to determine which receipts are income and which are principal, and which expenses should be paid out of the income account and which out of the principal account.[117]

**(h) The power to exclude the remainderman from the accounting process.** The trustee has a duty to render accounts at reasonable intervals not only to the income beneficiaries but also to the remaindermen.[118] The process of accounting to remaindermen can be expensive and time-consuming, particularly when interests are contingent or diffused.[119] Moreover, when remaindermen are unborn or unascertainable during a given accounting period, the involvement of a guardian ad litem may be required.[120] A trustee therefore welcomes an express power to

[115]*See* Restatement (Second) of Trusts §233 comment *p* (1959).

[116]In Old Colony Trust Co. v. Silliman, 352 Mass. 6, 223 N.E.2d 504 (1967), the court held that broad discretion in the trustee to decide whether accretions are to be treated as income or principal did not empower trustee to shift the beneficial interests. It noted that "[a] fair reading of the whole of most trust instruments will reveal a 'judicially enforceable, external, and ascertainable standard' for the exercise of even broadly expressed fiduciary powers." Id. at 9; id at 506.

[117]*See* R.P. Davis, Annot., Construction of specific provision of will or trust instrument giving executor or trustee power to determine what is income or what is principal, 27 A.L.R. 2d 1323 (1953).

[118]*See* §6.1.5 (Duty to Account to the Beneficiary).

[119]*See generally* Westfall, Nonjudicial Settlement of Trustees' Accounts, 71 Harv. L. Rev. 40, 49 n.34 and accompanying text (1957).

[120]Id.; *see also* Restatement (Second) of Trusts §214 comment *a* (1959).

exclude the remaindermen from the accounting process.[121] A word of caution: In some jurisdictions, the assent of the income beneficiary cannot bind the remaindermen no matter what the governing instrument may say, particularly when the assent relates to a shifting of beneficial interests.[122]

**(i) Special investment powers.** The trustee has a duty to invest the trust property prudently, balancing the obligation to preserve the principal for the remaindermen against the obligation to produce a reasonable rate of return for the income beneficiary.[123] Over the years, courts and legislatures have set down guidelines for trustees to follow in the carrying out of this duty.[124] A trustee who keeps within them will be protected regardless of how the portfolio actually performs.[125]

Many instruments, however, provide the trustee with powers to deviate from established guidelines, such as a power to speculate, or to hold wasting assets or assets that present a high degree of risk. As a practical matter, the more general the fiduciary's power to veer from established investment practice the more likely the power is illusory.[126] If a settlor, for example, wants the family business retained in trust even though such an investment may amount to a speculation under the common law, the trustee will want an express power of retention that makes reference to the business itself[127] as well as appropriate express powers to

[121]For sample language, *see* Bogert, Trusts and Trustees §1295 n.11.

[122]*See, e.g.*, In re Crane, 34 N.Y.S.2d 9 (1942); *see generally* Westfall, supra note 119. *See also* Matter of Odmark, N.Y.L.J. Feb. 5, 1996, at 29 (Surr. Ct.) (invalidating provision relieving trustee of duty to account to remaindermen).

[123]*See* §6.2.2.1 (The Harvard College Prudent Man Rule and Its Progeny).

[124]Id.

[125]Id.

[126]"A trust provision that authorizes investments to be made 'in the trustee's discretion,' or that confers on the trustee 'all of the powers of an owner' is not ordinarily to be construed as granting the trustee wider latitude than conferred by the prudent investor rule." Restatement (Third) of Trusts §228 comment *g* (1992).

[127]Id. §229 comment *e*; *see* M.L. Cross, Annot., Construction and effect of instrument authorizing or directing trustee or executor to retain investments received under such instrument, 47 A.L.R. 2d 187 (1956).

enable the trustee to run the business efficiently and cost-effectively. Absent express authority to hold the settlor's business in trust, the trustee is under a duty to liquidate the business.[128] Certainly a general authority to speculate is insufficient, because the trustee is at risk that some court would dismiss such language as "boilerplate" and then rule that the trustee's reliance upon it was unreasonable.[129]

**(j) The power to loan money to the trust and charge a reasonable rate of interest.** As the trustee has no inherent power under the common law to transact with the trust property for his own account, it would seem he has no inherent power to loan his own money to the trust at interest. The cases suggest otherwise, however.[130] All things being equal, however, it is preferable that the trustee refrain from such activity in the absence of statutory or regulatory authority or authority in the governing instrument.[131]

**(k) The power to terminate the trust.** The trustee has no inherent power to terminate the trust before its purposes have been fulfilled.[132] The settlor may wish to provide such a power should the trust become impractical or uneconomical to administer. Absent an express power of termination, for example, the trustee might feel obliged to seek judicial approval before terminating a trust that had become too small to cost-effectively manage.[133] Many jurisdictions now have statutes authorizing the nonjudicial termination of small trusts.[134] It is important to keep in mind, however, that for an express termination provision to

[128]Id.

[129]Id. §228 comment *g*. For a discussion of the trustee's obligations as they relate to investments in life insurance contracts, see U.S. Trust, 1994 Life Insurance Trusts and Related Matters, Practical Drafting 3588 (1994).

[130]*See generally* Bogert, Trusts and Trustees §543(L).

[131]Id.

[132]*See generally* 4 Scott on Trusts §337.

[133]*See* Procedures for Terminating Small Trusts: Report of the Committee on Formation, Administration and Distribution of Trusts, 19 Real Prop. Prob. & Tr. J. 988 (1984).

[134]Id.

have any utility, it must direct where the property is to go once the power of termination has been exercised.[135]

**(1) The power to administer distributions to minors.** Delivery of trust property into the hands of a minor beneficiary is misdelivery for which there is absolute liability. Thus the cautious trustee, faced with making a distribution to a minor, may well insist that a court-appointed guardian be in place to receive the property. Because of the general cost and inconvenience of the guardianship process, the prospective trustee will want to see a provision empowering the trustee to retain and administer property otherwise distributable to a minor for the minor's benefit. Typical language includes the power to deal with the minor's relatives and others who have not been formally appointed to oversee the minor's welfare. The prospective trustee should insist that any such provision address where the property is to go should the minor die prior to the final distribution.

## *§3.5.4 Nature of Trustee's Liability*

At common law, the trustee's liability was personal.[136] This is still the law when it comes to the trustee's internal dealings with the beneficiary.

### §3.5.4.1 Personal Liability

The trustee can take no benefit from ownership of the trust estate, nor deal with it for personal profit or for any purpose unconnected with the trust.[137] The trustee is nevertheless the "owner" of the property.[138] Thus, subject to certain exceptions

[135] Id.

[136] *See, however, generally,* Curtis, The Transmogrification of The American Trust, 31 Real Prop. Prob. & Tr. J. 251 (no. 2 1996) (suggesting that the trust is evolving into a "quasi-corporation" when it comes to the trustee's third party liability).

[137] *See* §6.1.3 (Duty to Be Loyal to the Trust).

[138] *See* §3.5.1 (Nature and Extent of the Trustee's Estate).

(statutory and otherwise),[139] the general rule is that the trustee is personally liable as owner to nonbeneficiaries such as contract creditors, tort creditors, and the federal, state, and local governments in the same way and to the same extent as if the property were owned by the trustee individually.[140] Moreover, the trustee is personally liable in equity to the beneficiaries for any breach of fiduciary duty,[141] subject however to a right of indemnity or exoneration from the trust estate for certain liabilities.[142]

### §3.5.4.2 Insuring Against Personal Liability

As owner of the legal interest, the trustee is vulnerable on two fronts when it comes to personal liability. As the *owner* of the trust estate, the trustee is personally liable to nonbeneficiaries for negligent and intentional torts committed by him and his servants against nonbeneficiaries in the course of the administration of the trust estate. As the *fiduciary*, the trustee is also personally liable to the beneficiaries for any negligent or intentional breaches of trust that cause injury to the trust itself.

As a practical matter, the individual trustee cannot obtain insurance that would cover the trustee's personal liability for intentional torts committed against nonbeneficiaries and for intentional breaches of trust.[143] Even if such insurance could be obtained, the premiums would have to be absorbed by the trustee personally as a cost of doing business — they may not be charged by the trustee to the trust estate.[144] The insurance company that underwrites the trustee's coverage for negligent acts against nonbeneficiaries essentially underwrites as well the costs of the trustee's defense against allegations that the acts were intentional.

[139] *See* §§3.5.2.3 (exoneration & reimbursement); 7.3 (Trustee's Liability as Legal Owner to Nonbeneficiaries).

[140] *See* §7.3.

[141] *See* §7.2 (Trustee's Liability as Fiduciary to the Beneficiary).

[142] *See* §3.5.2.3.

[143] *See generally* R. Keeton & A. Widiss, Insurance Law, Guide to Fundamental Principles, Legal Doctrines, and Commercial Practices, Practitioner's Edition §5.4 (1988) (suggesting that it would be against public policy to be able to obtain insurance against one's intentional tortious acts).

[144] *See generally* Bogert, Trusts and Trustees §599.

The individual trustee who is not also an attorney will have a hard time finding inexpensive fiduciary liability insurance that will cover the trustee's personal liability for negligent breaches of trust, particularly in the carrying out of investment and property disbursement responsibilities.[145] Such insurance falls outside the scope of coverage of most homeowner and umbrella policies. It is generally underwritten on a per trust basis, with the insurance company requiring the trustee, as part of the application process, to submit a copy of the governing instrument. If the terms of the trust are amendable in any manner that would change the potential liability of the trustee, a substantive amendment will terminate coverage unless approved in advance by the insurance company.

Many insurance companies have a substantial minimum premium for such fiduciary liability insurance. The individual trustee of a personal trust who seeks customized fiduciary liability insurance that would cover the trustee's negligent breaches of trust probably should start with those companies that write policies for fiduciaries of pension plans or directors and officers of corporations.[146] Remember that premiums for that type of coverage may not be charged against the trust estate.

The attorney acting as trustee has an advantage over the layman when it comes to coverage for negligent breaches of trust. Standardized legal malpractice policies are available to the lawyer who acts as trustee of trusts in the ordinary course of his or her practice. Most of these policies, however, exclude discrimination and environmental injury claims.

There are standardized insurance products available to corporate trustees. This type of insurance is known in the trade as Bankers Professional Liability Insurance or BPL Insurance. BPL Insurance covers both the *internal* risk of breach of fiduciary duty and the *external* risk of liability to third parties with whom the

[145]Phone interviews with insurers offering professional liability products yielded no insurer with a standard policy for the private trustee. Those insurers willing to consider underwriting policies would negotiate the price and the coverage.

[146]A list of such companies is published by the International Risk Management Institute, 12222 Merit Drive, Suite 1660, Dallas, Texas 75251, which can be reached at (214) 960-7693.

trustee comes in contact in the course of administering a trust. The following are some of the more common trust activities that are covered by a typical BPL Insurance contract:[147]

- Administering trusts
- Administering Individual Retirement Accounts and Keogh Plans
- Acting as trustee in bankruptcy
- Acting as an ERISA fiduciary
- Acting as tax planner and/or tax preparer to trusts, estates and individuals
- Acting as an investment or financial advisor
- Acting as an investment manager

The corporate trustee is the named insured under a BPL Insurance policy. Also covered under the policy are the corporation's owners, partners, officers, stockholders, directors, and employees. Their estates are covered as well. BPL Insurance generally covers economic injury occasioned by negligent acts. It will not cover punitive, exemplary, and multiplied damages. Nor will it cover fines and penalties. Some policies have "recourse provisions." This means that if a covered individual such as a trust officer *willfully* injures a trust, e.g., embezzles its funds, then the insurance company will not pay out under the policy if the corporate trustee can make itself whole in an action against the trust officer.

There are three types of exclusions found in BPL Insurance policies. They are exclusions for business risks; fraudulent, criminal and dishonest acts; and exposures covered under other policies.

The trust officer who is employed by a corporate trustee seems particularly exposed when it comes to liability for breaches of trust. While the doctrine of respondeat superior will inevitably draw in the corporate trustee as a codefendant, it is the employment contract itself that determines whether the employer must

[147]Bankers Professional Liability Policy Supplemental Application (American International Specialty Lines Insurance Company) 89-182 (3/89).

defend and indemnify the trust officer or obtain insurance that will achieve the same result. If the terms are nonexistent or ambiguous in this regard, the trust officer would be well advised to consult with his or her insurance carrier. Again, little comfort will be found in the terms of personal homeowner and umbrella policies.

The trustee's liability for injury to nonbeneficiaries occasioned by negligent acts (committed personally and by servants) is readily insurable, and in most cases its costs are chargeable to the trust estate. For example, the cost of insuring an automobile that comprises a part of the trust estate is properly a trust expense.

### §3.5.4.3 Bonds and Sureties

In most states, a *testamentary trustee* must execute a bond for the faithful performance of his duties.[148] (However, it is generally within the discretion of the court to require that the trustee of any type of trust give an appropriate bond.)[149] A fiduciary bond is a signed promise to be personally responsible for carrying out certain obligations. It neither increases nor decreases the trustee's general fiduciary responsibility nor does it affect the trustee's liability. It is essentially a standardized enforcement mechanism. If a trustee who has given bond misdelivers or embezzles, for example, he is subject to suit "on the bond." For a compilation of state statutes requiring certain trustees, including corporate trustees, to give bond, see §151 of Bogert, Trusts and Trustees.

It may be appropriate to have a surety on the bond.[150] A surety is either an individual or a company who agrees to be responsible (up to the dollar limits specified in the bond) in the event the beneficiary cannot be made whole in an action against the trustee. Surety fees are a proper trust expense generally charged to trust

[148] *See generally* Bogert, Trusts and Trustees §151; 76 Am. Jur. 2d *Trusts* §§427-440 (1992); *see also* §3.4.1 (Appointment of Trustee).

[149] Id.

[150] *See generally* Bogert, Trusts and Trustees §864; 76 Am. Jur. 2d *Trusts* §§427-440 (1992).

income. Usually corporate trustees, by statute, need not have sureties on their bonds.[151]

In some jurisdictions, the surety is entitled to receive an accounting from the trustee.[152] The surety, however, does not have standing to petition for removal of the trustee.[153]

[151]Id.
[152]Bogert, Trusts and Trustees §961.
[153]Bogert, Trusts and Trustees §522.

CHAPTER 4

# Interests Remaining with the Settlor



## §4.1 Interests and Powers Remaining with the Settlor by Operation of Law

Whether the law reserves for the settlor some interest in the trust property is a question of more than academic interest, particularly in the charitable context where property worth billions of dollars is currently held in trust.[1] If some property rights remain

**§4.1** [1]The three largest charitable foundations are The Ford Foundation ($6,600,562,000), the W. K. Kellogg Foundation ($6,034,576,655), and the J. Paul Getty Trust ($6,016,488,752). Feczko, The Foundation Directory: 100 Largest Foundations by Assets (18th ed. 1996). The best-endowed academic institutions are Harvard ($8,811,785,000), the University of Texas Systems ($5,697,150,000), and Yale ($4,853,010,000). Cambridge Associates, Inc., 1996 NACUBO: Endowback with the settlor at the time property is transferred in trust, then the settlor may have standing to compel the trustee to carry out the terms of the trust. Thus, for example, the trustee of a college endowment fund could be accountable not only to the attorney general but also to benefactors. Presently there is much authority to the effect that the settlor of an irrevocable trust has no interest that would allow him to bring an action against the trustee for breach of trust.[2] However, some case law and commentary suggest that the settlor may not be entirely out of the picture (*e.g.*, a spendthrift trust may not be terminated without the settlor's consent).[3] Moreover, some states have enacted legislation that directly address the issue.[4] Of course, in any state the settlor with

---

ment Study (1996). The aggregate sum for the 472 institutions that participated in the college and university study is $132.2 billion. (For further information, contact the National Association of Colleges and Universities at (202) 861-2500.) The so-called Bishop Estate is the wealthiest charity in the United States with $10 billion in assets. Freedman & Cohen, Bishop's Gambit, Hawaiians Who Own Goldman Sachs Stake Play Clever Tax Game, Wall St. J., Apr. 25, 1995, at A1, col. 6; Barrett, Tempest Erupts Over Secretive Hawaiian Trust, Wall St. J., Oct. 10, 1997, at B1 col. 3.

[2] *See, e.g.*, 3 Scott on Trusts §200.1; Bogert, Trusts and Trustees §42.

[3] *See, e.g.*, Carr v. Carr, 171 N.W. 785 (Iowa 1919) (holding that the donor of a trust has such interest therein as to entitle him to maintain a suit in equity to compel the carrying out of the terms thereof); 2A Scott on Trusts §151 ("It is held that even though the trust is a spendthrift trust, it can be terminated by the beneficiaries and the settlor if they all consent and are under no disability); 4 Scott on Trusts §340 ("It is clear, therefore, that in New York the trust can be terminated with the consent of the settlor and all the beneficiaries, even though a beneficiary may have an interest in the income that cannot be assigned by him.") Bogert, Trusts and Trustees §1006 n.13 and accompanying text; *see generally* Gaubatz, Grantor Enforcement of Trusts: Standing in One Private Law Setting, 62 N.C. L. Rev. 905, 941 (1984); Note, Right of a Settlor to Enforce a Private Trust, 62 Harv. L. Rev. 1370 (1949); Rounds, Social Investing, IOLTA and the Law of Trusts: The Settlor's Case Against the Political Use of Charitable and Client Funds, 22 Loy. U. Chi. L.J. 163 (1990); *see generally* Reid, Mureiko, Mikeska, Privilege and Confidentiality Issues When a Lawyer Represents a Fiduciary, 30 Real Prop. Prob. & Tr. J. 542, 588 (1966); Langbein, The Contractarian Basis of the Law of Trusts, 105 Yale L.J. 625, 664 (1995).

[4] In 1990, California enacted legislation granting the settlor of an irrevocable living trust the right to petition to have the trustee removed for cause. Cal. Prob. Code §15642(a) (West 1991). California also provides for settlor involvement in the modification or termination of irrevocable trusts. Id. §15404.

expressly retained interests or powers may bring an enforcement action against the trustee.[5]

## §4.1.1 *The Reversionary Interest*

If the settlor or the settlor's estate[6] is entitled by operation of law to a return of the trust property should the trust fail, it is said that the settlor possesses a *reversionary interest.* Moreover this right is vested in the settlor from the trust's inception whether or not the trust ever does fail.

### §4.1.1.1 The Noncharitable Trust

The governing instrument of a noncharitable trust — if properly drawn — designates those who take title to the property once the trust terminates. In the absence of such express or implied designation, or if the anticipated takers are not then in existence, the beneficial interest does not accrue to the trustee. Or to put it another way, the trustee may not walk away with the trust property. The property returns to the settlor or the settlor's estate upon a resulting trust.[7]

A *resulting trust* is the equitable mechanism that gets the title from the trustee back into the hands of the settlor or the settlor's estate when a trust fails. From the trust's inception, the settlor possesses the possibility of reverter, which is a fully transferable vested reversionary interest in the property.[8] This is nothing more than a beneficial interest in the property superior to that of the trustee and which may become possessory by operation of law through the mechanism of the resulting trust should the trust fail.

The resulting trust represents the law's commitment to protecting the settlor's property rights. The concept of the trust be-

[5] *See* Bogert, Trusts and Trustees §§42, 415.

[6] *See generally,* W.W. Allen, Annot., Time of ascertainment of settlor's heirs and distributees who take on failure of trust, 27 A.L.R. 2d 691 (1953).

[7] 5 Scott on Trusts §411. *See also* National Shawmut Bank v. Joy, 315 Mass. 457, 463, 53 N.E.2d 113, 119 (1944).

[8] J. Gray, Rule Against Perpetuities §§113, 603.9 (4th ed. 1942).

gins with the settlor, exists to fulfill the settlor's wishes, and ultimately ends with the settlor or the settlor's estate to the extent that the settlor's wishes cannot be fulfilled or are unknown. The trustee is the steward of someone else's property — in part the steward of the reversionary interest. The scrupulous trustee understands this.

#### §4.1.1.2 The Charitable Trust

Occasionally, the charitable purpose for which the settlor establishes a charitable trust will become impossible of fulfillment. This most often arises where the charity ceases to exist. In those cases a cy pres petition may be brought to determine if the settlor had a general charitable intent.[9]

A settlor possesses no reversionary interest under a trust with a general charitable purpose. Should such a trust become impossible of fulfillment, the court, instead of enforcing a resulting trust, will apply the doctrine of *cy pres.*[10] This involves the judicial modification of the terms of the trust so that a charitable purpose as near as possible to the one generally specified by the settlor can be carried out. The development of the concept of cy pres as an alternative to the resulting trust has had the effect of making general charitable intent and the reversionary interest mutually exclusive.[11] The settlor of a trust with a limited charitable purpose, however, does have a vested reversionary interest that becomes possessory if the purpose becomes impossible of fulfillment.[12]

### *§4.1.2 The Expectation Interest*

Let us assume for the sake of argument that a certain settlor reserves no power and no beneficial interest. Would that settlor nonetheless have any standing to seek judicial redress for a breach

[9] *See* §§9.4.3 (Cy Pres) and 8.15.5 (Statute of Frauds).

[10] Id.

[11] Id.

[12] J. Gray, The Rule Against Perpetuities §603.9 (4th ed. 1942); 4A Scott on Trusts §§399.3, 401.2-401.3.

of trust? It is generally assumed that neither the settlor nor the settlor's representatives can compel performance of the trust or redress a breach.[13] This assumption appears to take support from the Restatement of Trusts:

> Neither the settlor nor his heirs or personal representatives, as such, can maintain a suit against the trustee to enforce a trust or enjoin or obtain redress for a breach of trust. Where, however, the settlor retains an interest in the trust property, he can of course maintain a suit against the trustee to protect that interest. Thus, if the settlor is also a beneficiary of the trust, or if he has an interest by way of a resulting trust, or if he has reserved power to revoke the trust, he can maintain a suit against the trustee to protect his interest.[14]

Upon reflection, however, one realizes that while under this section the settlor of a trust with a general charitable purpose would lack standing to enforce the trust, perhaps the settlor of either a personal trust or a charitable trust with a limited purpose would not.

The settlor of a personal trust or a limited-charitable purpose trust retains a vested reversionary interest in the trust property that exists because of the possibility that the trust may fail at some future date for want of a purpose or beneficiary. Upon the trust's failure, a resulting trust arises in favor of the settlor or the settlor's estate. Thus the Restatement may support the proposition that the reversionary interest — an interest that becomes possessory should the trust fail — provides a settlor with sufficient standing to compel the trustee to carry out the provisions of his trust. On the other hand, the authors of the Restatement may have intended that the settlor acquire standing only in the event the trust actually fails.

Taking a different tack, in 1949, a Note in the Harvard Law Review questioned the now widely-held assumption that the settlor lacks standing to seek enforcement of the trust and suggested that Professor Scott's positions were unsupported by judicial decision.[15] Thirty-five years later Professor Gaubatz put forth in an

[13] *See generally* 3 Scott on Trusts §200.1; Bogert, Trusts and Trustees §42.
[14] Restatement (Second) of Trusts §200 comment *b* (1959).
[15] *See* Note, Right of a Settlor to Enforce a Private Trust, 62 Harv. L. Rev. 1370 (1949).

article the thesis that in some situations a settlor has standing to enforce a trust based on the settlor's "expectation interest" in having the terms of the trust carried out.[16]

Even the Uniform Management of Institutional Funds Act (UMIFA)[17] acknowledges that the donor of a gift to a charitable corporation is not entirely out of the picture. Section 7 of the Act, for example, provides that, "[w]ith the written consent of the donor, the governing board may release, in whole or in part, a restriction imposed by the applicable gift instrument on the use or investment of an institutional fund."[18]

To be sure, enforceability and accountability are two features that distinguish the trust from the *gift.*[19] If a settlor has an expectation interest in having the terms of the trust carried out — and thus standing to seek judicial redress — this may add an extra measure of accountability to the trust relationship consistent with the impo-

[16]Gaubatz, Grantor Enforcement of Trusts: Standing in One Private Law Setting, 62 N.C. L. Rev. 905 (1984). Professor Gaubatz suggests that "the grantor's standing is analyzed better on the basis of whether he has an interest, economic or otherwise, in the performance of the trustee's duties. If he possesses such an interest, and that interest is within the zone of interests sought to be protected by those duties, then the grantor can bring an action to enforce the trust. In a broad sense, if the grantor has an economic, *expectation* (emphasis added), or representational interest in the trust, such that he can be trusted to fully and fairly litigate the validity of the transactions that he challenges, and his interest was foreseeable at the time the trust was created, he can maintain an action." Id. at 940-941. *See generally* Reid, Mureiko, Mikeska, Privilege and Confidentiality Issues When a Lawyer Represents a Fiduciary, 30 Real Prop. Prob. & Tr. J. 541, 588 (1996); Langbein, The Contractarian Basis of the Law of Trusts, 105 Yale L.J. 625, 664 (1995). *But see* Sanders v. Citizens Natl. Bank of Leesburg, 585 So. 2d 1064 (Fla. 1991) (court, having denied a settlor standing to enforce a trust that he had impressed upon his property, made an oblique reference to Professor Gaubatz's article).

[17]7A U.L.A. 705. UMIFA has been adopted by 40 states and the District of Columbia.

[18]Id. at 723; *but see,* Carl J. Herzog Foundation, Inc. v. University of Bridgeport, 243 Conn. 1, 699 A.2d 995 (1997) (Section 7 does not bestow standing on benefactor to enforce restriction).

[19]*See generally* Restatement (Second) of Trusts §§25 comment *c*, comment *a* (1959). The settlor's standing, if any, to enforce a trust may have its roots in Anglo-Norman law. In the fourteenth century, if the *feoffee to uses* failed to perform his duties, the *feoffor* could seek enforcement in the Court of Common Pleas. Later, the *cestui que use* also gained a right to seek enforcement, but in the Court of Chancery. *See generally* W. F. Fratcher, 6 Intl. Encyclopedia of Comp. Law, at 14 (F. H. Lawson, ed. 1973).

sition of fiduciary duties. It is that imposition, after all, which distinguishes a trust from a gift. Without some right of enforcement remaining back with the settlor, there is no practical way to prevent the trustee from colluding with beneficiaries to effect a breach of trust. In the context of charitable trusts, an element of "privatization" is called for as attorneys general no longer have the resources to systematically police the administration of the nation's inventory of charitable trusts.[20] Moreover, in construing the terms of a trust, a court will attempt to divine the intent of the settlor as manifested at the time the interest was created.[21] Is there not then some irony when that settlor, himself, is denied standing to bring before the court issues relating to that intent?

One cannot deny the practical downside for the trustee if the settlor is to remain in the picture, particularly in situations where the trustee and settlor disagree as to how certain trust provisions should be interpreted and administered. And there will always be the situation where the settlor and beneficiaries are at loggerheads and the trustee is caught in the middle.

### *§4.1.3 Creditor Accessibility as a General Inter Vivos Power of Appointment*

It is becoming a general rule that a settlor's creditors may reach the trust property to the extent the settlor reserves a beneficial interest.[22] For example, a trust for the benefit of the settlor — fully discretionary as to income and principal — will expose the entire property to creditor attack.[23] The law thus bestows on the settlor the ability to indirectly extract value from the trust by incurring debts and leaving it to the creditors to collect.[24] This right to direct trust property to creditors conforms to the Restatement of Property's definition of a general inter vivos power of appointment.[25] The possession of such a right may have estate and

[20] *See generally* 4A Scott on Trusts §391.
[21] *See generally* Restatement (Second) of Trusts §164 comment *b* (1959).
[22] *See* §5.3.3.1 (Reaching Settlor's Reserved Beneficial Interest).
[23] Id.
[24] Id.
[25] Restatement (Second) of Property §11.4 (Donative Transfers).

gift tax consequences,[26] and may also bear on the settlor's eligibility for Medicaid and on the rights of the settlor's spouse to reach the trust property.[27]

In 1997, Alaska enacted a statute that may insulate reserved beneficial interests in certain irrevocable, "self-settled," independently-trusteed, discretionary trusts (created after April 1, 1997) from the reach of the settlors' creditors.[28] If a settlor of one of these Alaska asset protection trusts has reserved no express right of revocation and if the statute is effective in insulating the reserved beneficial interest from creditor attack, then it could be said that for gift and estate tax purposes the settlor has reserved no general inter vivos power of appointment over the transferred property.[29] Accordingly, although the transfer might have gift tax consequences, down the road the property itself, along with any appreciation, could be out of the settlor's Federal gross estate for estate tax purposes.[30] How the taxing authorities will respond to the Alaska legislation remains to be seen.

## §4.2 Expressly Reserved Beneficial Interests and Powers

A settlor may expressly reserve a beneficial interest in the income or the principal, or both, of the trust.[1] The settlor may

[26] *See* §5.3.3.1 (Reaching Settlor's Reserved Beneficial Interest).

[27] *See* §§5.3.5 (Medicaid eligibility) and 5.3.4 (spousal rights). The trustee will find helpful the chart entitled "Trusts Affected By The Omnibus Reconciliation Act of 1993" published in Kruse, Third-Party and Self-Created Trusts: A Lawyer's Comprehensive Reference 22-25 (1995). An earlier version of the chart can be found in the March 1995 issue of Trusts & Estates: Kruse, Self-Settled Trusts Following OBRA 1993, 134 Tr. & Est. 66, 68 (1995). *See also* Kruse, OBRA '93 Disability Trusts — A Status Report, 10 Prob. & Prop. 15 (No. 3) (1996).

[28] *See generally* §5.3.3.1(c) (Reaching Settlor's Reserved Beneficial Interest: . . . (c) Domestic Asset Protection Havens: Alaska).

[29] *See* Paolozzi v. Commissioner, 23 T.C. 182, 186 (1954) (gift tax); Outwin v. Commissioner, 76 T.C. 153 n.5 (1981) (estate tax).

[30] Id.

**§4.2** [1] *See generally* Restatement (Second) of Trusts §114 (1959).

reserve special and general powers of appointment.[2] If a power is exercisable by a will it is known as a *testamentary power.* A power exercisable by a deed is known as an *inter vivos power.* The settlor may reserve a power to amend the trust.[3] (This right is tantamount to a general inter vivos power of appointment because such a power can be inserted into the instrument through the amendment process.) At the outset, the settlor may appoint himself trustee or cotrustee by declaration or reserve the right to do so thereafter.[4] These are the traditional ways the settlor may remain in the picture.

Nowadays settlors are resorting to more limited, more subtle means of maintaining involvement, such as by reserving rights to control investments, to remove trustees, or to receive accountings. These reservations are less burdensome for the settlor than the assumption of a cotrusteeship, but not necessarily less burdensome for the trustee. The practice of reserving the right to direct investments is a particularly worrisome development from the trustee's perspective because the law is not entirely clear whether the trustee has some fiduciary responsibility to monitor and react to the settlor's investment activities.[5] Any ambiguity in the arrangement will pose a trap for the unwary trustee and an extraordinary burden for the cautious trustee. The trustee should not accept directed trust business unless these ambiguities can be resolved by express language in the governing instrument. There is some authority to the effect that, in the case of an irrevocable trust, a nontrustee in whom investment discretion has been allocated will be held to a fiduciary standard in the

[2] *See generally* National Shawmut Bank v. Joy, 315 Mass. 457, 53 N.E.2d 113 (1944); 4 Scott on Trusts §330.

[3] *See generally* 4 Scott on Trusts §§331, 331.1, 331.2.

[4] *See generally* 2 Scott on Trusts §100.

[5] *See generally* 2A Scott on Trusts §185; Restatement (Third) of Trusts §185 comments *b-h* (1992); Kemper, Construction and Operation of Will or Trust Provision Appointing Advisors to Trustee or Executor, 56 A.L.R.3d 1249 (1974); *see also* Cal. Prob. Code Ann. §16462 (1990) (providing that "a trustee of a revocable trust is not liable to a beneficiary for any act performed or permitted pursuant to written directions from the person holding the power to revoke, including a person to whom the power to direct the trustee is delegated."); *see generally,* Hatamyar, See No Evil? The role of the directed trustee under ERISA, 64 Tenn. L.R. 1, 38-41 (1996) (discussing the common law of directed trustees).

exercise of that discretion.[6] It should be emphasized, however, that this will in no way diminish the general fiduciary duties of the trustee.

As to devices aimed at riding herd on the trustee — reserved rights of removal, consultation, and disclosure — the law has not settled on what constraints, if any, are placed on the holders of these rights. If they are fiduciaries, they are like cotrustees and presumably assume the burdens commensurate with that office, such as the risk of surcharge for unreasonable behavior. If they are *not* fiduciaries, then what are they? How does the law protect the trustee from assertions of these rights that are arbitrary, unreasonable, or imprudent — in short, in ways that are not in the interest of the beneficiaries?

[6] *See supra* note 5.

CHAPTER 5

# The Beneficiary



## §5.1 Who Can Be a Beneficiary?

A trust beneficiary's interest is an equitable interest.[1] This interest, be it vested or contingent, is property.[2] Thus entities

**§5.1** [1]*See* Restatement of Property §6 comment *a* (1936); Restatement (Second) of Trusts §2 comment *f* (1959); *see generally* §3.5.1 (Nature and Extent of Trustee's Estate).

[2]*See generally* 2 Scott on Trusts §130 (the property subject to the trust); 1 Restatement of Property at 3 (1936) (introduction to chapter 1) (the equitable interest); *see* In re Catherwood's Trust, 173 A.2d 86, 91 (1961) ("A gift of an equitable life estate in income or of an estate in remainder does constitute a grant

capable of owning property are eligible to be trust beneficiaries; these are entities to whom enforceable personal rights with respect to tangible and intangible things may attach.[3] Such entities would include minors,[4] the insane,[5] certain corporations, [6] unincorporated associations, trustees, persons who are unborn or unascertained,[7] the United States or a state of the United States. In the noncharitable context, the equitable interests of the unborn and unascertained are represented by the guardian ad litem.[8] In the charitable context, future unascertained recipients of charity are entitled to beneficiary status because the attorney general is charged with enforcing trusts established on their behalf.[9]

The dead, who are without any status whatsoever under the common law, are entitled to beneficiary status provided the legislature authorizes trusts for the perpetual care of gravesites and legal mechanisms for their enforcement.[10] In the absence of such statutory authority, the relatives of the dead have common law standing to enforce gravesite protection trusts during the period permitted by the Rule Against Perpetuities.[11] It could be argued that for all intents and purposes such trusts would exist for the benefit of the relatives who themselves possess the common law right to visit, honor, and protect gravesites of their deceased relatives.[12]

---

of a vested property right of which the recipients cannot be divested by legislative action).

[3] *See generally* W. N. Hohfeld, Fundamental Legal Conceptions 23-124 (1923) (suggesting that property is a collection of rights, privileges, powers and immunities with respect to a thing rather than the thing itself); *see also* I Restatement of Property at 3 (1936) (introduction to chapter 1).

[4] *See* 2 Scott on Trusts §116.

[5] Id.

[6] *See* 2 Scott on Trusts §117.1.

[7] *See* 2 Scott on Trusts §112.1.

[8] *See* Restatement (Second) of Trusts §214 comment *a* (1959). *See generally* Begleiter, The Guardian Ad Litem in Estate Proceedings, 20 Willamette L. Rev. 643, 651-653 (1984); *see generally* §8.14 (When Is a Guardian ad Litem Needed?).

[9] *See* 4A Scott on Trusts §§364, 391.

[10] *See generally* P. Jackson, The Law of Cadavers and of Burial and Burial Places (2d ed. 1950); G. Newhall, Settlement of Estates and Fiduciary Law in Massachusetts §10 (4th ed. 1958); 4A Scott on Trusts §374.9.

[11] *But see* 2 Scott on Trusts §124.2.

[12] *See generally* Rounds, Protections Afforded to Massachusetts' Ancient Burial Grounds, 73 Mass. L. Rev. 176 (1988).

Under the definition of property adopted by the Restatement, the holder of a general inter vivos power of appointment would be a beneficiary because the holder would possess an enforceable equitable personal right relating to a tangible or intangible thing.[13] In the pre-Restatement world, when personal rights and property rights were considered mutually exclusive, a power holder had only a personal right.[14]

Where there is no beneficiary, there is no trust.[15] In the case of private trusts (as opposed to charitable or public trusts), the beneficiary must be definite.[16] This does not mean that the beneficiary specifically must be named — a designation by description is sufficient.[17] The beneficiary is sufficiently definite only if it is certain at the time when the trust takes effect that the beneficiary will be identified before the expiration of the period allowed by the Rule Against Perpetuities.[18]

Despite the usual rule that a beneficiary must be a definite ascertainable individual, it commonly is held that a trust for the benefit of the members of a class of persons is valid.[19] However, a trust created for the benefit of a class of persons which is not sufficiently definite to be capable of ascertainment within the period of the Rule Against Perpetuities will fail, and a resulting trust will be imposed.[20] Trusts for the benefit of animals or of inanimate objects have been sustained, even when not charitable.[21] These trusts, however, depend upon the honor of the trustee since there is no person who as beneficiary can apply to the court for enforcement.[22] If the named trustee does not carry out the

[13] *Supra* note 3. *See generally* 1 Restatement of Property at 43 (1936) (introduction to chapter 1).

[14] *See generally* National Shawmut Bank v. Joy, 315 Mass. 457, 472, 53 N.E.2d 113, 123 (1944) (suggesting that power of appointment is not property).

[15] Restatement (Second) of Trusts §66 (1959).

[16] Id. §112 (1959).

[17] Id. comment *b*.

[18] Id. comment *a*; *see generally*, §8.2.1 (The Rule Against Perpetuities).

[19] *See* id. §120.

[20] *See* id. §123; *see generally* 2 Scott on Trusts §123; *Joy*, 315 Mass. at 463, 53 N.E.2d at 118.

[21] *See generally* 2 Scott on Trusts §124.

[22] *See generally* Restatement (Second) of Trusts §124 comment *d* (1959).

trust, the property will be held upon a resulting trust.[23] In the case of charitable trusts, where the beneficiaries are indefinite, the attorney general is charged with the duty of informing the court of any breach of duty by the trustee.[24]

## §5.2 Class Designation: "Issue" and "Heirs"

When the settlor properly designates by name related beneficiaries such as children, there is little room for ambiguity as to who qualifies as a beneficiary. What is lost however is the flexibility, adaptability, and economy of language that comes when the beneficiaries are designated not by name but by group membership. Suppose a trust provides that the trustee, upon the death of the settlor's spouse, shall distribute the corpus outright and free of trust to "the children then living of the settlor." It would bring in children born after the trust was executed and exclude children predeceasing the spouse. Were the children specifically named, considerable additional language would be required to address such contingencies.

But class designations must be drafted properly or they will only cause problems for the trustee. Take for example the term *issue*, perhaps the most commonly used and most useful of the class designations:

(1) *Issue* includes not just children but the descendants of all generations of the designated ancestor, that is, grandchildren, great-grandchildren and the like.[1] Thus, the term *issue* can lead to unfortunate misunderstandings and misconceptions on the part of beneficiaries and amateur

[23] *See generally* id. §404.
[24] *See* §9.4.2 (Standing to Enforce Charitable Trusts).
**§5.2** [1] Uniform Probate Code §1-201(25), 8 U.L.A. 35 (1998); *see generally,* Fratcher, Class Gifts to "Heirs," "Issue," and Like Groups, 55 Alb. L. Rev. 1205 (1992).

trustees who are inclined to understand the term as meaning only someone's "children."

(2) *Issue* ought not to stand alone. It should be accompanied by language explaining the proportions in which the issue take, be it *equally* or *by right of representation* or *equally within a generation* (the new *equally near, equally dear* concept of the Uniform Probate Code).[2] The inherently contradictory phrase *issue in equal shares by right of representation* should be avoided at all costs.[3] Trustees unable to avoid administering such a provision will be faced with rationalizing this patently ambiguous phrase. It may well be that the phrase *in equal shares* refers to equality among the stocks ("stirpes") with the term *by*

[2]To illustrate the difference between *per stirpes* (by right of representation) and *per capita at each generation* (equally near, equally dear), let us assume that a settlor provided that his trust shall terminate at his death and that the property shall then pass to his then living issue, per stirpes. Let us also assume that the settlor had three children (*X*, *Y*, and *Z*) during his lifetime: *X* predeceased the trust's termination, leaving one child who survived the termination; *Y* predeceased the trust's termination, leaving two children who survived the termination; *Z* survived the termination as did her three children. Under the traditional per stirpital approach, *X*'s child would take one third, *Y*'s children would share one third, and *Z* would take one third (*Z*'s children would take nothing). *See generally* M. Reutlinger, Wills, Trusts, and Estates 18-23 (1993). On the other hand, if the settlor had provided that his then living issue were to take *per capita* (equally), then *Z* and all the then-living grandchildren would have taken equal shares.

A hybrid concept, known as *per capita at each generation* or *equally near, equally dear*, has recently been approved by the National Conference of Commissioners on Uniform State Laws. Uniform Act on Intestacy, Wills, and Donative Transfers, 8B U.L.A. 22 (1993). It is derived from the intestacy sections of the Uniform Probate Code, §2-106. It has been suggested that "[t]he per-capita-at-each-generation system is more responsive to the underlying premise of the original UPC system, in that it always provides equal shares to those equally related; the pre-1990 UPC achieved this objective in most but not all cases." 8 U.L.A. 85 (1998 Supp.). To continue with our example, if the classic pre-1990 per stirpital approach is applied, the child of *X* receives one third; under the new "equally near, equally dear" approach, the child of *X* receives $2/9$, because the children of deceased *X* and the children of deceased *Y* would share equally. *Z*, of course, would take to the exclusion of her children. Id.

[3]*See generally* U.S. Trust, 1992 New York Trusts and Estates Legislation: Meanings of "Per Stirpes" and "In Equal Shares per Stirpes," Practical Drafting 2939-2972 (1992).

*right of representation* referring to the proportions that the issue within each stock ("stirps") take.[4]

(3) Even without the reference to equal shares, a provision calling for distribution to someone's issue "by right of representation" ("per stirpes") may be ambiguous under certain circumstances; such as when the first generation of issue below that person dies before the time set for distribution. Let us take the following situation: The person has two children, *A* and *B*, both of whom have predeceased. *A* had one child (*X*) and *B* had two children (*Y* and *Z*). Do *X*, *Y*, and *Z* start the stocks ("stirpes") and share one third each? Or do we begin at the level of *A* and *B*, giving *X* one half and leaving *Y* and *Z* to share one quarter each? The Restatement of Property §301, comment h, suggests that where the intent of the settlor is unclear, the stocks ("stirpes") shall begin at the first generation where there is a living member at the time set for distribution. Thus, in our case, *X*, *Y*, and *Z* would share equally.[5] Some cases, however, have held otherwise.[6] Because the law is unsettled in this area, the prospective trustee will want the matter of "where to start the stocks" addressed in the governing instrument.

(4) Legislatures and courts are redefining the term *issue* and other such group designations to include persons adopted and born out of wedlock.[7] Such alterations in meaning should not apply retroactively to trusts already in existence — no matter how appealing on a personal level retroactivity may be. Such alterations in meaning should apply only prospectively, unless the settlor has expressed a contrary intention. Otherwise, this shifting of property interests from one group to another amounts to the state's "taking by redefinition" of property.

[4] *See, e.g.*, In re Will of Lewis, 434 S.E. 2d 472 (Ga. 1993).

[5] Restatement of Property §301 comment *h* (1940).

[6] *See, e.g.*, Weller v. Sokol, 271 Md. 420, 318 A.2d 193 (1974).

[7] *See generally* Restatement (Second) of Property §§25.2-25.5 (1988) (Donative Transfers). *See also* In re Trusts of Harrington, 311 Minn. 403, 250 N.W.2d 163 (1977) (adoptees deemed issue of the body); In Will of Hoffman, 53 A.D.2d 55, 385 N.Y.S.2d 49 (1976) (redefining the term *issue* to include illegitimates).

To illustrate the last point, let us assume that in 1900 an irrevocable trust was created that provided that, upon its termination at the death of the last survivor of the settlor's children, the property passes outright and free of trust to the "then living issue" of the settlor. Let us assume further that the term *issue* as understood in 1900 did *not* include persons who were adopted or who were born out of wedlock. At the time the trust was created, members of the class of the settlor's grandchildren and more remote descendants, whether born or unborn, acquired property rights in the form of equitable contingent remainders. It is a popular misconception that contingent interests under trusts are not property interests — nothing could be further from the truth. The office of the guardian ad litem itself has evolved to represent just such property interests on behalf of minors, the unborn, and the unascertained.[8] Thus when the state retroactively redefines a term such as *issue* to bring in persons not intended by the settlor, the state dilutes the property interests, contingent or otherwise, of the persons whom the settlor did contemplate, whether those persons are born or unborn.[9]

*Heirs* is another term that often appears in trust instruments.[10] That term, accompanied by appropriate qualifying language, can serve as a convenient formula for coming up with takers in default of named beneficiaries, but it can also carry with it all kinds of problems if it is used alone. To illustrate, let us assume that upon the death of a settlor's spouse the trustee shall distribute the trust property outright and free of trust to the settlor's "heirs."

[8]*See* §§5.1 (Who Can Be a Beneficiary?) and 3.5.3.2(h) (The Power to Exclude the Remainderman from the Accounting Process); Restatement (Second) of Trusts §214 comment *a* (1959).

[9]Wachovia Bank & Trust Co. v. Andrews, 264 N.C. 531, 142 S.E.2d 182 (1965) (holding that the state may not retroactively redefine a class to include adopteds and thus dilute the property interests of nonadopted members); *see* Continental Bank, N.A. v. Herguth, 248 Ill. App. 3d 292, 187 Ill. Dec. 395, 617 N.E. 2d 852 (1993) ("Because the settlor is presumed to have known these legal principles when he executed the trust, the terms "descendant" and "per stripes" unmistakably evidenced his . . . intent to limit the class of beneficiaries to his natural born progeny.").

[10]The Uniform Probate Code narrowly defines *heirs* as "those persons, including the surviving spouse, who are entitled under the statutes of intestate succession to the property of a decedent." Uniform Probate Code §1-201(21), 8 U.L.A. 35 (1998). *See also* §8.5 (Conflict of Laws).

Most courts will construe *heir* as someone who takes, or would take, under some statute dealing with intestate succession.[11] But the statute of which jurisdiction? And is it the statute in effect at the creation of the trust, the death of the settlor, or the death of the spouse?[12] What if the statute treats real property differently from personal property? And what is intended by the term if the settlor in fact died testate? Perhaps it imports the subjunctive, that is, those persons who would take the property of the settlor if he or she had died intestate.[13] The same issues are present when a distribution is to be made to the "heirs" of someone other than the settlor.[14]

A prospective trustee should insist that the term *heirs* be accompanied with appropriate assumptions, exclusions, and qualifications to wring out such gaps and ambiguities.[15] In 1939, Professor Casner offered the following "basic form" which was intended to do just that in the context of devises under wills. Over the years since then it has been revised and adapted to accommodate equitable interests under trusts:

[11] *See* Casner, Construction of Gifts to "Heirs" and the Like, 53 Harv. L. Rev. 207, 208-209 (1939): "When the devisees in a will are described as the 'heirs' . . . of a designated person, almost all courts agree that some statute dealing with the intestate succession of property is to be employed to ascertain the persons described, in the absence of additional language or circumstances which indicate a contrary intent on the part of the testator." *See also,* Fratcher, Class Gifts to "Heirs," "Issue" and Like Groups, 55 Alb. L. Rev. 1205 (1992) and §8.5 (Conflict of Laws).

[12] *See,* W.E. Shipley, Annot., Time as of which members of class described as grantor's or settlor's "heirs," "next of kin," "relations," and the like to whom a future gift is made are to be ascertained, 38 A.L.R. 2d 327 (1954).

[13] *See* National Shawmut Bank of Boston v. Joy, 315 Mass. 457, 462-467, 53 N.E.2d 113, 117-120 (1944) (construing a default clause to be in the subjunctive); *see generally* Casner, Construction of Gifts to "Heirs" and the Like, 53 Harv. L. Rev. 207 (1939); *See also* §§8.5 (Conflict of Laws), and 8.15.2 (Doctrine of Worthier Title).

[14] *See generally* W.W. Allen, Annot., Time of ascertaining persons to take, under deed or inter vivos trust, where designated as the "heirs," "next of kin," "children," "relations," etc. of the life tenant or remainderman, 65 A.L.R. 2d 1408 (1959); *see also,* W.W. Allen, Annot., Time of ascertaining persons to take where designated as the "heirs," "next of kin," "descendants," etc. of one other than the testator, trustor, grantor, life tenant, or remainderman, 60 A.L.R.2d 1394 (1958).

[15] *See generally* Casner, Construction of Gifts to "Heirs" and the Like, 53 Harv. L. Rev. 207 (1939); *See also* §8.5.

> . . . then to those persons, and in such shares, as would have taken real property owned by me and situated in State *X* if I had died immediately after the termination of all prior interests in the land which is the subject of this devise, intestate and domiciled in State *X*, unless all prior interests expire by their terms before the will has taken effect, in which case, to those persons and in such shares as would have taken real property owned by me and situated in State *X* if I had died intestate and domiciled in State *X*; my intention is to include all persons who would take on such assumed intestacy whether they are related to me by blood or not, whether legitimate or illegitimate, and whether or not they have received any interest under this will.[16]

If the trust instrument uses the term *heirs* without any language that qualifies the term, then prior to distribution the trustee should seek the advice of counsel. This will reduce the risk of misdelivery.

## §5.3 The Beneficiary's Property Interest

The beneficiary's equitable interest is an interest in property.[1] However, it is a type of interest that may, under certain circumstances, be inalienable or immune from attachment, or both.

### *§5.3.1 Nature and Extent of Property Interest*

"When uses were first enforced in England by the chancellors of the fifteenth century, it is clear that they looked at the use primarily as a personal relationship between the feoffee and the

[16] Id. at 249-250.

**§5.3** [1] *See* In re Catherwood's Trust, 173 A.2d 86, 91 (1961). ("A gift of an equitable life estate in income or of an estate in remainder does constitute a grant of a vested property right of which the recipients cannot be divested by legislative action.")

cestui que use."[2] Today, a beneficiary has more than mere rights against the trustee.[3] The beneficiary possesses an interest in the trust property itself that is either vested or contingent.[4] The outcome of a tax or other dispute may hinge on the beneficiary's legal relationship with the underlying trust property.[5]

The extent of the beneficiary's equitable interest is usually governed by the terms of the instrument. The settlor of the trust may create equitable interests that correspond to the comparable legal estates (*e.g.*, the beneficiary may be given an equitable life estate or an equitable estate for years). With respect to vested equitable interests, if the trust principal is personal property the beneficiary's interest is personal property, too, and follows personal property rules; if it is real estate, the beneficiary's interest is also regarded as realty.

The interest of the beneficiary may be a future interest, vested or contingent; may rest solely in the discretion of the trustee; it may be limited to the occupation of the trust property.

Co-owners of a beneficial interest ordinarily hold the interest jointly unless there is a statute to the contrary.[6] Of course, the terms of a governing instrument may specify how the beneficial interest is to be held (jointly or as tenants in common) notwithstanding any common law or statutory presumption.[7]

The issue of the beneficiary's relationship to the underlying property is separate from the issue of whether a particular equita-

[2] 2 Scott on Trusts §130. The phrase *cestui que trust* has evolved into a synonym for *beneficiary*. It is not known when this Norman-French phrase was introduced into our language, but it is believed to have been in the seventeenth century. For a discussion of such borrowings from the Norman French see Sweet, *'Cestui Que Use': 'Cestui Que Trust,'* 26 L.Q. Rev. 196 (1910).

[3] *See generally* 2 Scott on Trusts §130.

[4] *See generally* Bogert, Trusts and Trustees §182.

[5] *See, e.g.*, Cohen, Massachusetts Estate Tax Planning For Non-Massachusetts Residents Owning Real Estate in Massachusetts, 70 Mass. L. Rev. 124, 126 (1985) (tax); In re Grand Jury Subpoena, 973 F.2d 45 (1st Cir. 1992) (Fifth Amendment privilege not available to trustees of nominee trust).

[6] In many states such statutes have been enacted. *See generally* 2A Scott on Trusts §143. Many states' statutes impose a presumption of tenancy in common. *See, e.g.*, N.Y. Est. Powers & Trusts Law §6-2.2 (Consol. 1979); Ill. Ann. Stat. ch. 76, §§1-1a, 2 (Smith-Hurd 1987); Cal. Civ. Code §683 (West 1982); Mass. Gen. Laws. Ann. ch. 184, §7 (West 1987).

[7] *See, e.g.*, Anderson v. Bean, 220 Mass. 360, 107 N.E. 964 (1915).

ble interest is vested or contingent. A beneficiary's equitable interest, for example, may be so contingent as to be for all intents and purposes little more than a right of action against the trustee.

"Interests of beneficiaries of private express trusts run the gamut from valuable substantialities to evanescent hopes. Such a beneficiary may have any one of an almost infinite variety of the possible aggregates of rights, privileges, powers and immunities."[8] Equitable interests in trusteed IRAs and realty trusts tend to crowd the substantial end of the rights spectrum.[9] They are often distinguishable only in form from vested legal interests in the underlying property.[10] At the opposite extreme are the contingent interests in charitable trusts.[11] Such interests tend to be little more than evanescent hopes. A beneficiary's interest in a trust associated with a qualified employee benefit plan tends to move over time from the contingent end to the vested end of the rights spectrum.[12]

### *§5.3.2 Voluntary Transfers*

In the absence of restraint imposed by the trust instrument or by statute, the beneficiary's equitable estate may be transferred by the beneficiary as freely as might be done if it were a legal estate (beneficial interests after all being property interests).[13] (This is a matter separate from whether the beneficiary holds a power of appointment.[14]) The beneficiary may not transfer the equitable interest if it is subject to the discretion of the trustee or if it is inseparable from that of others.[15] These are restraints imposed by

[8]Farkas v. Williams, 5 Ill. 2d 417, 422-423, 125 N.E.2d 600, 603 (1955) (*citing* 4 Powell, The Law of Real Property, at 87).

[9]*See* §§9.5.2 (The IRA Trust), 9.6 (Trusts That Resemble Corporations or Agencies).

[10]Id.

[11]*See* §9.1 (The Grantor Trust).

[12]I.R.C. §§401(a)(7), 411; ERISA §203 (ERISA vesting standards).

[13]*See generally* Restatement of Property §5 (1936); id. at 3 (introduction to chapter 1); 2A Scott on Trusts §132; Restatement (Second) of Trusts §133 (1959); Brown v. Fletcher, 235 U.S. 589, 599 (1915).

[14]*See* §8.1 (Powers of Appointment).

[15]*See generally* 2A Scott on Trusts §§132, 155, 161; E. Griswold, Spendthrift Trusts §§435-445 (2d ed. 1947) (discussing the separability of the beneficial interests).

the instrument. Although not literally a restraint of the trust instrument, a beneficial interest may be so personal in nature as to be unassignable (e.g., support for the beneficiary's education).[16]

Unless it terminates with the beneficiary's death, the beneficial interest may pass by will or by intestacy, or be transferred by deed. The transfer may be in whole or in part, outright or by way of security, or in trust.[17] Requirements of capacity and intention are identical at law and in equity.[18] The transferee of a legal or equitable interest need not know of the transfer or assent to it, but both interests are of course disclaimable.[19] Testamentary transfers of beneficial interests as well as legal interests require compliance with the Statute of Wills.[20]

The Statute of Frauds may apply to the transfer of an equitable interest, particularly if the underlying property is realty.[21] Such a transfer may also require attention to the rules and regulations of the Securities and Exchange Commission.[22] On the other hand, some of the formalities required for the transfer of a legal interest may be dispensed with in the case of the transfer of the equitable interest. Thus, as a general rule, the transfer of a beneficial interest in a trust containing real estate need not be recorded in a registry of deeds.[23] This then raises the question whether assignments of beneficial interests take priority in the order made or in the order in which notice is given to the trustee. There is a division of authority on the issue.[24]

[16]*See generally* 2A Scott on Trusts §160.

[17]*See generally* id. §132; *see also* Blair v. Commissioner, 300 U.S. 5, 13 (1937) (holding valid life beneficiary's assignment of portions of trust income).

[18]*See generally* Restatement (Second) of Trusts §133 (1959); 2A Scott on Trusts §§133-134 (capacity, intention); Chase Natl. Bank v. Sayles, 11 F.2d 948, 955 (1st Cir. 1926) (a valid unrestricted assignment is irrevocable); Restatement (Second) of Trusts §134 (1959).

[19]*See generally* Restatement (Second) of Trusts §137 (1959); 2A Scott on Trusts §137; *see generally* §5.5 (Loss of the Beneficiary's Rights).

[20]*See generally* Bogert, Trusts and Trustees §188; 2A Scott on Trusts §132.1.

[21]*See generally* Bogert, Trusts and Trustees §190; Restatement (Second) of Trusts §138; *See generally* §8.15.5 (Statute of Frauds).

[22]*See* §§7.3.3.3 (Registration and Sale of Securities), 7.3.4.2(a) (Criminal and Civil Liability as Legal Owner: Securities Laws).

[23]*See generally* Bogert, Trusts and Trustees §249.

[24]*See generally* 2A Scott on Trusts §163; Bogert, Trusts and Trustees §195.

What if a trustee honors the beneficiary's assignment of an equitable interest in a spendthrift trust? Courts tend to absolve the trustee by treating the assignment as a revocable order to transfer accrued income or principal once it becomes possessory.[25] For this purpose, the trustee is essentially deemed an agent of the beneficiary. The relationship being an agency, it is revocable by the principal (in this case the beneficiary) up until the time accrued income or principal is transferred by the trustee outright and free of trust to the assignee.[26]

### *§5.3.3 Rights of Beneficiary's Creditors and Others to Trust Property*

In the case of involuntary transfers of the beneficiary's interest, the equitable estate is treated in many respects as if it were a legal estate.[27] Therefore, as a general rule a beneficiary's creditors and spouse may reach that portion of the equitable interest over which the beneficiary possesses an affirmative right of consumption.[28] There are three important exceptions to this rule.

(1) *Powers of appointment.* As a general rule, a nonsettlor holder of a general power of appointment cannot be compelled to exercise it.[29] This is a remnant of the pre-Restatement of Property distinction between personal rights and property rights.[30] However, if the power is exercised, the property subject to the power may be fair game

[25] *See* Restatement (Second) of Trusts §152 comment *i* (1959); *see,* John P. Ludington, L.L.B, Annot., Validity and construction of beneficiary's arrangement for payment to another, as they become due, of sums due under spendthrift trust, 83 A.L.R. 3d 1142 (1978).

[26] Id.

[27] Bogert, Trusts and Trustees §193.

[28] *See generally* 2A Scott on Trusts §§147, 157.

[29] *See* State Street Trust Co. v. Kissel, 302 Mass. 328, 333, 119 N.E.2d 25 (1939); Ritchie et al., Decedent's Estates and Trusts 961-964 (8th ed. 1993).

[30] Id.; *see also* National Shawmut Bank v. Joy, 315 Mass. 457, 472, 53 N.E.2d 113, 124 (1944); Jones v. Clifton, 101 U.S. 225, 231 (1879).

for the holder's creditors.[31] It should be noted that in a few states, statutes permit the creditors of the holder of a general power of appointment to reach the property even if the power is unexercised.[32] Property subject to a nongeneral power to appoint, of course, can never be reached by the holder's creditors, whether or not the power is exercised.

(2) *Employee benefit plans.* Even when employees have untrammeled access to their interests in trusts associated with qualified employee benefit plans, it does not necessarily mean that their creditors do as well. This is due to federal pension law.[33]

(3) *Indivisible equitable interests.* If the debtor-beneficiary holds the equitable interest jointly with another or as a tenant by the entirety, the creditors may not reach the trust property during the life of the cotenant.[34]

An example of an equitable interest that is vulnerable to involuntary transfer would be an irrevocable, nondiscretionary, income-only trust created by *A* for the benefit of *C*: where, after the expiration of ten years, the property passes outright and free of trust to *D*; where *B* is the trustee; where *D* is ascertained at the time the property is transferred to *B*; and where there is no spendthrift provision. Under such a trust, the income stream itself would be reachable and attachable by *C*'s spouse and creditors during the ten-year period. If *C* were to die intestate during the ten-year period, the income stream would inure to the benefit of *C*'s heirs at law for the balance of the period, subject to any rights of the creditors and the spouse to the equitable interest. In addition, the present vested right to the future unrestricted enjoyment of the property would be reachable by *D*'s

[31] Id.

[32] Bogert, Trusts and Trustees §233.

[33] *See* I.R.C. §401(a)(13) (1954) (trusts that are part of qualified plans must prohibit assignment or alienation of benefits); Patterson v. Shumate, 504 U.S. 753 (1992) (holding that assets held in a trust associated with a qualified plan may not be reached by the bankruptcy trustee though the trust would not qualify for spendthrift protection under state trust law); *see, however,* Marton, Gerson and Levine, Qualified Plans May Not Be Protected in Bankruptcy, 23 ACTEC Notes 75 (1997).

[34] *See generally* Bogert, Trusts and Trustees §230.

spouse and creditors during the ten-year period.[35] If *D* were to die intestate before ten years, the vested equitable remainder interest — that right of future enjoyment — would pass in accordance with the laws of distribution to *D*'s heirs at law, unless the underlying trust property were realty, in which case the equitable interest would pass to them by descent.[36] *D* could also designate by a will who is to succeed to *D*'s interest if death occurred during the ten-year period.

While a vested equitable interest may be vulnerable to creditor attack, it may also be entitled to the same statutory protections as legal interests.[37] Homestead exemptions, for example, apply to equitable as well as legal interests.[38]

An example of an equitable interest that probably would not be subject to involuntary transfer is a fully discretionary trust established by *A* for the benefit of *C* during *C*'s lifetime. Here *C* possesses no affirmative right to consume the income and principal: *C* gets whatever *B* chooses to release and no more, as do *C*'s spouse and creditors. Moreover, should *C* die intestate nothing would pass to *C*'s heirs at law, the interest having extinguished at *C*'s death. All bets are off, however, with respect to reserved equitable interests, even under discretionary trusts. Where the settlor is also a beneficiary, that is to say, where *A* and *C* or *A* and *D* are the same, the equitable interest is vulnerable to attack by *A*'s spouse and creditors. This is a manifestation of the public policy that if you are a settlor-debtor you may not eat your cake and have it too.[39] Alaska, however, has recently enacted legislation insulating certain such self-settled discretionary trusts from creditor attack.[40] Whether Alaska's action marks the start of a trend remains to be seen.

[35] *See generally* Bogert, Trusts and Trustees §193.

[36] 2A Scott on Trusts §142.

[37] Bogert, Trusts and Trustees §187.

[38] Id.

[39] *See generally* 2A Scott on Trusts §156; Restatement (Second) of Trusts §156 (1959); Ware v. Gulda, 331 Mass. 68, 117 N.E.2d 137 (1954) (holding the property of a fully discretionary trust to be reachable by the settlor-beneficiary's creditors); *see also* Wilson v. American National Bank of Pueblo, 42 P. 1037, 1040 (Colo. 1895); Vanderbilt Credit Corp. v. Chase Manhattan Bank, 100 A.D.2d 544, 546 (N.Y. 1984).

[40] A.S. 34.40.110(b)(2).

### §5.3.3.1 Reaching Settlor's Reserved Beneficial Interest

**Domestic Trusts.** In the United States, it has been a matter of public policy that the settlor cannot place property in trust for the settlor's own benefit and keep it beyond the reach of creditors. This has been true even though the trust may contain a spendthrift provision, even though the remaindermen may be harmed, even if the transfer was not procured by fraud, and even if the settlor has not retained the right to revoke or amend the trust.[41] The policy is reflected in §156(2) of the Restatement (Second) of Trusts,[42] which has been adopted by case law or statute in whole or in part by an ever-increasing number of jurisdictions: "[W]here a person creates for his own benefit a trust for support or a discretionary trust, his transferee or creditors can reach the maximum amount which the trustee under the terms of the trust could pay to him or apply for his benefit."[43] While unanimity across the jurisdictions on the rights of creditors to reach reserved beneficial interests has not been achieved, the law had been settling rapidly on the spirit, and in some cases even the language, of §156(2).[44] Recently, however, Alaska has seen fit by legislation to afford some creditor protection to certain "self-settled" discretionary trusts.[45] Whether this development marks the beginning of a trend remains to be seen. The Alaska initiative is discussed in greater detail in 5.3.3.1(c) of this handbook.

In jurisdictions that are following the letter or spirit of §156(2), a transfer to an irrevocable trust by the settlor for the settlor's own benefit will not be a completed inter vivos transfer for federal gift tax or estate tax purposes.[46] This is true even if the settlor is only a discretionary beneficiary.[47]

[41]*See* Restatement (Second) of Trusts §156 (1959); *see e.g.,* Spenlinhauer v. Spencer Press, Inc., 195 B. R. 543 (Bankr. D. Me. 1996); *aff'd* 103 F.3d 106 (1st Cir. (Me.) 1996).

[42]*See also Ware, supra* note 38.

[43]*See* Restatement (Second) of Trusts §156 appendix (1959).

[44]*See* 2A Scott on Trusts §156 n.1.

[45]45 A.S. 34.40.110(b)(2).

[46]Paolozzi v. Commissioner, 23 T.C. 182, 186 (1954); Outwin v. Commissioner, 76 T.C. 153 n.5 (1981); *see generally,* §4.1.3 (Creditor Accessibility as a General Inter Vivos Power of Appointment).

[47]Id.

**(a) The Vulnerability of Principal.** It is important to understand how radically §156(2) alters the common law of property and trusts. Let us assume that a settlor creates a trust for his own benefit giving the trustee discretion over income and principal. Under §156(2) the principal is vulnerable to attack by the settlor's creditors even if: (1) the trustee never chooses to exercise this discretion; (2) the trustee is independent; (3) the remaindermen are unrelated third parties; and (4) the original transfer in trust was *not* procured by fraud. Suppose the settlor reserves no beneficial interest, only a naked right of revocation. The current state of the common law seems to be that an unexercised, naked reserved right of revocation will not expose the principal to attack by the settlor's creditors.[48] The trustee however, should expect form to give way to substance sooner rather than later. Courts will be hard pressed to justify why, as a matter of public policy, the settlor's creditors should be thwarted by naked reserved rights of revocation under which settlors retain rights of consumption over the subject properties, but should not be thwarted by reserved beneficial interests in discretionary trusts where control is transferred to independent trustees.

Is principal safe from attack when the settlor creates an income-only trust for the settlor's own benefit? Probably so — at least for the foreseeable future.[49] There is a counter-argument, however: The principal — the engine that generates the income — is employed for the benefit of the settlor. Thus, because the entire principal is dedicated to the benefit of the settlor, the spirit and letter of §156(2) dictate that the principal itself should be vulnerable to creditor attack.[50] While the engine argument is essentially the rationale in the estate tax context for the reserved life estate sections of the Internal Revenue Code,[51] it has so far proven of little utility to the settlor's creditors.

[48] *See* Restatement (Second) of Trusts §330 comment *o* (1959); Jones v. Clifton, 101 U.S. 225, 230-231 (1879); for statutes providing otherwise, *see* 4 Scott on Trusts §330.12.

[49] *See generally* 2A Scott on Trusts §156 n.2 and accompanying text.

[50] *See generally* Rounds, The Vulnerability of Trust Assets to Attack by the Deceased Settlors Creditors, by the Commonwealth Should It Seek Reimbursement for Medicaid Payments, and by the Spouse, 73 Mass L. Rev. 67, 70 (1988).

[51] I.R.C. §2036 (a)(1) (1978), *rev'g* May v. Heiner, 281 U.S. 238 (1930); *see also* Omnibus Budget Reconciliation Act of 1993 §13611 (1993) (making the principal of self-settled income-only trusts countable for Medicaid eligibility purposes).

**(b) the postmortem creditor.** The current trend of the law favors allowing the settlor's postmortem creditors, and the surviving spouse as well, access to the principal of an inter vivos trust if the settlor reserved a power to consume the property at the time of the settlor's death.[52] This should be contrasted with the lot of the inter vivos creditor where the focus is on the retention of a beneficial interest rather than a power to consume.[53] Thus we have such anomalies as the naked reserved right of revocation exposing a trust to the reach of the settlor's postmortem creditor but not the inter vivos one.[54] In the future the law will evolve to the point where the settlor-beneficiary's inter vivos and postmortem creditors will have coextensive access to the property of an inter vivos trust, but until that time such subtle divergences in the law will continue to complicate the already complicated life of the trustee.

Life insurance proceeds paid to the insured's inter vivos trust upon the death of the insured may, by statute, be beyond the reach of the settlor's postmortem creditors.[55] Prior to paying the settlor's postmortem creditors from life insurance proceeds payable to the trustee by reason of the settlor's death, the trustee should consult counsel.

**(c) Domestic asset protection havens: Alaska and Delaware.** In 1997, Alaska enacted a statute that may insulate certain self-settled discretionary trusts created after April 1, 1997, from the reach of the settlor's creditors.[56] The reserved contingent equitable interest may be unavailable to the settlor's creditors if: (1) the trust is

[52] *See, e.g.*, State Street Bank v. Reiser, 7 Mass. App. Ct. 633, 389 N.E.2d 768 (1979) (power of consumption at time of debtor's death); Sullivan v. Burkin, 390 Mass. 864, 460 N.E.2d 572 (1984) (power of consumption during marriage); *see* "Summary of Case Law: Rights of Creditors Following Death of Settlor. Beneficiaries of Revocable Trusts," compiled by Clifton B. Kruse, Jr., 23 ACTEC Notes 155 (1997).

[53] *See* 4 Scott on Trusts §330.12; Restatement (Second) of Trusts §330 comment *o*(1959).

[54] *See Reiser*, 7 Mass. App. Ct. at 638, 389 N.E.2d at 771 (in the postmortem context, a reserved general inter vivos power may be enough to expose trust property to creditor attack); Restatement (Second) of Trusts §330 comment *o* (1959) (in inter vivos context a naked reserved general inter vivos power may *not* be enough to expose property to creditor attack).

[55] *See generally* 5 Scott on Trusts §508.4; Bogert, Trusts and Trustees §243.

[56] A.S. 34.40.110.

irrevocable, (2) the trust is fully discretionary as to income and principal at its inception, (3) the trustee with the discretionary authority is someone other than the settlor, (4) the transfer in trust is not established to "hinder, delay, or defraud" pre-existing creditors, (5) at the time of transfer, the settlor is not in default by 30 or more days of making payment due under a child support judgment or order, and (6) the trust is sited in Alaska.[57] The Alaska statute rejects the public policy at the heart of §156(2) of the Restatement (Second) of Trusts, namely "that a settlor cannot place property in trust for his own benefit and keep it beyond the reach of creditors."[58] Effective July 1, 1997, Delaware responded by enacting a similar but not identical statute.[59]

One hope is that this asset protection legislation will save estate taxes. Here is how: the property of a fully discretionary "self-settled" irrevocable inter vivos trust has been subject to estate tax upon the death of the settlor-beneficiary *not* because the settlor died with a reserved contingent equitable interest but because the property was reachable by the settlor's creditors.[60] The legislation aims to eliminate what makes such arrangements tax-sensitive, namely creditor accessibility.[61] The hope is that even if a gift tax should be owed at the time the trust is established, any subsequent appreciation in the value of the trust property would escape estate tax upon the settlor's death.

**Foreign Trusts.** Some non-U.S. jurisdictions have rejected the creditor-friendly policy of §156(2) of the Restatement of Trusts.

[57]Id.

[58]Ware v. Gulda, 331 Mass. 68, 117 N.E.2d 137 (1954).

[59]12 Del. Stat. §§3570-3575.

[60]A general inter vivos power of appointment is the power to appoint to oneself *or* one's creditors. If the property of an irrevocable discretionary self-settled trust is reachable by the settlor's creditors, then the settlor has reserved a general inter vivos power of appointment exercisable by the incurring of debts. *See generally* §8.9.3 (Tax-Sensitive Powers of Appointment).

[61]See Blattmacher, Practice Alert: Alaska Trusts Offer New Estate Planning Opportunities, 1997 RIA Estate and Financial Planners Alert, June 1997, pg. 3 (Discussing how the Alaska asset protection legislation might enhance the attractiveness of Crummey Trusts; Life Insurance Trusts; Unified Credit and GST Exemption Trusts; GRATs, GRUTs, and GRITs; QPRTs; Charitable Lead Trusts; and Charitable Remainder Trusts and also discussing how non-U.S. persons might find an Alaska Trust advantageous).

This has given rise to the so-called Offshore Asset Protection Trust discussed briefly in §9.10.

### §5.3.3.2 Reaching the Equitable Interest of Beneficiary Who Is Not the Settlor

The trustee should understand that because the equitable interests of nonsettlor trust beneficiaries and remaindermen are property interests, these interests may be subject to the claims of the beneficiaries' creditors.[62] If, however, the settlor has reserved beneficial interests or if the settlor has qualified the beneficiaries' equitable interests,[63] then the trust property may well not be available to the creditors of the nonsettlor beneficiaries.[64] Let us look at a classic creditor-vulnerable trust that contains no such reservations or qualifications: *A* establishes an income-only trust for the benefit of *C* for *C*'s life. The principal passes outright and free of trust to *D* at the death of *C*, *D* being a person ascertained at the time of the trust's creation. *C* has a vested property interest in the stream of net income.[65] *C*'s creditors can seize the stream itself.[66] *D* has a vested nonpossessory property interest in the remainder. That interest is reachable by *D*'s creditors even before *C* dies, although it would not be possessory until *C* dies.[67]

The trustee should understand that *all* equitable interests — contingent or otherwise — are *property* interests.[68] As such they may not be taken by the state without just compensation.[69] Some equita-

[62] *See* 2A Scott on Trusts §147.

[63] *See* §§5.3.3.1 (Reaching Settlor's Reserved Beneficial Interest), 5.3.3.3 (Discretionary Provisions and Other Restraints upon Voluntary and Involuntary Transfers Including the Spendthrift Trust).

[64] *See* Restatement (Second) of Trusts §§152, 155 (1959). *But see* id. §157.

[65] *See generally* Bogert, Trusts and Trustees §182 (section entitled "Vested and Contingent Interests").

[66] *See generally* id. §193.

[67] *See* 2A Scott on Trusts §147.2.

[68] *See* id. §130.

[69] *See* Webb's Fabulous Pharmacies, Inc. v. Beckwith, 449 U.S. 155 (1980); Sinibaldi, The Taking Issue in California's Legal Services Trust Account Program, 12 Hastings Const. L.Q. 463 (1985); *see also,* In re Catherwood's Trust, 173 A.2d 86, 91 (1961) ("A gift of an equitable life estate in income or of an estate in

ble interests, however, such as those under the just-described trust, may be reached by the beneficiaries' creditors. While an equitable interest in trust property may be vulnerable to the reach of creditors, property subject only to a power of appointment — even a general inter vivos power — may well not be vulnerable.[70] The trustee should be aware of this subtle but substantive difference in vulnerability, a difference that has its origins in a vestigial distinction between property rights (*e.g.*, the equitable interest) and personal rights (*e.g.*, the power of appointment).[71]

### §5.3.3.3 Discretionary Provisions and Other Restraints Upon Voluntary and Involuntary Transfers Including the Spendthrift Trust

The settlor may limit the circumstances under which income and principal shall benefit the holder of an equitable interest.[72] Some limitations can so qualify the equitable interest that the beneficiary, as a practical matter, has no transferable and attachable property right.[73] The trustee should keep in mind — and this bears frequent repeating — that these limitations are not likely to thwart the settlor-beneficiary's creditors,[74] and that, even in the face of such limitations, once income or principal is

---

remainder does constitute a grant of a vested property right of which the recipients cannot be divested by legislative action.") and Washington Legal Found. v. Texas Equal Access to Justice Found., 94 F.3d 996 (1996) (holding that clients have a cognizable property interest in the interest proceeds earned on their deposits in IOLTA accounts), *aff'd on appeal,* Phillips v. Washington Legal Found., U.S. Supreme Court, No. 96-1578, June 15, 1998 (1998 WL 309070 (U.S.)). *But see* Washington Legal Found. v. Massachusetts Bar Found., 993 F.2d 962 (1st Cir. 1993) (holding that the interest earned on certain funds entrusted by a client to his attorney is not the client's property; rather, it "belongs to no one").

[70] State Street Trust Co., Trustee v. Kissel, 302 Mass. 328, 19 N.E.2d 25 (1939).

[71] National Shawmut Bank v. Joy, 315 Mass. 457, 53 N.E.2d 113 (1944).

[72] Farkas v. Williams, 5 Ill. 2d 417, 422-423, 125 N.E.2d 600, 603 (1955) (*citing* 4 Powell, The Law of Real Property, at 87).

[73] *See, e.g.*, Brownell v. Leutz, 149 F. Supp 98 (1957) (the interest of permissible beneficiary of a discretionary trust who was German alien was held not to be property interest susceptible of seizure during wartime by Alien Property Custodian).

[74] *See* §5.3.3.1 (Reaching Settlor's Reserved Beneficial Interest).

distributed from the trust to the beneficiary (*i.e.*, once title passes from the trustee to the beneficiary), the distributed property becomes alienable by the beneficiary and is reachable by the beneficiary's creditors.

**(a) The discretionary trust.** The *discretionary trust* is perhaps the most effective means of keeping the beneficiary's creditors away from the equitable interest.[75] This is because the beneficiary has no enforceable right to an identifiable portion of the income stream or to the principal. The classic discretionary trust grants the trustee broad discretion to pay income and distribute principal to the beneficiary.[76] A cousin of the discretionary trust is the *support trust*, in which the trustee's discretion is limited by a standard such as health, maintenance, and support. No matter what the type of noncharitable discretionary trust, a member of the class of eligible beneficiaries would have standing to sue the trustee for abuse of discretion.[77] As a general rule a creditor, not being a beneficiary, would lack such standing and thus could not force the trustee to make discretionary distributions.[78] Limited exceptions to this general rule may include support trusts where the claimant is the beneficiary's spouse or child,[79] or a governmental entity.[80] When the beneficiary is not the settlor, the creditor will

[75] *See* Restatement (Second) of Trusts §155 comment *b* (1959); Pemberton v. Pemberton, 9 Mass. App. Ct. 9, 20, 411 N.E.2d 1305, 1308 (1980).

[76] *See* Bogert, Trusts and Trustees §228.

[77] *See* Restatement (Second) of Trusts §187 comment *k* (1959).

[78] *See* id. §155 comment *d*.

[79] *See generally* Dessin, Feed a Trust and Starve a Child: The Effectiveness of Trust Protective Techniques Against Claims for Support and Alimony, 10 Ga. St. U. L. Rev. 691 (1994) and Restatement (Second) of Trusts §157 (1959).

[80] *See* id. §157 (1959); *but see* Miller v. Department of Mental Health, 432 Mich. 426, 442 N.W.2d 617 (1989) (suggesting that Michigan may not seek reimbursement from discretionary trusts for public assistance rendered to nonsettlor beneficiaries but that support trusts may be vulnerable) and Simpson v. Kansas Dept. of Social Rehabilitation Servs. 906 P.2d 174 (Kan. Ct. App. 1995) (assets of an irrevocable discretionary trust for settlor's adult daughter not available to daughter for Medicaid eligibility purposes). *See generally* Silber, The Effect of a Trust on the Eligibility or Liability of the Trust Beneficiary for Public Assistance, 26 Real Prop. Prob. & Tr. J. 133 (1991); *but see also* United States v. O'Shaughnessy, 517 N.W.2d 574 (Minn. 1994) and Texas Commerce Bank Natl.

find it difficult if not impossible to reach property held in a fully discretionary trust because the trustee's fiduciary duty runs to the debtor-beneficiary, not to the creditor.[81]

**(b) Forfeiture provisions.** Another mechanism for thwarting a trust beneficiary's creditors is a provision that terminates altogether the beneficiary's equitable interest upon the happening of some event such as the beneficiary's entering a nursing home, assuming debtor status, or attempting the alienation of the income stream.[82] If the beneficiary has no property interest then there is nothing to alienate and nothing for the creditors to attach.

**(c) The spendthrift trust.** Unlike the settlor of a discretionary trust, the settlor of a *spendthrift trust* directly confronts the creditor by withholding from the trustee the right to honor assignments and attachments of the equitable interests.[83] What the beneficiary cannot alienate, the creditor cannot attach.[84] The rationale for upholding the spendthrift trust is that it is the prerogative of the settlor — the owner of the property — to determine what restrictions (if any) shall be placed on the use of his property.[85] It is a privilege that comes with ownership.[86] After all, the settlor need not have created the trust in the first place, but could have instead consumed the property or given it away outright and free of trust.

The express reference in many spendthrift clauses to creditors over the years has invited assaults on the very institution of

---

Assn. v. United States, 908 F. Supp. 453 (S.D. Tex. 1995) (each denying IRS access to a taxpayer-beneficiary's equitable interest in a discretionary trust).

[81] *See* 2A Scott on Trusts §154; Restatement (Second) of Trusts §170 (1959).

[82] *See generally* 2A Scott on Trusts §150.

[83] *See* 2A Scott on Trusts §151, §152 (restraint on alienation of income), §153 (restraint on alienation of principal); Bogert, Trusts and Trustees §222 n.59 (for the current status of spendthrift trusts in all states).

[84] Ritchie et al., Decedent's Estates and Trusts 630 (8th ed. 1993); 2A Scott on Trusts §152.3. *But see* Bank of New England v. Strandlund, 402 Mass. 707, 529 N.E.2d 394 (1988) (honoring restraint on involuntary alienation only).

[85] Broadway Natl. Bank v. Adams, 133 Mass. 170 (1882).

[86] Id.

the spendthrift trust.[87] Some assaults have been partially or wholly successful, leading to noteworthy divergences across the jurisdictions.[88] A few states, such as North Carolina, will not enforce a spendthrift provision.[89] On the other hand, Massachusetts will, with one possible divorce-related exception.[90] Some states allow spendthrift provisions to protect the income stream only,[91] while others allow principal to be protected as well.[92] Some spendthrift jurisdictions draw a line when it comes to the beneficiary's spouse and children[93] or to a creditor who has supplied "necessaries"[94] which has been held in some cases to include a government agency that has provided institutional care to the beneficiary.[95] A spendthrift provision will not prohibit the United States or a state from attaching the beneficial interest for taxes owed by the beneficiary.[96]

At this point a comment on *alienation restraints* is in order. It is a cardinal principle of the law that a restraint upon alienation of a legal fee simple, or of an absolute interest in personal property, is invalid.[97] Courts that enforce spendthrift provisions circumvent this rule by drawing a distinction between legal interests and equitable interests.[98] Because the spendthrift restraint goes to the equitable interest and not to the trustee's legal interest, the power of alienation under a spendthrift provision continues unimpaired.[99]

[87]*See* Bogert, Trusts and Trustees §222 (arguments for and against spendthrift trusts).

[88]Bogert, Trusts and Trustees §222 n.59.

[89]Id.

[90]*See* Lauricella v. Lauricella, 409 Mass. 211, 565 N.E.2d 436 (1991) (nonsettlor beneficiary's interest in realty trust subject to equitable division in divorce proceeding notwithstanding spendthrift clause); *see generally,* §5.3.4 (Rights of Beneficiary's Spouse to Trust Property).

[91]2A Scott on Trusts §152.

[92]Id. §153.

[93]E.g. California, Kentucky, Louisiana, Missouri, New York, Oklahoma, Washington, and Wisconsin by legislation afford the spouse and dependents, under certain circumstances, access to a beneficiary's equitable interest in a spendthrift trust. *See* 2A Scott on Trusts §157.1 n.2. *See generally* Dessin, *supra* note 78.

[94]*See* 2A Scott on Trusts §§157.1, 157.2.

[95]Id.

[96]Id. §157.4.

[97]*See* 2A Scott on Trusts §152.

[98]*See* Broadway Natl. Bank v. Adams, 133 Mass. 170 (1882).

[99]Id.

**(d) Trusteed employee benefit plans and IRAs.** An employee benefit plan may well include an associated trust that serves as a receptacle for employer and employee contributions. Under federal law, contributions and the income generated by their investment are entitled to favorable tax treatment, provided the plan meets certain requirements (is *tax-qualified*). One such requirement is that the associated trust contain a spendthrift provision.[100] An ERISA-mandated antialienation provision may prevent a trustee in bankruptcy from reaching the bankrupt's interest in a tax-qualified plan, even though the associated trust would not have enjoyed spendthrift protection under state trust law.[101] The trustee should be aware that no such federal spendthrift requirement applies to trusts associated with IRAs.[102] Thus state statutes and the common law of trusts will determine whether property held by an IRA trustee is reachable by the taxpayer's creditors.[103] In the Federal bankruptcy context, however, a wall against creditor attack is beginning to build around the IRA.[104]

The administration of employee benefit and IRA arrangements is a topic beyond the scope of this handbook. Trustees of property associated with tax-qualified employee benefit arrangements, however, should at least understand the federal and state

[100] *See* I.R.C. §401(a)(13) (1986).

[101] *See* Patterson v. Shumate, 504 U.S. 753 (1992); *but see,* Martin, Gerson, and Levine, Qualified Plans May Not Be Protected in Bankruptcy, 23 ACTEC Notes 75 (1997).

[102] *See* I.R.C. §408 (1986).

[103] The following states have enacted legislation expressly governing the reachability of IRA assets by the taxpayer's creditors: Arkansas (Ark. Code Ann. §16-66-220); Colorado (Colo. Rev. Stat. Ann. §13-54-102); Connecticut (Conn. Gen. Stat. Ann. §52-321a); Georgia (Ga. Code §18-4-22(a)); Illinois (Ill. Ann. Stat. ch. 735 §5/12-1006); Louisiana (La. Rev. Stat. Ann. §20:33); Maryland (Md. Code Ann., Cts. & Jud. Proc. §11-504): Massachusetts (Mass. Gen. L. Ann. ch. 235, §34A); Minnesota (Minn. Stat. Ann. §550.37); New Hampshire (N.H. Rev. Stat. Ann. §515:13-a); North Carolina (N.C. Gen. Stat. §IC-1601); North Dakota (N.D. Cent. Code §28-22-03.1); Ohio (Ohio Rev. Code Ann. §2329.66); Oklahoma (Okla. Stat. Ann. tit. 31, §1); Rhode Island (R.I. Gen. Laws §9-26-4); Texas (Tex. Prop. Code Ann. §42.0021); Virginia (Va. Code Ann. §51.1-124.4). *See, e.g.,* In re Barshak, 106 F.3d 501 (1997) (Under Pennsylvania statute, only $15,000 of debtor's rollover to IRA is exempt from attachment and execution). It has been suggested that because the so-called Roth IRA is governed by §408A of the I.R.C., it may not be covered by many state creditor protection statutes.

[104] *See generally,* Martin, Gerson, and Levine, Qualified Plans May Not Be Protected in Bankruptcy, 23 ACTEC Notes 75 (1997).

laws governing the rights of creditors to reach such property. And all trustees should be aware of how beneficiaries and their creditors may be affected by the movement of property from the shelter of tax-qualified employee benefit trusts to other types of trusts.[105]

### *§5.3.4 Rights of Beneficiary's Spouse to Trust Property*

**Divorce** If a trust is accessible to a beneficiary's creditors, it willbe accessible to the beneficiary's spouse for the spouse's support and will be subject to property division in the event of divorce.[106] Under certain circumstances, the spouse will have access while the creditors will not.[107] The spouse, for example, may be entitled to pierce a spendthrift trust for alimony and child support, even when the beneficiary is not the settlor.[108] Equitable interests of beneficiaries under such trusts have been subjected to division as marital property.[109] Some courts are viewing spouses and children as a class of claimant entitled to special deference.[110] The thought is that as a matter of public policy the beneficiary should not be permitted to enjoy the equitable interest while neglecting to support his dependents.[111] Some states have enacted statutes allowing the spouse and children access to the beneficiary's interest in a spendthrift trust.[112]

[105]I.R.C. §401(a)(13); *Patterson, supra* note 100.

[106]*See, e.g.,* Speed v. Speed, 263 Ga. 166, 430 S.E.2d 348 (1993).

[107]2A Scott on Trusts §157.1; Restatement (Second) of Trusts §157 (1959).

[108]Id.

[109]*See, e.g.,* Flaherty v. Flaherty, 138 N.H. 337, 638 A.2d 1254 (1994).

[110]*See* Wife v. Husband, 286 A.2d 256 (Del. Ch. 1971); Barcardi v. White, 463 So. 2d 218 (Fla 1985); and Albertson v. Ryder, 85 Ohio App. 3d 765, 621 N.E.2d 480 (1993).

[111]*See* Dessin, Feed a Trust and Starve a Child: The Effectiveness of Trust Protective Techniques Against Claims for Support and Alimony, 10 Ga. St. U.L. Rev. 691 (1994).

[112]Arizona: Rev. Stat. Ann. §14-7707(1); California: Prob. Code §15305; Georgia: Code Ann. §53-12-28; Illinois: S.H.A. 735 ILCS 5/2-1403; Kentucky: Rev. Stat. §381.180, as amended by Laws 1966, c. 61; Louisiana: R.S. §9:2005; Missouri: Rev. Stat. Ann. §456.080; New York: Estates, Powers and Trusts Law §7-1.5; Oklahoma:

As a general rule, the spouse and children of the beneficiary may *not* reach the beneficiary's interest in a fully *discretionary trust* created by someone other than the beneficiary.[113] (In a divorce proceeding, however, one court has deemed a beneficiary's contingent equitable interest in such a discretionary trust to be a marital asset belonging to the beneficiary for purposes of determining how the other items of marital property are to be allocated between the parties.[114]) Of course, the trustee voluntarily might decide that it is in the interests *of the beneficiary* to make distributions to the spouse or children, subject, of course, to the terms of the governing instrument and the facts and circumstances prevailing. In some states, equitable interests under a *spendthrift* or *support* trust may *not* be reached by the spouse and children of the non-settlor beneficiary.[115] The thinking is that if the settlor had wanted them in as beneficiaries, he would have named them as beneficiaries.[116]

Whatever the degree of the trust's vulnerability, always keep in mind that the trustee's primary allegiance is to the beneficiary, not to the nonbeneficiary spouse. Thus, when there is marital discord, the trustee must suppress any personal feelings as to who may be "at fault" and vigorously defend — within reason and to the extent the law allows — the beneficiary's equitable property interest.

***Postmortem.*** Upon the death of the nonsettlor beneficiary, his or her surviving spouse will not have access to the trust property unless the terms of the governing instrument expressly provide so,

---

Stats. Ann., tit. 60, §175.25; Pennsylvania: The Estates Act of 1947, §12 (20 Pa. C.S. Sec. 6112); Washington: R.C. §11.96.150; Wisconsin: Wis. Stat. Ann. §701.06.

[113]*See generally* Restatement (Second) of Trusts §155. *See also* Pemberton v. Pemberton, 9 Mass. App. 9, 411 N.E.2d 1305 (1980); Jones v. Jones, 812 P.2d 1152 (Colo. 1991); and §5.3.3.3(a) (The discretionary trust). *See generally,* Brezinsky, Trusts as Marital Property Still Safe, No Decisions Address Equitable Distribution, 6/30/97, N.Y.L.J. 7, (col. 1) (discussing New York's substantial body of matrimonial law with its ever-changing definition of marital property). *See also* M.L. Cross, Annot., Trust income or assets as subject to claims against beneficiary for alimony, maintenance, or child support, 91 A.L.R.2d 262 (1963).

[114]*See* Comins v. Comins, 33 Mass.App.Ct. 28, 595 N.E.2d 804 (1992).

[115]Id. *See also* Erickson v. Erickson, 266 N.W. 161 (Minn. 1936), Matter of Campbell's Trusts, 258 N.W.2d 856 (Minn. 1977); but see, Lauricella v. Lauricella, 409 Mass. 211, 565 N.E.2d 436 (1991) (holding beneficiary's interest in realty trust subject to equitable division notwithstanding spendthrift clause).

[116]Id.

or the trust distributes to the deceased beneficiary's estate.[117] In an ever-increasing number of jurisdictions, however, the spouse may be afforded postmortem access to the trust if it was created by the deceased spouse *and* if the deceased spouse had reserved the power to revoke or amend the trust or a general inter vivos power of appointment.[118] The law in this area is unsettled.[119]

### §5.3.5 *Medicaid Eligibility and Recoupment*

Medicaid (not to be confused with Medicare) is a medical assistance welfare program established under the federal Social Security Act, administered by the states, and supported by federal and state tax revenues.[120] To be eligible for Medicaid benefits (*e.g.*, reimbursement for nursing home costs), an applicant in theory must be "needy."[121] Over the years, attorneys have resorted to the trust device as a means of having their clients render themselves "needy" and thus "eligible" for Medicaid; legislatures and welfare bureaucracies have responded with statutes and regulations designed to thwart these efforts.[122]

Often trustees have been left to administer poorly drawn instruments long after the settlors have died and memories faded as to why such arrangements were made in the first place. The prospective trustee of a trust designed to render the settlor eligible

[117] *See* 2A Scott on Trusts §§144, 145, 146A.

[118] Bogert, Trusts and Trustees §233 (surviving spouse's marital rights). *See also* Sullivan v. Burkin, 390 Mass. 864, 460 N.E.2d 572 (1984); *but see* Friedberg v. Sun Bank/Miami, N.A., 648 So. 2d 204 (Fla. Dist. Ct. App. 1994) (denying surviving spouse access to assets of revocable inter vivos trust when seeking elective share).

[119] *See Sullivan,* 390 Mass. at 864 n.4, 460 N.E.2d at 572 n.4.

[120] *See* Dobris, Medicaid Asset Planning by the Elderly: A Policy View of Expectations, Entitlement and Inheritance, 24 Real Prop. Prob. & Tr. J. 1, 10 (1989).

[121] Id.

[122] *See* Rounds, The Vulnerability of Trust Assets to Attack by the Deceased Settlor's Creditors, by the Commonwealth Should It Seek Reimbursement for Medicaid Payments, and by the Spouse, 73 Mass. L. Rev. 67, 79 n.94 and accompanying text (1988); *see, e.g.*, 42 U.S.C. §1396p (1993) (deeming property in certain self-settled trusts to be countable for Medicaid eligibility); 42 U.S.C. §1320a-7b(a) (criminalizing certain transfers made for the purpose of achieving Medicaid eligibility); *see also* K. M. Coughlin, Here Come the Trustbusters: States Move to Restrict Medicaid Planning, The ElderLaw Report, Nov. 1992, at 1.

for Medicaid should pay particular attention to the provisions that kick in *after* the settlor has died. In addition, whether the trust is long- or short-term, the prospective trustee should be particularly wary of taking on a trust that contains a single illiquid asset such as a residence. How are the expenses and commissions to be paid?

While Medicaid planning issues are well beyond the scope of this handbook, several points are worth making here:

First, the trustee should understand that Medicaid planning has two parts: *eligibility* and *recoupment.* A trust, for example, that contains the settlor's residence may not jeopardize the settlor's eligibility for Medicaid assistance,[123] but the residence may be subject to postmortem recoupment by the state.[124] The two should not be confused.

The second point concerns whether the beneficiary is also the settlor. If so, then even the settlor-beneficiary's contingent interest in a discretionary trust is likely to cause the trust property to be considered "owned" by the beneficiary for Medicaid eligibility purposes (with the exception of certain structured settlement trusts).[125] Even the effectiveness of self-settled trusts with forfeiture provisions is now open to question when it comes to preserving Medicaid eligibility.[126] Moreover, there is no value discount for the contingency of the trustee exercising its discretion.[127] On the other hand, when the beneficiary is not the settlor, the rule of thumb is that the trust property will be countable for Medicaid eligibility purposes to the extent the property is accessible to the beneficiary's creditors.[128] Thus a true discretionary trust (*i.e.*, one that gives the trustee uncontrolled or absolute discretion over payment of income or distribution of principal) created by someone other than the beneficiary may not render a beneficiary ineligible for Medicaid. If the trust grants the trustee the discretion to pay income or distribute principal to the beneficiary for the beneficiary's support, then it is a matter of interpretation as to whether

[123] *See* Dobris, *supra* note 120, at 15.

[124] Id. at 17.

[125] *See* U.S. Trust, Practical Drafting 1746-1747 (April 1989); *See generally* §9.3 (The Structured Settlement Trust).

[126] *See generally* Cohen v. Commissioner, 423 Mass. 399, 668 N.E.2d 769 (1996).

[127] Id.

[128] *See* Dobris, *supra* note 120.

the assets of the trust will prevent the beneficiary from obtaining Medicaid.[129] In matters of Medicaid, the trustee should understand that the treatment of trusts created by the beneficiary is likely to be different from trusts created by a third party.[130]

Finally, when it comes to postmortem recoupment for lifetime Medicaid payments, the welfare department essentially has the status of a creditor.[131] The trustee thus should keep in mind the duty to the successor beneficiaries to allow the state only such access to the trust as the law requires. The trustee wishing to keep abreast of trust-related developments in the Medicaid area would do well to subscribe to the ElderLaw Report.[132]

## §5.4 Rights of the Beneficiary

The beneficiary has, by virtue of the equitable interest in the trust property, rights against the trustee. The trustee must perform certain duties or be held accountable to the wronged beneficiary.

### *§5.4.1 Certain Incidental Rights of the Beneficiary Against the Trustee*

The beneficiary's equitable interest is an interest in property, a property right being a bundle of personal rights associated with

[129] *See e.g.,* Simpson v. Kansas Dept. of Social and Rehabilitation Services, 906 P.2d 174 (Kan. 1995).

[130] *See* Dobris, *supra* note 120.

[131] *See generally* Rounds, *supra* note 122.

[132] Published 11 times a year, the ElderLaw Report is edited by Harry S. Margolis and published by Aspen Law and Business. The trustee will also find helpful the chart entitled "Trusts Affected by the Omnibus Budget Reconciliation Act of 1993" [OBRA-93], published in Clifton B. Kruse, Jr.'s ABA treatise, Third-Party and Self-Created Trusts: A Lawyer's Comprehensive Reference 22-25 (1995). An earlier version of the chart can be found in Kruse, Self-Settled Trusts Following OBRA 1993, 134 Tr. & Est. 66, 68 (1995); *see also* Kruse, OBRA '93 Disability Trusts — A Status Report, 10 Prob. & Prop. 15 (No. 3) (1996).

something of value.[1] It could be said that the various rights of the beneficiary are subsumed in the general right that fiduciary duties be carried out. However, to the trustee operating on the front lines, such a general description does not offer much practical guidance. Accordingly, this section addresses some of the more important specific rights incidental to that general right.

### §5.4.1.1 Right to Information and Confidentiality

A trustee has a duty to account to the beneficiary.[2] As a practical matter this duty translates into a right in the beneficiary to all information needed to protect the beneficiary's equitable interest.[3] The beneficiary has a right to full information about the concerns of the trust at all reasonable times[4] and may examine the trust property, accounts, vouchers, and *usually* the opinions of counsel consulted by the trustee in respect to trust affairs.[5]

The most important thing that the trustee must keep in mind is that the income beneficiary does not possess this right to information alone: The remaindermen, including in some cases those with contingent interests,[6] also share this right. Unless limited by the terms of the trust,[7] a trustee must not succumb to the pressure of a beneficiary to withold information about the trust from other

**§5.4** [1] *See* Restatement of Property §§1-5, 6 comment *a* (1936); 2 Scott on Trusts §130.

[2] *See* §6.1.5 (Duty to Account to the Beneficiary).

[3] *See* §6.1.5.1 (Duty to Provide Information); *see generally* Reid, Mureiko, Mikeska, Privilege and Confidentiality Issues When a Lawyer Represents a Fiduciary, 30 Real Prop. Prob. & Tr. J. 541 (1996).

[4] Bogert, Trusts and Trustees §§961, 861.

[5] *But see* 2A Scott on Trusts §173 n.5 and accompanying text; *see* §8.8 (Whom Does Counsel Represent?); *see* Revised Reg 9, reprinted in Appendix II, providing that a national bank administering a collective investment fund shall provide the fund's financial report to beneficiaries of participating trusts entitled to periodic accountings. 12 C.F.R. §9.18(b)(6)(iv) (1997).

[6] *See* id. §§172, 173; *but see* Bogert, Trusts and Trustees §961 n.23 and accompanying text.

[7] *See* Restatement (second) of Trust §173 (1959) (providing that beneficiaries may examine trust instrument unless its terms provide otherwise); *see, e.g.,* Taylor v. Nationsbank, 481 S.E.2d 358 (N.C. App. 1997), review granted, then withdrawn 493 S.E.2d 57 (12/15/97) and Fletcher v. Fletcher, 480 S.E.2d 488 (Va. 1997) (both affording beneficiaries full access to trust instruments).

beneficiaries. This situation usually occurs when the current beneficiary is a member of a generation older than the remainder interests and does not want the existence of the trust disclosed. Typically the current beneficiary is a parent of the beneficiaries who will take the remainder. To be sure, the settlor by express language may limit the rights of the remaindermen to information, but there is a limit to what a court will tolerate when it comes to limiting a beneficiary's right to protect the equitable interest. A trustee who may operate in secret is essentially unaccountable — a condition that is inimical to the concept of the trust.

On the other hand the beneficiary's right to information, under certain circumstances, may conflict with another beneficiary's right to confidentiality, the latter right being an incident of the trustee's duty of loyalty.[8] The conflict arises not in the context of the trustee's duty to refrain from making unnecessary disclosures of the affairs of the trust to third parties, which is virtually absolute; it arises in the context of balancing the interests of multiple classes of beneficiaries. Is someone with a remote contingent remainder interest, for example, entitled to all the information that the trustee was privy to when a discretionary distribution to a permissible life beneficiary was made? That information might include medical information or intimate details of the beneficiary's marital situation. The answer is "of course not." On the other hand, an abuse of the trustee's discretion could improperly eliminate the remainderman's property interest altogether.[9]

There are no easy answers. The trustee must exercise good judgment in distinguishing the fishing expedition from legitimate efforts to protect one's property. While the contingent remainder-

[8] *See* §6.2.3 (Duty of Confidentiality) and Reid, Mureiko, Mikeska, Privilege and Confidentiality Issues When a Lawyer Represents a Fiduciary, 30 Real Prop. Prob. & Tr. J. 541, 590 (1996) ("Like an umpire who must call a runner either safe or out, the trustee must make decisions that almost always could be considered adverse to some beneficiary's interest."); for a case illustrating the tension between the trustee's duty to disclose and the beneficiary's right to confidentiality, *see* Fletcher v. Fletcher, 480 S.E.2d 488 (Va. 1997) (the fact that plaintiff was beneficiary of one of three trust shares not grounds for denying him access to entire trust document and its schedule of assets).

[9] *See* Bogert, Trusts and Trustees §961 n.4 and accompanying text; 2A Scott on Trusts §173 n.3 and accompanying text.

men ought not to be furnished with all the details of the discretionary distribution, they at least are entitled to know that discretion has been exercised; they certainly are entitled to a copy of the governing instrument. The practice of furnishing certain classes of beneficiaries with excerpts only of a governing instrument is a questionable one, absent express, unambiguous authority in the governing instrument.

### §5.4.1.2 Right to Prompt and Efficient Administration

The beneficiary's equitable interest is an interest in property. Thus to the extent the trustee is dilatory or inefficient in the administration of his trust, he interferes with that property interest and is in breach of trust.[10] The beneficiary has a right to expect that his checks will arrive on time, that tax returns will be filled out properly and filed when due, that investment decisions will be made and executed in a timely fashion, and that accountings will be submitted at regular intervals.

### §5.4.1.3 Right to Income or Possession

It is a common law principle that a trust is *income only* unless the governing instrument clearly indicates that the settlor intended otherwise.[11] Thus, a trust for the "benefit" of C, remainder to D is income only absent additional language suggesting the contrary. Thus, a trust for the "benefit" of C, remainder to D is income only absent additional language suggesting the contrary. The beneficiary has no right to the possession of the trust property unless there is clear indication that the settlor intended otherwise.[12] If the trust requires a mandatory distribution of income to the beneficiary, the trustee must remit the net income at regular intervals.

[10] *See* Bogert, Trusts and Trustees §541 n.60 and accompanying text (the requirement of diligence applies to the uncompensated as well as the compensated trustee).

[11] Id. §812 n.72 and accompanying text; *see* §3.5.3.2(a) regarding application rather than direct payment of income.

[12] Id. §181 n.14 and accompanying text.

Ordinarily the right to possession of real estate and chattels belongs to the trustee,[13] but if the settlor intended that the beneficiary have the use of the property in specie, the beneficiary will be entitled to possession.[14]

The trustee should not make an *unsecured* loan of principal to the beneficiary of an income-only trust in the absence of express or implied authority to do so in the governing instrument. If the beneficiary defaults on the unsecured loan, the trustee would have participated in an unauthorized invasion of principal. Any loan that the trustee does make to the beneficiary should be *secured.* There should be written loan documentation that adequately spells out the rights, duties and obligations of the parties. To further protect the remaindermen's interest, the trustee may want to take out insurance on the beneficiary's life. The loan is a fixed income trust investment and should be carried as such on the trustee's schedule of assets. All this having been said, even a secured loan of principal to the beneficiary of an income-only trust is likely to be a bad idea. The trustee needs a compelling reason for putting the economic interests of the remaindermen at risk in this way. From the remaindermen's perspective, it is unlikely that such a high maintenance asset can be justified on investment grounds alone. If it cannot, it must fall to someone other than the remaindermen to absorb the initial and ongoing costs of the loan.[15] Again, all this assumes that the terms of the income-only trust do not address the matter of principal loans. If the settlor intends that such loans be made, then the trustee must take his cue from the governing instrument when it comes to such matters.

As mentioned, there is a presumption that a *trust* is income only, unless the governing instrument clearly indicates that the settlor intended otherwise. When it comes to the *charitable corporation,*[16] however, there is an opposite presumption. An unrestricted gift to a charitable corporation carries with it the presumption that principal as well as income may be devoted to its charitable purpose.[17]

[13]Id.

[14]Id.

[15]*See generally* §6.2.4.4 (What Expenses Are Allocated Entirely to Income, Entirely to Principal, and Apportioned Between Income and Principal?).

[16]*See generally* §9.8.1 (The Charitable Corporation).

[17]*See generally* 4A Scott on Trusts §348.1.

#### §5.4.1.4 Right to Enjoin Abuse of Discretion

By express language in the governing instrument, the settlor may provide — in lieu of the common law right to the income from or the use of the trust property — that the beneficiary shall have a right to income or principal or both, in the discretion of the trustee.[18] Usually the settlor provides some standard to guide the trustee in the exercise of discretion ("support" and "education" being some common examples).[19] While the general rule is that a court will not second-guess the trustee's exercise of discretion, a beneficiary does have the right to seek judicial relief should the trustee abuse that discretion.[20]

#### §5.4.1.5 Right to Remedies for Breaches of Trust

The beneficiary has standing to seek judicial enforcement of the terms of the trust and to have the trust made whole for any loss occasioned by the trustee's breach of trust.[21] This is true whether the beneficiary's interest is vested or contingent, or whether the beneficiary is a life beneficiary or a remainderman. The judicial remedies available to the beneficiary are covered elsewhere in this handbook.[22]

#### §5.4.1.6 Express Rights to Appoint, Remove, Direct, and Advise in the Absence of Fault

The trustee is not an agent of the beneficiary. Thus the beneficiary has no inherent common law right to appoint or remove the trustee, nor to direct the trustee or even have the beneficiary's

[18] *See* §3.5.3.2(a) (The power to make discretionary applications of income and principal).
[19] Bogert, Trusts and Trustees §182 (support or education), §229 (support).
[20] 2 Scott on Trusts §128.3.
[21] Bogert, Trusts and Trustees §871.
[22] *See* §7.2.3 (Types of Relief); *see also* Bogert, Trusts and Trustees §§861-871.

advice considered by the trustee.[23] The beneficiary can bring an action to remove the trustee, but there must be grounds for removal, and the ultimate decision rests with the court. The settlor, however, may bestow on the beneficiary by express language in the governing instrument any one or more of these rights as against the trustee. These rights may be exercised even when the trustee is not at fault, if such is the wish of the settlor. The prospective trustee should be aware of all such common law derogations that may lurk in a governing instrument. The existence of certain ones — such as the right to give investment directions — may bear on how the trustee's services should be priced or on the advisability of even taking on the trusteeship at all,[24] because the law has not yet settled on what monitoring obligations the trustee has in the face of such a right of direction in the beneficiary.[25]

### §5.4.1.7 Right to Conveyance

The remainderman has a right to conveyance of the trust property within a reasonable time after the trust has terminated, assuming title has not already vested in the remainderman by operation of law.[26]

Are there any circumstances under which a remainderman is entitled to a conveyance before the end of a trust's natural life? Assume the following transfer in trust: *A* to *B* for *C* for ten years, remainder to *C*; the trust is inter vivos; no other person has a beneficial interest; and *C* is of full age and legal capacity. Does *C* have a right to the property outright and free of trust before the expiration of the ten-year period? The American Rule is that if the trust has a purpose (*e.g.*, if it is a spendthrift or discretionary trust), *C* would have no such right.[27] (The English Rule is to the contrary.[28]) If the

[23] *See* 2 Scott on Trusts §§107.3, 185.

[24] Bogert, Trusts and Trustees §122.

[25] *See* §6.1.4 (Duty to Give Personal Attention (Not to Delegate)).

[26] Restatement (Second) of Trusts §345 comment *e* (1959); *see generally* §§3.5.1 (Nature and Extent of the Trustee's Estate) and 8.15.1 (Statute of Uses).

[27] *See* Claflin v. Claflin, 149 Mass. 19, 20 N.E. 454 (1889); Restatement (Second) of Trusts §337 (1959); *see generally* §8.15.7 (The Claflin Doctrine).

[28] Restatement (Second) of Trusts §337, reporter's notes (1959).

trust has no purpose, or its purpose had been accomplished, *C* would have a right to conveyance before the period's expiration.[29]

As a practical matter, *C* may be able to persuade the trustee to convey in the face of an unfulfilled trust purpose. However, some have suggested that the settlor ought to have a cause of action against the trustee for interfering with the settlor's expectation interest in having the terms of the trust carried out.[30] In any case, while *C* may succeed in obtaining the property, there is no enforceable right to a premature conveyance in the face of an unfulfilled purpose as would be the case under the more liberal English Rule.[31] Therefore, if the aid of the court is sought in accelerating *C*'s remainder interest, it will not be given.[32]

In any event, nothing less than the whole of an absolute estate will entitle the beneficiary to a conveyance, even under the English Rule.[33] Therefore, if there are contingent or unascertained interests there can be no agreement to convey, and a beneficiary who has a life estate, with power of disposition by a will, has not such an absolute estate as entitles him to a conveyance. Thus the settlor can prevent the beneficiary's call for a conveyance even under the English Rule by the simple expedient of making a small provision for some person unascertained.[34]

Under a traditional "net income only to *C* for life, remainder to *D*" type of trust, may the trustee make a loan *of trust principal* to the remainderman (*D*) before the trust has terminated even if the interest rate is reasonable? Probably not, unless there is express authority to do so in the governing instrument or all parties who have, or could have, income and remainder interests (or their personal representatives) give informed consent. The effect of such a loan is to constructively delegate to the remainderman

[29] *See* Bogert, Trusts and Trustees §1006, 1007.

[30] *See* §4.1.2 (The Expectation Interest). *But see* Bogert, Trusts and Trustees §1006 n.13 and accompanying text (premature terminations upheld when the trustee and beneficiary joined in a transfer of trust property outright and free of trust back to the settlor). *See also* §1008 (implying that settlor has standing to litigate issues of premature termination).

[31] Id. §1008.

[32] *See* id.

[33] *See* id. §1007 n.7 and accompanying text.

[34] *See* id. §1007 n.9 and accompanying text.

aspects of the trust's administration.[35] Moreover, by making such loans the trustee is asking for trouble. If the remainderman is slow to make the interest payments or pay back the principal, the equitable interests of the income beneficiaries (*C*) are compromised. If the remainderman defaults, the trust is prematurely terminated to the detriment of the income beneficiaries and in contravention of the intentions of the settlor. If something should go wrong, it is guaranteed that the income beneficiaries will call the trustee to account for having made the loan. Why could the remainderman not obtain a bank loan? In the absence of consent by all parties or express authority in the governing instrument, the prudent trustee usually will want authority of the court before making pre-termination loans of trust assets to remaindermen.

May the trustee, without express authority in the governing instrument, make a pre-termination loan *of his own funds* to the remainderman and secure the loan with trust assets? If the trust is a spendthrift trust, the answer is no. If the remainderman's equitable interest is non-vested, the answer is also no. If the trust is not a spendthrift trust and the remainderman's equitable interest is vested, then the concerns relating to constructive premature termination expressed in the prior paragraph would still apply to a loan of the trustee's own funds that is secured by trust assets. Consideration should also be given to the loyalty issues attendant when such loans are secured by trust assets.[36] There is probably no impediment, however, to a trustee making a loan at interest to the remaindermen of his own funds, either unsecured or secured by non-trust assets, provided the transaction is fair and untainted by undue influence.[37]

### §5.4.2 *Rights of the Beneficiary Against Those Other Than the Trustee (The BFP and Others)*

The trustee holds the legal title for the benefit of the beneficiary; each person who receives the legal title from the trustee in breach of trust also holds the property in trust, unless the

[35] *See generally* §6.1.4 (Duty to Give Personal Attention (Not to Delegate)).
[36] *See generally* §6.1.3.1 (Trustee Benefiting as Borrower and Lender).
[37] *See generally* §6.1.3.5 (Duty of Loyalty to the Beneficiary in Nontrust Matters).

transferee has a special and valid equitable claim of his own.[38] The law has concluded that the transferee has such an equitable claim when title is acquired in a wholly innocent manner in exchange for value.[39] Whenever a person acquires the title under these circumstances, the equity court declines to interfere.[40] This is the doctrine of *bona fide purchase*; it is substantially a rule of inaction.[41] Thus, if the trustee transfers trust property to a bona fide purchaser (BFP) (that is, one who has no actual or constructive knowledge of the trust), the purchaser acquires the title free of trust.[42] In many jurisdictions the rule has been codified. For the transferee to be protected each of the rule's three conditions must be satisfied: actual acquisition of title, the payment of value, and a lack of notice.[43]

Thus, even when the trustee wrongfully contracts to sell the trust property to an innocent purchaser, the beneficiary's right remains unclouded if the purchaser then learns of the trust relationship before the transfer.[44] To enforce the contract under these circumstances would be to order a breach of trust.

One who receives the trust property by *gift* must disgorge it, even when the donee is ignorant of the trust's existence.[45] The innocent donee who has restored the property to the trust is under no further duty.[46] The donee who sold it need only restore the proceeds. Should the donee, while still ignorant of the trust, in turn give it away to someone else, he or she is not liable.[47] If on the other hand the innocent donee sells or gives away the property after acquiring knowledge of the trust, liability attaches.[48]

The innocent donee who has consumed the trust property

[38] *See* 4 Scott on Trusts §288.

[39] *See* id. §284.

[40] Id.

[41] Id.

[42] Id; *see generally,* §8.21 (Duty of Third Parties to Investigate Whether Trustee Has Power to Act or Is Properly Exercising the Power).

[43] Bogert, Trusts and Trustees §885 (title), §887 (value), §891 (notice), §894 (facts putting on inquiry).

[44] *See* Restatement (Second) of Trusts §311 (1959).

[45] Id. §289.

[46] *See* 4 Scott on Trusts §292.

[47] *See* id. §292.1.

[48] *See* id. §292.3.

may be liable if these expenditures qualify as "ordinary";[49] if they are "extraordinary," and if the donee has changed position detrimentally in reasonable reliance upon the transfer, then the donee may not be liable.[50]

A person who actually pays for and receives title and possession knowing that the transfer is in violation of the beneficiary's prior rights holds the property in constructive trust for the beneficiary.[51] This holds true if the person ought to have known of the outstanding beneficial interest.[52]

### *§5.4.3 Beneficiary's Right to Legal Fees from Trust Estate*

In litigation involving a good faith difference of opinion among the parties to a trust as to the meaning of a material trust term, the beneficiaries may be entitled to reimbursement for their legal fees *from the trust estate.* This matter is covered in §8.13.

## §5.5 Loss of the Beneficiary's Rights

The trustee has an affirmative equitable duty to act solely in the interest of the beneficiaries. Thus a former or present trustee may not acquire the property of the trust by adverse possession.[1] In theory, however, the trustee may acquire the property with the informed consent of all beneficiaries.[2] Likewise, their informed consent, ratification, or release may be sufficient to discharge the trustee from breaches of trust.[3]

[49]Restatement (Second) of Trusts §292 comment *j* (1959).
[50]Id.
[51]5 Scott on Trusts §462.4.
[52]Bogert, Trusts and Trustees §894.
**§5.5** [1]5 Scott on Trusts §495; *see* §6.1.3 n.14 (Duty to Be Loyal to the Trust).
[2]Id. §496.
[3]Id. §216; *see generally,* W.W. Allen, Annot., Beneficiary's Consent To, Aquiescence In, or Ratification of Trustee's Improper Allocation or Distribution of Assets, 29 A.L.R. 2d 1034 (1953).

It is clear, however, that such discharge is not binding if given in reliance upon fraudulent representations or under circumstances of concealment of material facts.[4] It equally is well settled that the beneficiary must be of full age and legal capacity else the beneficiary's consent is not binding.[5] In acts involving the shifting of beneficial interests, the assent of one beneficiary will not bind the others,[6] nor is the assent of the income beneficiaries binding on the remaindermen.[7] Thus it is impossible for a trustee to obtain release by private agreement when there are beneficiaries who are unborn, unascertained, or under some legal disability.[8] (Such would certainly be the case for most cemetery trustees and trustees of charitable trusts.[9]) On the other hand the assent of the beneficiary who holds a general inter vivos power of appointment or reserved right of revocation may well be binding on all other beneficiaries, including the unborn and unascertained.[10]

Delay on the part of the beneficiary in compelling a trustee to redress negligent breaches of trust apparent from a scrutiny of the trustee's accounts may constitute laches sufficient to release the trustee from such liabilities.[11] A cause of action against a trustee for breaches of the duty of loyalty, however, is not barred by laches until a reasonable time after *all* beneficiaries become aware of the breach and fail to take appropriate action.[12] What constitutes laches depends upon the circumstances of each case, but the mere lapse of time alone will not bar the beneficiary where the position of others has not been changed.[13] Circumstances indicating an intention to abandon one's equitable remedies, along with a lapse

[4] Id.

[5] Id. §216.3.

[6] Id. §216.2; *see also* In re Crane, 34 N.Y.S.2d 9 (1942).

[7] 3 Scott on Trusts §216.2.

[8] *See* Bogert, Trusts and Trustees §1007 n.9 and accompanying text.

[9] Rounds, Protections Afforded to Massachusetts' Ancient Burial Grounds, 73 Mass. L. Rev. 176 (1988).

[10] *See* 3 Scott on Trusts §216.2; *see generally* §8.11 (What Are the Duties of the Trustee of a Revocable Inter Vivos Trust?).

[11] *See* id. §219; *see also* Bogert, Trusts and Trustees §964.

[12] *See* Lawson v. Haynes, 170 F.2d 741 (10th Cir. 1948); Bogert, Trusts and Trustees §543(u); *see also* §6.1.3.5 (Duty of Loyalty to the Beneficiary in Nontrust Matters).

[13] *See* Bogert, Trusts and Trustees §§948, 949.

of time, will be sufficient to bar a recovery.[14] A beneficiary with a contingent remainder interest may interfere to protect the estate during the life tenancy but is not guilty of laches or acquiescence until the estate comes into the beneficiary's possession. Even the contingent remaindermen are well advised to take action immediately upon receiving notice of a breach, whether or not prior interests have terminated.[15]

What does the trustee do when a beneficiary cannot be found? He looks for a state statute, for example, one that applies to abandoned property.[16] Also, in some states, by statute, the trustee, after a specified period of time, may bring an action to have the equitable interest pass to those who would be entitled to it if the beneficiary had died.[17]

A beneficiary at common law, or by statute, may disclaim an equitable interest, provided the beneficiary has not accepted the interest.[18] For estate, gift, and generation-skipping tax avoidance purposes, however, a disclaimer must comply with I.R.C. §2518.[19] It must be made not later than the date which is nine months after the later of the day on which the transfer creating the interest in the disclaiming beneficiary is made, or the day on which he or she attains age 21.[20] Generally, the equitable interest will then pass as if the beneficiary had predeceased the time of transfer.[21]

A "no-contest" ("in terrorem") clause in a will or trust provides for the forfeiture or reduction of the interest of a beneficiary who "contests" the arrangement.[22] Some courts have upheld such

[14] Id. §949 n.36 and accompanying text.

[15] *See* id. §949 n.66 and accompanying text; 3 Scott on Trusts §219.4.

[16] 2A Scott on Trusts §142.3, n.3

[17] Id. n.1

[18] I Scott on Trusts §36.1

[19] *See generally* Roche & Carlson, The Dynamic Disclaimer, 14 New Eng. L. Rev. 399 (1979); *see also,* Connelly, Constructing Qualified Disclaimers, 11 Prob. & Prop. 47 (Jul./Aug. 1997).

[20] Roche & Carlson, *supra* n. 19, at 416-441.

[21] Id. at 410

[22] *See generally* Annot., Validity and enforceability of provisions of will or trust instrument for forfeiture or reduction of share of contesting beneficiary, 23 A.L.R.4th 369 (1983).

clauses.[23] Others have not.[24] In the case of the trust, there are really three avenues of attack. One can contest the circumstances surrounding a trust's creation, its purposes, or *how* it is being administered, or any combination thereof. Assuming that the settlor intended to impress a trust upon the property, not to make a gift to the "trustee," then it would seem inconsistent with the concept of the trust for a court to apply a "no contest" clause to the third category, e.g., good faith actions brought by beneficiaries to construe the terms of governing instruments or to remedy breaches of trust.[25] Accountability, after all, is the glue that holds the institution of the trust together.[26]

## §5.6 Liabilities of the Beneficiary

With the possible exception of those trusts under which the beneficiary for all intents and purposes controls the trustee (*e.g.*, the revocable inter vivos trust, the realty trust, the nominee trust), the beneficiary incurs no liabilities arising inherently out of ownership of the beneficial interest, except for taxes.[1] The trustee is not an agent of the beneficiary. In the absence of agreement, the beneficiary is not personally bound to indemnify the trustee for trust administration expenses.[2] The beneficiary may voluntarily undertake to make himself liable to the trustee by, for example, furnishing funds to enable the trustee to improve the trust estate or by litigating in order to collect insurance proceeds.

If a beneficiary wrongfully deals with trust property, any loss

[23]Id.

[24]Id.

[25]*See, e.g.,* Hillyard v. Leonard, 391 S.W.2d 211 (Mo. 1965) (in a trust for the benefit of the settlor's widow, a general no-contest clause covering actions to partition the trust did not cover an action to partition brought by the beneficiaries *after* the widow's death).

[26]*See generally* §6.1.5 (Duty to Account to the Beneficiary).

**§5.6** [1]*See* 3A Scott on Trusts §274.

[2]*See* Bogert, Trusts and Trustees §718.

can be made up from the beneficiary's interest;[3] in the case of overpayment, the beneficiary may be personally liable.[4] Where an innocent overpayment has been made, there may be a change of position by the beneficiary which makes it inequitable to compel repayment.[5] A trustee makes distribution at his peril: An overpayment that is not repaid by the beneficiary is a personal obligation of the trustee.

A beneficiary is liable to the same extent as any other person for participation or collusion in a breach of trust.[6] If beneficiary *X* persuades the trustee improperly to lend or distribute to him trust property, *X* may be liable to beneficiaries *Y* and *Z*.[7] *X*'s own interest in the trust estate may be subjected to an equitable lien in their favor.[8]

The beneficiary would be ill advised to instruct the trustee in matters concerning management of the trust estate.[9] The trustee would be equally ill-advised to blindly follow the beneficiary's instructions.[10] The trustee is in no way excused from liability merely because some of the beneficiaries insisted upon an improper action — except perhaps as to a claim presented by those who did the insisting.[11] Moreover, the interfering beneficiaries may be held to have colluded in the breach of trust.[12] If a beneficiary engages in frivolous litigation against the trustee or the trust, that beneficiary's interest may be charged with payment of the costs.[13]

[3]Restatement (Second) of Trusts §253 (1959).

[4]Id. §254.

[5]Id; *but see,* First Union National Bank v. McGill,, 684 So.2d 845 (Fla. App. 1996) (trustee's improper allocation of capital gains to the income account shall be made up by a remedial allocation to principal of future income payments, rather than by surcharging the trustee).

[6]Id. §256.

[7]Id.

[8]Id.

[9]Id. §216.

[10]Id. §256(2) (one beneficiary's consent to a breach of trust will not relieve trustee from liability to the other beneficiaries); 1 Scott on Trusts §8 (trustee not an agent of the beneficiary).

[11]Restatement (Second) of Trusts §216 comment *g* (1959).

[12]Id. §256.

[13]*See* 3 Scott on Trusts §188.4 n.13 and accompanying text.

Except perhaps in certain cases where the beneficiary controls the trustee, the beneficiary will not be held liable as the owner of the trust estate.[14] Thus in matters involving the trust estate, the beneficiary is liable neither in contract[15] nor in tort;[16] neither criminally for a nuisance on the trust property,[17] for a trustee's unlawful acts of discrimination,[18] nor as a stockholder.[19] The beneficiary may not be forced to contribute personal funds in order to prevent the trust property from being taken by foreclosure.[20] Nor is the trustee "entitled to a charge on the beneficiary's interest in the trust to secure a liability of the beneficiary to the trustee not connected with the administration of the trust, unless the beneficiary contracts to give him such a charge."[21]

[14]*See* 3A Scott on Trusts §§274, 274.1.
[15]*See* id. §275.
[16]*See* id. §276.
[17]*See* id. §265.3.
[18]*See* Bogert, Trusts and Trustees §731.
[19]*See* 3A Scott on Trusts §265.2.
[20]*See* 2A Scott on Trusts §176.
[21]Restatement (Second) of Trusts §250 (1959).

CHAPTER 6

# The Trustee's Duties



## §6.1 General Duties

When property is transferred from one person to another, the transferee's legal status with respect to the property will depend in large part on the transferor's intent. If the intent is to make a gift, then the transferor imposes no duties on the transferee with respect to the property. If the intent is to create an agency, contract, bailment, or trust, then the transferor imposes certain enforceable duties on the transferee with respect to the transferee property. A trust relationship brings with it five fundamental duties:

1. the duty to be generally prudent (to include the duty to segregate the property)

2. the duty to carry out the terms of the trust
3. the duty to be loyal to the trust
4. the duty to give personal attention to the affairs of the trust
5. the duty to account to the beneficiary

If any one of these duties is totally lacking, there is a good chance that the transferee's legal status with respect to the property is something other than that of a trustee.

### §6.1.1 *Duty to Be Generally Prudent*

The trustee has a duty to act reasonably and competently in all matters of trust administration, not just in investment matters.[1] With respect to investments, this standard of prudence is a standard of *conduct*, not *performance*.[2] A trustee's action or inaction will not be judged in hindsight. As a general rule, the amateur trustee must exercise "such care and skill as a man of ordinary prudence would exercise in dealing with his own property."[3] On the other hand, one who holds oneself out as a professional with special skills is under a duty to employ those skills.[4] Thus the trustee's administration had better be as advertised.

standard of conduct → not performance.

**§6.1** [1]A distinction should be drawn here between this overarching duty to act reasonably and competently in all matters of trust administration and the so-called *prudent man rule* that provides the trustee with a standard of conduct for the investment of trust assets. *See* §6.2.2.1. (The Harvard College Prudent Man Rule and Its Progeny). The more general duty to act reasonably and competently in all matters of trust administration requires the trustee to exercise caution, reasonable care, and at least the skill of a person of ordinary intelligence in the fulfillment of all duties arising under the trust; the "prudent man rule" is a more specific application of this general duty.

[2]Harvard College v. Amory, 26 Mass. (9 Pick.) 446, 461 (1830); Restatement (Third) of Trusts §§204, 227 (1992); 3 Scott on Trusts §§204, 227.

[3]Restatement (Second) of Trusts §174 comment *a* (1959); 2A Scott on Trusts §174; *Harvard College, supra* at 461; *but see* Uniform Probate Code §7-302, 8 U.L.A. 507 (1998) (holding trustee to standard of "a prudent man" dealing with the property of another).

[4]2A Scott on Trusts §174.1; Uniform Probate Code §7-302, 8 U.L.A. 507 (1998).

### *§6.1.2 Duty to Carry Out the Terms of the Trust*

The trustee has an overarching duty to carry out the intentions of the settlor as they have been communicated in the governing instrument.[5] The wishes of the beneficiaries are subordinate to those of the settlor. While legally the trustee is neither an agent of the settlor nor an agent of the beneficiary,[6] it can do no harm for trustees to consider themselves agents of their settlors. Take for example a spendthrift trust. Let us assume that notwithstanding its antialienation provisions, the beneficiary intends to assign the beneficial interest. Moreover it may be in the beneficiary's interest to do so. The trustee's first and foremost duty, however, is to the intentions of the settlor as they have been set forth in the governing instrument. The assignment must not be honored;[7] the trustee is not an agent of the beneficiary.

If the trustee honors the assignment, the settlor ought to have recourse. Would not the trustee's obligation to carry out the settlor's intentions be an illusory one if only the beneficiary could seek its enforcement? Certainly the beneficiary will not be raising any objections in the situation just described. As for the settlor, the matter of what rights, if any, are lodged with the settlor is covered in Chapter 4.

### *§6.1.3 Duty to Be Loyal to the Trust*

> A trustee is held to something stricter than the morals of the marketplace. Not honesty alone, but the punctilio of an honor the most sensitive, is then the standard of behavior. As to this there has developed a tradition that is unbending and inveterate. Uncompro-

[5]Restatement (Second) of Trusts §164 comment *a* (1959); 2A Scott on Trusts §§164, 164.1. *But see* 2A Scott on Trusts §§165-168 (deviation from terms of trust permitted in cases of impossibility, illegality, or a change in circumstances). Unless the settlor has reserved a power to modify or revoke the trust, however, subsequent oral expressions of the settlor are not admissible to vary the terms of the trust. Id. at §164.1.

[6]Restatement (Second) of Trusts §8 (1959); 1 Scott on Trusts §8.

[7]*See, e.g.*, Restatement (Second) of Trusts §164 (1959).

mising rigidity has been the attitude of courts of equity when petitioned to undermine the rule of undivided loyalty by the "disintegrating erosion" of particular exceptions.[8]

A trustee is under a duty to act solely in the interest of the beneficiaries as to matters that directly and indirectly involve the trust property.[9] This duty springs from the trust relationship rather than from any provision of the trust instrument. It is the bedrock of the trust relationship; it is a duty of undivided loyalty.

The trustee must not allow personal interests to compete with the interests of the beneficiaries arising under the trust.[10] The trustee who has an interest adverse to the trust that he intends to assert must resign the trust[11] unless all the beneficiaries are informed and consent to his retention of the office.[12] Likewise, the trustee of a business may not enter into a competing business for personal benefit.[13] It is also the case that a trustee of land may not assert a claim of adverse possession against the trust.[14] A trustee of two trusts may sell property from one trust to the other only if neither trust is disadvantaged.[15]

The duty of loyalty, however, does not make the trustee an agent of the beneficiary. The trustee thus may not yield to a demand by the beneficiaries to commit a breach of trust, for that

[8]Meinhard v. Salmon, 249 N.Y. 458, 464, 164 N.E. 545, 546 (1928) (Cardozo, C.J.).

[9]*See* Restatement (Third) of Trusts §170(1) (1992); 2A Scott on Trusts §170; The Employee Retirement Income Security Act (ERISA), 29 U.S.C. §§1104(a)1, 404 (1974) codifies this duty for fiduciaries of employees' pension plans; Revised Reg. 9 (effective January 29, 1997 and reprinted in Appendix II) provides that a national bank exercising fiduciary powers shall adopt and follow written policies and procedures that address, where appropriate, the bank's methods for preventing self-dealing and conflicts of interest. *See* 12 C.F.R. §9.5(c).

[10]*See* Restatement (Second) of Trusts §170 comment *p* (1959); 2A Scott on Trusts §170.23.

[11]*See* 2A Scott on Trusts §170.23.

[12]*See* Restatement (Second) of Trusts §216 comment *g* (1959); 3 Scott on Trusts §§216, 216.2.

[13]*See* Restatement (Third) of Trusts §§170 comment *p*, 206 comment *l* (1992); 2A Scott on Trusts §§170.23, 206.

[14]Railroad Co. v. Durant, 95 U.S. 576 (1877); Smith v. Dean, 240 S.W.2d 789 (Tex. Civ. Ct. App. 1951).

[15]*See* Restatement (Third) of Trusts §170 comment *r* (1992); 2A Scott on Trusts §170.16.

would be putting the interests of the trustee before the interests of the trust.[16]

The duty of loyalty is not a passive one. It requires affirmative action by the trustee, who must do all that can honestly be done for the furtherance of the interests of the trust.[17] The trustee cannot consent to a judgment invalidating the trust nor pay a creditor who has a claim that cannot be enforced by suit. All demands must be pressed, even to the extent of bringing suit, unless it is evident that it is useless to do so. The trustee must not unreasonably fail to appeal adverse decisions.[18] The trustee must defend the trust. If a successful action is brought by a third party against the trust, the trustee is under a duty to the beneficiary to appeal to a higher court if it is reasonable to do so.[19]

A trustee is entitled to take a reasonable fee from the trust estate for all fiduciary services.[20] This is an inherent conflict, but it is nonetheless permitted since it would be unreasonable to expect trustees to serve without compensation. (At early English common law the trustee did not have a right to compensation.[21])

The trustee is also entitled to reimbursement for reasonable expenses,[22] but the general rule is that, apart from the right to reasonable compensation, a trustee may not receive direct or indirect economic benefit from the trust estate unless authorized to do so by the settlor of a revocable trust, by the nonsettlor holder of a general inter vivos power of appointment, by the terms of the trust instrument,[23] by the court, by statute, or by all of the beneficiaries including the remaindermen after full and

[16]In Estate of Carmean, Los Angeles Super. Ct. Civ. P374331 (1984) (unpublished), the court held that the duty of loyalty was breached when a trust officer imprudently diverted income from the maintenance of the trust property to the beneficiaries in order to keep them quiet, that is, in order to "rid herself of the burden of handling requests and listening to hard luck stories."

[17]*See* Restatement (Second) of Trusts §2 comment *b*, §170 (1959).

[18]*See* id. §177 comment *d*.

[19]*See* id. §178 comment *a*; 2A Scott on Trusts §178.

[20]*See* §3.5.2.4 (Right in Equity to Compensation).

[21]*See* 3A Scott on Trusts §242.

[22]*See* §3.5.2.3 (Right in Equity to Exoneration and Reimbursement).

[23]*See generally*, J.D. Perovich, J.D., Annot., Validity and Construction of Trust Provision Authorizing Trustee to Purchase Trust Property, 39 A.L.R. 3d 836 (1971).

fair disclosure.[24] As a practical matter, the trustee bent on transacting with the trust estate "for his own account" seldom will find the last option (beneficiary consent in a nonjudicial setting) a viable one. Most trusts will have some beneficiaries who are unborn, unascertained, or under legal disabilities such as minority or mental incapacity, thereby making the consent of all the beneficiaries unobtainable.

So rigorous is the duty of loyalty that an act of self-dealing will be regarded as constructively fraudulent and, at the option of the beneficiary, will be set aside.[25] The trustee is not given an opportunity to justify his action; an untrammelled choice of affirmance or rejection rests with the beneficiary.[26] If the beneficiary elects to affirm the transaction, the trustee must account for all profit; if the beneficiary disaffirms, the trustee must make good all losses.[27] Thus if a trustee, motivated by divided loyalties, imprudently acquires or retains on behalf of the trust a particular investment, the trustee will be held liable for any resulting loss suffered by the trust whether or not the investment is a sound fiduciary investment. Moreover the trustee — at the election of the beneficiaries — may be liable even for the difference between the highest unrealized value of the investment and its realized value.[28]

It is obvious that the trustee should scrupulously avoid the assumption of so serious a risk; no intelligent person desires to become an insurer against loss under such circumstances. The trustee's invariable rule should be to avoid dealing with the trust property in this way.

This rule sounds almost unreasonably harsh, but it is required because of the demonstrated fallibility of humanity. There are no exceptions, although there are limits. Thus if the trustee honestly

[24] *See* Restatement (Third) of Trusts §§170 comment *w*, 206 (1992); 2A Scott on Trusts §170.

[25] *See* Restatement (Second) of Trusts §206 comment *b* (1959); 3 Scott on Trusts §§206, 208.4.

[26] *See* 2A Scott on Trusts §170.2.

[27] *See* Restatement (Second) of Trusts §206 comment *b* (1959); 2A Scott on Trusts §§170.2, 206.

[28] *See* §§7.1, 7.2.3.1-7.2.3.2 (Liabilities of Trustee).

sells the trust property to a third person and *there is no scheme to repurchase*, the trustee is not conclusively forbidden from acquiring it in his individual capacity later on.[29] So also after the trustee has stepped down.[30]

### §6.1.3.1 Trustee Benefiting as Borrower and Lender

Nothing good can come of a trustee's borrowing from the trust estate no matter how competitive the interest rate may be and no matter how complete the paper trail, with perhaps the limited exception of the short-term deposit of funds awaiting distribution on the commercial side of the trustee bank.[31] The thief when caught asserts it is only a loan. Even when borrowing is duly authorized, it will always bring with it the appearance of impropriety, the trustee being on both sides of the transaction.[32] Was the authority

[29] *See* Restatement (Third) of Trusts §170 comment *e* (1959); 2A Scott on Trusts §170.6.

[30] *See* Restatement (Second) of Trusts §170 comment *g* (1959). But if the trustee steps down for the purpose of purchasing the trust property, then the sale can be set aside at the election of the beneficiary. 2A Scott on Trusts §170.8.

[31] Comptroller of the Currency Regulation 9, Fiduciary Funds Awaiting Investment or Distribution, 12 C.F.R. §9.10(b) (self-deposits) (1997). The Employee Retirement Income Security Act (ERISA) permits the fiduciary ("a bank or similar financial institution supervised by the United States or a State") under an employee's pension plan to invest all or part of the plan's assets in deposits with itself that bear a reasonable rate of interest if either a provision of the plan expressly authorizes it to do so or the plan covers only employees of the fiduciary. ERISA §408, 29 U.S.C. §1108(b)(4) (1974). Most banks now have the operational capability of "sweeping" uninvested trust cash into short-term investments on a daily basis, thus reducing substantially the occasions when it would be appropriate for a bank trustee to deposit trust funds in noninterest-bearing accounts. *See, e.g.*, Upp v. Mellon Bank, N.A., 799 F. Supp. 540 (E.D. Pa. 1992), *rev'd*, 994 F.2d 1039 (1993); Revised Reg. 9 (effective January 29, 1997 and reprinted in Appendix II) provides that a national bank exercising fiduciary powers shall adopt and follow written policies and procedures that address, where appropriate, the bank's investment of funds held as fiduciary, including short-term investments and the treatment of fiduciary funds awaiting investment and distribution. *See* 12 C.F.R. 9.5(e) (1997).

[32] The case of John Zaccaro, husband of former vice-presidential candidate Geraldine Ferraro, and his handling of the estate of an elderly woman in New York illustrates the pitfalls of fiduciaries borrowing from their estates and trusts.

fairly obtained? Why didn't the trustee go to the marketplace? Who represented the trust in the transaction? Will the trust be thought of first if the trustee's personal financial situation begins to sour? Who will represent the trust in the event of default? What happens if the trustee goes bankrupt?

Moreover, from the perspective of the trustee, when a portion of the trust assets is invested in a personal obligation the trustee ventures outside the safe harbor of the Prudent Man Rule (which is a rule of conduct, not performance) to become an insurer of the value of the portion.[33]

The *no further inquiry rule*[34] should continue to apply to unauthorized trustee borrowings, and the courts should resist the temptation to recognize "fairness" and "benign intentions" as legitimate defenses to such activity. To do otherwise is to tempt the honest and afford avenues of escape to the dishonest. The law should be absolutely unambiguous in this regard and ignorance of it should never be a judicially recognized excuse.

On the other hand there is some social utility in allowing the trustee to lend *to the trust* if there is sensitivity to the loyalty considerations attendant even when funds flow from the trustee to the trust. A strict definition of self-dealing would encompass trustee lending in that the trustee receives from the trust estate not only fee compensation but also interest income.[35] Moreover, if for some reason the credit-worthiness of the trust erodes, does the

---

Mr. Zaccaro had borrowed from the estate $175,000 which he paid back with interest. Nonetheless, he was removed as conservator of the woman's estate. The judge in the case, New York Supreme Court Justice Edwin Kassof, wrote, "Thus it is generally accepted that the fiduciary is not permitted to use estate funds for his own benefit or for investments in his own business. There is no necessity for finding malicious intent, deliberate wrongdoing or criminal conduct. The mere appearance of impropriety must be assiduously avoided. This standard has been applied with uncompromising rigidity by the courts." Washington Post, Aug. 31, 1984, §1, at A1.

[33] *See* §§6.1.1 (Duty to Be Generally Prudent), 6.2.1 (Duty to Take Active Control of, Segregate, Earmark, and Protect Trust Property).

[34] *See* Estate of Rothko, 43 N.Y.2d 305, 372 N.E.2d 291 (1977), *aff'g* 56 A.D.2d 499, 392 N.Y.S.2d 870 (1977), *aff'g* 84 Misc. 2d 870, 379 N.Y.S.2d 923 (1975). *See generally* 3 Scott on Trusts §206.

[35] *But see* First Natl. Bank of Boston v. Slade, 379 Mass. 243, 399 N.E.2d 1047 (1979); Bullivant v. First Natl. Bank of Boston, 246 Mass. 324, 141 N.E. 41 (1923). *See generally* 2A Scott on Trusts §170.20; Bogert, Trusts and Trustees §543(L).

duty of loyalty require some forbearance on the part of the lending trustee? The outcome of a particular case is likely to depend on its own set of facts and circumstances.[36] It is recommended, however, that unless the trust instrument specifically permits the trustee to lend funds to the trust, the trustee should refrain from engaging in such activity.[37]

In the context of the corporate fiduciary with general banking powers the trust should specifically permit the trustee to enter into a loan with its commercial department. Even if the trust specifically permits the trustee to lend funds to the trust, the terms of the loan must be competitive. With respect to a trustee's loan to a corporation that is owned and controlled by the trust, the law is somewhat ambiguous as to whether the trustee may protect its position to the detriment of the corporation and of course the trust.[38] What if the lending trustee calls the loan, driving the corporation into bankruptcy and the trust into oblivion?[39] In this context may the commercial side and the trust side of a bank be treated as separate entities? As the corporation has only one management pyramid and one set of shareholders, the answer has to be no.[40] Thus it is recommended that lenders attempt to avoid loans to corporations that are controlled by their trusts. As a practical matter, the attorney for the trust will find it a difficult task leading the lending trustee through a gauntlet of federal insider trading compliance requirements on one side and state-imposed fiduciary obligations on the other.

#### §6.1.3.2 Trustee Invests in Its Own Stock

When trustees lend to themselves without authority they breach the duty of loyalty. Are things any different if a corporate trustee invests trust assets in itself, in its own stock? This situation usually arises inadvertently when bank stock pours over by will into

[36] *See generally Slade, supra* note 34; *Bullivant, supra* note 34; Bogert, Trusts and Trustees §543(L); 2A Scott on Trusts §§170.20, 170.23A, 170.24.

[37] *See,* §3.5.3 2(c) (The power to borrow on behalf of the trust or to pledge or mortgage the trust property).

[38] *See supra* note 36.

[39] Id.

[40] 2A Scott on Trusts §170.18.

a trust of which the bank is a trustee or as an incident to the bank's merger with or acquisition of another bank. Again, nothing good can come of such entanglements. If the corporate entity is publicly traded, the entity as trustee may not exploit inside information on behalf of the trust.[41] Independent judgment in the voting of proxies is virtually impossible.[42] If the bank gets into trouble its trust department may be tempted to hold onto its own stock for any number of business considerations unrelated to the welfare of its trusts, such as supporting the stock's price in order to maintain the confidence of trust or commercial customers.[43] In either case, such nonfeasance constitutes a continuing act of self-dealing arising out of the bank's divided loyalties. Moreover, even in the face of duly obtained authority, the trustee is saddled with the overarching obligation to be prudent. Thus express retention language in the governing instrument cannot relieve the trustee of its duty to monitor the investment.[44] Such entanglements never should be initiated by the trustee and, when they inadvertently develop, should be ended as soon as it is prudent to do so.[45] If the stock is part of the holdings of a revocable trust and the donor wants the trustee to hold the trustee's stock, the trustee at a minimum should require a letter from the donor directing retention of the stock and holding the trustee harmless from the consequences of so doing.

### §6.1.3.3 Trustee Benefiting as Buyer and Seller

Any act that appears to be in the interest of the trustee instead of the trust estate may constitute a breach of trust for which the remedies are as complete as the equity court can make them. The

[41] *See generally* §§7.3.3.3 (Registration and Sale of Securities), 7.3.4.2(a) (Criminal and Civil Liability as Legal Owner . . . (a) Securities Laws).

[42] *See generally* Report, Voting by Corporate Trustee of Its Own Stock Held in Trust, 3 Real Prop. Prob. & Tr. J. 517 (1968); Barclay, Voting Bank's Own Stock Held in Trust (pts. 1-2), 106 Tr. & Est. 70, 678 (1967).

[43] *See generally* 2A Scott on Trusts §170.15.

[44] *See* Restatement (Second) of Trusts §231 comments *a, b* (1959); Mueller v. Mueller, 28 Wis. 2d 26, 135 N.W.2d 854 (1965).

[45] *See generally* American Bar Association, A Fiduciary's Guide to Federal Securities Laws 46 (1994).

trustee cannot make any profit out of the use of the trust property or gain any advantage, direct or indirect, by its purchase or sale. The trustee — individual or institutional — must not sell trust property to himself personally,[46] sell his own property to the trust,[47] sell property under circumstances where his personal interest might affect his judgment,[48] renew the trust lease in his own name,[49] buy property for himself which he ought to have bought for the trust,[50] or be guided by the interests of any third person including other trusts.[51]

A gray area has developed in the law, namely the selling by the trustee of legal, brokerage, and consulting services to the trust.[52] Again, as with the sale of goods, such transactions fall within the strict definition of *self-dealing* in that economic benefit is accruing to the trustee from the trust estate over and above the trustee fees. In England the practice is forbidden,[53] but in most American jurisdictions it is not.[54]

The practice is troubling. The trustee is on both sides of the service contract, so the arrangement on its face is the product of divided loyalties. At the very least such transactions put great stress on the trustee's independent judgment. Thus, to avoid even the appearance of impropriety, the trustee should not charge for routine legal or consulting tasks,[55] and should turn over to the trust

[46] *See* Restatement (Third) of Trusts §170 comment *b* (1992).

[47] *See* id. comments *h*, *i*.

[48] *See* id. comments *c*, *d*, *e*.

[49] *See generally* 2A Scott on Trusts §170.23.

[50] *See* Restatement (Third) of Trusts §170 comment *k* (1992).

[51] Id. comment *q*.

[52] *See* id. comment *o*; Restatement (Second) of Trusts §242 comment *d* (1959); 2A Scott on Trusts §§170.22, 242.2.

[53] *See* Robinson v. Pett, 3 P. Wms. 249 (1734). *See generally* Bogert, Trusts and Trustees §975.

[54] *See* Restatement (Second) of Trusts §242 comments *d*, *k* (1959); 3A Scott on Trusts §242.2; Bogert, Trusts and Trustees §975. *Cf.* Tellier, Annot., Right of Executor or Administrator to Extra Compensation for Legal Services Rendered by Him, 65 A.L.R.2d 809 (1959).

[55] The author acknowledges that there is a divergence of opinion over whether the trustee who renders legal services to his or her trust is entitled to additional compensation. In recent years, bills have been filed in both the California and New York legislatures aimed at what is perceived by the sponsors to be "double dipping." *See* Pollock, State Legislators Move to Curb Double Dipping by Estate Lawyers, Wall St. J., June 23, 1993, at B5, col. 1. The American

any routine brokerage commissions that are generated as a consequence of these transactions with the trust estate.[56] Extraordinary legal, consulting, and brokerage services should be purchased by the trust at arm's length from independent third parties.[57] When the trustee is also the service vendor, accountability is reduced: The trust is deprived of the benefit of independent advice, and the beneficiaries are deprived of the benefit of the checks and balances inherent in arm's-length contractual relationships.[58] When the trustee, for example, acts also as attorney, it must fall to the court or to the beneficiaries to monitor the quality of the legal work, the commitment to the expeditious resolution of the legal matter, and the reasonableness of the legal fees. Because court oversight is inefficient and beneficiary oversight often illusory, neither alternative is particularly satisfactory.

### §6.1.3.4 Indirect Benefit Accruing to the Trustee

Vast wealth is concentrated in the hands of the nation's relatively small corps of trustees.[59] With wealth comes patronage and with patronage comes the opportunity and the temptation to bene-

---

Bar Association, however, has opposed any legislative initiatives to limit or regulate the practice of lawyer-trustees taking double compensation. *See* Link, Developments Regarding the Professional Responsibility of the Estate Administration Lawyer: The Effect of the Model Rules of Professional Conduct, 26 Real Prop. Prob. & Tr. J. 1 (1991); Bogert, Trusts and Trustees §975.

[56] *See* Restatement (Third) of Trusts §§170, comment *o* (1992); Restatement (Second) of Trusts §206 comment *k* (1959); 2A Scott on Trusts §170.22.

[57] *See generally* Brown, The Punctilio of an Honor the Most Sensitive, 131 Tr. & Est. 24 (1992). *See also* First Natl. Bank of Boston v. Brink, 372 Mass. 257, 268, 361 N.E.2d 406, 412 (1977) (Liacos, J., concurring in part and dissenting in part) (commenting on the perceived or actual conflicts of interest that can arise when an attorney and fiduciary are one and the same).

[58] *See* §§3.2.2-3.2.3; *see generally* Blake v. Pegram, 109 Mass. 541, 553 (1872) (charges to the trust of legal fees by the lawyer/trustee are "open to serious question, because of the liability to abuse, or, at least to the suspicion of abuse," this because the lawyer/trustee "is his own client.").

[59] It is estimated that more than $600 billion worth of property is held in personal trusts and $10.6 trillion is held in corporate, charitable, and other nonpersonal trusts. Schultz, Banks Get New Competition for Trusts, Wall St. J., Nov. 24, 1995, at C1.

fit indirectly from its dispensation. The opportunities are virtually unlimited and the benefits to be gained subtle and often difficult to detect. Nevertheless, the conscientious and ethical trustee resists the temptation to benefit personally from the economic power that comes with the right to control the property of others.

Trustees should think twice before selling or loaning trust property to — or purchasing goods and services with trust property from — their spouses, relatives, business associates,[60] attorneys, as well as persons in a position to offer indirect considerations. Trustees should not accept benefits of a pecuniary or nonpecuniary nature from a service vendor,[61] and should always strive to avoid the hint of impropriety. Like Caesar's wife, the trustee must be above suspicion. When the trustee yields to these temptations it is not long before rationalizing takes over and the interests of the beneficiaries are compromised.

The practice of *social investing* illustrates how seductive this economic power can be. Social investing has been defined by Professor Langbein and Judge Posner as the "pursuit of an investment strategy that tempers the conventional objective of maximizing the investor's financial interests by seeking to promote nonfinancial social goals as well."[62] A trustee who voluntarily undertakes to practice social investing uses the trust estate to promote the trustee's own political and social goals — a clear case of indirect self-dealing.[63] The trustee who yields to third-party

[60] *See, e.g.,* Inter First Bank Dallas N.A. v. Risser, 739 S.W.2d 882 (Tex. App. 1987) (Trustee bank assessed punitive damages and actual damages and was removed for selling trust assets to a commercial customer).

[61] *See, e.g.,* In re Estate of Rothko, 43 N.Y.2d 305, 372 N.E.2d 291 (1977), *aff'g* 56 A.D.2d 499, 392 N.Y.S.2d 870 (1977), *aff'g* 84 Misc. 2d 830, 379 N.Y.S.2d 923 (1975) (a case in which independent judgment was called into question because of professional advantages and financial opportunities that accrued to coexecutors from the sale of estate assets); Brown, *supra* note 57 (referring to a case, ultimately settled, involving an executor who selectively revealed information regarding real property in the estate in order to give an advantage to a friend participating in the subsequent auction of that piece of property).

[62] Langbein & Posner, Social Investing and the Law of Trusts, 79 Mich. L. Rev. 72, 73 (1980).

[63] *See* Rounds, Social Investing, IOLTA, and the Law of Trusts: The Settlor's Case Against the Political Use of Charitable and Client Funds, 22 Loy. U. Chi. L.J. 163, 170-172 nn.27, 31 (1990).

pressure to practice social investing is acting on divided loyalties; the trustee who seeks the acclaim of particular constituencies, or at least the cessation of their criticisms, may be subordinating the interest of the trust to the interest of the trustee.[64] If social investing has any place in the law of trusts, it is incumbent upon the courts and the legislatures to define this exception to the trustee's duty of undivided loyalty in a way that establishes reasonable limits on the trustee's right to promote with the trust estate personal, political or social goals or the goals of third parties.[65]

Florida's adoption in 1978 of an IOLTA program[66] has brought a state-imposed exception to the duty of loyalty. In furtherance of the IOLTA concept, the judiciaries of a number of states[67] are now authorizing or compelling attorney-trustees to

[64]Langbein & Posner, *supra* note 59, at 96-104. "We conclude that the duty of loyalty . . . forbid[s] social investing in its current form." Id. at 76. *But see* 29 C.F.R. §2509.94-1 (1995). Section 2509.94-1, the U.S. Labor Department's Interpretive Bulletin relating to ERISA, states that §§403 and 404 of ERISA do not prevent trustees of private employee benefit trusts who comply with ERISA prudence requirements from investing in Economically Targeted Investments (ETIs). Section 2509.94-1 defines ETI's as investments "selected for the economic benefits they create apart from their investment return to the employee benefit plan." Id. On May 9, 1995, U.S. Representative Jim Saxton (R-N.J.) introduced a bill that would effectively rescind the Interpretive Bulletin. *See* H.R. 1594, 104th Cong., 1st Sess. (1995). For an analogous controversy in the corporate area, see Medical Committee for Human Rights v. SEC, 432 F.2d 659, 681 (D.C. Cir. 1970), wherein the court noted "that there is a clear and compelling distinction between management's legitimate need for freedom to apply its expertise in matters of day-to-day business judgment, and management's patently illegitimate claim of power to treat modern corporations with their vast resources as personal satrapies implementing personal political or moral predilections"; *see also* Cryan v. Crocker National Bank, No. 721368 (Cal. Sup. Ct., March 10, 1981) (Bank trustee surcharged for selling trust property to a charity on whose board a trust committee member was serving).

[65]With the abolition of South Africa's system of apartheid, the debate over social investing has now turned to investments by trustees of private employee benefit trusts in so-called Economically Targeted Investments (ETIs). *Compare* 29 C.F.R. §2509.94-1 (1995) (permitting trustees of private employee benefit trusts to invest in ETIs) *and* H.R. 1594, 104th Cong., 1st Sess. (1995) (seeking to restrict 29 C.F.R. §2509.94-1 (1995)).

[66]*See generally* Comment, IOTA — Overcoming Its Current Obstacles, 18 Stetson L. Rev. 415 (1989). *See also* §9.7.2 (IOLTA Trusts).

[67]*See* A.B.A. IOLTA Clearinghouse, IOLTA Profiles, 7 IOLTA Update 1, 4-7 (1991). It should be noted, however, that there is legislative involvement in the Maryland, New York, Ohio and Pennsylvania IOLTA programs. The IOLTA Update is a valuable resource for statistics relating to the various state programs.

apply the income earned by certain client trust accounts to charitable and professional organizations. In the First Circuit, the concept has withstood a challenge on First, Fifth, and Fourteenth Amendment grounds.[68] The Federal Court of Appeals for the Fifth Circuit, however, has held that IOLTA income is the property of the client. On appeal, the U.S. Supreme Court has affirmed holding that, "for purposes of the Takings Clause of the Fifth Amendment," IOLTA income is the property of the client.[69]

The corporate trustee (*e.g.*, a bank) is a collection of human beings performing a myriad of tasks in furtherance of a myriad of corporate purposes. Thus there is ample opportunity for the corporation and the individual employees to directly and indirectly self-deal. The breaches can be subtle. They are often hidden in a thicket of complicated financial transactions and thus difficult to sort out, let alone prevent and detect by those not privy to the inner workings of the institution.[70] As a general rule, neither the corporate trustee nor its employee should directly or indirectly transact with the trust property.[71] Unless authorized by the terms of the governing instrument or by statute, the corpo-

[68] *See, e.g.*, Washington Legal Found. v. Massachusetts Bar Found., 993 F.2d 962 (1st Cir. 1993) (holding in part that an IOLTA account is not a "formal" trust and that the "interest earned on IOLTA accounts belongs to no one"); *but see* Ritchie et al., Decedents' Estates and Trusts 1318 (8th ed. 1993) ("Funds received by a lawyer on behalf of a client are held in trust for the client."); Sinibaldi, The Taking Issue in California's Legal Services Trust Account Program, 12 Hastings Const. L.Q. 463 (1985) ("the laudable purpose of California's [IOLTA] program should not sustain it against a Takings Clause challenge").

[69] *See* Washington Legal Found. v. Texas Equal Access to Justice Found., 94 F.3d 996 (1996); *see* Phillips v. Washington Legal Found., U.S. Supreme Court, No. 96-1578, June 15, 1998 (1998 WL 309070 (U.S.)).

[70] *See* Brown, The Punctilio of an Honor the Most Sensitive, 131 Tr. & Est. 24, 24-25 (1992). Author Peter O. Brown suggests a simple test to govern individual ethical conduct in trust administration to avoid any resulting conflicts: "If an intended act is even faintly suggestive of impropriety, don't do it." Id. at 26. *See also* Comptroller of the Currency Regulation, Self-Dealing, 12 C.F.R. §9.12 (1963) (list of prohibited transactions arising from conflict situations; for example, §9.12(b) states that "[p]roperty held by a national bank as a fiduciary shall not be sold or transferred, by loan or otherwise, to the bank or its directors, officers, or employees").

[71] The duty of loyalty extends to employees and agents of the trustee. The focus is on the functions performed, not the mere title of trustee. *See* Bogert, Trusts and Trustees §543 n.21 and accompanying text. *See, e.g.*, Matter of People (Bond & Mtge. Guar. Co.), 303 N.Y. 423, 103 N.E.2d 721 (1952).

IOLTA

soft dollars

rate trustee should not direct trust business to its in-house real estate sales operation, its discount brokerage operation, or its proprietary mutual funds.[72] When the corporate trustee receives "soft dollars"[73] from its security trading activities or "financial

[72]At the very least, a trust company should establish strong ethical policies to ensure compliance with both fiduciary and business ethics. Brown, *supra* note 70, at 31. *See* Comptroller of the Currency Trust Interpretation No. 273 (Sept. 25, 1992), concerning trust department purchase of securities through affiliated discount brokerage companies. 12 C.F.R. §9.5(a) and (c). Revised Reg. 9 (effective January 29, 1997 and reprinted in Appendix II) provides that a national bank exercising fiduciary powers shall adopt and follow written policies and procedures that address, where appropriate, the bank's brokerage placement practices and methods for preventing self-dealing and conflicts of interest). The following states have enacted legislation allowing banks, under certain circumstances, to invest trust assets in mutual funds for which the banks act as investment advisors: Alabama (Ala. Code §19-3-120.1); Alaska (A.S. §06.05.180 (1994)); Arizona (Ariz. Rev. Stat. Ann. §6-246, as added by Laws 1992, ch. 328, §1 and amended by Laws 1994, ch. 53, §1); Arkansas (Ark. Code Ann. §28-71-104); California (Cal. Fin. Code §1561.1 (1995)); Colorado (Colo. Rev. Stat. §11-10-107)); Connecticut (Conn. Gen. Stat. Ann. §45a-209); Delaware (Del. Code Ann. tit. 12, §3312(a)); Florida (Fla. Stat. Ann. §660-417, as added by Laws 1992, ch. 92-303, §147); Georgia (Ga. Code Ann. §53-8-2(e)); Hawaii (Haw. Rev. Stat. §412:8-400 (Banks & Fin. Inst.) (1993)); Idaho (Idaho Code §68-404(A)); Illinois (Ill. Ann. Stat. ch. 760, para. 5/5.20); Indiana (Ind. Code Ann. §28-1-12-3(i)); Iowa (Iowa Code Ann. §633.123(2)); Kansas (Kan. Stat. Ann. §§17-5004, 17-5005 (1994)); Kentucky (Ky. Rev. Stat. Ann. §386.020(1)(g)); Louisiana (La. Rev. Stat. Ann. §9:2127(c)); Maine (Me. Rev. Stat. Ann. tit. 18-A, §7-408); Maryland (Md. Code Ann., Est. & Trusts §15-106(c)(1)); Massachusetts (Mass. Ann. Laws ch. 167G, §3(11)); Michigan (Mich. Stat. Ann. §23.710(185)); Minnesota (Minn. Stat. Ann. §48.38(6)); Mississippi (Miss. Code Ann. §81-5-33); Missouri (Mo. Rev. Stat. §362.550(11), as amended by Mo. Legis. H.B. 34 (1995)); Nebraska (Neb. Rev. Stat. Ann. §30-3205(2)); Nevada (Nev. Rev. Stat. Ann. §669.225); New Jersey (N.J. Rev. Stat. Ann. §3B:14-23(w)); New Mexico (N.M. Stat. Ann. §§45-2A-14, 45-7-401, 46-2A-1 (1996)); New York (N.Y. Est. Powers & Trusts Law §11.2.2(b)(1)); North Carolina (N.C. Gen. Stat. §36A-66.2); North Dakota (N.D. Cent. Code §6-03-02 (1997)); Ohio (Ohio Rev. Code Ann. §1109.10(11)); Oklahoma (Okla. Stat. Ann. tit. 60, §175.55, as amended by Okla. Legis., ch. 351, §26 (1995)); Oregon (Or. Rev. Stat. §709.175(2)); Pennsylvania (20 Pa. Cons. Stat. Ann. §7314.1); Rhode Island (R.I. Gen. Laws §19-9-16); South Carolina (S.C. Code Ann. §62-7-302(a)(6)); South Dakota (S.D. Codified Laws Ann. §55-1A-9); Tennessee (Tenn. Code Ann. §35-3-117(h), as added by Laws 1991, ch. 386, §1); Texas (Tex. Prop. Code Ann. §113.053(g), as added by Laws 1993, ch. 933); Utah (Utah Code Ann. §75.7-402); Virginia (Va. Code Ann. §26-44.1); Washington (Wash. Rev. Code §11.100.035 (1994)); West Virginia (W. Va. Code §44-6-9(b)); Wisconsin (Wis. Stat. Ann. §881.01(4)).

[73]*Soft dollar purchases* occur when "a national bank chooses to purchase products or services and pay for them with brokerage commissions arising from securi-

incentives for doing business on behalf of fiduciary accounts with third-party vendors,"[74] issues of indirect self-dealing present themselves.

When a trustee of a trust makes a "soft dollar" arrangement with a broker, the trustee uses the trust's property (in the form of nondiscounted brokerage commissions) to purchase investment research that may benefit the trustee's other trusts, or even the trustee personally.[75] The practice was not an issue for fiduciaries until 1975, when the current negotiated rate system replaced a fixed rate system. With the unbundling of brokerage and research products, it was thought that trustees who entered into "soft dollar" full-commission arrangements might be breaching their duty of loyalty. Should they not be purchasing investment research products with their own funds? After all, a trustee may not use trust funds to pay for services that the trustee ought personally to perform.

In 1975, the U.S. Congress squarely addressed the issue when it added §28(e) to the Exchange Act.[76] Section 28(e), *which preempts state trust law insofar as applicable*, provides a "safe harbor" for those trustees with investment discretion. Thus when such a trustee enters into a "soft dollar" full-commission transaction with a broker on behalf of his trust, the trustee will not be in breach of his common law duty of loyalty, provided he has determined "in good faith that [the] commission [is] reasonable in relation to the value of the brokerage and research services . . . viewed in terms of either that particular transaction or his overall responsibilities with respect to the accounts as to which he exercises investment discretion."[77]

In investment matters, the trust officer, as an employee of the trustee, has a common law duty of loyalty to the trust, which

---

ties transactions for trust accounts . . ." Comptroller of the Currency Regulation TBC-17 Banking Issuance 267 (1990). *See generally* Pickard, Institutional Portfolio Execution: Soft Dollar Arrangements, 8 Prentice Hall L. & Bus. 22 (1990).

[74]Brown, *supra* note 70, at 27.

[75]*See generally* American Bar Association, A Fiduciary's Guide to Federal Securities Laws 192 (1994).

[76]Id.

[77]Id. at 194.

coexists with the 1934 Securities Exchange Act's narrow insider trading proscriptions.[78] The nature and scope of these proscriptions[79] have been poorly explained by securities lawyers to the fiduciary community, with the result that trust officers have been frightened into an obsessive concern with avoiding the act's criminal sanctions. In fact, this obsession has led to allegations of breaches of the common law duty of loyalty.[80] The " '34 Act," for example, does not abrogate the trust officer's common law duty to exploit public information (even information derived from colleagues on the commercial side) in furtherance of the interests of the trust.[81] The failure to utilize such information out of an irra-

[78] *See* §7.3.4.2(a) (Criminal and Civil Liability as Legal Owner — Securities Laws); Revised Reg. 9, reprinted in Appendix II, provides that, "unless authorized by applicable law, a national bank may not invest funds of a fiduciary account for which a national bank has investment discretion in the stock or obligations of, or in assets acquired from: the bank or any of its directors, officers, or employees; affiliates of the bank or any of their directors, officers, or employees; or individuals or organizations with whom there exists an interest that might affect the exercise of the best judgment of the bank 12 C.F.R. §9.12(a) (1997).

[79] *See* §7.3.3.3 (Registration and Sale of Securities); *see generally* American Bar Association; A Fiduciary's Guide to Federal Securities Laws 228, 229 (1994).

[80] In a suit against the FDIC by the beneficiaries of a testamentary trust containing a large concentration of stock in the insolvent parent corporation of the bank cotrustee, it was alleged that the bank breached its fiduciary duty by failing to evaluate, manage, or analyze the stock during a period when the stock went from a high of $6,030,726 in June 1986 to a low of $260,605 in August 1990. The Bank in its answer had suggested that the Bank lawfully "could not" have evaluated, managed, or analyzed the stock and accordingly had not done so. The case was settled before trial. *See* Godfrey v. FDIC, Civil No. 90-0290-B-C (D. Me. 1990).

[81] *See* Comptroller of the Currency Regulation, 12 C.F.R. §9.7(d) (1963) **(This has been superseded by a full revision, effective January 29, 1997. Revised 12 C.F.R. Part 9 provides that a national bank exercising fiduciary powers shall adopt and follow written policies and procedures that in part should address methods for ensuring that fiduciary officers and employees not use material inside information in connection with any decision or recommendation to purchase or sell any security.)**:

> The Chinese Wall provision [embodied in 12 C.F.R. §9.7(d)] has been misinterpreted at times as an absolute barrier. The doctrine does not require the total separation of trust and commercial functions within the bank. Neither does it prohibit the integration of joint marketing and servicing of fiduciary and commercial department customers. The original and continuing intent of the Chinese

tional fear of criminal sanction is in itself a breach of the duty of loyalty.

On the other hand, the trust officer may not exploit any inside information relating to the trust itself directly or indirectly for personal benefit. The general rule is that as much relevant information as is legally permissible should flow to the trust and as little as possible should flow out of the trust.[82] Confidential information, as with light in a black hole, stays in the trust officer's file. The trust officer conducting an auction of trust property, for example, violates the duty of loyalty by disclosing nonpublic information relating to asset value to certain bidders with whom the officer has a direct or indirect relationship and not to the others.[83]

Moreover, as with the trust company itself, the trust officer should refrain from directly or indirectly transacting with the trust property.[84] This will usually take the form of contracting on behalf of the trust for goods and services with persons in a position to directly or indirectly further the personal interests of the trust officer.

### §6.1.3.5 Duty of Loyalty to the Beneficiary in Nontrust Matters

As we have seen, a trustee is under a duty to act solely in the interest of the beneficiaries as to matters that directly and indirectly relate to the trust property.[85] The trustee, however, may have occasion to deal with a beneficiary in matters *unrelated to the trust property*, such as selling the beneficiary life insurance or providing the beneficiary with brokerage or legal services. Such activity is

---

Wall was to prevent the passage of material inside information between a bank's fiduciary and commercial departments in violation of securities laws and regulations.

Comptroller's Handbook for Ficuciary Activities, Fiduciary Activities — Conflicts of Interest, 71,72 (Sept. 1990).

[82] *See* §6.2.3 (Duty of Confidentiality).

[83] *See* Brown, *supra* note 70, at 24-25.

[84] *See* Bogert, Trusts and Trustees §543 n.21; 4 Scott on Trusts §326.3.

[85] *See supra* note 9 and accompanying text.

permissible, but the trustee must be scrupulously fair.[86] While such dealings may not be forbidden per se, they carry with them the presumption, albeit rebuttable, of undue influence.[87] This is because the trustee-beneficiary relationship is a confidential one, as solemn as that of priest-penitent, physician-patient, and attorney-client.[88] A judicial finding of undue influence, at the very least, would entitle the beneficiary to disaffirm the transaction.[89]

Nor may the trustee through abuse of confidence gain a direct or indirect advantage in outside transactions with beneficiaries.[90] Unlike dealing with a stranger, the trustee may not take advantage of his peculiar knowledge or position, either for personal gain or for the profit of some of the beneficiaries to the exclusion of others.[91]

The best course is for the trustee to avoid commercial and financial dealings with the beneficiaries altogether; if such activity must be pursued, it should be done only after full disclosure of all relevant information and only after they have obtained competent independent advice on those matters that directly and indirectly relate to the activity.[92] The trustee always has the burden of showing that the beneficiaries were fully informed and thoroughly understood the matter and that no advantage of position or influence was taken,[93] or face the consequences of abusing the confidential relationship.

It goes without saying that the trustee should never solicit gifts or other favors from beneficiaries. At the very least such solicitations would have the appearance of extortion. Nor should the trustee accept unsolicited gifts or favors from the beneficiaries, for to do so cannot help but cloud independent judgment — particu-

[86] *See* Restatement (Third) of Trusts §170(2) (1992); Bogert, Trusts and Trustees §544.

[87] *See* Bogert, Trusts and Trustees §544.

[88] *See* Restatement (Second) of Trusts §2 comment *b* (1959); Bogert, Trusts and Trustees §544 nn.15-23; *see generally* Restatement (Third) of Trusts, Tent. Draft & No. 1 (April 5, 1996), Reporter's Notes on §2, pp. 34-38.

[89] Id.

[90] *See* Bogert, Trusts and Trustees §544.

[91] Id.

[92] Id.

[93] Id. *See* §7.2.3 (Types of Relief).

larly should the wishes of the settlor as manifested in the governing instrument and the wishes of the beneficiaries come in conflict. Matters are worsened if unsolicited gifts or favors from fewer than all beneficiaries are accepted, because then the trustee's ability to be impartial is called into question.[94] The trustee's duty of impartiality in matters relating to the beneficiaries is an incident of the general duty of loyalty, so it goes without saying that the trustee ought not to act as an agent (*e.g.*, as attorney-at-law) for a beneficiary whose interests are in conflict with the interests of the other trust beneficiaries, whether or not the conflicting interests are trust-related.[95]

### §6.1.4 Duty to Give Personal Attention (Not to Delegate)

Because the trustee's relationship with the trust beneficiaries is a personal one, the administration of the trust may not be delegated.[96] If the trustee can avoid responsibility by delegating fundamental duties to a third party, then the settlor's intention in selecting a particular trustee will be thwarted. On the other hand, the trustee has a fiduciary obligation to seek whatever assistance necessary to execute the efficient and competent administration of the trust.[97] As a general rule, the trustee may never delegate to others the responsibility to coordinate the trust's administration and to supervise agents.[98] Moreover, some specific functions are nondelegable no matter how intense the supervision,[99] such as discretion as to how income and principal may be used in further-

[94] *See* Restatement (Third) of Trusts §183 (1992); 2A Scott on Trusts §183; §6.2.5 (Duty of Impartiality).

[95] Id; *see generally* §8.8 (Whom Does Counsel Represent?).

[96] *See* Restatement (Third) of Trusts §171 (1992); 2A Scott on Trusts §171.

[97] *See* Restatement (Third) of Trusts §§171 comment *a*, 227 comment *j* (1992); 2A Scott on Trusts §§171.2, 227.1.

[98] *See* Restatement (Third) of Trusts §171 comments *e*, *k* (1992); 2A Scott on Trusts §171.1.

[99] *See* Restatement (Third) of Trusts §171, comment *e* (1992); 2A Scott on Trusts §171.1; Bogert, Trusts and Trustees §555.

ance of the purposes of the trust.[100] The consequences of improper delegation are severe: The trustee becomes liable for the errors and omissions of his agents.[101]

On the other hand, asset custody, record keeping, and other such ministerial tasks generally may be delegated to others.[102] An agent may be allowed to collect dividends and rents, keep the books, and act for the trustee where a "prudent man of business" would employ an agent.[103] Thus the trustee employs a stockbrokerage to purchase stocks and pays for the same through it.[104] In such cases, the trustee will not be held liable for the default of an agent, unless due care in selecting that agent was not exercised.[105] Likewise, a trustee who has employed a reputable conveyancer is not responsible for a flaw in the title that the conveyancer overlooked. If, however, a loss occurs through the careless failure of the trustee to see that the agent uses due diligence, it really is the trustee's own negligence that triggers liability. The trustee may vote stock by proxy at shareholder meetings, unless the block of stock represents a controlling interest or there are other than routine matters on the table.[106] Many states have statutes to that effect.[107] As to controlling interests or nonroutine matters, delegation by means of a general proxy is inappropriate.[108]

[100]2A Scott on Trusts §171.2.

[101]*See* Restatement (Second) of Trusts, §225(2)(b) (1959); 2A Scott on Trusts §§171.1, 225.1.

[102]*See* Restatement (Third) of Trusts §171 comment *f* (1992); 2A Scott on Trusts §171.2; Bogert, Trusts and Trustees §555.

[103]Id.

[104]*See* 2A Scott on Trusts §171.2.

[105]It would be unreasonable to require the trustee to be a guarantor of the conduct of the agent where the delegation was proper and the trustee has otherwise acted prudently. *See* Restatement (Second) of Trusts §225(2)(c) (1959); 2A Scott on Trusts §§171.2, 225.1; Bogert, Trusts and Trustees §557.

[106]*See* Restatement (Second) of Trusts 193 comment *b* (1959); 3 Scott on Trusts 193.3. See also Bogert, Trusts and Trustees 556 nn. 97-98 and accompanying text for a list of local statutes authorizing trustees to vote stock by proxy. In its Interpretive Bulletin 94-2, the U.S. Department of Labor suggests that ERISA plan fiduciaries have a duty to vote proxies where proxy voting decisions will affect the value of an investment. *See* Department of Labor Interpretive Bulletin 94-2, 29 C.F.R. 2509.

[107]3 Scott on Trusts §193.3.

[108]Id.

In the gray area is the matter of asset selection. In the past, investment discretion was considered a nondelegable function.[109] The principle was best illustrated by the sale of real estate or personal property: The trustees could not delegate the essential matters of the sale (*i.e.*, the determination of the price and terms and the central question whether the sale had best be made).[110] Similarly, the trustees could not give a general power of attorney to make sales or purchases of trust securities, but having reached a decision to sell certain trust securities they ordinarily would deliver a special power of transfer, thus employing an agent to perform a purely ministerial act.[111]

The modern trend is to permit the trustee to delegate some investment discretion to investment advisers and others, provided there is adequate supervision by the trustee.[112] This allows the trustee to retain an investment advisor and to pay for the advisor's services from the trust. The theory of the early common law that the trustee needs no assistance in investment matters has been discarded. This relaxation of the prohibition against delegation in the investment context is embodied in §171 of the Restatement (Third) of Trusts (the *Prudent Investor Rule*), which recognizes that some "fiduciary authority" may with adequate supervision be delegated.[113] "The trustee," however, "personally must define at least the trust's investment objectives."[114] The trustee must also make the decisions that establish the trust's investment strategies and programs, at least to the extent of approving plans developed by

[109] *See* Restatement (Second) of Trusts §171 comment *h* (1959); 2A Scott on Trusts §§171.2, 227.9A.

[110] *See* Restatement (Second) of Trusts §171 comment *g* (1959); 2A Scott on Trusts §171.2; Bogert, Trusts and Trustees §556; *see generally,* Trustee's Power to Employ Broker or Agent to Sell or Lease Estate Property, 47 A.L.R. 2d 1379 (1995).

[111] Id.

[112] *See* Restatement (Third) of Trusts §171 comment *f* (1992); *see, however,* Curtis, The Transmogrification of the American Trust, 31 Real Prop., Prob. & Tr. J. 251 (No 2-1996) (Suggesting that this relaxation of the trustee's duty not to delegate "has diminished the protections afforded trust assets and has fundamentally changed the relationship between the trustee, beneficiary, and other parties").

[113] Id.

[114] Id. comment *h.*

agents and advisers.[115] Section 171 thus gives trustees the flexibility to carry out their investment duties and does away with the general prohibition against trustees' delegating investment discretion.[116] As long as trustees are prudent in selecting their advisors, participate in setting trust investment objectives, and routinely monitor the advisors' performance, they should not be liable for delegating to advisors.[117]

It is now settled law that a trustee may prudently invest in a mutual fund without breaching the duty not to delegate.[118] But what about the practice of incorporating the trust estate itself? The argument has been advanced that if the trust estate is incorporated, the trustees are thereafter freed from the inherent limitations of the trust and even from their liability for the continued administration. A trust, however, is a personal confidence. Thus, the better view is that the corporation will act simply as an agency to carry out the trust[119] and that the trustees are in no way liberated from their responsibility in the premises.[120] A trustee who holds the working control of the stock is accountable as a fiduciary for the administration of corporate affairs absent express language in the governing instrument to the contrary. Corporate transactions will be treated as though they were the trustee's.[121]

As stated above, the trustee has an affirmative fiduciary obligation — and therefore the implied authority — to seek out the advice of experts if it is prudent to do so. If the specialized

[115] Id.

[116] Id. comment *f*.

[117] Id.

[118] Id. §227 comment *m*; 3 Scott on Trusts §227.9A; Bogert, Trusts and Trustees §673; Langbein & Posner, Market Funds and Trust-Investment Law, 1976 Am. B. Found. Res. J. 1, 22 (1976).

[119] *See generally* 3 Scott on Trusts §190.9A.

[120] Id. *See also* 3 Scott on Trusts §225.

[121] *See* 2A Scott on Trusts §§171.1, 171.4; Annot., Trustee's Power to Exchange Trust Property for Share of Corporation Organized to Hold the Property, 20 A.L.R.3d 841 (1968); *see also* Uniform Trustees' Power Act §3(c)(3), 7 U.L.A. 746 (1988), which provides that a trustee has the power "to continue or participate in the operation of any business or other enterprise, and to effect incorporation, dissolution, or other change in the form of the organization of the business enterprise."

services of lawyers, accountants, genealogists, private investigators, and the like are necessary for the proper administration of the trust, then the trustee has a duty to consult them at trust expense on behalf of the trust.[122] As can be seen, the trustee must walk the fine line between improper delegation and improper failure to delegate. The "amateur" trustee, for example, should guard against the natural inclination to turn over the entire administration of the trust to "experts" such as lawyers, investment advisors, brokers, financial planners, and institutions acting as agents for fiduciaries.[123] There is more to trust administration than a series of legal tasks; than making investment decisions; than security custody and record keeping. Conscientious and reasonable "amateurs" make excellent trustees, provided they actively coordinate and supervise.[124]

A trustee should not only guard against delegating the entire administration to "experts" and others but also to the cotrustee.[125] Cotrustees hold the trust property in joint tenancy;[126] accordingly there is authority that one of them alone may demand and receive interests, rents, dividends, and other sums of money due the trust.[127] It has been stated to be the rule, in the absence of any knowledge of unfitness, that the "other" trustees may permit one of their number to exercise the trust powers and will not be liable if the designee abuses them.[128] It also has been

[122] *See generally* Restatement (Third) of Trusts §171 (1992); 2A Scott on Trusts §171.2.

[123] *See* Restatement (Third) of Trusts §227 comment *j* (1992). *See, e.g.*, Shriners Hospitals v. Gardiner, 152 Ariz. 527, 733 P.2d 1110 (1987) (holding that express authority to employ and compensate attorneys, accountants, agents and brokers merely a recognition of the trustee's obligation to obtain expert advice, not a license to remove himself from the role as trustee).

[124] *See generally,* J.R. Kemper, L.L.B., Annot., Construction and Operation of Will or Trust Provision Appointing Advisors to Trustee or Executor, 56 A.L.R. 3d 1249 (1974).

[125] *See* Restatement (Third) of Trusts §184 (1992); 2A Scott on Trusts §184; Bogert, Trusts and Trustees §555.

[126] *See* Bogert, Trusts and Trustees §145, 554.

[127] "[I]f the performance of an act may be properly delegated by the trustee he may give such power to a cotrustee as well as to any other qualified person." Bogert, Trusts and Trustees §555. *See also* id. §554; Restatement (Second) of Trusts §194 comment *b* (1959); 3 Scott on Trusts §194.

[128] *See* Restatement (Second) of Trusts §224 (1959); 3 Scott on Trusts §224.

said that in cases where the trust duties cannot conveniently be exercised by joint action, the trustees may make a reasonable apportionment of them and that an individual trustee will not, under these circumstances, be liable for the loss of funds caused by the neglect of the other.[129] Although the rule forbidding delegation has thus been relaxed, there are distinct limitations. In fact it is very dangerous for one cotrustee to fall into the habit of leaving the trust business to another. It is the duty of all trustees, unless excused by the instrument,[130] to participate in the trust administration.[131] May one cotrustee allow the other cotrustee to make and execute investment decisions without prior consultation or approval? Typically, this issue arises when a trust has a professional cotrustee and a nonprofessional co-trustee. In the context of a nonprofessional delegating to a professional cotrustee, the answer is probably yes. The Prudent Investor Rule would now seem to permit this delegation, but this may not be the rule in all jurisdictions.[132]

The question which is difficult, in practice, is the extent to which one of several cotrustees may be subject to surcharge as a result of allowing one or more of the others to assume custody and control of part or all of the trust property. These cases ordinarily do not involve an active participation in a wrongful act. Nevertheless the ensuing loss may well have been "made possible" by the "neglect" of the inactive trustee.[133] It is improper for a trustee to allow a cotrustee to act generally as the trustee's agent[134] and to do alone what ought to have been done jointly (*e.g.*, allowing the cotrustee to invest the trust funds without consultation or supervision[135] or by standing by and allowing the cotrustee to commit a

[129] *See* Bogert, Trusts and Trustees §589.

[130] *See* Restatement (Third) of Trusts §184 comment *c* (1992); 2A Scott on Trusts §§184, 185.

[131] *See* Restatement (Third) of Trusts §184 (1992); 2A Scott on Trusts §184; Bogert, Trusts and Trustees §584.

[132] *See* Restatement (Third) of Trusts §171 comment *f* (1992).

[133] *See* Restatement (Second) of Trusts §224(2)(d) (1959); 3 Scott on Trusts §224.3.

[134] *See* Restatement (Second) of Trusts §224(2)(b) (1959); 3 Scott on Trusts §224.2.

[135] *See* Restatement (Third) of Trusts §171 comments *f*, *k* (1992); 3 Scott on Trusts §224.3.

breach of trust).[136] If one trustee commits a breach of trust, the cotrustee is liable if redress is not sought.[137]

As may be expected, it is doubly dangerous for one trustee to allow a cotrustee to have exclusive management of the trust estate after the latter has proved unreliable. Thus in one case the trust instrument provided that each trustee was to be held liable for his own defaults only (a fairly common clause). The active management of the estate was entrusted to a person who had been the testator's financial advisor. This person collected and embezzled $30,000, which the inactive trustee discovered. The inactive trustee nevertheless allowed the cotrustee to continue to manage the estate, and the latter then embezzled additional monies from the trust estate. The inactive trustee was not held liable for the first embezzlement but was surcharged with the amount of the second.[138]

A delegation issue is raised by the practice, now commonly followed by corporate cotrustees, of retaining exclusive possession of the trust property and of issuing checks and making distributions without signature of the remaining trustees. It is probable that the courts will approve this practice under most circumstances.[139] Yet the principle remains unshaken that the trustee will be liable if the trust property is unjustifiably left in the exclusive control of the cotrustee and is lost.[140] The representations of the cotrustee as to the status of the property may not be relied upon; personal investigation is required.[141] It is not clear whether trustees may delegate access to a safe deposit box to one of their number. Professor Scott cites several state statutes which

[136] *See* Restatement (Second) of Trusts §224(2)(d) (1959); 3 Scott on Trusts §224.3.

[137] *See* Restatement (Second) of Trusts §224(2)(e) (1959); 3 Scott on Trusts §224.5; *see generally,* Lee R. Russ, J.D., Annot., Award of Attorney's Fees Out of Trust Estate in Action by Trustee Against Co-Trustee, 24 A.L.R. 4th 624 (1981).

[138] In re Mallon's Estate, 43 Misc. 569, 89 N.Y. Supp. 554 (1904), *aff'd sub nom.* In re Howard, 110 App. Div. 61, 97 N.Y. Supp. 23 (1905), *aff'd,* 185 N.Y. 539, 77 N.E. 1189 (1906).

[139] *See* Restatement (Second) of Trusts §194 comment *b* (1959); 3 Scott on Trusts §194; Bogert, Trusts and Trustees §555.

[140] *See* Restatement (Second) of Trusts §224(2)(d) (1959); 3 Scott on Trusts §224.3.

[141] *See* Restatement (Third) of Trusts §227 comment *j* (1992).

indicate approval.[142] Good practice suggests access by more than one person, as by one trustee and a deputy or agent of another.

Occasionally trustees adopt a program of divided custody and responsibility. Thus a trustee who is particularly skilled in real estate matters is given charge of that part of the trust portfolio or one who lives near a fraction of the trust property is expected to manage that fraction. It is, of course, possible to make these arrangements and yet to avoid criticism, if all of the trustees keep themselves informed of the facts and problems as they arise and participate in all decisions of significance. The habit is not a salutary one in the absence of express permission.

There has been developing in the law a principle that the professional or corporate fiduciary is held to a standard higher than that of an amateur.[143] This concept of a higher standard for professional trustees has matured to the point where it is now a part of the Restatement:

> On the other hand, it follows from the requirement of care as well as sound policy that, if the trustee possesses a degree of skill greater than that of an individual of ordinary intelligence, the trustee is liable for a loss that results from failure to make reasonably diligent use of that skill. So also, if a trustee, such as a corporate or professional fiduciary, procured appointment as trustee by expressly or impliedly representing that it possessed greater skill than that of an individual of ordinary intelligence, or if the trustee has or represents that it has special facilities for investment management, the trustee is liable for a loss that results from failure to make reasonably diligent use of that skill or of those special facilities.[144]

The professional should take heed; the amateur should behave as if there is only one standard: the highest one.

[142] 3 Scott on Trusts §224.2.

[143] *See generally,* James L. Rigelhaupt, Jr., J.D., Annot., Standard of Care Required of Trustee Representing Itself to Have Expert Knowledge or Skill, 91 A.L.R. 3d 904 (1980).

[144] Restatement (Third) of Trusts §227 comment *d* (1992); *see also* Bogert, Trusts and Trustees §612; *see also,* James L. Rigelhaupt, Jr., J.D., Annot., Standard of Care Required of Trustee Representing Itself to Have Expert Knowledge or Skill, 91 A.L.R. 3d 904 (1980).

Express allocations of fiduciary responsibilities can raise troubling issues. If, for example, the governing instrument allocates investment discretion to one trustee, to what extent does the "other" trustee have a fiduciary obligation to monitor the activities of the investing trustee?[145] The California courts were asked to consider this perplexing issue in *Kirkbride v. First Western Bank.*[146] In *Kirkbride* a corporate fiduciary was held liable for the speculative investments of a cotrustee, even in the face of explicit allocations of investment responsibilities to the cotrustee.[147] The speculations with trust assets were made when the trust was revocable by the settlor who at all relevant times was of full age and legal capacity and fully informed. To be sure the California legislature responded to *Kirkbride* by amending the California Probate Code to provide trustees some limited prospective relief from the holding.[148] It now provides that "a trustee of a revocable trust is not liable to a beneficiary for any act performed or permitted pursuant to written directions from the person holding the power to revoke, including a person to whom the power to direct the trustee is delegated."[149] Nevertheless, the message of the California courts and legislature is clear: In the face of express allocation of certain responsibilities to one trustee, the "other" trustee should be careful not to inadvertently delegate coordinating and supervising functions, regardless of how protective and exculpatory the language in the governing instrument. This is particularly necessary when the trust is irrevocable. If a prospective "other" trustee practically or politically would be unable to supervise the acting trustee and appropriately respond to any breaches of trust, including if necessary the solicitation of judicial involvement, or if the prospective "other" trustee could not be adequately compensated for the extra effort and liability attend-

[145] *See generally,* Hatamyar, See No Evil? The Role of the Directed Trustee Under ERISA, 64 Tenn. L. Rev. 1, 38–41 (1996) (Discussing the common law of directed trustees).

[146] Civ. No. 58254, Super. Ct. No. 101232 (Cal. App. 2d 1981) (unpublished).

[147] Id.

[148] Cal. Prob. Code §16462 (West 1991); *see generally* §8.11 (What Are the Duties of the Trustee of a Revocable Inter Vivos Trust?).

[149] Id.

ant with such divisions of responsibility, then serious consideration should be given to declining the business.

This discussion of delegation would be incomplete without reference to the ultimate delegation breach: the resignation of the trustee without a qualified successor in place, even when the governing instrument purports to grant the trustee such authority.[150] A resignation provision is never a license to abandon a trust once accepted.

## *§6.1.5 Duty to Account to the Beneficiary*

The trustee assumes enforceable obligations. Without enforceability, there is no trust; beneficiaries would be unable to protect their interests. Thus the trustee's general duty to account to someone other than himself is an indispensable one.

### §6.1.5.1 Duty to Provide Information

An incident of the trustee's general duty to account is the duty to provide the beneficiary with all the information which is needed to protect the beneficiary's equitable interest.[151] Secrecy and accountability are incompatible.

### §6.1.5.2 Duty to Keep and Render Accounts

An incident of the trustee's general duty to account and the trustee's particular duty to provide information is the trustee's duty to keep written accounts that show the nature, amount, and administration of the trust property.[152] All doubts are resolved

[150] *See* Bogert, Trusts and Trustees §511; 2A Scott on Trusts §171.1.

[151] *See* Restatement (Second) of Trusts §173 (1959); 2A Scott on Trust §173; *see* §5.4.1.1 (Right to Information and Confidentiality) and §8.8 (Whom Does Counsel Represent?).

[152] *See* Restatement (Second) of Trusts §172 (1959); 2A Scott on Trusts §172; Bogert, Trusts and Trustees §962. For a comprehensive list of local statutes

against the trustee who does not keep accurate accounts.[153] A trust provision that states that the trustee does not have to account will not be enforced.[154] The courts consider such a provision as being against public policy, so it is without effect. Jurisdictions will vary as to the necessary form of an account, but in every trust account there should be a clear showing of seven fundamental sets of facts: income received, income paid, balance of income, additions to principal, deductions from principal, principal on hand, and changes in investments. The account will ordinarily be presented with debtor and creditor sides.

Some states require the testamentary trustee to file an inventory with the court soon after appointment.[155] The trustee of a testamentary trust should take care to ensure that the inventory is accurate. The balance of personal and real property set forth on the inventory will be the beginning balances of a testamentary trustee's first account. Also, the values of the property on the inventory establish the trustee's financial responsibility for those assets. Even in the case of the inter vivos trust where there is usually no court involvement, the inventory is indispensable from every standpoint. It is the starting point for all subsequent accounts.

To reiterate, on failure to keep adequate accounts, all doubts are resolved against the trustee, and the trustee may be denied compensation.[156] The beneficiary may demand an accounting.[157] Compelling an accounting is within the jurisdiction of a court of equity.[158]

The trustee is entitled periodically to a discharge of liability by means of the judicial settlement of accounts[159] (*allowance of the*

---

regulating the duty of a trustee to account in court for the administration of a trust, *see* Bogert, Trusts and Trustees §§965-968. *See also* 2A Scott on Trusts §172 n. 10 and accompanying text.

[153] *See* Restatement (Second) of Trusts §172 comment *b* (1959); 2A Scott on Trusts §172; Bogert, Trusts and Trustees §962.

[154] *See* 2A Scott on Trusts §172 n.16 and accompanying text.

[155] *See* Bogert, Trusts and Trustees §597.

[156] *See* Restatement (Second) of Trusts §243 (1959); 2A Scott on Trusts §§172, 243; Bogert, Trusts and Trustees §962.

[157] *See* Restatement (Second) of Trusts §172 comment *c* (1959); 2A Scott on Trusts §172.

[158] *See* 2A Scott on Trusts §172; Bogert, Trusts and Trustees §963.

[159] *See* Bogert, Trusts and Trustees §970.

*account*). The trustee is discharged of any liability for transactions covered by the account.[160] A careful examination of local statute and case law should be made to determine the extent to which the judicial allowance of the trustee's account acts as a discharge from further obligation for the transaction covered thereby. Commonly the statutes require notification of the interested parties, either by personal service, mailing, or publication.[161] The procedure followed in most states provides for the appointment of a guardian ad litem to represent persons unborn or unascertained and often to represent persons under some legal disability.

The final decree allowing a trustee's account can be reopened only under circumstances that would allow the reopening of an ordinary decree of the equity or probate court (*e.g.*, to correct fraud).[162] Finality in the settlement of accounts furthers the public interest that there be honest people willing to serve as trustees. Thus a decree allowing an account ordinarily cannot be questioned in a collateral proceeding in law or in equity.[163] Of course, for a decree to be final the court must have jurisdiction to make the decree, and the machinery for giving notice must satisfy due process.[164]

Inter vivos trust instruments often provide for periodic accountings in a nonjudicial setting,[165] with discharge of further liability upon assent of certain adult beneficiaries.[166] Some provide

[160] *See* id. §974.

[161] *See* Restatement (Second) of Trusts §220 comment *d* (1959); 3 Scott on Trusts §220; Bogert, Trusts and Trustees §974.

[162] *See* Restatement (Second) of Trusts §220 comment *a* (1959); 3 Scott on Trusts §220; Bogert, Trusts and Trustees §974. For a case involving the reopening of allowed accounts for "constructive fraud," *see* National Academy of Sciences v. Cambridge Trust Co., 370 Mass. 303, 346 N.E.2d 879 (1976), which involved a trustee's good faith representation on its accountings that a widow had not remarried and thus was entitled to income payments when in fact she had remarried and under the governing instrument was not so entitled. The court found that the trustee had made "no reasonable efforts to ascertain the true state of the facts it [had] misrepresented in the accounts."

[163] *See* 3 Scott on Trusts §220.

[164] *See* Restatement (Second) of Trusts §220 comment *c* (1959); 3 Scott on Trusts §220. *See, e.g.*, Mullane v. Central Hanover Bank & Trust Co., 339 U.S. 306 (1950).

[165] *See generally* Westfall, Nonjudicial Settlement of Trustees' Accounts, 71 Harv. L. Rev. 40 (1957).

[166] Id. at 60-63.

for release upon the beneficiary's failure to object within a certain period, usually within 60 days of receipt.[167] It is unsettled whether, in a nonjudicial setting, the assent of present beneficiaries can bind future beneficiaries, remaindermen, and others including minors, the unborn and the unascertained. In this regard, the law is particularly uncertain when it comes to the nonjudicial settlement of accounts that reflect a shifting of beneficial interests. Given this uncertainty, it may be unwise for a trustee to place too much reliance on these provisions. From the perspective of the beneficiary, however, the privacy attendant with a nonjudicial settlement is preferable to the publicity, time, and expense attendant with a judicial proceeding.

## §6.2 Specific Duties Incident to General Duties

The trustee has a myriad of duties that are offshoots of the general duties to be prudent, to carry out the terms of the trust, to be loyal to the trust, to give personal attention, and to account.[1] Some particular duties are offshoots of other particular duties. The duty to follow the Prudent Man Rule, for example, is not only an offshoot of the general duty to be prudent, but also of the specific duty to protect the trust property, the specific duty to make the trust property productive, and the specific duty to balance the interests of income beneficiaries and remaindermen.

### *§6.2.1 Duties to Take Active Control of, Segregate, Earmark, and Protect Trust Property*

The trustee's duty to take active control of, segregate, earmark, and protect the trust property is implicit in all the trustee's

[167] Id.
**§6.2** [1] *See* §6.1 (General Duties).

general duties. If the trust is to do its job, the trust property must be kept safe.

### §6.2.1.1 Duty to Take Active Control of Trust Property

It is axiomatic that the trustee must take reasonable steps to take control of all property due the trust,[2] and face liability for loss that occurs during or because of delay in so doing.[3] This duty includes redressing breaches of trust by predecessor fiduciaries,[4] including executors of pour-over wills,[5] and may even include the trustee's suing to collect insurance proceeds. The trustee however has no obligation to fund such litigation personally unless indemnified by the trust beneficiaries, although there may be an affirmative duty to solicit their voluntary indemnity.[6] The trustee takes control of the trust property by re-registration, through agents, or by acquiring physical possession, as appropriate.[7] For example, it is now a standard practice of mutual funds to evidence ownership by means of the computer-generated account statement rather than a paper certificate. Re-registration would therefore be enough. On the other hand, with respect to closely held corporations where paper certificates remain the standard means of evidencing ownership, physical possession would be required as well.[8]

### §6.2.1.2 Duty to Segregate and Earmark Trust Property

It is the duty of the trustee to earmark the trust property and to keep it separate from the trustee's own property and from other

[2] *See generally* Restatement (Second) of Trusts §175 (1959).

[3] *See generally* 2A Scott on Trusts §175; Bogert, Trusts and Trustees §§583, 594.

[4] *See* Restatement (Second) of Trusts §223(2)(a) (1959); 2A Scott on Trusts §177; Bogert, Trusts and Trustees §583.

[5] *See, e.g.*, Pepper v. Zions First Natl. Bank, N.A., 801 P.2d 144 (Utah 1990).

[6] *See generally* Bogert, Trusts and Trustees §582; 2A Scott on Trusts §175.

[7] *See generally* Bogert, Trusts and Trustees §583; 2A Scott on Trusts §175.

[8] Id.

property not subject to the trust (including funds of different trusts).[9] Most of the evils of trust mismanagement will be avoided if this rule is strictly observed. Unless authorized by statute, decision, or the governing instrument, the trustee should not commingle.

Mingling the trust funds with funds belonging to the individual trustee generally is held to be a breach of trust.[10] Many states have statutes covering such activity, which is a *criminal act* in some states.[11] Even if commingling is not a per se breach of trust, the trustee nevertheless invites full personal responsibility if anything goes wrong.[12] Additions to a trust fund, whether by the settlor or others, ought to be permissible as not the type of commingling contemplated by the prohibition.[13] Separate management of additions seems unnecessary and in most cases not in the economic interest of the beneficiaries. However, there may be generation-skipping transfer tax considerations that warrant having additions to a trust segregated.

The trustee should deposit trust funds only in a properly identified trust account.[14] If the deposit is made in the individual name of the trustee, however, the trustee will be treated as a guarantor of the solvency of the bank even though due care was

[9] *See generally* Restatement (Second) of Trusts §179 (1959); 2A Scott on Trusts §179.3; Bogert, Trusts and Trustees §596; *see* §8.15.11 (addressing who is entitled to what when withdrawals are made from an account containing funds that have been wrongfully commingled); Revised Reg 9, reprinted in Appendix II, provides that a national bank shall keep the assets of fiduciary accounts separate from the assets of the bank. 12 C.F.R. §9.13(b) (1997). *See also,* §8.18 (Regulation 9 Revised).

[10] *See generally* Restatement (Second) of Trusts §§179 comment *d,* 205 comment *f;* Bogert, Trusts and Trustees §§596, 707.

[11] *See* 2A Scott on Trusts §179.1 n.5 for a collection of state statutes criminalizing the commingling of trust funds.

[12] *See, e.g.,* Kirby v. Frank, 132 N.J. Eq. 378, 28 A.2d 267 (1942) (a trustee is held strictly accountable when he commingles trust funds with those of his own, and any doubt will be resolved against him).

[13] *See* 2A Scott on Trusts §179.2; Smith v. Stranahan, 314 Mass. 329, 50 N.E.2d 397 (1943) ("The futility of having two or more parallel trusts in the hands of the same trustee to accomplish the same objects in the same way is plainly apparent.").

[14] *See generally* Bogert, Trusts and Trustees §598; Restatement (Second) of Trusts §180 (1959).

used in the choice of the bank and the funds were not in any way misused.[15]

All negotiable securities, and even partially negotiable securities such as registered coupon bonds, should be deposited in a safe deposit vault.[16] If that is inconvenient, they should be kept in a separate strongbox and properly identified as trust property. Trust securities ought not be kept in the trustee's personal safe-deposit box even if they are in a separate envelope. The particular danger to be avoided here is the commingling of assets of the trust estate with the trustee's own property.[17]

More often than not, a single trust instrument will provide for the creation of more than one trust. A single discretionary trust, for example, might be established at the outset under the terms of the instrument, and there might then be a provision for the trust to divide into separate trust shares at some future time, perhaps when no child of the settlor is both alive and under the age of 21. It is likely that the terms of the trust would then authorize the trustee to manage the properties of the various separate trust shares as a common fund[18] — not to be confused of course with a common trust fund[19] — in order to reduce the administrative costs of running separate trusts. Despite the existence of this permissive provision, however, there is a practical downside: The effectiveness of the trustee's defense against an allegation of breach of trust may depend upon the faithful and productive management of each of the individual trust shares. Thus managing separate trusts as a common fund might cause a

[15] *See generally* 2A Scott on Trusts §180.2; Bogert, Trusts and Trustees §596.

[16] *See generally* Bogert, Trusts and Trustees §598.

[17] *See* Bogert, Trusts and Trustees §596, providing the following reasons for the duty to earmark: (1) to facilitate identification of trust property were the trustee to die in office; (2) to deter a trustee from using trust funds for personal benefit; (3) to facilitate an equitable enforcement action by beneficiaries or creditors against a trustee who is uncooperative, disloyal, or insolvent.

[18] *See generally* 2A Scott on Trusts §179.2; Maxwell, Comment, Statutory Procedures for the Combination or Division of Trusts, 21 Real Prop. Prob. & Tr. J. 561 (1986).

[19] *See generally* Bogert, Trusts and Trustees §677; 2A Scott on Trusts §227.9; and §9.7.1 (The Common Trust Fund).

problem involving only one trust to spread throughout the instrument's entire system of trusts.

Over the years, it has become apparent that it is in the economic interest of trustees and beneficiaries alike that some commingling be permitted.[20] Legislatures and courts from time to time have responded by relaxing somewhat the general prohibition against commingling.[21] The most obvious example of this relaxation is the *common trust fund.*[22]

From the beneficiary's standpoint, a small fund, whether initially small or the tag end of a trust, offers little possibility of diversification or of yield and would be better off commingled with other trust funds similarly situated.[23] Thus in the early part of the twentieth century was born the concept of the common trust fund.[24] As time went on, many states were prepared through legislation to exempt the arrangement from the common law prohibition against commingling.[25] Aside from the segregation duty, however, rose the question whether a common trust fund would be deemed an association for federal income tax purposes.[26] Beginning in 1936 the tax roadblock was removed: The Federal Revenue Act of 1936 (now §584 of the 1986 Code) allows a pass-through of the income tax liability to the participating trusts.[27] Today thousands of common trust funds are administered by hundreds of banks across the country.[28]

The Internal Revenue Code defines a common trust fund as a fund maintained by a bank exclusively for the collective investment and reinvestment of monies contributed thereto by the bank in its capacity as a trustee, executor, administrator, or guardian and in

[20] *See generally* Bogert, Trusts and Trustees §677.
[21] Id.
[22] Id.
[23] *See generally* Bogert, Trusts and Trustees §677.
[24] *See* Bogert, Trusts and Trustees §677.
[25] Id.
[26] *See* Brooklyn Trust Co. v. Commissioner of Internal Revenue, 80 F.2d 865 (2d Cir. 1936), *cert. denied,* 298 U.S. 659 (1936) (holding that a common trust fund was essentially conducting an investment business for profit, and thus, is "taxable as an association").
[27] *See generally* Bogert, Trusts and Trustees §261.
[28] *See* id. §677 n.34.

conformity with federal rules and regulations.[29] The Comptroller of the Currency regulates national banks in the exercise of their trust powers.[30] This includes the administration of their common trust funds.[31] The compilation of the regulations applicable to the fiduciary activities of national banks is known in the trade as "Regulation 9" or simply "Reg. 9."[32] Since no common trust fund gains the §584 income tax advantage unless it conforms to the requirements of federal law, common trust funds administered by state banks, as a practical matter, must also comply with Reg. 9's provisions with respect to common trust funds.[33]

The common trust fund itself is a trust with its own governing instrument.[34] Its trustee is a bank, and can only be a bank.[35] When the bank's own trust accounts — its fiduciary customers if you will — invest or participate in the common trust fund, funds from a number of trusts come together. The resulting commingling would place the bank, as trustee of the various participating trusts, in breach of its duty to segregate were it not entitled to the statutory common trust fund exemption.

Over the years, the cost of generating, storing, and transferring paper stock and bond certificates has prompted courts and legislatures, in furtherance of the economic interests of trustees and beneficiaries alike, to relax somewhat the common law duty to earmark.[36] The practice of holding certificates in bulk with book entry, in special purpose depository institutions, in the name of nominees, and in street name has been the result.[37] Moreover, it is clear that electronic data entry will make paper certificates go the

[29] *See* 2A Scott on Trusts §227.9.

[30] *See* revised 12 C.F.R. Part 9 (effective January 29, 1997).

[31] *See* Bogert, Trusts and Trustees §§677, 270.25.

[32] *See generally* id. §134; 2 Scott on Trusts §96.5; *see also* Appendix II (Regulation 9).

[33] *See generally* Bogert, Trusts and Trustees §677.

[34] *See* Revised 12 C.F.R. §9.18(b)(1) (effective January 29, 1997) (reprinted in Appendix II).

[35] *See* Bogert, Trusts and Trustees §677.

[36] *See* id. §596.

[37] *See generally* 1 Whitney, Trust Department Administration and Operations §3.01[11] (1995); *see also* §3.5.3.2(e) (The power to hold the trust property in the name of a third party or in the trustee's own name without disclosing the fiduciary relationship).

way of the carbon copy.[38] The law of trusts should be able to accommodate most such innovations, with the exception of those that entail the commingling of trust property with the personal assets of the trustee or the nominee. Thus the trustee should still think twice before placing trust property in "street name" with a broker.[39]

### §6.2.1.3 Duty to Protect Trust Property

The trustee must take all reasonable steps to protect and conserve the trust property.[40] This duty is not delegable.[41] A necessary part of this general duty encompasses vigilant protection of the trust property against deterioration or loss.[42] Thus it is implicit in the so-called *prudent man rule* in all its manifestations, including the Restatement's recently adopted *prudent investor rule*, that the trustee, in investing the trust estate, must strive to protect trust principal from the ravages of inflation.[43] The trustee at trust expense should insure the trust property to the extent it is reasonable to do so.[44] Property taxes should be paid in a timely fashion to

[38] *See generally* Group of 30, Clearance and Settlement Systems in the World's Securities Markets (1988) (recommending a worldwide move to "dematerialize" securities); *see also* Peers, "Paperless" Wall Street, Wall St. J., June 7, 1994, at C1.

[39] *See generally* In re Bevill, Bresler & Schulman, Inc., 59 B.R. 353, 374 (1986) ("Customers . . . who [leave]securities with a broker in street name or in negotiable form do not retain full property ownership of the securities in the event a SIPA liquidation proceeding is initiated against the broker. These customers are treated as preferred creditors entitled to receive a ratable share of customer property (plus an appropriate SIPC allowance.")); *see generally* Mooney, Beyond Negotiability: A New Model for Transfer and Pledge of Interests in Securities Controlled by Intermediaries, 12 Cardozo L.R. 305, n. 4 ("Street Name" generally refers to the practice of securities intermediaries holding fungible bulks of securities in their own names, or that of their nominees, even though the securities may be beneficially owned by their customers.). *See also* Don and Wang, Stockbroker Liquidations Under the Securities Investor Protection Act and Their Impact on Securities Transfers, 12 Cardozo L.R. 509 (1990).

[40] *See* Bogert, Trusts and Trustees §582; 2A Scott on Trusts §176.

[41] *See generally* 2A Scott on Trusts §171.

[42] *See* Restatement (Second) of Trusts §176 comments *b, c* (1959).

[43] *See* Restatement (Third) of Trusts §227 comment *e* (1992).

[44] *See* Bogert, Trusts and Trustees §599.

avoid a tax sale.[45] Also, the trustee may be liable if he permits stock subscription rights to expire.[46]

Claims owned by the trust estate must be enforced whether against strangers or against a predecessor trustee or the settlor's estate.[47] Thus a trustee who has reason to suspect that a cotrustee is depleting or about to deplete the trust property must take reasonable steps to prevent him from doing so.[48]

It is the duty of the trustee to defend actions affecting the trust estate.[49] Pursuant to this duty, the trustee has full power to sue on behalf of the trust estate and to defend suits in which it is involved or in which the trustee is involved as trustee.[50] All demands must be pressed, even to the extent of bringing suit,[51] or else the trustee will be liable for any loss caused by unjustified forbearance.[52] Under some circumstances, it may be in the economic interest of the beneficiaries, and therefore prudent and reasonable, to forbear or to compromise a claim or submit it to arbitration.[53] Because of the attendant expense to the trust, the patently futile prosecution of a claim itself can constitute a breach of the specific duty to protect the trust property.[54] State statutes authorize a trustee to compromise, usually with court approval.[55]

### *§6.2.2 Duty to Make Trust Property Productive*

The trustee has a specific duty to make the trust property productive, unless the settlor intended otherwise or it is impracti-

[45] *See* id. §602; 2A Scott on Trusts §176.

[46] *See* 2A Scott on Trusts §176 n.28 and accompanying text.

[47] *See* id. §177; Bogert, Trusts and Trustees §§592, 594.

[48] *See* Restatement (Third) of Trusts §184 comment *a* (1992).

[49] *See* 2A Scott on Trusts §178; Bogert, Trusts and Trustees §581; §6.2.6 (Duty to Defend the Trust Against Attack; Duty Not to Attack the Trust).

[50] *See* Bogert, Trusts and Trustees §§594, 869; §6.2.6.

[51] *See* 2A Scott on Trusts §177; §6.2.6.

[52] Id.

[53] *See* Restatement (Second) of Trusts §192 (1959).

[54] *See* Restatement (Second) of Trusts §192 comment *c* (1959); 3 Scott on Trusts §192; §6.2.6. (Duty to Defend the Trust Against Attack; Duty Not to Attack the Trust).

[55] *See* 3 Scott on Trusts §192.

cal to do so.[56] This specific duty is an offshoot of the trustee's general duty to be prudent and the general duty to carry out the terms of the trust, particularly if the terms make provision for income beneficiaries.[57] Inherent in the duty to make the trust property productive is the duty, as well as right, to invest the trust property.[58] The "prudent man rule" in its original manifestation,[59] and as it has evolved in the various jurisdictions by statute and decision,[60] is designed to provide a safe harbor for the trustee carrying out investment responsibilities by holding the trustee to a standard of *conduct* rather than *performance.*[61]

### §6.2.2.1 The *Harvard College* Prudent Man Rule and Its Progeny

In *Harvard College v. Amory,*[62] the Supreme Judicial Court of Massachusetts set forth the following rule:

> All that can be required of a trustee to invest, is, that he shall conduct himself faithfully and exercise a sound discretion. He is to observe how men of prudence, discretion and intelligence manage their own affairs, not in regard to speculation, but in regard to the permanent disposition of their funds, considering the probable income, as well as the probable safety of the capital to be invested.[63]

This is a "default" rule in that it applies absent an expression of a contrary intention in the governing instrument or preemption by some other body of law (*e.g.*, ERISA). Essentially, the

[56]Restatement (Third) of Trusts §§181 comment *a*, 227 comment *a* (1992). *See generally* Bogert, Trusts and Trustees §611.

[57]Restatement (Third) of Trusts §227 comment *i* (1992).

[58]Id. comment *a.*

[59]Harvard College v. Amory, 26 Mass. (9 Pick.) 446, 461 (1830).

[60]*See generally* 3 Scott on Trusts §227.13.

[61]Restatement (Third) of Trusts §227 comment *b* (1992) (the Prudent Investor Rule). *See also* Bogert, Trusts and Trustees §612 n.23 and accompanying text. *But see* Washington Legal Found. v. Massachusetts Bar Found., 795 F. Supp. 50, 53 (D. Mass. 1992) ("[under Massachusetts law ]the extent of a putative beneficiary's property interest is limited by the so-called 'prudent man doctrine' ").

[62]26 Mass. (9 Pick.) 446 (1830).

[63]Id. at 461.

trustee is to strike a reasonable balance between the extreme of the nonincome producing speculation that subverts the interests of the income beneficiary and the extreme of the wasting asset that subverts the interests of the remainderman. A middle ground, that allows for a reasonable flow of income and a reasonable rate of growth is the goal.[64] Down through the years, many jurisdictions, either judicially or legislatively, have adopted some form of the rule. Some have adopted the rule almost verbatim;[65] others have tinkered with its language.[66] A few have rejected the rule in favor of the *legal list* and then returned to the rule with a renewed appreciation for its flexibility.[67]

The *Harvard College* Prudent Man Rule has proved remarkably adaptable to changing economic environments.[68] In 1974 Congress included a modified version of the rule in the Employee Retirement Income Security Act (the *Federal Prudent Man Rule*).[69]

Concern has been expressed that "much of the apparent and initially intended generality and adaptability of the *Harvard College* prudent man rule [has been] lost as it [has been] elaborated in the courts and applied case by case."[70] To be sure, certain investment practices, as a practical matter, have come to be off-limits to even the most careful, skillful, and cautious of trustees (*e.g.*, engaging in futures and option trading and venture capital programs).[71] Moreover, the clear distinction between income and

[64] *See e.g.*, Sarlin v. Sarlin, 430 S.E. 2d 530, 532 (S.C. Ct. App. 1993) (trustee faulted for investing almost exclusively for growth).

[65] *See generally* 3 Scott on Trusts §227.5; Restatement (Third) of Trusts topic 5 (Investment of Trust Funds) introduction 3 (1992); Bogert, Trusts and Trustees §§612-613.

[66] *See, e.g.*, Bogert, Trusts and Trustees §§612 n.17 comment, 613 n.14.

[67] *See* 3 Scott on Trusts §227.13 (New York is a good example); today only two states have legal lists limited to debt securites. Ala. Const. art. IV, §74 (1901, amended 1939); Ala. Code §19-3-120-128 (1994); Ky. Rev. Stat. Ann. §§386.020-070 and 386.800(3) (Michie/Bobbs-Merrill 1994).

[68] *See* Bergquist, The Prudent Man Rule in Massachusetts Today, 122 Tr. & Est. 44 (Dec. 1983).

[69] *See* 29 C.F.R. §2550.404a-1 (1974); Bogert, Trusts and Trustees §612 n.20; Restatement (Third) of Trusts §227 reporter's note 66-67 (1992).

[70] *See* Restatement (Third) of Trusts topic 5 (Investment of Trust Funds) introduction 3 (1992).

[71] *See* id. §227 comment *f.*

principal implicit in the *Harvard College* Prudent Man Rule is being blurred by two relatively recent developments: (1) the eclipse of the income-only trust by the discretionary trust, and (2) the practice of gauging investment performance not only by the income that is produced but also by how much the principal has appreciated (the *total return* concept).[72] A consensus may be emerging that investment prudence either may be (or perhaps even should be) judged not on the basis of each individual security in isolation but on the basis of the portfolio as a whole.[73] In 1992, the American Law Institute, in an effort to respond to these concerns and developments, published its *Prudent Investor Rule*:

**§277 General Standard of Prudent Investment**

> The trustee is under a duty to the beneficiaries to invest and manage the funds of the trust as a prudent investor would, in light of the purposes, terms, distribution requirements, and other circumstances of the trust.
>
> (a) This standard requires the exercise of reasonable care, skill, and caution, and it is to be applied to investments not in isolation but in the context of the trust portfolio and as a part of an overall investment strategy, which should incorporate risk and return objectives reasonably suitable to the trust . . .[74]

What specific investments, then, are suitable for a trustee? That is a subject beyond the scope of this handbook and far better covered by others.[75] Suffice it to say that the traditional trust portfolio consists of a mix of equities (common stock) and indebtedness (*e.g.*, bonds, debentures, promissory notes, and money

[72] *See* id. §227 comment *i*; *see* §6.2.4.6 (a portfolio's total return is the sum of income, *e.g.*, dividends, interest, and the like, and realized and unrealized capital gains); *see generally*, Dobris, New Forms of Private Trusts for the Twenty-First Century, 31 Real Prop. Prob. & Tr. J. 1 (Spring 1996).

[73] Id.; *see* Revised Reg. 9, reprinted in Appendix II, providing that in determining whether investing fiduciary assets in a collective investment fund is proper, the bank may consider the fund as a whole and, for example, shall not be prohibited from making that investment because any particular asset is nonincome producing. 12 C.F.R. §9.18(a) n. 1 (1997).

[74] Id. §227.

[75] Id. §227 comment *k*.

market instruments).[76] At one time, the prevailing practice was to weight the mix in favor of fixed income securities; today, the prevailing practice is to weight the mix in favor of equities.[77]

While investing in fixed income securities presumably generates a predictable stream of income, they can lose some of their real value in periods of inflation.[78] Equities, on the other hand, tend to keep pace with inflation but can lose their value in periods when the market is down.[79] "Do what you will, the capital is at hazard."[80] Thus the prudent trustee not only calls for a reasonable balance between equities and fixed income securities, but also diversification among economic sectors, geographical areas, and maturity dates, of course taking into account in the formulation of investment objectives the settlor's intentions.[81] There is even a school of thought that advocates funds designed to hold a basket of securities that approximates the diversification of some index of market performance such as Standard and Poor's 500 is the way to go.[82] These funds are known as *index* or *market funds*.[83] The trustee should be particularly careful not to improperly retain property received from the settlor or a prior fiduciary; the closely held business, the stock with sentimental value, and the unproductive real estate holding are common traps for the unwary.[84]

What specific investments are then improper for trustees? The drafters of the Prudent Investor Rule would say that it de-

[76]Id. *See also* comments *l* and *m*.

[77]Id. comment *l*.

[78]Id.

[79]Id.

[80]*Harvard College*, 26 Mass. at 461.

[81]*See* Restatement (Third) of Trusts 227 comments *e-h* (1992); In re Dickinson, 152 Mass. 184, 25 N.E. 99 (1890). *But see* In re Adriance's Estate, 145 Misc. 345, 260 N.Y.S. 173 (Sur. Ct. 1932) ("It is entirely true that many financial authorities advocate wide diversity of investment. It is equally true that others as strenuously affirm the contrary, and agree with the familiar admonition of the late Andrew Carnegie: 'Put all your eggs in one basket and watch the basket.' "). It should be noted that in 1995 New York adopted a version of §227, including its diversification requirements. N.Y. Est., Powers & Tr. Law §11-2.3 (1995). *See generally* Estate of Cooper, 913 P.2d 393 (Wash. Ct. App. 1996) (trustee surcharge for imprudent asset balance).

[82]Langbein & Posner, Market Funds and Trust-Investment Law (pts. 1-2), 1976 Am. B. Found. Res. J. 1 (1976); 1977 Am. B. Found. Res. J. 1 (1977).

[83]Id.

[84] *See generally* 3 Scott on Trusts §230.

pends on the facts and circumstances of the particular trust[85] — *no* investment is considered per se imprudent or prudent.[86] It must be noted that the Restatement's rule is not the law in the majority of states.[87] Up to now, at least, some investments have been deemed per se imprudent: enterprises lacking in seasoned performance as to safety and yield;[88] junior mortgages;[89] wasting assets (*e.g.*, leaseholds, royalties, patents, oil wells, natural gas wells, timberlands, and coal mines);[90] most family businesses;[91] other speculations of one sort or another.[92] It goes without saying that under any rule, investments in an enterprise in which the trustee has a personal interest is off-limits.[93] In any case, it should always be remembered that these rules are default rules. They apply in a given situation absent an expression of a contrary intention in the governing instrument or preemption by some other body of law (e.g., ERISA).

Once the trust property is well invested, the investments should not be changed without good reason. The trustee should strive to assess market panics or dramatic inflations in market

[85] *See* Restatement (Third) of Trusts §227 comment *k* (1992).

[86] *See* id.

[87] Several states, however, have adopted the Restatement's rule. *See* Ariz. Rev. Stat. §§14-7601 thru 14-7611; Cal. Prob. Code §§16045-16054 (Deering 1995); Colo. Rev. Stat. §15-1.1-101-115 (1995); Conn. P.A. No. 97-140 (approved June 13, 1997); Fla. Stat. Ann. §§518.11, 518.112, and 660.431 (1993); Ill. Stat. ch. 760, §515 (Smith-Hurd Supp. 1992); Iowa Code Ann. §633.123 (West 1992); Kan. Stat. Ann. §17-5004 (1994); Me. Rev. Stat. Ann. tit. 18-A, §7-302 (West 1997); Minn. Rev. Stat. Ann. §§501B.151, 501B.152 (West 1997); N.M. Stat. Ann. §45-7-603 (1995); N.Y. Est. Powers & Trusts Law §11-2.3 (1995); 60 Okla. Stat. §175.60-175.72 (1995); Or. Rev. Stat. §128.192-128.218 (1995); R.I. Gen. Laws §§18-15-1 thru 18-15-13 (1996); S.C. Code Ann. §62-7-302 (Law. Co-op. 1989 & Supp.); S.D. Codified Laws Ann. §55-5-7 (1995); Tex. Prop. Code Ann. §112.035 (Vernon 1984 & Supp. 1992); Utah Code Ann. §75-7-302 (1995); Va. Code Ann. §26-45.1 (1992); Wash. Rev. Code Ann. §11.100.010 (West 1995); W. Va. Code §§44-6c-1 thru 44-6c-15 (1996). *See generally* Restatement (Third) of Trusts §227 Reporter's Notes (1992).

[88] *See generally* Bogert, Trusts and Trustees §§612, 679. *But see* Restatement (Third) of Trusts §227 comment *l* (1992).

[89] *See* Bogert, Trusts and Trustees §674. *But see* Restatement (Third) of Trusts §227 comment *n* (1992).

[90] *See* Bogert, Trusts and Trustees §827.

[91] Id. §§571-577.

[92] Id. §612.

[93] Id. §543.

values with professional detachment. It is not the duty of the trustee to follow the ticker as might a speculator. However, when a company in which trust funds are invested shows a threatened lack of earnings or there is an actual suspension of interest or dividends, the investment should be liquidated, but not before tax and transaction costs are estimated and duly considered.

If a trust security has acquired a speculative value much above its true value as an investment, it is obviously time to reduce the trust's position in that investment, if not sell out altogether.[94] And yet a mere increase in market value is not enough, for the doctrine "can readily be pressed so far as to sanction a practice of trading and trafficking in trust securities, which would be attended with dangerous results to the trust fund."[95]

#### §6.2.2.2 The Prudent Investor's Code of Conduct

The *Harvard College* Prudent Man Rule and its progeny are rules of conduct, not performance. While the prudence of the trustee's conduct will be judged in light of the facts and circumstances applicable in a given situation, there are some long-accepted indicia of prudent conduct. At minimum the trustee should always:

(1) decide whether to accept a trust only after making an exhaustive examination of the trust portfolio and only after a thorough audit of the accountings of the prior fiduciary is completed;[96]

(2) require, before taking on a trusteeship, that a predecessor fiduciary remedy any breaches of fiduciary duty and cleanse the portfolio of improper investments, absent compelling reasons to do otherwise;[97]

[94] *See* 3 Scott on Trusts §231.

[95] New England Trust Co. v. Eaton, 140 Mass. 532, 537, 4 N.E. 69, 72 (1886).

[96] *See generally* Bogert, Trusts and Trustees §684; Revised Reg. 9, reprinted in Appendix II, provides that, before accepting a fiduciary account, a national bank shall review the prospective account to determine whether it can properly administer the account. 12 C.F.R. §9.6(a) (1997).

[97] *See generally* Restatement (Second) of Trusts §223 (1959).

(3) upon accepting a trusteeship, immediately take control of all property belonging to the trust and set about cleansing the portfolio of improper investments;[98]
(4) understand the intentions of the settlor as they are expressed in the governing instrument and invest accordingly;[99]
(5) investigate each investment, personally monitor the portfolio on a regular basis, and respond to changed circumstances in a timely fashion to the extent a response is deemed appropriate;[100]
(6) obtain expert investment advice as appropriate;[101]
(7) maintain prudent diversification at all times, unless it is clearly the intention of the settlor that this not be done;[102]
(8) maintain an adequate cushion of liquidity so that the cash needs of the trust may be accommodated in an orderly fashion;[103]
(9) understand that no capital is risk-free and that even insured bank accounts and fixed income government issues are "at hazard" in that their value erodes with inflation, and act upon that understanding;[104]

[98]Bogert, Trusts and Trustees §583; *see also,* Revised Reg. 9 applicable to national banks, 12 C.F.R. §9.6(b) (1997) (Initial post-acceptance review).

[99]Id. §683.

[100]Id. §612; *see* Uniform Prudent Investor Act §2(c), 7B U.L.A. 18 (1997) (listing "circumstances" that a trustee shall consider in investing and managing trust assets).

[101]Id. *See also* §§555, 556, 701. *See generally* Restatement (Third) of Trusts §171 (1992).

[102]*See* 3 Scott on Trusts §228; Restatement (Third) of Trusts §227 (1992); *see generally,* P.G. Guthrie, Annot., Duty of trustee to diversify investments, and liability for failure to do so, 24 A.L.R.3d 730 (1969); *see e.g.,* In re Lincoln First Bank, 630 N.Y.S.2d 472 (N.Y. Surr. Ct. 1995) (trustee surcharged $6 million for failing to diversify), 223 A.D.2d 20, 643 N.Y.S.2d 972, *aff'd* 659 N.Y.S.2d 165, 681 N.E.2d 332 (1997) (damage amount modified on appeal to $4,065,029); *See also,* Estate of Maxedon, 946 P.2d (104 (Kan. Ct. App. 1997) (suggesting a common law duty to diversify absent language in governing instrument to contrary).

[103]*See generally* Bogert, Trusts and Trustees §612.

[104]*See* id. §612 n.90. *See also* Restatement (Third) of Trusts §227 comment *e* (1992).

(10) invest for the long term unless there is a legitimate reason not to do so;[105]
(11) keep all trust property invested at all times unless there is a legitimate reason not to do so;[106]
(12) keep meticulous permanent records of all investment research, deliberations, and decisions;[107]
(13) assess the tax consequences of contemplated investment changes; and
(14) assess the transaction costs of contemplated investment changes.

Adherence to this code of conduct does not mean that the trustee will be immune from suit for improper investing, but it will help to show that the trustee's conduct was prudent.

#### §6.2.2.3 The Prudent Investor and the Charitable Corporation

It has been suggested that there is no compelling reason to maintain the trust's traditional line of demarcation between income and principal when it comes to tax-exempt funds managed by charitable corporations, except when private beneficiaries are involved. Assuming that to be the case, then it follows that a charity's day-to-day cash requirements ought not to influence one way or another the implementation of a reasonable growth investment strategy. Accordingly, §2 of the Uniform Management of Institu-

[105] *See generally* Bogert, Trusts and Trustees §612.

[106] *See generally* id. §611; Revised Reg. 9, reprinted in Appendix II, provides that with respect to a fiduciary account for which a national bank has investment discretion or discretion over distributions, the bank may not allow funds awaiting investment or distribution to remain uninvested and undistributed any longer than is reasonable for the proper management of the account and consistent with applicable law. 12 C.F.R. §9.10(a) (1997).

[107] *See generally* id. §962; *see* Revised Reg. 9, reprinted in Appendix II, setting forth the recordkeeping responsibilities of national banks in the conduct of their fiduciary activities, 12 C.F.R. §9.8 (1997).

tional Funds Act ("UMIFA")[108] allows for some tapping of principal appreciation:

> The governing board may appropriate for expenditure for the uses and purposes for which an endowment fund is established so much of the net appreciation, realized and unrealized, in the fair value of the assets of an endowment fund over the historic dollar value of the fund as is prudent under the standard established by Section 6. This Section does not limit the authority of the governing board to expend funds as permitted under other law, the terms of the applicable gift instrument, or the charter of the institution.[109]

#### §6.2.2.4 The Non-Charitable Unitrust: Investment Considerations

There is a school of thought that even in the non-charitable context, the rigid demarcation between income and principal is counter productive when it comes to trust investments. The trustee is caught in the middle between the life beneficiaries who are clamoring for more income and the remaindermen who are clamoring for more growth. Under these conditions, a total return investment strategy aimed at growth rather than income is difficult. Certain high-performing, low income-producing stocks are effectively off limits to the trustee of a traditional trust. Moreover, when it comes to investment performance, the trustee is unfairly compared with those investors who are not shackled by a traditional trust's income requirements. For some, the non-charitable "unitrust" is the way to go. Instead of the traditional "all net income to *C*, remainder to *D*" design, a typical "unitrust" governing instrument will provide that all trust accounting net income shall be added to principal and the life beneficiary in a given year shall then receive a fixed percentage (typically 5%) of the net market value of the trust estate valued at the end of the prior year.

[108] 7A U.L.A. 712, 716 (1985). This act has been adopted in 41 states including the District of Columbia.

[109] Id.

There are many variations on the theme.[110] The point is that now both constituencies, the life beneficiaries and the remaindermen, at least will be pounding on the trustee for the same thing: growth.

### *§6.2.3 Duty of Confidentiality*

An offshoot of the trustee's general duty of loyalty is the specific duty to keep all the affairs of the trust confidential.[111] The trustee's duty to act solely in the interest of the beneficiaries means that third parties are told only what the law requires the trustee to divulge or what furthers the interests of all the beneficiaries.[112] An unauthorized disclosure of information pertaining to the trust or pertaining to a beneficiary is a breach of the duty of loyalty and, at minimum, grounds for removal.[113]

### *§6.2.4 Duty to Separate Income from Principal and the Right to Income*

Unless a contrary intention is expressed in the governing instrument, one class of beneficiaries will get the net income or use of the trust property and another will ultimately get the principal free of trust.[114] As a matter of law, unless the settlor intended otherwise, a life beneficiary is entitled to the net income as it accrues.[115] It must be distributed periodically at reasonable inter-

[110] *See* Wolf, Defeating the Duty to Disappoint Equally — the Total Return Trust, 23 ACTEC Notes 46 (1997).

[111] *See* Restatement (Third) of Trusts §170 comment *s* (1992); *see also* §§5.4.1.1 (Right to Information and Confidentiality) and 8.8 (Whom Does Counsel Represent?).

[112] Id. §170; *see also* 2A Scott on Trusts §170.

[113] *See* Bogert, Trusts and Trustees §527.

[114] *See generally* 3A Scott on Trusts §232.

[115] Note, however, that a life beneficiary is entitled to income in the form of corporate distributions to stockholders once the distribution becomes payable to shareholders of record on a designated date after the creation of the beneficial interest. *See generally* Restatement (Second) of Trusts §236. Income in the form of periodic payments such as interest and rents, however, is treated as accruing from

vals.[116] Thus one offshoot of the trustee's general duty to carry out the terms of the trust will likely be the specific duty to separately account for income and principal.[117]

This is a critical duty. The determination where to credit a receipt or debit an expense directly affects the property interests of the life beneficiary and the remainderman: A receipt credited to income will benefit the life beneficiary whereas a receipt credited to principal will benefit the remainderman. Similarly, a decision where to charge an expense directly affects the beneficiary's property interests. Failure to properly credit a receipt or charge an expense is a breach of trust.

A trustee is also under a duty to act impartially. Thus the trustee must be careful to distinguish between principal and income with regard both to receipts and expenditures so that neither the life beneficiary nor the remainderman will be deprived of what is due to each.

The trustee must decide what qualifies as income and what qualifies as principal for trust accounting purposes. For guidance the trustee should look to the law that governs the administration of the trust.[118] Some jurisdictions have comprehensive legislation that, unless contrary to the governing instrument, determines

---

day to day. *See generally* Restatement (Second) of Trusts §235 comment *a* (1959). *See also* Revised Uniform Principal and Income Act §4, 7B U.L.A. 157 (1985).

[116]Although the trustee is not obligated to distribute income upon receipt, it is reasonable, where the trust does not specify the frequency of income payments, to distribute income semiannually or quarterly. *See generally* 2A Scott on Trusts §182; Bogert, Trusts and Trustees §814. It might in fact be reasonable in certain instances for the trustee to withhold income to build up a reserve for payment of future expenditures. Id.

[117]*See generally* 2A Scott on Trusts §183. *See also* Bogert, Trusts and Trustees §816.

[118]When the terms of the trust provide neither for the allocation of receipts and expenses nor for the applicable law, a conflict of laws question may arise. *See* 4A Scott on Trusts §586. The trustee or court may resolve such questions by ascertaining the intention of the settlor. Otherwise, matters of administration might be resolved through application of the law of the place of administration, and matters of construction might be resolved through application of the law of the settlor's domicile. Id. *See generally* J. A. Schoenblum, 1 Multistate and Multinational Estate Planning §17 (1982).

allocation issues and apportionment issues.[119] Others rely less on a statutory framework and more on the common law and the generally accepted practices of the jurisdiction.[120] Of course if the terms of the trust direct where a receipt is to be credited or where an expense is to be debited, then the trust term controls.[121] Deviation by the trustee, without any special circumstances or prior court approval, would be a breach of trust. Above all the trustee must understand that the rules governing what is income for tax purposes are separate from the rules governing what is allocated to income for trust accounting purposes.[122] A receipt of Income in Respect of a Decedent (IRD), for example, may be income for tax purposes but principal for trust accounting purposes.[123] And of course, *when in doubt, the prudent trustee allocates receipts to principal and expenses to income.*

**Most states have adopted versions of either the 1931 Uniform Principal and Income Act or the 1962 Revised Uniform Principal and Income Act. The reader should be aware, however, that in 1997, the National Conference of Commissioners on Uniform State Laws has approved a new version of the model statute.[124] The 1997 version would allow trustees who are authorized and inclined to pursue total return investment strategies to make appropriate**

[119]For a catalog of state legislation applicable to the allocation of income and principal and the apportionment of expenses, see Bogert, Trusts and Trustees §816 nn.64-66.

[120]*See generally* Bogert, Trusts and Trustees §816 n.67 and accompanying text.

[121]*See generally* 2A Scott on Trusts §164.

[122]*See* Bogert, Trusts and Trustees §816. The trustee should note that the economic theories that form the basis for principles of accounting for tax purposes and of accounting for trust purposes differ substantially. *See* Bogert, Trusts and Trustees §816 n.63 and accompanying text.

[123]Receipt of income in respect of a decedent (*IRD receipt*) is income received to which a decedent had rights prior to death but which was not payable or collected until after death. *See generally* M. C. Ferguson et al., Federal Income Taxation of Estates, Trusts, and Beneficiaries §3.3 (2d ed. 1993). Once the receipt is paid, it must be included in the gross income of the estate or trust of the decedent for the taxable year when received. I.R.C. §691(a)(1) (1992). For trust accounting purposes, however, the receipt is treated as principal. *See* Revised Uniform Principal and Income Act §4(b)(1), 7B U.L.A. 157 (1985) ("receipts due but not paid at the date of death of the testator are principal").

[124]Uniform Principal and Income Act (1997), http://www.law.upenn.edu/library/ulc/upaia/princin3.htm.

**reallocations between the income and principal accounts in furtherance of these strategies. Trust accounting rules relating to a number of asset categories, including S corporation stock, partnership interests, derivatives, and timber, have been amended, clarified or expanded.**

### §6.2.4.1 What Receipts Are Entirely Allocated to Income for Trust Accounting Purposes?

The ordinary current receipts of a trust are income. They should be credited to the income account and distributed, after making provision for ordinary expenses, to the beneficiary who is entitled to receive income.[125] This includes: routine rents; ordinary and extraordinary cash dividends; items of current interest;[126] accrued increment on bonds or other obligations issued at discount;[127] shares in a corporation other than the distributing corporation;[128] a pro rata share of the income earned during administration of the settlor's estate.[129] As to extraordinary cash dividends, the majority rule is that they belong to income, although some jurisdictions have held that they are apportionable between income and principal.[130]

[125]Ordinary current receipts will generally include the earnings, profits, and products that result from use or investment of the trust corpus. *See* 3A Scott on Trusts §233.1. Ordinary receipts that indicate merely a change in the form of the corpus, however, are not to be credited to the income account but are retained as principal. Id. *See also* Bogert, Trusts and Trustees §816. The Revised Uniform Principal and Income Act provides rules for the allocation of most receipts. Revised Uniform Principal and Income Act §3, 7B U.L.A. 154 (1985). For a catalog of states where the Act has been adopted, *see* Bogert, Trusts and Trustees §816 nn.64, 65.

[126]*See* 3A Scott on Trusts §233.1.

[127]*Id. See also* Revised Uniform Principal and Income Act §7, 7B U.L.A. 165 (1985).

[128]A dividend in the form of shares in a corporation other than the distributing corporation is generally allocable as income unless the dividend is declared out of capital. 3A Scott on Trusts §236.5; *see, e.g.,* Mass. Gen. L. C 203, §21a.

[129]*See* 3A Scott on Trusts §234.4.

[130]*See* id. §236.4.

### §6.2.4.2 What Receipts Are Entirely Allocated to Principal for Trust Accounting Purposes?

Proceeds from the sale of trust property are considered principal; thus, realized capital gains, although income for tax purposes, are considered items of principal for trust accounting purposes.[131] So also are most distributions of stock, including ordinary and extraordinary stock dividends, subscription rights, and dividends in liquidation.[132] Additional shares resulting from stock splits are of course items of principal, as are capital gain distributions from mutual funds.[133]

### §6.2.4.3 What Receipts Are Apportioned Between the Income and Principal Accounts?

The money received by way of "yield" from a wasting investment presents a peculiar problem.[134] Such a yield involves a

[131]Bogert, Trusts and Trustees §§822-823 (1984).

[132]For a discussion of the rules of allocation for ordinary and extraordinary stock dividends, including the distinction between the "Massachusetts rule" and the "Pennsylvania rule," *see* 3A Scott on Trusts §§236.3-236.8. For a discussion of the treatment of rights to subscribe to shares of stock and the treatment of dividends in liquidation, *see* id., §§236.9-236.10. The recent trend among jurisdictions has been adoption of the "Massachusetts rule" which holds that stock dividends, whether announced as stock dividends or as stock splits, are principal. *See* 3A Scott on Trusts §236.3. There are, however, some jurisdictions where legislation provides guidelines for apportionment. *See* id. §236.3 n.7 (citing New York and Pennsylvania legislation that provides that both stock splits and stock dividends are treated as income if made at the rate of six percent or less of the existing shares); *see* John P. Ludington, Annot., Modern status of rules governing allocation of stock dividends or splits between principal and income, 81 A.L.R.3d 876 (1977); *see also* §8.15.14 (The Massachusetts Rule of Allocation).

[133]*See e.g.*, Tait v Peck, 346 MA.521, 194 N.E.2d 707 (1963) (Capital gains from mutual funds are principal); *see also*, Annot., Allocation between income and principal of "Capital Gains" Dividend of Mutual Fund or Investment Trust or Corporation, 98 A.L.R.2d 511 (1964).

[134]A *wasting asset* is one whose value will depreciate or be destroyed in time because it currently benefits the life beneficiary at the expense of the remainderman, leaving the remainderman with an asset of little or no value. *See generally* 3A

continuing dissipation of principal to the economic detriment of the remainderman.[135] In order to be impartial, therefore, the trustee should set aside some part of the yield to protect the remainderman from this gradual loss.[136] Examples of wasting investments are copyrights, patents, royalties, leaseholds, and property subject to depletion.[137]

The apportionment of wasting assets is purely a matter of calculation. It may be done by fixing the value of the property at the time of creation of the trust and paying the life tenant from time to time that part of the yield which would equal the usual rate of return in trust investments.[138] It also may be done by apportioning the proceeds of sale when the property is sold.[139] The decisions in cases involving mining operations, quarries, and oil wells are numerous and diverse in their holdings.[140] Obviously if the instrument shows that the life beneficiary is to enjoy all benefits of wasting property, neither amortization of receipts nor apportionment of proceeds is necessary.[141]

Under the common law, the trustee had a duty to the remainderman to amortize bond premiums.[142] Thus the purchase of a bond at a price in excess of its face amount called for the allocation of some of the bond income, as it was received, to the principal account.[143] The Revised Uniform Principal and Income Act has relieved the trustee of this duty.[144] It should be noted that, for

---

Scott on Trusts §239; Bogert, Trusts and Trustees §827; Revised Uniform Principal and Income Act §§9-11, 7B U.L.A. 168 (1985).

[135]*See* 3A Scott on Trusts §239; Restatement (Third) of Trusts §239.

[136]Id. The Revised Uniform Principal and Income Act sets specific guidelines for apportioning receipts from wasting assets such as minerals and other natural resources, timber, royalties, patents, and so forth. *See* Revised Uniform Principal and Income Act §§9-11, 7B U.L.A. 168 (1985); Restatement (Third) of Trusts §239.

[137]*See generally* 3A Scott on Trusts §239.

[138]*See* id. §§239 n.4, 241.4.

[139]*See* id.

[140]For a general discussion of the wide range of holdings among the jurisdictions in this area, *see* 3A Scott on Trusts §239.3.

[141]*See generally* id. §239.1.

[142]Id. §239.2.

[143]Id.

[144]The Act provides that no provision is required for amortization of bond premiums except for bonds payable in the future in accordance with a fixed

purposes of tax accounting, premiums on purchases on tax-exempt bonds must be amortized.[145]

The Act treats the matter of wasting assets in this way:

> Except as provided in sections 9 and 10, if the principal consists of property subject to depletion, including leaseholds, patents, copyrights, royalty rights, and rights to receive payments on a contract for deferred compensation, receipts from the property, not in excess of 5% per year of its inventory value, are income, and the balance is principal.[146]

Sometimes, the trust property includes a building that generates income. Should a trustee apportion some of this income to principal to establish a depreciation reserve? The majority of cases on this issue hold that a trustee is not required to establish a reserve for depreciation.[147] Furthermore some cases hold that it is not proper for the trustee to establish a reserve.[148] Thus, absent a contrary intention, it appears a trustee has no power to establish a reserve.[149]

On the other hand, nonincome producing property works a hardship on the beneficiary.[150] Thus, upon the sale of such property, an appropriate portion of the proceeds should be allocated to the income account unless a fair reading of the governing instrument suggests that the settlor intended otherwise.[151] Likewise the

---

appreciation schedule. Revised Uniform Principal and Income Act §7, 7B U.L.A. 165 (1985).

[145]For the federal tax treatment of premiums paid in purchasing tax-exempt bonds, *see* I.R.C. §171 (1992).

[146]Revised Uniform Principal and Income Act §11, 7B U.L.A. 172 (1985).

[147]For a catalog of cases that hold that the trustee has no duty to establish a reserve for depreciation of a building held by a trust, *see* 3A Scott on Trusts §239.4 n.2.

[148]For a catalog of cases that hold it improper for a trustee to establish a reserve for the depreciation of a building held by a trust, *see* 3A Scott on Trusts §239.4 n.4. *But see,* Revised Uniform Principal and Income Act §13(a)(2), 7B U.L.A. 176 (1985).

[149]*See* id. §239.4.

[150]Id. Restatement (Third) of Trusts §240.

[151]As a general rule, where unproductive property is sold by the trustee, the net proceeds are apportioned between principal and income by determining the principal amount that, when earning interest at the current rate of return on

proceeds from the settlement of a note long in default should be appropriately apportioned between both accounts.[152] When the proceeds are brought into the hands of the trustee, a calculation is made which attempts to award to the life tenant the income which would have been received if the unproductive property actually had produced at a current rate of return.[153] In the case of unproductive property, an income allocation is appropriate even when a particular investment has resulted in a capital loss.[154]

Absent a contrary intention expressed in the instrument, a trustee is under a duty to the income beneficiary to sell the unproductive property within a reasonable time.[155] The rules expressed herein also apply to *under*productive property.[156] Thus if property that produces income substantially less than the current rate of return on trust investments is held, the trustee, absent a contrary intention, should make an apportionment when the property is sold.[157] Also, absent a contrary intention,

---

trust investments for the amount of time during which the nonproductive asset was held by the trust, will yield interest equal to the net proceeds minus that principal amount. The principal amount is allocated to principal. The net sale proceeds minus the principal amount is allocated to income. On the other hand, the income account receives no portion of proceeds from the sale of unproductive property that the trustee, in the governing instrument, is directed or specifically authorized to retain. *See* Restatement (Third) of Trusts §241. *See also* Bogert, Trusts and Trustees §824; Restatement (Second) of Trusts §241(2) (1959). *Cf.* Revised Uniform Principal and Income Act §12, 7B U.L.A. 173 (1985) (income should be determined as if principal had been invested to yield four percent per annum).

[152] A default in interest payment on a bond may be an example of a productive asset which becomes nonproductive. *See generally* 3A Scott on Trusts §§240.3, 241.3-241.3A.

[153] *See supra* note 151.

[154] Restatement (Third) of Trusts §241 comment *b* (1992).

[155] 3A Scott on Trusts §240; *see also* Restatement (Third) of Trusts §240 (1992).

[156] *See* 3A Scott on Trusts §240; Restatement (Third) of Trusts §240 comment *b* (1992).

[157] The trustee, when allocating proceeds from the sale of underproductive property, must modify the general rule for allocating proceeds from the sale of unproductive property (as explained *supra* note 151) to account for the small income received as well as for the associated carrying charges of the underproductive asset. *See* 3A Scott on Trusts §241.1.

the trustee should within a reasonable time sell underproductive property.[158]

### §6.2.4.4 What Expenses Are Allocated Entirely to Income, Entirely to Principal, and Apportioned Between Income and Principal?

Expenses that are connected with the everyday administration of the trust property are chargeable entirely to income. Examples include ordinary repairs to real estate, annual real property taxes, insurance premiums, premiums on the trustee's bond, and legal expenses incurred in collecting income.[159] Income taxes attributable to trust accounting income are charged to income.[160]

Expenses incurred primarily for the protection and preservation of the principal are chargeable entirely to principal. This includes legal expenses that relate to the interpretation of the trust, the appointment or removal of the trustee, and litigation; alterations and additions to real estate; expenses for preparation of property for rental or sale; income taxes on capital gains; brokers' commissions; the costs of a guardian ad litem appointed to represent remainder interests; and the expenses of making final distribution.[161]

Some expenses are chargeable in part to income and in part to principal, such as trustee's fees and costs of periodic accountings that pertain both to the income and the remainder interests.[162]

[158] *See supra* note 155.

[159] The Revised Uniform Principal and Income Act provides that "ordinary expenses" are chargeable against income. Revised Uniform Principal and Income Act §13(a), 7B U.L.A. 175 (1985). *See generally* 3A Scott on Trusts §233.2; Bogert, Trusts and Trustees §802.

[160] Revised Uniform Principal and Income Act §13(a)(6), 7B U.L.A. 176 (1985).

[161] Id. §13(c). *See generally* 3A Scott on Trusts §233.3.

[162] Revised Uniform Principal and Income Act §13(a)(3), 7B U.L.A. 176 (1985). Ordinary practice is to pay the trustee a commission on income earned that is chargeable against income. *See* 3A Scott on Trusts §233.3. The trustee is also ordinarily paid a commission, either upon acceptance of the trust or upon

The trust may include property that does not produce any current income. Where should the expenses of the unproductive property be charged? The answer to this difficult question depends upon the terms of the trust. Generally, the current as well as extraordinary expenses of unproductive property are payable from principal unless the terms of the trust provide otherwise.[163] It should be noted that some jurisdictions require a trustee to adjust the income and principal amounts when certain tax elections upset the equilibrium between the competing equitable interests.[164] Let us take a residuary testamentary trust, for example. Administration expenses paid from the principal of the probate estate are elected to be taken as an income tax deduction, rather than as an estate tax deduction. This reduces the taxable income of, but not the income actually paid to, the life beneficiary. Some jurisdictions require that some income be transferred to the principal account so that the trust remainderman is compensated for not benefitting from an estate tax deduction (and so that the income beneficiary is not given a free ride.)[165]

---

the distribution of principal, which is chargeable against principal. Id. To determine how any other service is to be charged, the nature of the service must be considered. Id. *See also* Bogert, Trusts and Trustees §975. *Cf.* Revised Uniform Principal and Income Act §13(a)(5), 7B U.L.A. 176 (1985) ("one half of trustee's regular compensation, whether a percentage of principal or income, and all expenses reasonably incurred for current management of principal and application of income" are chargeable against income).

[163]Where the trustee by terms of the trust is directed to sell unproductive property, and the property is not immediately sold, the ordinary expenses of carrying the property should generally be charged to principal. *See* 3A Scott on Trusts §233.4. *See also* Restatement (Second) of Trusts §233 comment *m* (1959). However, if the terms of the trust direct the trustee to retain unproductive property, it is assumed that the settlor intended carrying costs to be paid out of income. 3A Scott on Trusts §233.4.

[164]*See, e.g.*, Matter of Warms, 140 N.Y.S.2d 169 (Sur. Ct. 1955) (the "Warm's adjustment").

[165]*See generally* M. L. Ferguson et al., Federal Income Taxation of Estates, Trusts and Beneficiaries §4.2.6 (1993); *see also* In re Estate of Holloway, 323 N.Y.S.2d 534 (Sur. Ct. 1971), *modified*, 327 N.Y.S.2d 865 (Sur. Ct. 1972) (when a trust accounting principal distribution from an estate to a trust carries out distributable net income (DNI), *i.e.*, is taxable as income, then the income account must reimburse the principal account for the tax benefit) (the "Holloway Adjustment"); *see generally* Boyle, Equitable Adjustments and GST Taxes, 6 Probate Practice Reporter 1 (Nov. 1994).

### §6.2.4.5 When Does Income Begin and What Happens to Accrued but Undistributed Income When the Trust's Term Expires or the Beneficiary Dies?

The beneficiary of a trust is entitled to income earned on the trust property computed back to the date the trust is deemed to arise.[166] Thus, in the case of a trust that will receive a portion or all of the residue of the settlor's estate, income will accrue to the trust beneficiary from the date of the settlor's death even though there will be some time thereafter before the trust actually receives a distribution from the settlor's estate.[167] Conversely, E bond interest accrued to date of testator's dealth is likly to be characterized as principal should it become subject to a testamentary trust.[168.1]

In most states this includes income earned on funds used to pay enforceable debts, taxes, and expenses of administration.[168] A specific devise of property or a specific legacy of property to a trustee carries with it the income earned on the property.[169] In some cases the settlor will create a trust by a general pecuniary legacy. When the executor distributes the pecuniary legacy to the trustee, the general rule has been that is the trustee is entitled to a proportionate share of the income earned by the estate during its administration, possibly without taking into account the residue's diminishing value occasioned by the payment of debts, taxes, and expenses.[170] When estate property is transferred to a trustee by the settlor's executor the trustee has a duty to review the executor's account to determine that the trust has received its share of

[166] *See* 3A Scott on Trusts §234.

[167] Id.; *see e.g.*, Old Colony Trust Co. v. Smith, 266 Mass. 500, 165 N.E. 657 (1929).

[168.1] *See* Estate of Berger, 696 So. 2d 412 (Fla. Dist. Ct. App. 1997).

[168] For a catalog of states where income earned by the assets of the estate used to pay debts, taxes, and administrative expenses is payable to the life beneficiary, see 3A Scott on Trusts §234.4 n.1. *See generally* Revised Uniform Principal and Income Act §5, 7B U.L.A. 160 (1985); *see,* D.E. Buckner, Annot., Allocation, as between Income and Principal of Income on Property Used in Paying Legacies, Debts and Expenses, 2 A.L.R.3d 1061 (1965).

[169] *See* 3A Scott on Trusts §234.1; *see, e.g.*, M.G.L. Ch. 197 §26.

[170] *See* 3A Scott on Trusts §§234.2, 234.4; but see §202(b)(1) of the Univorm Principal and Income Act (1997).

income.[171] Periodic rental, interest, and annuity payments that continue after the testator's death accrue on a daily basis.[172] Thus periodic payments accruing to the testator before his or her death are items of trust principal, and payments accruing afterward are items of trust income.[173] "In all other cases, any receipt from an income producing asset is income even though the receipt was earned or accrued in whole or in part before the date when the asset became subject to the trust."[174]

On termination of an income interest under a trust that is up and running, the beneficiary or his estate receives income then having been earned but undistributed.[175] If the day fixed by a corporation for determining which stockholders of record are entitled to a dividend comes before the termination date of the trust, the dividend goes to the beneficiary or the beneficiary's estate even though the dividend is not mailed out until after the termination date.[176] Unpaid rents, interest, and annuities accrue on a daily basis to the beneficiary up to the date of termination.[177] If the beneficiary's death triggers the termination, then accrued income will be paid to the beneficiary's estate.[178] These income accrual rules apply unless the settlor expressed a contrary intention in the governing instrument.[179] As most modern trust instruments will address the matter of undistributed and accrued income, the trustee is likely to find the answers to most accrual questions simply by reading the governing instrument.

### §6.2.4.6 Rethinking Traditional Principles of Income Allocation

The Drafting Committee of the National Conference of Commissioners on Uniform State Laws is redrafting the Revised Uni-

[171] *See generally* id. §177. *See also* Bogert, Trusts and Trustees §817 n.11.

[172] Revised Uniform Principal and Income Act §4(b)(2), 7B U.L.A. 157 (1985).

[173] Id.

[174] Id. §4(c).

[175] Id. §4(d).

[176] Id. §4(e).

[177] Id. §4(d).

[178] Restatement (Second) of Trusts §235A (1959).

[179] *See generally* 3A Scott on Trusts §234.

form Principal and Income Act-1962 (the "1962 Act").[180] The 1962 Act has been adopted, in one form or another, in 34 states.[181] It is expected that there will be modifications in the 1962 Act to accommodate "total return" or growth investment strategies. A portfolio's total return is the sum of income (*e.g.*, dividends, interest, and the like) and realized and unrealized capital gains.[182] Specifically, it is expected that the new act will give a trustee the power to reallocate between income and principal in order to compensate income beneficiaries for shifts in beneficial interest occasioned by the pursuit of certain "total return" and growth investment strategies. The new act would also mandate equitable adjustments absent an expression of contrary intent in the governing instrument.

### §6.2.4.7 The Non-Charitable Unitrust: Applying Income to Principal

It is not only in the charitable context that one sees the erosion of traditional principles of income segregation and allocation. In order to facilitate "total return" and growth investment strategies,[183] practitioners are beginning to draft non-charitable "unitrust" instruments. A typical "unitrust" calls for a trustee to apply all net trust accounting income to principal. The trustee then distributes to the life beneficiaries in a given year a fixed percentage (typically 5%) of the net market of the trust estate valued at the end of the prior year. There are many variations on the theme.[184]

[180] *See generally* Schaengold, New Uniform Principal and Income Act in Progress, 133 Tr. & Est. 42 (1994).

[181] Revised Uniform Principal and Income Act-1962, 7B U.L.A. 1 (West Supp. 1997).

[182] *See generally* Dobris, New Forms of Private Trusts for the Twenty-First Century — Principal and Income, 31 Real Prop. Prob. & Tr. J. 1 (Spring 1996).

[183] *See generally* §6.2.2.1 (The Harvard College Prudent Man Rule and Its Progeny).

[184] *See* Wolf, Defeating the Duty to Disappoint Equally — the Total Return Trust, 23 ACTEC Notes 46 (1997). *See, however,* Dobris, Why Do Trustee Investors Often Prefer Dividends, 32 Real Prop. Prob. & Tr. J. 255, No. 2 (1997).

### §6.2.5 *Duty of Impartiality*

A difficult aspect of the trustee's general duty of loyalty is the specific duty to treat all beneficiaries impartially, that is, not to favor one beneficiary over another unless authorized to do so by the governing instrument.[185] And even when so authorized the trustee's discretionary acts favoring one beneficiary over another must be in furtherance of the intentions of the settlor, not in furtherance of the trustee's own biases and predilections.[186] In a dispute between two parties claiming to be beneficiaries, a trustee may not advocate for either side or assume the validity of either side's position.[187]

The trustee runs a major risk of breaching the duty of impartiality in the context of the competing interests of income beneficiaries and remaindermen.[188] In the absence of the settlor's contrary intention, the trustee has a duty to separate income from principal and then to distribute the net income to the income beneficiary and eventually to turn over the principal free of trust to the remaindermen.[189] This is implied by the trustee's general duty to carry out the terms of the trust. The general duty of loyalty however, requires that the trustee balance the interests of the income beneficiaries and the remaindermen — in other words, *the trustee must be impartial when dealing with those with conflicting equitable interests.*[190] This is easier said than done: For example, who should bear the burden of the insurance premium, the income account or the principal account?[191] The difficulty in balancing competing equitable interests manifests itself most dramatically, however, in matters of *investment* and of *disclosure of information.*

With respect to investments, the trustee has traditionally

[185]2A Scott on Trusts §183; Restatement (Third) of Trusts §183 (1992).

[186]*Supra* note 176.

[187]In re Doris Duke Trust, 702 A.2d 1008, 1023-1024 (N.J. Super. Ch. 1995).

[188]3A Scott on Trusts §232; Restatement (Third) of Trusts §232 comment *b* (1992).

[189]*See* §6.2.4 (Duty to Separate Income from Principal and the Right to Income).

[190]2A Scott on Trusts §183; Restatement (Third) of Trusts §183 (1992).

[191]*See* §6.2.4.4 (What Expenses are Allocated Entirely to Income, Entirely to Principal, and Apportioned Between Income and Principal?).

walked a tightrope. Investing for maximum income may sacrifice growth, to the displeasure of the remainderman;[192] investing for maximum growth may cause the income beneficiary to complain.[193] This is an inevitable outgrowth of the traditional distinction between income and principal, a trust accounting concept that takes no account of the investment concept of *total return.*[194]

The *Harvard College* Prudent Man Rule and its progeny[195] acknowledge these conflicting interests and attempt to balance them. It was first enunciated at a time when the psychological wall between the income beneficiary and the remainderman was higher than it is today. Then, income-only trusts and use-only trusts involving land were the rule;[196] now, settlors tend to bestow on their trustees considerable discretionary authority, particularly the authority to invade principal for the benefit of the life beneficiary and to accumulate income for the benefit of the remaindermen.[197] Also, in the last 50 years the discretionary trust has come into its own,[198] bringing about some practical blurring of the distinctions between the life beneficiary and the remainderman. However it remains the general rule that a trustee has a duty to be impartial in investment matters.

[192] *See* Dennis v. Rhode Island Hosp. Trust Natl. Bank, 744 F.2d 893, 897 (1st Cir. 1984) (In holding the trustee liable to the remaindermen the court said: "[T]here is evidence that the trustee did little more than routinely agree to the requests of the trust's income beneficiaries that it manage the trust corpus to produce the largest possible income.").

[193] In in re Francis M. Johnson Trust, 211 Neb. 750, 320 N.W.2d 466, 469 (1982), the trustees held onto stock in a corporation that paid no dividends and upon dissolution of the corporation allocated a part of the gain to income. A minor beneficiary challenged the allocation. Although the court held the allocation to be a proper exercise of discretion, it did say: "Trustees may not, however, sacrifice income for the purpose of increasing the value of the principal of the trust."

[194] *See* Restatement (Third) of Trusts §227 comment *e* (1992); *see, however,* §6.2.4.6 (Rethinking Traditional Principles of Income Allocation), §6.2.2.4 (The Non-Charitable Unitrust: Investment Considerations) and §6.2.4.7 (The Non-Charitable Unitrust: Applying Income to Principal).

[195] *See* id.; Harvard College v. Amory, 26 Mass. (9 Pick.) 446, 461 (1830). *See also* 3 Scott on Trusts §227.

[196] Bogert, Trusts and Trustees §§5-8.

[197] *See generally* Restatement (Third) of Trusts §227 comment *i* (1992).

[198] 2A Scott on Trusts §155.

When it comes to the disclosure of information, the conflicting interests of the income class and the remainder class can put the trustee between a rock and a hard place. As we have seen, an incident of the trustee's general duty to account is the specific duty of disclosure,[199] while at the same time an incident of the trustee's general duty of loyalty is the specific duty of confidentiality.[200] What is a trustee to do if disclosures to the remainderman would violate the confidences of the income beneficiary? Suppose the income beneficiary's alcoholism was the basis for a proper exercise of the trustee's discretion to invade principal. Should the income beneficiary's medical history be disclosed to the remainderman? In theory the answer lies in another specific duty: the duty to balance the interests of the life beneficiary and the remainderman. Probably the best way out of this impasse is for the trustee to provide the remaindermen with only so much information about the income beneficiary as they need to protect their interest, in this case to determine whether the trustee has committed an abuse of discretion.[201] In the example at hand, what this means is harder to say. They are certainly not entitled to the medical file, but they should not be stonewalled either.

### *§6.2.6 Duty to Defend the Trust Against Attack; Duty Not to Attack the Trust*

The trustee has a duty to defend the trust.[202] The trust may be attacked by those who have an economic interest in bringing about its cancellation or termination.[203] It may be attacked by those who oppose its purposes.[204] To fail to mount a vigorous defense is to

[199] *See* §6.1.5 (Duty to Account to the Beneficiary).

[200] *See* §6.2.3 (Duty of Confidentiality).

[201] *See generally* Bogert, Trusts and Trustees §961; 2A Scott on Trusts §173; §8.8 (Whom Does Counsel Represent?).

[202] *See generally* Bogert, Trusts and Trustees §581; *see also* 2A Scott on Trusts §178.

[203] Id.

[204] Id.

thwart the intentions of the settlor and may be grounds for the trustee's removal. Moreover, the trustee would be liable to the beneficiaries for any injury occasioned by an unwarranted capitulation.[205]

However, if it is clear to a reasonable person who has sought and obtained independent, competent legal advice that an attack is warranted or that resistence would be futile, then a defense should not be mounted.[206] This exception would not apply when there is reasonable uncertainty as to the facts or the law.[207]

The trustee must do what is necessary within the bounds of law and reason to defend the trust and thus may retain counsel for that purpose and is entitled to have the costs of such representation absorbed by the trust.[208] All reasonable appeals should be taken.[209] The trustee who is unprepared to go the distance should seek to have the trusteeship transferred to someone who is. He probably should not have accepted the trust in the first place.

It goes without saying that the trustee, occupying a position of confidence, may not mount an attack against his own trust.[210] It has been said that the trustee, having accepted the trust, is "estopped" from setting up its invalidity.[211] At minimum, such acts of betrayal are grounds for removal.

## §6.3 Governmental Reporting Obligations

The trustee must be attentive to federal and state governmental reporting obligations. In addition to those obligations arising

[205]Id.

[206]Id.

[207]Id.

[208]Id.

[209]Id.; *see* P.H. Vartanian, Annot., Right of Trustee of Express Trust to Appeal from Order or Decree Not Affecting His Own Personal Interest, 6 A.L.R.2d 147 (1949).

[210]Id. *See general,* Bogert, Trusts and Trustees §581; *See also* 2A Scott on Trusts §178.

[211]Id.

under the tax and securities laws, the trustee of a pension trust may be required to file periodic reports with the Department of Labor; the trustee of a charitable trust with the state attorney general; the corporate trustee with the Comptroller of the Currency or state banking commissioner; and so forth. Do not forget property tax filings with City Hall and of course abatement notices. The list of governmental reports and filings is long and will vary from jurisdiction to jurisdiction. A caution is therefore in order: This handbook presents only a few of the more common reports and filings.

### *§6.3.1 Tax Filings*

**(a) Domestic Trusts.** After a trust becomes irrevocable it is likely to be treated as a separate taxable entity for federal and state tax purposes.[1] If the trust does not already have an Employer Identification Number at that time, one must be applied for on Form SS-4.[2] For any year in which the trust has taxable income or gross income exceeding $600, the trustee must file a federal fiduciary income tax return, Form 1041, on April 15 of the following year.[3] Beneficiaries are notified of taxable and nontaxable distributions on the form's Schedule K-1. While the K-1 must be in the hands of the beneficiaries by April 15, it is good practice for the trustee to do so sooner in order that the beneficiaries may prepare their own tax returns in a timely fashion. The trust's estimated tax payments are due April 15, June 15, September 15, and January 15.[4] The trust's federal income tax must be carefully estimated, since the trustee who substantially and negligently overpays may be personally liable for interest on the overpayment, while the consequences of substantially and negligently underpaying taxes

**§6.3** [1]In matters involving the income taxation of trusts, the trustee is referred to Ch. 10 of this handbook and Ferguson, Freeland & Ascher, Federal Income Taxation of Estates, Trusts, and Beneficiaries (2d ed. 1993). For state income taxation of trusts, *see* Gutierrez, Oops! The State Income Taxation of Multi-Jurisdictional Trusts, 25 U. Miami Est. Plan. Inst. ch 12 (1991).

[2]*See* 26 C.F.R. §301.6109-1 (1992).

[3]*See* Bogert, Trusts and Trustees §265.

[4]Id.

include personal liability for any penalties that may be assessed as a result of the underpayment. Further, many states impose a tax on the trust's taxable income. This may impose certain state tax reporting and payment obligations on the trustee. The matter of the income taxation of trusts is covered in greater depth in Chapter 10 of this handbook.

The generation-skipping tax on certain transfers is a relatively new tax which places additional tax-reporting burdens on trustees.[5] A federal GST tax payment obligation may arise upon one or more of the following events: (1) a trust's creation, (2) a trust's termination, and (3) a distribution of principal or income from a trust.[6] If either the trust itself or the recipient of the property interest enjoys an exemption, a federal GST tax may *not* be due.[7] The tax is generally separate from and independent of the federal estate, gift, and income tax. Under certain circumstances, the trustee may be obliged to file a GST tax return[8] as well as pay the tax due. For some GSTs, the trustee files an informational return and provides the recipient with data that the recipient will need to prepare the GST tax return and pay the tax. In matters related to the GST tax the prudent trustee communicates and coordinates with the settlor's executor and the trust beneficiaries as appropriate, and raises any cash needed to pay the tax in an orderly and timely fashion.

The trustee of an Individual Retirement Account or Simplified Employee Plan IRA (SEP-IRA) is required to make yearly reports to the IRS and to the taxpayer on the status of the account.[9] Employee benefit plan trustees must report distributions to participants on Form 1099-R.[10]

**(b) Foreign Trusts.** A U.S. person who creates a foreign trust

[5]I.R.C. §2601; *see generally* Stephens et al., Federal Estate and Gift Taxation ¶12.03[1] (6th ed. 1991).

[6]Id. at ¶13.02.

[7]Id.

[8]Id. at ¶18.02. For information on when and under what circumstances such returns must be filed, as well as other matters related to the federal generation-skipping-transfer tax, the trustee is referred to Stephens et al., *supra* note 5.

[9]*See* Treas. Reg. §§1.408-5-1.408-9.

[10]A complete list of federal tax forms (as well as the forms themselves) may be found in *IRS Forms,* published by Tax Management Inc., a subsidiary of the

or transfers property directly or indirectly to the trustee of a foreign trust must report to the IRS within 90 days the amount of money or other property transferred and the identity of the recipient trust, its trustees and its beneficiaries.[11] The death of a U.S. citizen who possessed a beneficial interest under a foreign trust is also a reportable event.[12] A U.S. person treated as the owner of a foreign trust under the foreign grantor trust rules must ensure that the trustee files an annual report with the IRS.[13] A U.S. person yearly must report to the IRS all distributions made to him or to her from foreign trusts.[14]

### *§6.3.2 SEC Filings*

When the trust acquires voting rights or a power of disposition over more than five percent of a class of registered securities, the trustee *may* have to report the event to the Securities and Exchange Commission, the issuer, and each exchange on which the security is traded.[15] The same may be necessary when the trust acquires voting rights or a power of disposition over more than ten percent of a class of registered securities.[16] As to whether the trustee, himself, need register with the Commission as an investment advisor, *see* §8.15.10 (The Loring Exemption).

---

Bureau of National Affairs, Inc., 1231 25th St. NW, Washington D.C. 20037-1197 (1-800-372-1033).

[11]I.R.C. §6048(a). The penalty for failure to report the transfer to a foreign trust is 35 percent of the gross value of the transfer. *See* I.R.C. §6677(a). Additional penalties may be levied as well for chronic failure to report. *See* I.R.C. §6677(a)(2).

[12]I.R.C. §6048(a).

[13]I.R.C. §6048(b)(1)(A). The penalty for failing to file the annual report on the foreign trust is five percent of the value of the portion of the trust assets treated as owned by the U.S. person. *See* I.R.C. §6677(b), (c). Additional penalties may be levied as well for chronic failure to report. *See* I.R.C. §6677(a)(2).

[14]I.R.C. §6048(c)(1). The penalty for failure to report a distribution is 35 percent of the gross amount. I.R.C. §6677(a), (c). Additional penalties may be levied as well for chronic failure to report. *See* I.R.C. §6677(a)(2).

[15]*See generally* American Bar Association, A Fiduciary's Guide to Federal Securities Laws (1994).

[16]Id.

### *§6.3.3 Bank Regulatory Filings*

Each national bank that exercises fiduciary powers must periodically submit reports to a myriad of governmental agencies,[17] including the Comptroller of the Currency.

[17] *See* Victor P. Whitney, 2 Trust Dept. Admin. & Operations §15.20 (1995) for a list of these reports.

CHAPTER 7

# The Trustee's Liabilities



## §7.1 Trustee's Liabilities Generally

The trustee is liable to the beneficiary for injury caused by negligent and intentional breaches of trust. There are some breaches, however, for which the trustee may be held absolutely liable even when acting in good faith. The trustee, for example, is absolutely liable for injury to the beneficiary's equitable interest occasioned by misdelivery[1] or by the trustee's misconstruing the nature and extent of the trustee's powers.[2] There are also some

**§7.1** [1] *See* Restatement (Second) of Trusts §226 comments *a, b* (1959).

[2] *See* Restatement (Second) of Trusts §201 comment *b* (1959); *see,* R.D. Hursh, Annot., Trustee's Liability for Payments of Trust Funds to One Whose Interest Has Terminated, 48 A.L.R.2d 1252 (1956).

breaches for which the trustee may be held liable even in the absence of a causal connection between the injury and the breach,[3] such as the failure to segregate and earmark[4] and engaging in unauthorized acts of self-dealing. As a general rule, however, the trustee is not liable to the beneficiary if the trust sustains economic injury (*e.g.*, investment losses or poor investment performance) unless there has been a breach of trust.

Under the common law, the trustee, as holder of the legal title to the trust property, is liable in contract and in tort to nonbeneficiaries as if the trustee were the absolute owner of the property,[5] although under certain circumstances indemnification and reimbursement from the trust estate for such third-party liability may be possible.[6]

## §7.2 Trustee's Liability as Fiduciary to the Beneficiary

The trustee is accountable to the beneficiary for breaches of fiduciary duties. These duties are enumerated and discussed in Chapter 6 of this handbook. Much difficulty could be avoided if the trustee took the time to learn each of these many duties. Specificity is the key. A general uninformed concern about "fiduciary duty" will not keep the trustee out of trouble. On the other hand, the beneficiary who puts forth the general allegation of "breach of fiduciary duty" should be called upon to elaborate. Which duty? How was it breached? Was the breach intentional or negligent?

The remedies available to the beneficiary are not available to a stranger to the trust. They are available, however, to anyone

[3] *See generally* 3 Scott on Trusts §205.1.

[4] *See* Restatement (Third) of Trusts §205 comment *f* (1992).

[5] *See generally* Bogert, Trusts and Trustees §712 (contractual liability), §731 (tort liability); Restatement (Second) of Trusts §261 (1959); 3A Scott on Trusts §261; *see generally* §3.5.1 (Nature and Extent of the Trustee's Estate).

[6] *See* §3.5.2.3 (Right in Equity to Exoneration and Reimbursement).

having a right to represent the interest of the beneficiary, including an assignee or a creditor with a lien.[1] Even persons to whom income or principal is payable at the discretion of the trustee would have standing to bring the matter of the trustee's abuse of discretion before the court.[2] If the trustee refuses to sue or defend on behalf of the trust estate, the beneficiary may proceed against the trustee and the third party as codefendants, but the trustee must be shown to be in default.[3]

### §7.2.1 *Intentional Breaches*

In the world of trusts, an intentional breach is usually two breaches: a breach of the duty of loyalty coupled with some other breach. For example, when a trustee without authority borrows from the trust estate at no interest, both the duty of loyalty *and* the duty to make the trust property productive have been breached, as well as the duty to segregate and earmark. The breach of the duty of loyalty never travels alone. Moreover, the element of self-dealing tends to make the associated breach a continuing one. Thus the self-dealing menu of damage theories may be more extensive than the negligence menu.[4]

### §7.2.2 *Negligent Breaches*

Like the intentional breach, the negligent breach is actually two or more breaches: a breach of the duty to be generally prudent in conducting the affairs of the trust coupled with some other breach. Let us assume, for example, that the trustee negligently makes an unauthorized distribution of principal to an income

**§7.2** [1]*See* Bogert, Trusts and Trustees §970 (creditor of beneficiary or of trust itself has standing to demand an accounting); 3 Scott on Trusts §200.

[2]*See* Bogert, Trusts and Trustees §871 n.10 and accompanying text; *see generally* 2 Scott on Trusts §128.3.

[3]*See* Bogert, Trusts and Trustees §869 n.35 and accompanying text.

[4]*See* 3 Scott on Trusts §205.1.

beneficiary. Here the trustee has breached both the duty to be prudent and the duty to carry out the terms of the trust.

## *§7.2.3 Types of Relief*

If the trustee commits an intentional breach or falls below the required standard of care, the law seeks to place the beneficiary at least in the position that would have been occupied had there been no breach of trust. The liabilities imposed upon the defaulting trustee are designed to attain this objective and are not necessarily mutually exclusive.

### §7.2.3.1 Tracing and Accounting for Proceeds and Profits

It is fundamental that the trust property and any income earned on it be kept within the trustee's control.[5] This obligation extends not only to the property in its original form but to any new form into which it has been changed or converted. For example, if the trustee, in breach of trust, allows the trust property to pass to a purchaser for value who is innocently unaware of the beneficiary's equitable interest in the property, then the purchaser is entitled to keep the property.[6] The trustee may be accountable to the beneficiary for the proceeds and liable for damages, but if the transferee is not a bona fide purchaser for value, then the beneficiary is entitled to have the property (if traceable) returned to the trust.[7] If the property is not traceable, then the trust is entitled to a recovery of the proceeds. Recovery is usually effected judicially by the imposition of a constructive trust upon the proceeds.

[5] *See generally* 2A Scott on Trusts §175; §6.2.1.2 (Duty to Segregate and Earmark Trust Property).

[6] *See* Restatement (Second) of Trusts §284 (1959); §8.3.2 (Purchasers for Value of Trust Property).

[7] *See generally* Bogert, Trusts and Trustees §§866, 921, 922; §8.3.2 (Purchasers for Value of Trust Property).

A plaintiff seeking relief for the misappropriation of property may prefer a return to the status quo to money damages and thus may assert that the wrongdoer is a constructive trustee in the hopes of having the property traced and retrieved. Even if the plaintiff is successful in asserting a trust relationship, however, the property must still be identified with reasonable precision if tracing is to be an available option.[8] If by ordinary accounting methods the beneficiary can show that trust cash has been deposited to the personal bank account of the trustee a lien may be placed upon all the funds in the account.[9]

All profits gained by use of the trust fund belong to the trust estate and not to the trustee. This is true whether the profits have been gained rightfully or wrongfully. "The principle is that, in the management of a trust, the trustee may lose but cannot gain."[10]

### §7.2.3.2 Damages

The wronged beneficiary is not necessarily limited to the remedy of tracing and recovery. If tracing is impractical, damages from the trustee's personal assets may be sought. As a general rule, damages would be computed on the basis of any loss occasioned by a breach to include the value of any subsequent earnings and gains which would have accrued to the trust were it not for the breach and to include interest thereon if appropriate.[11] An improper delay on the part of the trustee in liquidating an investment is the type of breach for which the remedy of damages may be appropriate.

The matter of improper delay in selling provides a useful illustration of how the introduction of an element of self-dealing into a fact pattern could provide the plaintiff-beneficiary with a

[8] *See* id. §921.

[9] *See generally* id. §924.

[10] Baker v. Disbrow, 18 Hun 29, 30 (1879), *aff'd mem.* 79 N.Y. 631 (1880).

[11] *See generally* Bogert, Trusts and Trustees §862; for a discussion of when compound interest, as opposed to simple interest, is appropriate, *see* Bogert, Trusts and Trustees §863; *see e.g.*, Matter of Judicial Settlement of Account of Lincoln First Bank, NA 223 A.D.2d 20, 643 N.Y.S.2d 972 (Allowing for compounding of interest).

theory of damages more generous than would otherwise be available in a simple negligence context. Let us assume that the trust owns 20 percent of the stock of a company and the trustee personally owns 10 percent of the same stock. Let us also assume that there is a rising market and the trustee negligently allows the stock to ride up in value to the point where it comprises 50 percent of the trust's portfolio. It is clear that, as the stock grows as an ever-larger percentage of the value of the trust portfolio, a prudent trustee, concerned about inadequate diversification, would have been chipping away at the stock unless the settlor had given clear express or implied retention instructions.[12]

Suppose the stock then gradually loses its value, with the company eventually going bankrupt at the bottom of the value curve. The portfolio has lost 50 percent of its value. A trustee who negligently (or in trust parlance, imprudently) retains a certain stock in a declining market is liable for the difference between the depressed value of the stock and the economic value that would have accrued to the trust if the stock were prudently liquidated and the proceeds then prudently invested.[13] This hypothetical "prudent liquidation" point is likely to be fixed somewhere between the highest and lowest point on the stock's value curve. If, on the other hand, the improper retention is occasioned by an act of self-dealing — perhaps part of the trustee's effort to buttress the price of the trustee's own holding in the stock — then the hypothetical "prudent liquidation" point might be fixed on the value line closer to the top of the curve.[14] If the trustee intentionally declined to diversify when the stock reached its highest price because of the effect sales would have on the trustee's own holding, then the beneficiary is entitled to damages computed as if the stock were sold at its highest price. After all, if the trustee had liquidated the stock and embezzled the proceeds, then the trustee would be expected to return the economic value that was lost to the trust at the time of the embezzlement; can it not be said that

[12] *But see* 3 Scott on Trusts §231.

[13] *See generally* 3 Scott on Trusts §§209, 230.

[14] *Cf.* Restatement (Second) of Trusts §179 comment *d* (1959) (trustee absolutely liable for any losses occasioned trust during period when trustee failed in bad faith to earmark).

our hypothetical trustee has appropriated the trust's stock to his own use when — in order to protect the price of his personal holding — the trustee fails to diversify?

Trustees may not reduce their liability for a breach of trust with a gain from a separate and distinct breach of trust.[15] If, however, a trustee makes a profit and also suffers a loss through the *same* breach of trust, the beneficiaries are entitled only to the amount of the profit less the amount of the loss or they may charge the trustee with the loss reduced by the amount of the profit.[16]

### §7.2.3.3 Punitive or Exemplary Damages

The courts of equity had no power to award punitive damages. It therefore followed that an award of damages for breach of fiduciary duty could not have a punitive element to it, the office of trustee itself being a creature of equity.[17] The absence of any mention of punitive damages in the Restatement of Trusts would tend to suggest that this is the modern state of the law as well. Recently, however, courts have begun to assess punitive damages against trustees and these assessments are being upheld, particularly in cases where the breach of fiduciary duty involves fraud or malice.[18] Courts, however, have always considered it within their equitable powers to reduce or deny compensation — and reimbursement for expenses as well — to trustees who are held to be in breach of trust.[19]

[15] *See* Restatement (Third) of Trusts §213 (1992).

[16] Id.

[17] *See generally* 22 Am. Jur. 2d *Equity* §738 (1990).

[18] *See* Bogert, Trusts and Trustees §862 n.34 and accompanying text; *see also* 3 Scott on Trusts §205 n.1 and accompanying text; *see generally* Campisi et. al., Emerging Damages Claims and the Right to Jury Trials in Fiduciary Litigation, 27 Real Prop. Prob. & Tr. J. 541, 542-553 (1992) (containing a review of availability of punitive damages and appreciation damages in fiduciary litigation in the various states); *see, e.g.,* InterFirst Bank of Dallas, N.A. v. Risser, 739 S.W.2d 882 (Tex. 1987) ($10 million in punitive damages assessed against trustee bank which sold trust property to a debtor of the bank).

[19] *See* Bogert, Trusts and Trustees §861 n.60 and accompanying text; *see also* Restatement (Third) of Trusts §205 comment *a* (1992).

#### §7.2.3.4 Injunction and Specific Enforcement

The beneficiaries' rights are fundamentally equitable; their remedies are correspondingly broad. They include: the right to a decree of specific performance, injunction, restitution, general accounting, the appointment of a receiver, and removal of the trustee.[20] Moreover, equity will impel a court that has taken jurisdiction to retain jurisdiction until the entire matter is "cleaned up" once and for all.

#### §7.2.3.5 Statutory Penalties Accruing to Beneficiaries

The trustee must monitor not only developments in the common law of trusts but also in the judicial construction of certain criminal and civil statutes that perhaps were not written with the personal trust in mind. The racketeering and consumer protection statutes should be of particular concern because of their generous treble damage provisions. Such provisions provide the trial bar with an economic incentive to take on the smaller breach of fiduciary duty cases.

**(a) Consumer protection.** In suits by beneficiaries against professional trustees,[21] it is now common practice to allege violations of the consumer protection statutes, which in some jurisdictions can bring treble damage recoveries to successful consumer-beneficiaries.[22] The defendant professional trustee should take such allegations particularly seriously when they are made by settlors of funded revocable trusts. This is because the professional trustee of such a trust is likely to have, or have had, a contractual relationship with the settlor and because the professional trustee advertises fiduciary services to the public.

[20] *See generally* Bogert, Trusts and Trustees §861.

[21] *See* §7.3.3.1 (Consumer Protection); *see generally* 17 Am. Jur. 2d *Consumer Protection* §§280-305 (1990).

[22] *See generally* Sovern, Deceptive Trade Practices, 52 Ohio St. L.J. 437, 448 n.66 and accompanying text (1991).

Apart from matters of litigation, there are innumberable consumer-oriented laws and regulations governing transactions between the trustee and the settlor and the trustee and beneficiary. At the point when a trust is established, for example, the trustee may be required to make certain disclosures to the settlor such as the trustee's prevailing fee structure.

**(b) RICO.** In suits by beneficiaries against trustees for breaches of fiduciary duty, it is now not unusual to see a count alleging that the trustee engaged in a pattern of racketeering activity in violation of Title IX of the Organized Crime Control Act of 1970 (the "RICO Statute").[23] A successful civil RICO action against a trustee could result in the beneficiary being awarded treble damages.[24] In addition to the federal RICO statute, over 20 states now have "little RICO" statutes.[25]

### §7.2.3.6 Removal

The court will remove a trustee if it is in the interest of the trust to do so.[26] Removal may be ordered because of hostility between the trustee and a beneficiary or a cotrustee, although relief has been denied if the trustee's duties are essentially ministerial or if the proper administration of the trust is not jeopardized by the hostility.[27] Hostility alone, however, is not grounds for removal.[28]

The court has removed trustees, or said that it would do so, for the following reasons: insanity, habitual drunkenness, crimi-

[23] "Racketeer-Influenced and Corrupt Organizations," 18 U.S.C. §§1961-1968 (1988); *see generally* D. Abrams, The Law of Civil RICO (1991).

[24] 18 U.S.C. §1964; *see generally* 31A Am. Jur. 2d *Extortion, Blackmail* §227 (1989).

[25] *See generally* id. §§241-259.

[26] *See* Restatement (Second) of Trusts §107 comment *a* (1959). *See also* 2 Scott on Trusts §107; *see generally,* E. Le Fevre, Annot., Removal of trustee of voting trust, 34 A.L.R.2d 1136 (1954).

[27] *See* Bogert, Trusts and Trustees §527; *see, e.g.,* Symmons v. O'Keeffe, 419 Mass. 288, 644 N.E.2d 631 (1995). (The mere fact that there is friction or hostility between the trustee and beneficiaries is not necessarily a sufficient ground for removal, because otherwise the beneficiaries would be quarreling with the trustee with the intent of forcing his removal).

[28] Id.

nality involving moral turpitude, failure to obey trust-related court orders, thwarting the purposes of the trust, chronic inactivity, unauthorized commingling, failure to account, a personal interest adverse to the trust, the taking of excessive and unauthorized compensation, and embezzlement, as well as a myriad of other serious and material breaches of trust too numerous to mention here.[29] Most jurisdictions have statutes covering one or more of the above cases.[30]

The court has declined to remove trustees for the following causes: irregularity in the way a trustee was appointed, personal insolvency, nonresidency, good faith error in judgment, and isolated acts of negligence.[31]

By the terms of the trust instrument, power to remove the trustee may be lodged in one or more individuals. A power granted to a beneficiary or some other person to terminate the trust has been said to involve a power to remove the trustee.[32] The trustee of an irrevocable trust should be aware that the retained power in a settlor (or the power in a beneficiary) to remove and replace the trustee may, under certain circumstances, subject the trust property to estate taxes upon the power holder's death.[33]

### §7.2.4 *Cofiduciary and Predecessor Liability and Contribution*

The trustee will be liable for an improper delegation of a duty;[34] on the other hand, it is well settled that a trustee is not responsible for a cotrustee's breach of trust unless the trustee participated in, approved, acquiesced in, or concealed the breach, or failed to take what steps were necessary to compel the co-trustee

[29] Id.; 2 Scott on Trusts §107.

[30] *See generally* Bogert, Trusts and Trustees §527 nn.7, 8; 2 Scott on Trusts §107 n.22; *see, e.g.*, Cal. Prob. Code §15642 (West 1994) (court may remove trustee for, among other things, excessive compensation, failure to act, and insolvency).

[31] *See generally* Bogert, Trusts and Trustees §527.

[32] *See* 2 Scott on Trusts §107.3. *See also* Restatement (Second) of Trusts §107 comment *i* (1959).

[33] *See generally* Estate of Wall v. Commissioner, 101 T.C. 300 (1993); Rev. Rul. 95-58, 1995-36 I.R.B. 16.

[34] *See* Restatement (Third) of Trusts §171 (1992).

to redress the breach.[35] "If several trustees unite in a breach of trust, they are jointly and severally liable and the entire claim of the beneficiary may be satisfied from the property of one trustee."[36] A trustee who has made good a loss occasioned by a breach of trust is entitled to contribution from those cotrustees participating in the wrong,[37] but in this day and age a professional trustee may well find it difficult to persuade a court to order a participating "amateur" cotrustee to make contribution.[38]

It long has been stated as the general rule that the successor trustee is in no way liable for the acts of the predecessor.[39] This statement undoubtedly is correct, but there is an equally well-settled rule that the successor trustee has a positive duty, upon taking over the trust estate, to see that the predecessor has properly accounted for the whole of it. Indeed, failure to prosecute any claim that may exist against the predecessor may constitute a breach of trust on the part of the successor.[40] Moreover, with the array of criminal statutes on the books covering everything from money laundering to hazardous waste, the successor trustee now more than ever cannot afford to dispense with an examination into the doings of his predecessor in office and into the condition of the trust property, particularly if it is real property. Due diligence is the order of the day.

At minimum, the successor should require an accounting if one has not been formally made.[41] Copies of the fiduciary income tax returns for the previous three years should be scrutinized. If the property is coming from the settlor's estate the successor should also obtain copies of federal and state estate tax returns. This matter is of growing practical importance especially since so many inter vivos trusts are conducted without formal accountings. The person pro-

[35]*See* Restatement (Second) of Trusts §224 (1959); *see* Lee R. Russ, J.D., Annot., Award of Attorneys' Fees Out of Trust Estate in Action by Trustee Against Cotrustee, 24 A.L.R.4th 624 (1983), *see also* F.M. English, Annot., Right of Coexecutor or Trustee to Retain Independent Legal Counsel, 66 A.L.R.2d 1169 (1959).

[36]Bogert, Trusts and Trustees §862 n.25 and accompanying text.

[37]Id. §862 n.29 and accompanying text.

[38]*See generally* Restatement (Third) of Trusts §227 comment *d* (1992).

[39]*See* Restatement (Second) of Trusts §223 (1959).

[40]*See* id. §223 comment *d*; §6.2.1.1 (Duty to Take Active Control of Trust Property).

[41]*See generally*, §6.2.2.2 (The Prudent Investor's Code of Conduct).

posed as successor trustee should insist, whenever it is reasonably possible, that accounts of the predecessor be made up and allowed or the assents obtained as provided in the trust instrument. Furthermore, it is often possible (and always desirable) to require that unsuitable holdings in the trust portfolio be removed before the succession is completed, or at least marked for very early removal after the succession. It is of little importance to a successor trustee whether the theoretical basis for surcharge is the predecessor's malfeasance or the successor's nonfeasance in prosecuting the trust's just claims against the predecessor. Moreover the bringing of a suit against a predecessor may have unpleasant collateral social and financial consequences for the successor, particularly if the predecessor is a relative, friend, business associate, or customer of the successor. The prudent person makes certain, before succeeding to the trust office, that all things are in order, and does not rely on any express language in the governing instrument purporting to relieve a successor of the duty to investigate the acts of the predecessor.

### §7.2.5 *Insurance and Indemnification for Liability Arising Out of a Breach of Fiduciary Duty to the Beneficiary*

Unless the trustee is an attorney or a bank, fiduciary liability insurance will be exceedingly difficult, if not impossible, to obtain for coverage for breaches of fiduciary duty; if it *is* obtained, the premium costs must be borne personally by the trustee[42] and not by the trust estate. Moreover, it goes without saying that a trustee may not be indemnified from the trust estate for an adverse judgment arising out of a breach of fiduciary duty.

### §7.2.6 *Exculpatory Provisions Covering Breach of Fiduciary Duties to the Beneficiary*

Many trust instruments contain provisions that purport to limit the trustee's liabilities to the beneficiary. In New York such provi-

[42] *See* §3.5.4.2 *See also* Bogert, Trusts and Trustees §599 (Insuring Against Personal Liability).

sions in testamentary trusts are void as against public policy.[43] In those jurisdictions where they are not, courts will go only so far in giving them force and effect.[44] As a general rule, anything beyond exculpation for ordinary negligence is of doubtful validity.[45] No provision, for example, can relieve a trustee from liability for a breach of the duty of loyalty. Nor can a trustee hide behind a provision that has been improperly inserted.[46]

An issue of the improper insertion of an exculpatory provision is likely to come up when the drafting attorney is also the named trustee.[47] When the attorney-trustee drafts into the instrument a provision limiting liability, there is at best an appearance of impropriety and conflict of interest. After all, he has a duty to represent the interests of the settlor, his client — not his own interests. In situations where the drafting attorney is the named trustee, the best practice is for the attorney to insist that the settlor seek competent, independent legal advice on the matter of trustee exculpation.[48] The benefit to the settlor is self-evident; the benefit to the trustee is that the exculpation is less vulnerable to attack than it would be otherwise. The next best practice is for the attorney to fully disclose to the settlor the existence and import of such a provision.[49] In no event should the drafting attorney casually dismiss as mere boilerplate an exculpatory provision — neither in practice nor in response to client inquiries.[50] That practice is unacceptable.

[43] *See generally* Whitman, Exoneration Clauses in Wills and Trust Instruments, 4 Hofstra Prop. L.J. 123 (1992); Bogert, Trusts and Trustees §542; 3 Scott on Trusts §222; Restatement (second) of Trusts §222 (1959).

[44] Id.

[45] Id.

[46] *See generally* Elizabeth A. Reece, Exculpatory Clauses Inserted in Trusts by the Attorney/Fiduciary, Exhibit B (Apr. 5, 1995) (51-jurisdiction survey of the effectiveness of exculpatory clauses) (unpublished study, available from author at Fleet National Bank, Boston, Massachusetts, (617) 346-2593). *See also* Young, Exculpatory Clauses, 13 Prob. L.J. 63 (1995).

[47] *See* Restatement (Second) of Trusts §222, comment *d* (1959).

[48] Id.

[49] *See* Marsman v. Nasca, 30 Mass. App. 789, 573 N.E.2d 1025 (1991), *review denied*, 411 Mass. 1102, 579 N.E.2d 1361 (1991) (exculpatory clause upheld in face of unrefuted testimony that the settlor asked the attorney-trustee to insert the clause).

[50] *See* Jonathan v. Irving Trust Co., 151 Misc. 107, 270 N.Y. Supp. 721 (1934), *aff'd*, 243 A.D. 691, 277 N.Y.S. 955 (1935); *see generally* Rutanen v. Ballard, 424 Mass. 723, 678 N.E.2d 133 (1997) (Citing §7.2.6 of this handbook).

While there are important similarities between the charitable trust and the charitable corporation,[51] fiduciary exculpation is one area where there is a fundamental difference. *Settlors* of charitable trusts generally control the insertion of exculpatory provisions into trust instruments, not the trustees. When it comes to charitable corporations, however, it is the *directors* — the fiduciaries themselves — who generally have authority, by statute,[52] to determine whether there is fiduciary exculpation.

### §7.2.7 *Beneficiary Consent, Ratification, and Release*

The beneficiary's informed consent, ratification, or release is sufficient to discharge the trustee from liability to the beneficiary for breaches of trust.[53] The trustee must understand that the term *beneficiary* means *all* the beneficiaries: those with remainder interests as well as those with income interests; those with contingent interests as well as those whose interests have vested.[54] The matter of the limitation of a trustee's liability to the beneficiary through the beneficiary's own actions or inactions is covered elsewhere in this handbook.[55]

### §7.2.8 *Liability Without Economic Injury to the Beneficiary*

A trustee is liable for intentional breaches of trust, whether or not the breach caused economic injury to the trust. This is particularly the case when it comes to breaches of the duty of loyalty. Lack of economic injury is no more a defense to a trustee's breach of the duty of loyalty than is the failure to steal a defense to the crime

[51] *See* §9.8.1 (The Charitable Corporation).

[52] *See* Revised Model Nonprofit Corporation Act Subchapter E comment 1 (1987); *see also* Moody, State Statutes Governing Directors of Charitable Corporations, 18 U.S.F. L. Rev. 749, 782-783 (1984) (tabulating state indemnification provisions applicable to nonprofit corporations).

[53] *See* Restatement (Second) of Trusts §§216-218 (1959).

[54] *See generally* 3 Scott on Trusts §216.2.

[55] *See* §5.5 (Loss of the Beneficiary's Rights).

of breaking and entering. While money damages may not be an available remedy in the absence of economic harm, there is always injunction, removal, and assessment of costs — and possibly even criminal sanction.[56]

Negligent breaches also can bring liability without economic injury. Let us take, for example, the trustee who negligently concentrates the trust estate in only one stock. Last year the stock's performance was well below the market average; this year its performance is, and continues to be, well above the market average. The beneficiary, concerned that the portfolio is at an unacceptable level of risk, retains counsel who finally manages either by litigation or negotiation to get the trustee to diversify. While ultimately the trust suffered no resulting economic injury, the trustee nonetheless was in breach of the duty to diversify. Thus while money damages may be inappropriate, it would be appropriate for the trustee personally to bear the burden of all legal fees and associated costs incurred by the beneficiary and others in getting the trustee to prudently diversify.[57] Had the trustee sold when the stock was down, there would have been realized losses that could have formed the basis for an assessment of damages.[58] There is some irony here. Had the stock been sold in a down market in a conscientious — albeit belated — effort to carry out the duty to diversify, the trustee's liability could well be keyed to those losses.[59]

### §7.2.9 *Personal Liability of Trust Officers*

There are instances where trust officers have been sued personally, along with their corporate employers, for breaches of

[56] *But see* Bogert, Trusts and Trustees §861 n.57 and accompanying text.

[57] *See generally* §8.13 (In litigation Pertaining to a Trust, When Is the Beneficiary Entitled to Reimbursement from the Trust Estate for Legal Fees?)

[58] *See* Restatement (Third) of Trusts §205 (1992).

[59] In one case, a bank trustee was held liable for the failure to diversify even though "the value of the trust principal increased and 'substantial income' was earned throughout the bank's tenure as trustee." First Alabama Bank of Huntsville, N.A. v. Spragins, 515 So. 2d 962 (Ala. 1987). Liability was based on the difference between the actual increase and the increase that might have been achieved with a diversified portfolio. *See also* Restatement (Third) of Trusts §§209-211 (1992).

fiduciary duty, notwithstanding the fact that the corporate employer was the named trustee. True, the trust company may be held liable for the acts of the trust officer under the doctrine of respondeat superior. It does not follow from this, however, that the trust officer is then relieved of liability.[60] A trust officer is at some financial risk if the trust company does not carry employee liability insurance; the trust company is financially weak, bankrupt or otherwise unable or unwilling to indemnify the trust officer; or the trust officer's homeowner's policy does not cover acts performed in the course of employment.

## §7.3 Trustee's Liability as Legal Owner to Nonbeneficiaries

It has been seen that the trustee, so far as concerns the outside world, is the owner of the trust property and that the duty to account to the beneficiary is primarily an internal matter.[1] It follows that in dealing with strangers the trustee is the responsible party, even though the trustee has no beneficial interest in the trust property. It is still ill-advised to regard the trustee as an agent or to assume that the trust estate or beneficiary will be primarily liable; for the most part the trustee has full and primary liability.[2] The beneficiary ordinarily has no liability, except in the case where the trustee has been stripped of substantial control over management of the trust property and the law of the jurisdiction finds the essence of the relationship to be that of principal-agent.[3]

[60] *See* Bogert, Trusts and Trustees §901 n.10 and accompanying text; 4 Scott on Trusts §326.3.

**§7.3** [1] *See* §3.5.1 (Nature and Extent of Trustee's Estate).

[2] *See generally* Restatement (Second) of Trusts §261 (1959) and §3.5 (Trustee's Relationship to the Trust Estate). In recent years, in matters of delegation and third party claims, the trust has begun to take on some corporate-like aspects. *See generally,* Curtis, The Transmogrification of the American Trust, 31 Real Prop., Prob. & Tr. J. 251 (1996).

[3] *See* Bogert, Trusts and Trustees §§247E-247F (discussing the liability of beneficiaries of certain business trusts); §9.6 (Trusts That Resemble Corporations or Agencies).

Because the trustee must bear this burden of full personal responsibility and because all gains must accrue to the trust estate, the trustee who has acted properly is given certain rights against the trust estate. These rights are equitable in nature and include the right of reimbursement and exoneration.[4] In cases where the creditor, whether in contract or in tort, finds difficulty in collecting directly from the trustee, may the trust estate be reached instead? Or should the creditor be limited, by subrogation, to whatever rights of indemnity the trustee may have? These and other such questions are considered below. However, it should be noted:

> Where a liability to third persons is imposed upon a person, not as a result of a contract made by him or a tort committed by him but because he is the holder of the title to the trust property, a trustee as holder of the title to the trust property is subject to personal liability, but only to the extent to which the trust estate is sufficient to indemnify him.[5]

### *§7.3.1 Liability as Legal Owner in Contract to Nonbeneficiaries*

Under the common law, when the trustee enters into a contract with a nonbeneficiary, even though he does so rightfully and on behalf of the trust estate, it nevertheless is the trustee's contract and not that of the trust estate.[6] Thus, a suit at law upon the contract is against the trustee personally; judgment issues against the trustee individually;[7] execution upon such a judgment cannot issue against the trust assets.[8] Trust assets can be reached upon execution only through subrogation to whatever equitable rights of indemnity the trustee may have against the trust estate.[9] In some

[4] *See* Restatement (Second) of Trusts §244 (1959); §3.5.2.3 (Right in Equity to Exoneration and Reimbursement).

[5] Id. (Restatement) §265.

[6] Bogert, Trusts and Trustees §712.

[7] Id.

[8] Id.

[9] Id. §716.

jurisdictions, however, either by statute or on different theories of law, the trust assets may be reached directly.[10]

The creditor's access to the trust estate will be measured strictly by the extent of the trustee's authority to act.[11] It follows that a creditor who intends to contract with the trustee should ascertain that the trustee has the authority to enter into the transaction on behalf of the trust. In the absence of such authority, the creditor may only look to the trustee's personal assets. Thus the prudent prospective creditor calls for the trust instrument and examines its provisions. Even when the trustee lacks the authority to enter into a particular contract on behalf of the trust, however, the creditor may look to the trust estate to the extent the trust benefits from the transaction.[12]

### *§7.3.2 Agreements with Nonbeneficiaries to Limit Contractual Liability*

The trustee may contractually limit personal liability in matters involving nonbeneficiaries[13] or have it limited to the extent of the trust estate.[14]

Thus a trustee may contract in such a way as to preclude personal liability by adding after his signature the qualification "as trustee, but not individually."[15] (With respect to negotiable instruments, a duly authorized trustee is not personally liable if he simply signs "as trustee," provided the instrument identifies

[10]Id. §712; *see* Curtis, The Transmogrification of the American Trust, 31 Real Prop. Prob. & Tr. J. 251 (1996) (Suggesting that the trend to allow direct actions against trustees in their representative capacities diminishes "the protections afforded trust assets and has fundamentally changed the relationship between the trustee, beneficiary, and other parties").

[11]*See* 3A Scott on Trusts §268.2.

[12]*See* id. §269.1.

[13]Id. §263.

[14]*See generally* Bogert, Trusts and Trustees §714 (rev. 2d ed. 1984). *But see* Restatement (Second) of Trusts §263, comment *a* (1959) (words "as trustee" or "as trustee for" without more may not be enough to limit the trustee's contractual personal liability).

[15]Restatement (Second) of Trusts §263 comment *a* (1959); *see generally* Uniform Commercial Code §3-403, 2A U.L.A. 22 (1991).

the trust.[16]) Trust instruments sometimes are recorded and often contain clauses exempting the trustee from personal liability;[17] in such cases a reference to the trust in the contract may suffice to do away with the trustee's liability.[18] Any creditor who is on actual notice of the existence of such a clause should be taken to have excused the trustee.[19] It will not do, however, in the present state of the law, for a trustee to rely upon a provision in the instrument of which the creditor has no notice.[20]

### §7.3.3 *Liability as Legal Owner in Tort to Nonbeneficiaries*

The trustee is as responsible for the torts which he commits in the course of administering the trust estate as he would be for those committed in the course of administering his own affairs.[21] Thus the trustee is personally liable to nonbeneficiaries for any injury to them occasioned by a failure to keep the trust property in proper repair.[22] Moreover, if servants are employed on behalf of the trust, the trustee's personal liability for their torts is determined exactly as though they were employed for the trustee's own affairs.[23] This liability is personal to the trustee; execution therefore runs against the trustee irrespective of whether he has a right to indemnity from the trust fund.[24] On the other hand, successor trustees do not succeed to this liability[25] nor is a trustee in bankruptcy necessarily liable for the torts of his agents.[26]

[16] *See* Uniform Commercial Code §3-403, 2A U.L.A. 22 (1991). *But see* 3A Scott on Trusts §263.1 n.2 and accompanying text.

[17] *See generally* Bogart, Trusts and Trustees §714.

[18] Id.

[19] Id.

[20] *See generally* 3A Scott on Trusts §263.2.

[21] *See* Restatement (Second) of Trusts §264 (1959).

[22] *See* 3A Scott on Trusts §264.

[23] *See* Restatement (Second) of Trusts §264 comment *b* (1959).

[24] *See generally* 3A Scott on Trusts §264.

[25] *See generally* Bogert, Trusts and Trustees §731 n.19 and accompanying text.

[26] *See generally* 3A Scott on Trusts §264; *but see* Bogart, Liability of Directors of Chapter 11 Debtors in Possession: "Don't Look Back — Something May Be Gaining on You," 68 Am. Bankr. L.J. 155, 208-212 (1994).

The right of the tort creditor to reach the trust estate has been a matter of great confusion in the cases. The principal difficulty lies in the fact that the trustee's right of indemnity is not clear.[27] It seems to be settled that if the trustee was not personally at fault *and* was not negligent in the selection of his agents, he has a right to exonerate himself from the trust estate, and the tort creditor has the right to levy against the trust property.[28] If a tort is committed while the trustee is acting beyond the scope of his duties, trust assets cannot be reached and judgment will be against the trustee personally.[29]

In jurisdictions that have adopted §7-306(b) of the Uniform Probate Code, the trustee would be liable to nonbeneficiaries in tort "only if he is personally at fault."[30] As a procedural matter, §7-306(c) permits claims to be asserted against the trust estate by proceeding against the trustee in his fiduciary capacity, whether or not the trustee is personally liable therefore. While the sections are intended to offer some protection to the trustee, it is difficult to see the practical advantage to the trustee of their adoption. The careful plaintiff will not only sue the trustee in his representative capacity but also sue the trustee in his individual capacity. The plaintiff need only allege "personal fault." Moreover, it will be the rare case where a judgment for the nonbeneficiary plaintiff contains no finding whatsoever of "personal fault" on the part of the trustee. Even when the wrongful acts were committed by the trustee's agents, there is the matter of their negligent selection and supervision.[31] And there is the matter of divided loyalty: when a trustee asserts the absence of "personal fault," he is calling for imposition of the economic burden of the tort on the trust estate and indirectly on the beneficiaries whose interests he is charged with protecting. Because of this conflict, it is important that the beneficiaries be represented in the litigation by separate independent counsel.

[27] *See generally,* Curtis, The Transmogrification of the American Trust, 31 Real Prop. Prob. & Tr. J. 251, 276-294 (1996).

[28] *See generally* 3A Scott on Trusts §264; *but see* Bogart, Liability of Directors of Chapter 11 Debtors in Possession: "Don't Look Back — Something May Be Gaining on You," 68 Am. Bankr. L.J. 155, 208-212 (1994).

[29] Id. §271A.2.

[30] *See generally* Bogert, Trusts and Trustees §732.

[31] Id. §731.

As a matter of practice, the wise trustee insures himself both as an individual and as trustee against nonbeneficiary claims in tort arising from the ownership or operation of the trust estate. The expense of such insurance is a proper charge against the trust estate.[32]

In the past 30 years a number of federal and state statutes have been enacted into law that are designed to protect consumers and redress acts of discrimination against certain classes of individuals. The trustee who deals with nonbeneficiaries on behalf of the trust estate may be bound by the requirements of these statutes and personally subject to their sanctions.

### §7.3.3.1 Consumer Protection

A substantial majority of the states have enacted, in one form or another, statutes designed to protect consumers from unfair or deceptive trade practices.[33] Most if not all of these consumer protection statutes will cover trustees who render goods and services to the public on behalf of their trusts.[34] If an unincorporated automobile dealership, for example, were operated out of a trust, the trustee might be held personally liable to customers for statements by employees of the trust that the automobiles are of a particular quality when they are not, that repairs may be needed when they are not, or that there is a specific price advantage when there is not.[35] Under some state statutes, consumers have a private right of action,[36] while under others the attorney general must bring the action on behalf of the consumers.[37] In some states both options are available.[38] Private relief usually takes the form of

[32] Id. §803.

[33] *See generally* 17 Am. Jur. 2d *Consumer Protection* §280 (1990); *see also* Dunbar, Comment, Consumer Protection: The Practical Effectiveness of State Deceptive Trade Practices Legislation, 59 Tul. L. Rev. 427, Tab. III at 441-448 (1984) (listing and analyzing consumer protection statutes by state).

[34] Id. §285.

[35] Id. §297.

[36] Id. §302.

[37] Id. §300.

[38] Id. §301.

rescission, restitution, and consequential damages.[39] In a number of jurisdictions, customers are entitled to treble damages and the recovery of attorneys' fees.[40]

If the dealership were incorporated, legal liability for damages under the statute might run in the first instance to the corporate enterprise. The trust beneficiaries however would have a right in equity to compel the trustee personally to make good any loss to the trust occasioned by the assessment of damages against the dealership, provided the loss could be tied to a breach of trust.

Not all consumer protection statutes cast the broad "unfair and deceptive" net. Some target specific activities such as odometer tampering, pyramid schemes, and telephone sales solicitations.[41]

### §7.3.3.2 Discrimination Based on Race, Color, Religion, Sex, Age, or Disability

As a general rule, the trustee may not discriminate on the basis of race, color, religion, sex, age, or disability in transactions with nonbeneficiaries on behalf of the trust.[42] This includes not only discrimination in the sale of goods and services to the public but also in matters relating to the hiring and employment of the trust's servants.[43] There are numerous exceptions and exemptions, which are beyond the scope of this handbook. Persons subject to unlawful discrimination may recover compensatory damages from the trustee, and in some cases punitive damages.[44]

The trustee's liability to nonbeneficiaries for intentional acts of discrimination is not indemnifiable from the trust estate.[45] If liability runs to a corporation held in the trust, the trustee may be

[39] *See generally* J. Sovern, Deceptive Trade Practices, 52 Ohio St. L.J. 437 (1991).

[40] Id. n.66. (1991).

[41] *See generally* 17 Am. Jur. 2d *Consumer Protection* §299 (1990).

[42] *See generally* 14 C.J.S. *Civil Rights* §§43-101 (1991).

[43] Id. §§143-217.

[44] Id. §§222-475.

[45] *See generally* Bogert, Trusts and Trustees §734.

compelled in equity to reimburse the trust estate for any resulting economic loss to the extent the loss is attributable to a breach of trust.

#### §7.3.3.3 Registration and Sale of Securities

The trustee may not engage in the interstate sale of securities held in the trust — or of securities representing beneficial interests in the trust itself — unless the securities are registered under the Federal Securities Act of 1933 or unless the sale falls under one or more of a number of statutory exemptions.[46] The determination of whether a particular interest constitutes a security and, if it does, whether it needs to be registered requires the specialized expertise of a securities lawyer. It certainly is not a job for the layman. The trustee who sells securities representing interests held by the trust, or beneficial interests in the trust itself, in violation of the registration requirements of federal law could be held personally liable to purchasers for their investment losses.[47] There are state registration requirements as well; known collectively as *Blue Sky Laws*, they carry their own private rights of action.[48]

The trustee also could incur personal civil liability to nonbeneficiaries for the unlawful insider trading of securities held in the trust estate.[49] This is the case even when the trustee acts solely in the interests of the beneficiaries, that is, when the trustee in no way profits personally.[50] *Insider trading* is trading in the securities markets while in possession of nonpublic information that would

[46]*See generally* American Bar Association, A Fiduciary's Guide to Federal Securities Laws, 5-59 (1994). A bank administering a collective investment fund may not issue any certificate or other document representing a direct or indirect interest in the fund, except to provide a withdrawing account with an interest in a segregated investment. 12 C.F.R. §9.18(b)(11) (1997) (Revised Reg. 9 reprinted in Appendix II).

[47]Id. (A Fiduciary's Guide to Federal Securities Laws).

[48]*See generally* Bogert, Trusts and Trustees §247R.

[49]*See supra* note 46. *See also* M. P. Malloy, Can 10b-5 for the Banks? The Effect of an Antifraud Rule on the Regulation of Banks, 61 Fordham L. Rev. 523 (1993).

[50]Id.

be important to a reasonable investor in making a decision to buy or sell a security.[51] Section 10(b) of the Securities Exchange Act of 1934 and Rule 10(b)(5) provide the legal framework for private rights of action in the insider trading context.[52] The trustee must make the trust whole for any losses to it occasioned by running afoul of the securities laws; and of course the trustee, not the trust, must bear the burden of attorneys' fees and other litigation costs that are a consequence of the illegal activities.[53]

## §7.3.4 *Liability as Legal Owner to the Sovereign*

The trustee as titleholder has certain duties and obligations not only to the beneficiaries and to third parties but also to the city, the state, and the United States.

### §7.3.4.1 Liability for Property Taxes

In the absence of statute, the trustee as legal owner would be personally liable for any taxes owed on tangible, intangible, and real property held in the trust.[54] In most cases, however, the trustee, as legal owner, is relieved by statute of personal liability either through the imposition of such liability on the beneficiary or on the property itself.[55] Consequently, as a practical matter, most property tax obligations are now directly imposed by statute on the trust estate.[56] Even if the trustee could not resort to a statute relieving him of personal liability for property taxes, he would have an equitable right to reimbursement from the trust estate.[57]

[51] Id.
[52] Id.
[53] *See* Bogert, Trusts and Trustees §801 n.15 and accompanying text.
[54] *See generally* 3A Scott on Trusts §265.
[55] Id. §265.1.
[56] Id.
[57] *See generally* Bogert, Trusts and Trustees §807; §3.5.2.3 (Right in Equity to Exoneration and Reimbursement).

### §7.3.4.2 Criminal and Civil Liability as Legal Owner

It has always been the case that the trustee may be held criminally liable for misappropriation of the trust funds.[58] This century, however, has seen a proliferation of statutes designed to regulate the advertising and sale of products and services to the public. These statutes have broadened substantially the trustee's opportunity to incur criminal liability in the course of administering a trust.

**(a) Securities laws.** The trustee as holder of the title to the trust portfolio has ample opportunity to run afoul of the criminal laws pertaining to the issuance, acquisition, and transfer of securities. Accordingly, the trustee should have near at hand a copy of A Fiduciary's Guide to Federal Securities Laws.[59]

(1) *Insider Trading (SEC)*. The trustee may be held criminally liable for insider trading in violation of the federal securities laws even in those cases where the trustee does not profit personally.[60] Conviction can result in substantial fines being levied against the trustee — and this would include the corporate trustee and its officers, directors, and supervisory personnel. In addition, conviction can bring long jail terms.[61] The key, however, is that the information must be nonpublic. The trustee may — and has a duty to — use public information in furtherance of the interests of the trust.

(2) *Securities Registration*. The trustee who transfers unregistered or restricted securities held in the trust in violation of the securities laws may be criminally liable.[62] Moreover

[58] *See generally* 2A Scott on Trusts §179.1 (intentional misappropriation constitutes the crime of embezzlement).

[59] *See generally* American Bar Association, A Fiduciary's Guide to Federal Securities Laws (1994) (hereinafter "the Guide").

[60] Id.

[61] *See* id.

[62] *See generally* id.

a transferable share of beneficial interest in the trust itself may be a "security" subject to regulation.[63]

(3) *Ownership Disclosure.* When a trust acquires more than five percent of a class of registered securities, the trustee may be required to file certain disclosure forms with the Securities and Exchange Commission and with the Exchanges.[64] Determining who is and what securities are subject to these disclosure obligations is a complicated matter. It is a topic that falls beyond the scope of this handbook and beyond the ken of most trust attorneys as well. However, because the cost of noncompliance could be criminal sanctions, the trustee should consult a qualified securities lawyer if there is reason to believe that a holding is approaching (or has exceeded) the five-percent point.

(4) *'40 Act Registration.* The Investment Advisers Act of 1940 may require the trustee, himself, to register with the Securities and Exchange Commission, file annual reports with the Commission, and conduct his business in certain specified ways. This matter is covered in §8.15.10 (The Loring Exemption).

**(b) Environmental protection.** As holder of the title to the trust property, the trustee is likely to face criminal sanctions if he intentionally or negligently, in the course of his administration, violates environmental statutes. In addition to a number of major federal environmental statutes on the books, each state as well has its own set of environmental laws.

While most environmental statutes require intent or negligence on the part of the trustee, under the federal Comprehensive Environmental Response, Compensation, and Liability Act (CERCLA), as initially enacted,[65] an innocent trustee's liability as the "owner" for the clean-up of hazardous waste on or within the trust

[63] Id. *See also* Bogert, Trusts and Trustees §247R (registration of beneficial interests under state securities laws).

[64] *See generally* the Guide, *supra* note 59.

[65] 42 U.S.C. §9601 et seq. (1983).

property may not have been limited by the trust's ability to indemnify the trustee *except when the property [was] contaminated at the time of acquisition and the trustee [undertook] promptly to correct the situation* or *when the trustee [had] no control over the use of the trust property* — at least one federal district court had so held.[66] In other words, the trustee under certain circumstances may well have been held strictly (and personally) liable as title holder for the full clean-up costs even if those costs *exceeded* the value of the trust estate.

In September 1996, CERCLA was amended to relieve a trustee of personal liability for the release or threatened release of a hazardous substance merely because the trustee held the legal title.[67] The amendment shifted the risk of CERCLA liability from the trustee personally to the trust estate itself, except for environmental injury resulting from the trustee's intentional or negligent acts.[68] The amendment is effective for any claim against a trustee which had not been finally adjudicated as of September 30, 1996. Because the amendment does nothing to alleviate the trust estate itself from the economic risk of CERCLA remedies and because the trustee would still be personally liable for negligent and intentional violations of CERCLA, it will still behoove the prudent prospective trustee to commission an exhaustive and comprehensive environmental inspection of land comprising the trust estate before deciding whether to accept its trusteeship. A trustee of clean real estate will not want to infect a trust with contaminated real estate. Nor will a trustee of contaminated real estate want to accept additions of clean real estate. Liability might well attach to a trustee who negligently failed to disclaim the clean property, or otherwise insulate it from having to contribute to the costs of bringing the contaminated property into conformance with environmental laws. Finally, the amendment does nothing to change environmental laws that may be on the books in the state in which the land is located.

[66] *See* City of Phoenix v. Garbage Servs. Co., 827 F. Supp. 600 (D. Ariz. 1993); *see generally* Graham & Lindquist, The Application of CERCLA and Other Strict Liability Environmental Statutes to Fiduciary Relationships — Putting City of Phoenix in Context, 29 Real Prop. Prob. & Tr. J. 1 (1994).

[67] 42 U.S.C. §9607(n).

[68] 42 U.S.C. §9607(n)(2); 42 U.S.C. §9607(n)(3).

**(c) Unauthorized practice of law.** The nonlawyer-trustee, whether a corporation or an individual, should leave the drafting of the trust instrument to the settlor's lawyer.[69] To be sure, practicing law without a license is a crime in some jurisdictions.[70] But what is perhaps of greater practical concern is that the nonlawyer-trustee (be it an individual or an institution like a bank) will be held to the standard of a competent trust lawyer in any *civil* action brought for negligent drafting.[71] Unlike the licensed attorney, however, the nonlawyer-trustee will have no legal malpractice insurance to fall back on.

## §7.4 Trustee's Discharge in Bankruptcy

How are the interests of beneficiaries having claims against trustees affected when the trustees, themselves, file for bankruptcy? First, any claims *for money damages* for fraud, embezzlement, defalcation, or other such acts of willful and malicious injury to a trust are not dischargeable.[1] Second, insofar as *the trust property* itself is concerned, if it can be traced, the trustee in bankruptcy will hold the property subject to the trust.[2] The beneficiary then will have priority over the general creditor with respect to that property.[3]

[69] *See generally* Bogert, Trusts and Trustees §136 nn.7-10 and accompanying text.

[70] *See* Powell, The Problem of the Parachuting Practitioner, 1992 U. Ill. L. Rev. 105, 123-24 nn.97-98 and accompanying text (listing state unauthorized practice of law statutes with respective enforcement systems); *see, e.g.,* Akron Bar Association v. Miller, 684 N.E.2d 288 (Ohio 1997) and Trumbull County Bar Assoc. v. Hanna, 684 N.E.2d 329 (Ohio 1997) (Enjoining the marketing of standardized living trust documentation).

[71] Harper, James & Gray, 3 The Law of Torts §16.6 (1986).

**§7.4** [1] 3 Scott on Trusts §221.

[2] 3 Scott on Trusts §221.1

[3] Id.

CHAPTER 8

# Miscellaneous Topics of General Interest to the Trustee

## §8.1 Powers of Appointment

### *§8.1.1 In General*

A power of appointment is a power of disposition.[1] It is a power given by the settlor to someone — usually a beneficiary, sometimes a third party — to short circuit, alter, or extend the terms of the trust. A power of appointment, as it is usually understood in the non-tax context, is not a discretionary power *in* a trustee to invade principal for the benefit of the beneficiary.[2] For purposes of this handbook, with the exception of §8.9.3 (Tax-Sensitive Powers), a power of appointment is not a power *in the trustee*; it is a power *to give directions to* the trustee.

The settlor determines the nature and extent of the power and how it is to be exercised by the power holder. For example, a general inter vivos power would give the power holder the right while alive to direct the trustee to turn over the trust property to the holder, the holder's creditors, or to anyone else.[3] A general testamentary power would give the power holder the right by will to direct the trustee to turn over the trust property to the power holder's estate, the estate's creditors, or to anyone else.[4] On the

**§8.1** [1]Restatement (Second) of Property §11.1 (1986) (Donative Transfers).
[2]*But see* id. §11.1 comment *d.*
[3]*See* id. §11.4.
[4]Id. In a few states, a general residuary clause in a will is presumed to exercise a *general* testamentary power of appointment, unless the settlor (the donor of the

other hand, the holder of a limited inter vivos or testamentary power may appoint only to the members of a class of permissible takers.[5] This class can be large enough to include everyone in the world except the power holder, his creditors, his estate, and the creditors of his estate; otherwise for all intents and purposes the power would be a general one.[6]

The trustee should keep in mind that a power of appointment is not always labeled as such in the governing instrument. It sometimes travels in disguise. For example, a general inter vivos power might take the form of a reserved right of revocation, a beneficiary's right to have his debts satisfied from the trust estate, or simply an unrestricted right in someone to demand principal.[7]

A prospective trustee should make sure there are provisions in default of exercise. Let us take as an example the following trust: *A* to *B* for *C* for life, with *C* possessing a general testamentary power of appointment. What happens if *C* were to die intestate? The instrument being silent, it is likely that the death of *C* would trigger a resulting trust in favor of *A* or *A*'s estate.[8] Were *C* to possess instead a limited power, there is a split of authority as to whether a resulting trust is triggered or whether the property passes in equal shares to the permissible appointees.[9] In any case, the settlor's counsel should have supplied the trust with terms that would become operative in the event *C* fails in whole or in part effectively to exercise the power.[10]

When a settlor makes himself a beneficiary *and* bestows on himself a *general* inter vivos power to appoint the trust property (*e.g.*, a reserved right of revocation), his creditors may have

---

power) indicated a contrary intention in the instrument that created the power. *See generally* Ritchie, et al., Decedents' Estates and Trusts 929 (8th ed. 1993); *see generally* §8.15.12 (Doctrine of Capture).

[5] Restatement (Second) of Property §11.4 comment *b* (1986) (Donative Transfers).

[6] Id.

[7] Id. §12.1 comment *a* & Reporter's Note to §12.1.

[8] Id. §24.1.

[9] *See generally* 1 Scott on Trusts §27.

[10] *See* Bogert, Trusts and Trustees §1064 for a sample provision in default of the exercise of a power of appointment (art. fourth, section 3).

access to the property whether or not the power is ever exercised.[11] This is consistent with the longstanding public policy that one may not place property beyond the reach of one's creditors and still retain the right to enjoy it.[12] It is the settlor's *right* of exercise which makes the property vulnerable; not the fact of exercise. The right of exercise is treated as equivalent to an ownership interest in the property subject to the power. On the other hand, if the holder of the general inter vivos power is not the settlor and absent a statute to the contrary, the property is creditor- accessible only to the extent that the holder in fact exercises the power.[13] This restriction on access may not apply to the trustee in bankruptcy.[14] With respect to a *limited* power to appoint trust property, the holder is treated as though an agent of the settlor; thus the holder's creditors would have no access to the property whether the limited power is ever exercised.[15]

Right of Exercise

### *§8.1.2 Exercises of Power of Appointment in Further Trust*

If the governing instrument is silent on the issue, may the holder of a *general* power of appointment exercise it in further trust (*e.g.*, instead of appointing the property outright and free of trust to *X*, appoint it to a trustee for the benefit of *X*)? The answer is yes.[16] This is inherent in the holder's overarching right to appoint to anyone, including himself. Even if the holder of a general power were not entitled to appoint in further trust, the same result could still be achieved in two steps: by first appointing to himself and then by impressing a trust upon the property for the benefit of *X*.

[11]2A Scott on Trusts §156; *see also* §5.3.3.1 (Reaching Settlor's Reserved Beneficial Interest). *But see* 4 Scott §330.12 (suggesting that property subject to an unexercised naked reserved right of revocation may not be reachable by the settlor's creditors).

[12]*See generally* 2A Scott on Trusts §156.

[13]*See generally* id. §147.3.

[14]Id.

[15]*See* id.; Restatement (Second) of Property §13.1 (1986) (Donative Transfers).

[16]*See generally* 1 Scott on Trusts §§17.2, 21.

Authority is split over whether, absent express authority in the governing instrument, the holder of a *limited* power may appoint in further trust.[17] If the holder may appoint to members of a class comprised of *X*, *Y*, and *Z*, some courts would hold an exercise in further trust to be impermissible, because title would pass to the trustee who would be someone other than a designated member of the class.[18] The matter of appointments in further trust should be addressed in the governing instrument. When it is not, the trustee should next check for an applicable statute before turning to the cases.[19]

If a *general* power is exercised in further trust, is a new trust created or are the terms of the original trust merely altered or extended? Unfortunately, the question is not susceptible of any easy answer.[20] It may well depend upon who wants to know. Let us assume, for example, that *A* transfers property inter vivos to *B* in trust for *C*, who is given a *general* testamentary power of appointment. *C* exercises the power by providing in his or her will that *B* shall continue to hold the property in trust for the benefit of *X*. In this case *C* has expressed the intention that no new trust be created and that the terms of the original trust are merely to be extended. On the other hand, the creditors of *C* might demand that *B* turn the trust property over to *C*'s estate so that it may be available to satisfy their claims. Once the claims are satisfied, a new trust presumably would arise for the benefit of *X*. Moreover, the court having jurisdiction over *C*'s estate might assert that this new trust is now a testamentary trust requiring its continuing supervision.

Regardless of the form of the arrangement, that is to say, whether there is a continuing trust or the termination of one and the starting up of another, when it comes to substantive rights there are two trusts. The donee who exercises the general power for all intents and purposes is the settlor of a new trust to which his or her creditors, spouse, the taxing authorities — perhaps even

[17] *See generally* id. §17.2.
[18] *See* id. §17.2 n.5 and accompanying text.
[19] *See* id. §17.2 n.7 and accompanying text.
[20] *See generally* id. §17.2.

the welfare department — all may have access.[21] Even for purposes of the Rule Against Perpetuities, the holder of a general inter vivos power is deemed to have a vested interest in the property subject to the power.[22]

The form of the arrangement seems to be up to the settlor. If the settlor expresses an intention that the power holder may appoint new trustees upon an exercise in further trust, then such an appointment will be honored.[23] But could the exercise of a *general* testamentary power of appointment have the effect of converting an inter vivos trust into a testamentary trust requiring subsequent periodic accountings to the court?[24] The attendant publicity and expense would make this an unfortunate result. Moreover it would fly in the face of the very concept of the power of appointment — a power of disposition, a power to direct. The holder who exercises the general testamentary power in further trust is either directing that the property stay with the current trustee or directing one trustee to transfer title to another. In neither case is it expected that the estate of the power holder will take unto itself more of an interest in the property (nor that the court will acquire more supervision over the new arrangement) than is reasonably necessary to accommodate the interests of those having a claim against the estate.[25]

With respect to the exercise of a *limited* testamentary power of appointment in further trust, there should be no excuse whatsoever for a court's converting an inter vivos trust into a testamentary trust. The deceased holder is for all intents and purposes no more than an agent of the settlor, the holder's estate having no ownership interest, constructive or otherwise, in the property subject to the power.

[21] *See generally* 2A Scott on Trusts §147.3.

[22] Leach, Perpetuities in a Nutshell, 51 Harv. L. Rev. 638, 654 (1938).

[23] *See* Lovejoy v. Bucknam, 299 Mass. 446, 13 N.E.2d 23 (1938).

[24] *See generally* Restatement (Second) of Property §11.1 comment *b*, §13.4 comment *b*(1986) (Donative Transfers).

[25] Id.; *see also* In re Estate of Wylie, 342 So. 2d 996 (Fla. Dist. Ct. App. 1977); Aurora Natl. Bank v. Old Second Natl. Bank, 59 Ill. App. 3d 384, 375 N.E.2d 544 (1978).

On the other hand, the exercise in further trust of a general testamentary power created under a *testamentary* trust as a practical matter might bring about a transfer of jurisdiction over the testamentary trust to the court supervising the administration of the power holder's estate. This however is as much a conflict of laws issue as it is an issue rooted in the nature of the power of appointment itself.

If the holder of a *general* power of appointment attempts to exercise the power in further trust and the "new" trust fails at the outset (or is established but some time thereafter fails), the property passes as a resulting trust to the power holder or his estate. It does *not* pass back to the settlor of the "original" trust or his estate, unless the "original" trust instrument provides for a different disposition or unless the power holder provided otherwise.[26] It is said that the property has been *captured* by the power holder or his estate.

If the holder of a *limited* power of appointment attempts to exercise the power in further trust and the "new" trust fails at the outset (or is established but some time thereafter fails), there is no capture. There are instead three possibilities, depending on the terms of the original trust or the law of the applicable jurisdiction: the property passes (1) to the takers in default, (2) in equal shares to the class of permissible appointees, and (3) back to the settlor of the "original" trust or his estate.[27] In no event can the trustee keep the property.

As the above discussion suggests, the subject of powers of appointment in multijurisdictional settings is too complex to discuss in a book of this scope. It would be equally impractical to attempt a discussion of what exercises in further trust will and will not violate the Rule Against Perpetuities.[28] Suffice it to say that the trustee confronted with these issues should consult with counsel.

[26] 5 Scott on Trusts §426.

[27] Id. §427.

[28] *See generally* §8.2.1 (The Rule Against Perpetuities); Leach, *supra* note 22, at 651-654; Bogert, Trusts and Trustees §213.

## §8.2 Termination of the Trust and Final Distribution

The law places a limit on how long a noncharitable trust may continue. This constraint has come to be known as the *Rule Against Perpetuities* (hereinafter "the Rule"). As long as the Rule is not violated, the settlor is entitled to set forth in the governing instrument when and under what circumstances the trust shall terminate. If the settlor fails to do so, the trust shall terminate when its purposes are fulfilled. If the terms of the governing instrument are silent on what then happens to the trust property, the property shall pass back to the settlor or the settlor's estate upon a resulting trust. As to the related *Rule Against Accumulations, see* §8.15.8.

### §8.2.1 *The Rule Against Perpetuities*

> No interest is good unless it must vest, if at all, not later than twenty-one years after some life in being at the creation of the interest.[1]

The Rule Against Perpetuities places a limit on how long certain types of trusts may continue. During the life of a trust (*i.e.*, during the period when the trustee has legal title to the property), ascertained and unascertained beneficiaries and remaindermen have equitable interests in the trust property.[2] If during that time there is a condition which must be fulfilled before someone may acquire an equitable interest, that equitable interest is said to be a *contingent* one. (The condition of survivorship is perhaps the most common such condition precedent the trustee is likely to encounter today.) In the context of trusts, the Rule thus governs how long equitable contingent interests may remain outstanding before they must extinguish or be converted into vested interests (interests which are held by someone unconditionally).[3]

**§8.2** [1]J. C. Gray, The Rule Against Perpetuities §201 (4th ed. 1942).
[2]*See generally* Bogert, Trusts and Trustees §181.
[3]Id.

The Rule is against the remoteness of *vesting in interest,* not remoteness of *vesting in possession.*[4] To illustrate the difference between the two, let us assume *A* transfers property to *B* in trust for *C* for life, remainder to Mrs. Jones, who currently lives in Washington, D.C. From the time the trust is created Mrs. Jones's interest is *vested,* though not possessory. This is because at the time the trust is created, she is ascertained and during the life of *C* there is no event that will extinguish her interest. At the death of *C*, the trust property passes outright and free of trust either to Mrs. Jones or to her estate.[5] In other words, Mrs. Jones then gets possession of the property, be she dead or alive.

On the other hand, were *A* to make a simple unconditional gift of the property outright and free of trust directly to Mrs. Jones, bypassing the trustee altogether, Mrs. Jones's interest at the time of transfer would be both *vested* and *possessory.* For purposes of the Rule, however, vesting only is what matters.

An exhaustive study of the Rule is beyond the scope of this book; moreover it would duplicate the efforts of others.[6] Rather, the trustee should use the guidelines that follow to assist in developing a methodology for ruling out Rule problems and for framing appropriate questions for counsel when such problems are encountered. Hopefully, the trustee will be able to confront the Rule efficiently and cost- effectively, with courage and with confidence.

It should first be made clear that if property becomes the subject of a charitable trust within the period of the Rule, such a trust may last forever.[7] Thus it is said that the Rule does not apply to charitable trusts.[8] Let us take as an example a scholarship trust fund for gifted and needy U.S. citizens. Each U.S. citizen, born and unborn, has a contingent equitable interest in the trust. The interests are contingent because certain conditions precedent—

[4] Id. §213.

[5] *Cf.,* U.P.C. §2.707 (providing that property would pass to the "descendents" of Mrs. Jones); *see generally* Halbach and Waggoner, The UPC's New Survivorship and Antilapse Provisions, 55 Albany L. Rev. 1091, 1131-1133 (1992) and Dukeminier, The Uniform Probate Code Upends the Law of Remainders, 94 Mich. L. Rev. 148, 149-150, 166 (1995).

[6] *See* id. §213 nn.1, 2 and accompanying text.

[7] *See generally* 4A Scott on Trusts §365.

[8] *But see* Bogert, Trusts and Trustees §341.

prior conditions as it were — must be satisfied before the citizen may receive a scholarship distribution from the trust. The conditions are that the citizen must be alive, gifted, needy, a scholar, a U.S. citizen, duly selected, and so forth. The beneficial interests are equitable not legal because legal title to the property is in the trustee. As a matter of public policy the use of the trust property for such a charitable purpose perpetually may be subject to such conditions.[9] Not so, however, with noncharitable trusts.

Under the common law, a contingent interest in a noncharitable trust must extinguish by vesting or otherwise within the period allowed by the Rule. That period is 21 years after the death of certain people who are alive at the time the contingent interest is created. These people are known as *measuring lives* or *lives in being.*[10] If at the time the interest is created one could conjure up a possible fact or circumstance — a worst case scenario as it were — that would cause a condition precedent to remain outstanding beyond the period of the Rule, there may be a common law Rule problem that the trustee will have to confront. At the very least, the trustee will have some analytical work to do as it is more than likely there are provisions in the governing trust instrument or somewhere in a state statute that will have some bearing on whether the trustee actually has a perpetuities problem with the trust.

How does one go about determining whether a particular contingent equitable interest violates the Rule in its classical form? First, determine when the contingent interests were created. Second, determine who the lives in being are. Third, determine who under the terms of the trust are to take vested interests. And finally, calculate whether such a vesting, under a worst-case scenario, could occur more than 21 years after the time when the last survivor of the lives in being dies. To illustrate the process and to expose uninitiated readers to the complexity and subtlety of the Rule's application, throughout this section the following hypothetical trust will be subjected to the four-step analysis:

[9] *See generally* id. §351.

[10] *See generally* Dukeminier, Perpetuities: The Measuring Lives, 85 Colum. L. Rev. 1648 (1985); Becker, A Methodology for Solving Perpetuities Problems Under the Common Law Rule: A Step by Step Process That Carefully Identifies All Testing Lives in Being, 67 Wash. U. L.Q. 949 (1989).

A settlor transfers property inter vivos to a trustee. The settlor reserves an inter vivos right to the net income as well as a right of revocation. Upon the death of the settlor the trust converts to an irrevocable discretionary trust. The provisions of the discretionary trust are that the trustee may apply income and invade principal for one or more of the settlor's grandchildren, whenever born, who are alive when a particular discretionary distribution from the trust is made. At the point in time after the death of the settlor when no grandchild of the settlor is both alive and under the age of 30 years, the trust shall be held for the benefit of the youngest then-living great-grandchild of the settlor. That great-grandchild, if there is one, shall have a right to all the net income in all events as well as a general inter vivos power to appoint the trust property. Any property remaining in the trust at the death of that great-grandchild shall be paid to the executor of the great-grandchild's estate.

A time line of the trust would look like this:

| | | | |
|---|---|---|---|
| Transfer to Trustee | Death of Settlor | No Grandchild Both Alive and Under Thirty | Death of the Great-Grandchild |

### §8.2.1.1 The Creation of the Interest

It is self-evident that because a will speaks at death, a contingent equitable interest under a testamentary trust cannot be created before the testator dies. (Thus the testator can never be the life in being at the time of the creation of the testamentary trust.) With respect to any trust, whether testamentary or inter vivos, insofar as the Rule is concerned, contingent interests do not exist while a trust is revocable, that is, while there is an outstanding unexercised general inter vivos power to appoint the trust property.[11] Thus contingent interests are created at the time when a trust becomes irrevocable — a time which will not always coincide with when property is transferred to the trustee.

[11] *See* Leach, Perpetuities in a Nutshell, 51 Harv. L. Rev. 638, 654 (1938).

In our hypothetical trust, the equitable contingent interests of the grandchildren and great-grandchildren, born and unborn, are created at the death of the settlor when the reserved right of revocation (assuming it is never exercised) extinguishes. At that time certain of the settlor's issue receive equitable interests that are contingent upon survivorship and the trustee's exercise of discretion. During the lifetime of the settlor of our hypothetical trust, the settlor alone, as holder of the power, is deemed to hold unconditionally all the equitable interests and is deemed to possess a vested interest in the property. Therefore, as the Rule is concerned with when vesting must occur, there cannot be a Rule violation until after the extinguishment, by the settlor's death or otherwise, of the power.

#### §8.2.1.2 The Worst Case Life in Being

It is unfortunate, but a mastery of the many nuances of worst case life in being identification takes good intuition and much practice.[12] By way of illustration, the worst case life in being in our hypothetical trust is the last survivor of the children of the settlor who were alive at the death of the settlor, assuming the reserved right of revocation — which is tantamount to a general power of appointment — is never exercised. Why must some child of the settlor be the life in being? Because, taking the period of gestation into account and ignoring, for purposes of the Rule, recent developments in the science of postmortem reproduction, the child cannot come into existence after the settlor's death, which is when the reserved right of revocation is extinguished and when the contingent interests are created. A child cannot be conceived from the grave.

Why is that child the worst case life in being? Because that child, after the death of all other lives in being (namely the settlor and the settlor's issue living at the time of the settlor's death) could then produce non-lives-in-being grandchildren of the settlor whose equitable interests during the discretionary phase of the trust are contingent and whose ages will govern the time when the remainder interests will ultimately vest in a great-grandchild.

[12] Id. at 641-642.

What is the worst case? The worst case is that the only child of the settlor dies immediately after conceiving a grandchild of the settlor, the conception having taken place *after* the settlor's death. At that point all lives in being at the death of the settlor are dead and vesting now must occur before the expiration of 21 years. Had another life in being been in existence at that time (for example, another child of the settlor), then the day of reckoning could have been postponed.

Professor Leach, with characteristic clarity and economy of language, went to the heart of the problem in his article entitled *Perpetuities in a Nutshell*, when he wrote that the lives in being "need not be mentioned in the instrument, need not be holders of previous estates, and need not be connected in any way with the property or the persons designated to take it."[13] In our hypothetical trust, the children of the settlor are neither mentioned nor holders of previous estates; yet they are lives in being for purposes of the Rule, assuming that at the death of the settlor there is at least one child of his then living and at least one grandchild of his then alive and under the age of 30. The trustee wishing to learn the art of life in being identification would do well to begin by studying the representative measuring life illustrations in Part III of Professor Leach's article.[14]

### §8.2.1.3 The Vesting of Interests Under Trusts

A trust beneficiary's interest is vested if the interest is not subject to a condition precedent such as survivorship.[15] When an ascertained person is entitled, whether dead or alive, to an ascertained portion of the trust property, the interest in that portion is vested. What the trustee may find difficult to grasp about the vesting aspect of the Rule is that an interest may vest in someone for purposes of the Rule; yet the person may not get the use of the interest before death.[16] It is the person's probate estate that will

[13] Id. at 641.
[14] Id. at 641-642.
[15] *See* J. C. Gray, The Rule Against Perpetuities §§101-103 (4th ed. 1942).
[16] Id. at §102.

ultimately get the use of the property. The trustee cannot begin to understand the Rule without having solved the vesting riddle.[17]

In our hypothetical trust, the words *then living* make the interests of conceived and unconceived great-grandchildren contingent in part on their being born before and not dying before the trust terminates. These contingencies — or conditions precedent — will remain outstanding during that phase of the trust's life after the death of the settlor when there exists a grandchild of the settlor who is both alive and under the age of 30 years. The instrument provides that at the point in time after the settlor's death when no grandchild of the settlor is both alive and under the age of 30, someone is then either going to hold a vested remainder interest or a vested reversionary interest under a resulting trust. The remainder interests will then be vested for two reasons, of which either one is sufficient vesting for purposes of the Rule: (1) the subsequent death of the great-grandchild, if any, who met the implicit conditions of birth, survivorship, and age will not extinguish his or her interest, because in that event the trust property would merely find its way into the great-grandchild's probate estate; (2) the qualifying great-grandchild will be the holder of an inter vivos power of appointment which, for purposes of the Rule, is tantamount to the great-grandchild's possessing a vested interest in the trust property which is the subject of the power. If there is no great-grandchild around to take when there is no grandchild both alive and under the age of 30, the property will pass to the settlor's probate estate upon a resulting trust, the reversionary interest having been vested in the settlor and the settlor's estate during the entire life of the trust.[18]

### §8.2.1.4 A Possible Vesting Beyond the Period of the Common Law Rule

Applying the Rule to our hypothetical trust, we assume the settlor and all the settlor's descendants who were alive at the

[17] The trustee may wish to consult chapter 3 of Thomas F. Bergin and Paul G. Haskell's Preface to Estates in Land and Future Interests (2d ed. 1984), which has a useful section on the "concept of vestedness." *See also* id. at 66-73 and Gray at §99-118.

[18] *See* Gray, *supra* note 15, §327.1.

settlor's death have died, except for one child of the settlor. After the death of the settlor, that child produces a grandchild of the settlor. The child then dies when the grandchild is a day old. Now all lives in being are dead and we have a day-old non-life in being grandchild of the settlor. If we can conjure up only one scenario whereby there could be a vesting in someone later than a day after the grandchild's twenty-first birthday, we have a common law Rule violation. We can. Here is one such scenario: At the age of 25, the grandchild receives a discretionary distribution of income or principal from the trust. Here is another: The grandchild has a thirtieth birthday at which point the property vests in a non-life in being great-grandchild of the settlor. In both cases, property would vest in non-lives in being more than 21 years after the death of the life in being child of the settlor.

### §8.2.1.5 Consequences of a Violation of the Common Law Rule

If an equitable contingent interest fails, it does not mean necessarily that the entire trust fails.[19] The tainted interests are constructively stricken from the instrument and the trustee will continue to administer any remaining equitable interests that may be in compliance with the Rule. In our hypothetical trust, for example, the provisions for the benefit of the settlor are valid because he had reserved to himself a right of revocation in the nature of a general inter vivos power of appointment which, for purposes of the Rule, is tantamount to retaining a vested interest in the trust property. If the instrument had provided that the settlor's children were to have beneficial interests in the discretionary trust, the trustee could continue to administer their interests as they would be lives in being. Unfortunately the instrument did not so provide. Therefore, effective immediately upon the death of the settlor — which is when the interests are created under our hypothetical trust — the contingent equitable interests of the settlor's grandchildren during the discretionary

[19] *But see* Leach, *supra* note 11, at 1336 (if equitable contingent interest is an "integral part of the dispositive scheme," then entire trust may indeed fail).

phase of the trust are deemed *nonexistent* because of the possibility of a discretionary distribution of income or principal to a non-life in being grandchild more than 21 years after the death of the last life in being child of the settlor. As vesting in a "then-living" grandchild may occur beyond the permissible period of the Rule, the remainder provision fails as well.

What are the consequences of these failures? The consequences are that upon the death of the settlor the trust stops — drops off into thin air as it were. By operation of law there are no more terms governing the disposition of income and principal. Thus the life of the trust has come to an end. The trustee, however, may not consume the property.[20] Rather the trustee, now holding the property upon a resulting trust,[21] must transfer title to the executor or administrator of the settlor's probate estate. The trust property will then follow the fortunes of the settlor's probate estate, passing either in accordance with the terms of the settlor's will or under the laws of intestacy.[22] Had the children of the settlor, along with the grandchildren, been permissible beneficiaries during the discretionary phase of the trust, the life of the trust would have continued (for the benefit of the children only, however) until the death of the last life in being child of the settlor; then the trust would fail. Our hypothetical trust instrument, however, contained no such provision for the benefit of the settlor's children.

### §8.2.1.6 The Perpetuities Savings Clause

Today, a trust instrument is likely to contain a so-called perpetuities savings clause that triggers the termination of the trust at a time certain, unless the trust in the ordinary course of things terminates at an earlier time.[23] This time certain provision is designed to trigger a vesting within the period of the common law Rule no matter what.[24] Most such clauses operate by providing for

[20] *See* Restatement (Second) of Trusts §345 comment *i* (1959).
[21] *See generally* Bogert, Trusts and Trustees §468.
[22] Id.
[23] *See, e.g.,* Bogert, Trusts and Trustees §1046 (section VIII(k)).
[24] Id.

a termination in all events 21 years after the death of the last survivor of specified lives of being, at which point the property is distributed outright and free of trusts to remainderman specified in the savings clause.[25]

If such a provision were in the governing instrument of our hypothetical trust — perhaps providing for termination 21 years after the death of the last survivor of all issue of the settlor alive at the death of the settlor — then there is no way that a non-life in being might receive a discretionary distribution or a vested remainder interest more than 21 years after the death of the last survivor of all lives in being.

The lesson here is: *Check for a savings clause.* The trustee should be faulted — if not held liable — for allowing a perpetuities panic to build before someone discovers that there is a valid governing savings clause, particularly if the trust is charged for any legal and administrative expenses attributable to the nonfeasance.

### §8.2.1.7 Perpetuities Legislation

Since the Second World War there have been waves of legislative initiatives designed to corral and mitigate the harshness of the Rule. It was Professor Leach who more than anyone else was responsible for setting things in motion when, in 1952, he published several law review articles calling for legislative modification of the Rule.[26] He suggested that the Rule be applied on the basis of events that actually happen and that offending provisions be reformed to approximate as near as possible the settlor's intent.[27] Whether the ensuing legislation has had or will have any social utility is a matter beyond the scope of this book. What is clear however is that these initiatives have added additional complexities to the Rule. Take for example the Uniform Statutory Rule

[25] Id.

[26] Leach, Perpetuities: Staying the Slaughter of the Innocents, 68 L.Q. Rev. 35 (1952); Leach, Perpetuities in Perspective: Ending the Rule's Reign of Terror, 65 Harv. L. Rev. 721 (1952).

[27] Id.

Against Perpetuities[28] (USRAP), which has already been adopted in 24 states.[29] It essentially grafts onto the common law Rule a 90-year wait-and-see provision and provides for judicial reformation in lieu of the imposition of a resulting trust.[30] Thus even in a USRAP jurisdiction the trustee may not ignore the common law Rule. In our hypothetical trust, for example, the USRAP would allow discretionary distributions to the settlor's grandchildren for a 90-year period beginning with the settlor's death. The interest of a great-grandchild would be good if it were to vest within that period.

There is another lesson here for a trustee faced with a common law Rule violation: If a review of the governing instrument does not turn up a savings clause, do not forget to check for an applicable statute.

### §8.2.1.8 Perpetuities and Powers of Appointment

Care must be taken that the exercise of a power of appointment in further trust not violate the Rule. However, a discussion of the matter is extremely technical and thus beyond the scope of this Handbook. For two excellent treatments of the subject, the trustee is referred to Professor Leach's *Perpetuities in a Nutshell*[31] and Professor Becker's *Perpetuities and Estate Planning.*[32]

### §8.2.1.9 Abolition of the Rule Against Perpetuities

In 1969, Wisconsin abolished the common law Rule Against Perpetuities.[33] Alaska abolished the rule in 1997.[34] South Dakota

[28]Uniform Statutory Rule Against Perpetuities, 8B U.L.A. 333 (1993).
[29]Id. at 44 (Supp. 1997).
[30]*But see* In re Estate of Keenan, 519 N.W.2d 373 (Iowa 1994).
[31]51 Harv. L. Rev. 638, 651-654 (1938).
[32]Becker, Perpetuities and Estate Planning §2.5 (1993).
[33]Wis. Stat. §700.16.
[34]A.S. 34.27.050 (a).

and Idaho, also, have abolished the Rule.[35] In 1995, Delaware abolished the Rule for trusts of personal property.[36] A competition among the states seems to be underway, in part to attract the trust business of those wishing to leverage the $1 million Federal generation-skipping transfer tax exemption, particularly through the use of life insurance products.[37] Bear in mind that a trust under which the trustee does *not* have a power of sale will likely still be subject to the Rule in those jurisdictions that are said to have "abolished" the Rule. The practicality and utility of a private perpetual dynastic trust with a relentlessly expanding class of beneficiaries (e.g., the "issue" of the settlor) remains to be seen, however:

> Historians say that 26 of the 102 people who crossed the Atlantic on the Mayflower in 1620 and later celebrated the first Thanksgiving had children who had children who had children. Today, approximately 12 generations later, the Mayflower passengers may well have 25 million descendants. "It could be one out of every 10 people on the street," says Cay Lanham, the governor general of the General Society of Mayflower Descendants.[38]

### §8.2.2 *When the Trust May Be Terminated*

A trust, once established, ordinarily cannot be altered, amended, revoked or terminated in mid-course except pursuant to its own provisions.[39] Such a provision might take the form of a reserved right of revocation, a general power of appointment, a right to demand principal, or a right in the trustee to invade principal. Only in a few states is a trust revocable by the settlor unless there is express language in the governing instrument to the contrary.[40]

[35] S.D. Codified Laws Ann. §43-5-8; Idaho Code Ann. §55.111.

[36] Del. Code Ann. tit. 25, §503.

[37] *See generally* Dukeminier, Dynasty Trusts: Sheltering Descendants From Transfer Taxes, 23 Est. Plan. 417(1996).

[38] The Wall Street Journal, Wed., Nov. 25, 1987, page 1, col. 4.

[39] *See generally* 4 Scott on Trusts §330.1.

[40] California and Texas are among these states. *See* id. §330.1 n.6 and accompanying text.

The termination of a trust also may be achieved if all the equitable and all the legal interests have been merged in one person,[41] if its purposes are impossible of fulfillment, or if its purposes have been fully accomplished.[42] Some states have enacted statutes providing for the termination of small trusts.[43] In the United States, the coalescing of all *beneficial* interests in one person who is not the trustee ordinarily will not trigger a termination of the trust unless the purposes of the trust have been accomplished.[44] A trust may be cancelled because it was created through fraud or undue influence or mistake,[45] although cancellation perhaps belongs more in the category of annulment than termination.

### §8.2.2.1 Mid-course Termination of the Irrevocable Trust

If all the beneficiaries including the remaindermen are in existence and of full age and legal capacity, may they (or in the case of a charitable trust, may the attorney general) collude with the trustee to terminate an inter vivos trust even if its purposes have yet to be accomplished? Would the settlor or the settlor's estate have any standing to object? One could well imagine, for example, a situation whereby the spendthrift adult children of a settlor collude with the trustee to break the provisions of an income-only spendthrift trust that was established for their benefit by the parent.[46] Some commentators have argued that the settlor, as a matter of public policy, ought to have standing to compel the

[41] *See generally* id. §341; §8.7 (Merger).

[42] *See generally* id. §335.

[43] *See generally* Committee on Formation, Administration, and Distribution of Trusts, Procedures for Terminating Small Trusts, 19 Real Prop. Prob. & Tr. J. 988 (1984).

[44] *See generally* 4 Scott on Trusts §337.1; *see generally* §8.15.7 (The Claflin Doctrine).

[45] *See generally* 4 Scott on Trusts §§333.1 (fraud), 333.3 (undue influence), 333.4 (mistake); *see* Rebidas v. Murasko, 677 A.2d 331 (Pa. Super. 1996) (suggesting an abuse of confidential relationship on part of lawyer/co-trustee).

[46] *See* 2A Scott on Trusts §151 ("It is held that even though the trust is a spendthrift trust, it can be terminated by the beneficiaries and the settlor if they all consent and are under no disability.").

trustee faithfully to carry out the terms of his trust.[47] Others, most notably Professor Scott, would seem to disagree.[48]

In this day and age of enormous pressure on the elderly and the handicapped to divest themselves of their property, the trustee should exercise due diligence before accepting an irrevocable inter vivos trust. He should assure himself that he is neither buying a lawsuit nor expected to violate that trust.

### §8.2.2.2 The Revocable Trust

The settlor of a trust may reserve a right of revocation.[49] Inherent in that right is the lesser right to amend the trust; inherent in the right to amend is the right to insert by amendment into the trust instrument a revocation provision. A legally incapacitated settlor cannot exercise a reserved right of revocation.[50] May, however, the settlor's agent, acting under a Durable Power of Attorney,[51] exercise it? In theory, yes, provided three conditions are met: (1) the applicable Durable Power of Attorney statute authorizes such an agency, (2) the Durable Power of Attorney under which the agent purports to act is either sufficiently broad or sufficiently precise to cover the purported act of revocation, and (3) the governing trust instrument itself contains a provision that authorizes revocation by proxy.[52] The trustee honors at his peril a revocation by proxy, unless all three conditions have been met. Close attention to matters of authority are warranted as well if the trustee is in receipt of an instrument of revocation submitted by the settlor's conservator or guardian.[53]

Suppose the governing trust instrument contains a revocation provision that *excludes* revocation by proxy. Would such a qualified revocation effectively foreclose revocation by a guardian or agent operating under a Durable Power of Attorney? Why not? Presumably it is the intention of the settlor that during periods of

[47] *See* §4.1 (Interests and Powers Remaining with the Settlor by Operation of Law).

[48] Id.

[49] *See* 4 Scott on Trusts §330.

[50] *See generally* id. §330 n.7 and accompanying text.

[51] Uniform Probate Code §5-501, 8 U.L.A. 419 (1998) (as amended in 1984).

[52] *See* Kline v. Utah Dept. of Health, 776 P.2d 57 (Utah 1989).

[53] *See, e.g.,* In re Bo, 365 N.W.2d 847 (N.D. 1985).

incapacity the trust be irrevocable and that the revocation provision be suspended so that there is no basis of authority on which the agent or guardian can act.[54] To the extent the agent or guardian is foreclosed from terminating an irrevocable trust created before incapacity, so too should it be foreclosed from terminating a trust where the power of revocation is suspended.

### *§8.2.3 Distribution Issues*

The trustee who distributes the wrong amount or pays it to the wrong person must bear the loss.[55] The cases which surcharge the trustee for making erroneous distribution are peculiarly distressing. It has been held that if the trustee pays the wrong person even under advice of counsel, the trustee will be obliged to refund the amount with interest. Particular care must be taken when a power of attorney or order for payment or assignment is presented. It is as dangerous to pay over to one whose interest has terminated as to pay over on an invalid assignment.

The trustee ought not to pay a minor's share to the minor or the minor's natural parent, lest the trustee be required to pay again when the minor comes of age. Payment should be made only to the minor's formally appointed guardian (which may of course be the child's natural parent) or to someone informally appointed pursuant to the terms of a statute enacted to facilitate the distribution of trust property to minors.[56] A well-drafted trust instrument will make provision for retaining the minor's share in trust until the minor reaches the age of majority. Such a provision, however, is not helpful when small amounts are involved.

The fact that the trustee has been diligent or has taken advice will not be of any help when it comes to misdelivery. The trustee's only protection for misdelivery is if it were done under a court

[54] "Where the settlor reserves a power to revoke the trust under certain circumstances, he can revoke it only under those circumstances." 4 Scott on Trusts §330.8.

[55] Restatement (Second) of Trusts §§226, 345 comment *j* (1959).

[56] *See, e.g.*, Uniform Transfers to Minors Act, 8B U.L.A. 497 (1993).

order obtained without fraud and with proper notice having been given to all interested parties.[57]

Prior to making distributions the trustee should make certain that all taxes due with respect to the property have been paid, including income, estate, and generation-skipping-transfer taxes. The trustee who distributes property needed to satisfy a tax obligation may be personally liable for all or a portion of the tax.[58] The key to an orderly and satisfactory settlement of the trust's tax obligations is timely coordination with the settlor's executor, the beneficiary, or the beneficiary's executor, as appropriate.

Upon termination of the trust, it is the trustee's duty to distribute the trust principal to the remainder beneficiaries. The trust instrument will often contain specific provisions directing the method of distribution. If there are none, the method of distribution intended by the settlor may be inferred from the general language of the instrument. Generally, the remainder beneficiaries may determine the method, as long as all are in agreement as to what it should be. Even if the trustee is directed by the terms of the trust to use a particular method of distribution, the remainder beneficiaries acting in concert may require that a different method be employed.[59]

Absent specific provisions, general guiding language, or agreement among the remainder beneficiaries, the proper method of distribution depends upon all the facts and circumstances. Where a single beneficiary is entitled to the trust property, the trustee would be expected to distribute the property in kind.[60] Where there are several remainder beneficiaries, three methods of distribution are possible: (1) transferring the trust property in kind to the remainder beneficiaries as tenants in common, (2) dividing the trust property into equal shares and distributing the trust property in kind to each remainder beneficiary, or (3) selling the trust property and

[57] *See generally,* §§6.1.5.2 (Duty to Keep and Render Accounts) and 7.1 (Trustee's Liabilities Generally).

[58] *See generally* Bogert, Trusts and Trustees §265 (income tax); Stephens et al., Federal Estate and Gift Taxation ¶8.02 (estate tax) and ¶12.03 (generation-skipping tax) (6th ed. 1991).

[59] *See* 4 Scott on Trusts §347.1; Restatement (Second) of Trusts §346 (1959).

[60] *See* Restatement (Second) of Trusts §345 comment *d* (1959).

dividing the proceeds among the remainder beneficiaries.[61] If appropriate, distribution might be made partly in cash and partly in kind. The proper method of distribution depends upon what is reasonable under all the circumstances.[62] The trustee should consider the nature of the assets, the number of remainder beneficiaries, market conditions, tax implications, and so forth.[63] When making a distribution, be it in cash or in kind, the trustee is under a duty to the remainder beneficiaries to act impartially.

## *§8.2.4 Trust Termination Checklist*

Winding up the affairs of a trust that has terminated can be a difficult and time-consuming process. Who qualify as remaindermen is not always clear; tax filings can get complicated; valuing and splitting the portfolio can be tricky. And then there are the remaindermen who have been waiting in the wings for years. Now that the life beneficiary has died, they want their property. The trustee does not want the process to drag on; for there is always the danger that a remainderman will die during the process. That can only further complicate and delay things. The following is a trust termination checklist designed to help the trustee get through this difficult period as quickly as possible, bearing in mind that there is absolute liability for misdelivery. Upon the event that triggers the termination, for example, the death of the life beneficiary, the trustee should:

### Legal

(1) Notify counsel for the trust, as well as the tax accountant (or tax officer) and the broker, if any, that the trust has terminated;

(2) If the trust was revocable, confirm that it was properly executed and valid.[64]

[61] Id. §347 comment *a*.

[62] Id. comment *c*.

[63] Id. *See also* Boston Safe Deposit & Trust Co. v. Boone, 21 Mass. App. Ct. 637, 489 N.E.2d 209 (1986).

[64] *See generally* Nunan, Trustee Liability: The Ghost of Distributions Past, 9 Prob. & Real Prop. 8 (Nov/Dec 1995); *see also* Jay M. Zitter, J.D., Liability of

(3) Ascertain who is entitled to undistributed income that has accrued to the time of termination;
(4) Obtain for the file a written legal opinion (and, if necessary, a judicial determination) that specifies who are the remaindermen;
(5) Check for QTIP elections, GST elections, disclaimers, and assignments that may have been made in the past with respect to the trust;
(6) Prepare and have approved (or judicially allowed, if necessary) accountings for the period beginning immediately after the period covered by the last approved account and ending at the time of termination;
(7) If the trust contains real estate, ascertain whether some action must be taken pursuant to some environmental statute or regulation;

**Tax**

(8) Early on, estimate the federal tax consequences for the trust estate *and for the remaindermen* of termination distributions (transfer tax) and posttermination sales (income tax);
(9) Early on, estimate the state tax consequences for the trust estate *and for the remaindermen* of termination distributions (transfer tax) and posttermination sales (income tax);
(10) Early on, understand the tax consequences, if any, of making distributions in one year rather than another;
(11) Early on, ascertain whether prior tax returns will have to be amended;
(12) Early on, ascertain whether there is a need to file for tax rebates;
(13) Meet regularly and often with the tax accountant (or tax officer) to make sure that no tax balls are being dropped;

---

Trustee for Payments or Conveyances Under a Trust Subsequently Held to be Invalid, 77 A.L.R. 4th 1177 (1990).

### Operations

(14) Locate and gather in one easily accessible location all past accountings, tax returns, brokerage statements, portfolio valuations, and legal opinions that pertain to the trust and keep the file current going forward;

(15) Early on, get the current full names, current full addresses, current telephone and fax numbers, and the social security numbers of the remaindermen (or the Tax I.D. numbers of personal representatives of any deceased remaindermen), and double-check the information for accuracy;

(16) Early on, obtain complete and accurate written transfer instructions from each remainderman;

(17) Early on, obtain complete tax cost information on the trust assets and put that information in a format that the remaindermen and their tax advisors can understand;

(18) Prepare an estimate of the termination costs that must be borne by the trust, such as accrued trustee fees, distribution fees, court filing fees, attorneys' fees, tax return preparation fees, brokerage commissions, and taxes;

(19) Early on, prepare a game plan for raising cash, dividing the portfolio, and dealing with fractional shares, odd lots, and illiquid items;

(20) Establish an appropriate reserve for meeting estimated termination costs, a reserve that has a little extra in it to accommodate the unforeseen;

(21) Keep income carefully segregated from principal and make sure each termination expense is charged to the appropriate account;

(22) If a broker has custody of the portfolio, make sure he or she has the operational capability to separately account for income and principal;

### Public Relations

(23) Early on, furnish the remaindermen with a provisional timetable outlining when partial and final distributions

are expected to be made and thereafter, at reasonable intervals, keep them informed as to how things are going;

(24) Early on, furnish the remaindermen with tax cost information;

(25) Early on, if appropriate, warn the remaindermen that *they* may be responsible for paying certain tax obligations *of the trust* and advise them to so notify their tax advisors;

(26) Early on, consult with the remaindermen on post-termination investment strategy;

(27) Unless inappropriate for some reason, circulate to the remaindermen drafts of accountings for their review and comment;

(28) Once an appropriate reserve has been established, immediately begin the process of making partial distributions and paying bills, unless there is a good reason not to do so (e.g., ongoing litigation);

(29) Do not procrastinate in tying up the final loose ends: As soon as possible, get the final accounts prepared and approved (or judicially allowed, if appropriate);

(30) If a remaindermen with a vested beneficial interest in the trust has died before final distribution, ascertain whether you are that remainderman's inadvertent executor.[65]

## §8.3 The Transfer of Trust Property

When the trustee transfers trust property to a bona fide purchaser, title passes free of trust.[1] Such a transfer forecloses the beneficiary's rights against the transferee, though not necessarily against the trustee. Any rights the beneficiary may have against nonbeneficiary takers of the trust property, including those who fail to qualify as bona fide purchasers, are covered elsewhere in this

[65] *See generally* §8.16 (The Trustee of Revocable Trust as "Inadvertent Executor").

**§8.3** [1] Restatement (Second) of Trusts §284 (1959); *see generally* 4 Scott on Trusts §284.

handbook.[2] Recall, however, that a transferee only secures the protection and status afforded a bona fide purchaser if title to the property is obtained for value and without notice.

### §8.3.1 *The Trustee's Personal Creditors and the Trustee's Spouse*

As a general rule, an attachment of the trust property by the trustee's personal creditor is subject to the rights of the beneficiary.[3] The rationale is that the creditor does not pay value to the trust nor does the attachment give the creditor legal title. Certain attachments of real estate, however, may be exempted by statute from this general rule. Many states, for example, now have statutes subordinating the interest of the beneficiary to that of the trustee's personal creditor when the attached real estate is held in an unrecorded trust.[4] Thus it is of primary importance for the trustee of an inter vivos trust containing real estate to record the governing instrument; timely recording effectively deprives the personal creditor of the trustee any access to the trust's real estate. Under most such statutes, the attaching creditor who has no notice of an unrecorded trust of real estate will prevail over the beneficiary even though the creditor receives notice before taking the property on execution.[5]The statutes that give this unusual right do not ordinarily apply to personal property.[6]

As a general rule, the trustee's spouse will have no present or future rights to the trust property.[7] This holds true, both in the divorce context and upon the death of the trustee.[8]

[2]*See* §5.4.2 (Rights of the Beneficiary Against Those Other Than to Trustee (the RFP and others)).

[3]Restatement (Second) of Trusts §308 (1959); *see generally* 4 Scott on Trusts §308.

[4]*See* Restatement (Second) of Trusts §308 comment *b*(1959).

[5]*See generally* 4 Scott on Trusts §308.2.

[6]*See generally* Bogert, Trusts and Trustees §884.

[7]*See generally* Bogert, Trusts and Trustors §146.

[8]Id.

### *§8.3.2 Purchasers for Value of Trust Property*

In the case of real estate, the prospective purchaser ordinarily has notice that the property is held in trust since the instrument is a matter of record. The purchaser must then determine whether the trustee has the power of sale.[9] If the trustee has that power, the transferee will take clear title even though the trustee thereafter misappropriates the proceeds.[10] In England and in many American jurisdictions the purchaser expressly is exempted by statute from monitoring the application of the purchase price.[11]

In the relatively few cases of unrecorded trusts of real estate and in nearly all cases of trusts of personal property, the first matter to be determined is whether the purchaser had notice of a trust's existence. There being no instrument of public record this question becomes one of fact. In the case of *real estate,* for example, the purchaser may be put on notice of the trust as a result of the explicit use of the word *trustee* in a previous deed,[12] material information communicated to the purchaser orally, or the existence of some peculiar circumstance, such as occupation of the property by a person who claims to have a beneficial interest in it.[13] In the case of *securities,* the word *trustee* appearing upon the face of the certificate is sufficient to put the purchaser to his inquiry not only as to the existence of the trust but also as to whether the proposed transfer is within the trustee's powers.[14]

The prospective purchaser who learns that a trust exists must demand to see the trust instrument to determine whether the proposed sale is authorized.[15]

[9] *See* §3.5.3 (The Powers of the Trustee in Equity to Manage the Trust Estate).
[10] *See generally* 4 Scott on Trusts §321.
[11] Id.
[12] *See generally* id. §297.3.
[13] Id.
[14] Id. However, under the Uniform Commercial Code, the issuer or its transfer agent registering a security for transfer is not bound to inquire into the trustee's power. U.C.C. §8-404, 2C U.L.A. 121 (1997 Supp.); *see also* Uniform Act for Simplification of Fiduciary Security Transfers §2, 7B U.L.A. 689 (1985).
[15] Restatement (Second) of Trusts §297 comments *d, k-n* (1959).

### *§8.3.3 Pledgees of Trust Property*

Let us assume that the trustee pledges trust property to secure the trustee's own personal obligation. What are the rights of the pledgee as against the beneficiary? The pledgee is in a critical position: He may be a bona fide purchaser and fully protected in his security rights or, if the circumstances are against him, he may be at the extreme opposite pole, in the position of colluding in a breach of trust with full responsibility to the beneficiary as a constructive trustee. Thus a person who in good faith lends money to the trust and accepts a pledge of trust property will be fully protected despite a subsequent misappropriation of the proceeds of the loan.[16] However, if the lender accepts a pledge of known trust property to secure what the lender knows to be the trustee's personal indebtedness, the lender colludes in a breach of the trustee's duty of loyalty. It should be noted that a pledgee of stock would be put upon inquiry by the presence of the word *trustee* on the face of the certificate.[17]

### *§8.3.4 Banks Receiving Deposits from Trustees*

A bank generally is not bound to see that the trustee properly administers the trust's bank account even when it has notice that the money belongs to the trust.[18] It would be impossible to conduct business under any other rule. Therefore, in cases where the trustee, apparently acting in the ordinary course of business, draws funds from the trust account and deposits them in his own account, or in situations where the trustee deposits a trust check in his own account, the bank is not in any way liable.[19] If, on the other hand, the trustee, in breach of trust, attempts to satisfy his personal obligation to the bank with trust funds, and

[16] Id. §284 comment *g*.
[17] *See generally* 4 Scott on Trusts §297.3.
[18] *See generally* id. §324; Restatement (Second) of Trusts §324 (1959).
[19] *See generally* 4 Scott on Trusts §324.3.

the bank is on notice of the trust, then the bank must give up the funds.[20]

### *§8.3.5 Stock Transfer Agents*

The stock transfer agent who is asked to effect transfer of a trust's shares in a corporation, and the corporation itself, are placed in an unpleasant position whenever the trustee is engaged in a wrongful assignment or sale of the shares. The underlying rule is that any person who knowingly assists in the wrongful disposition of the trust property is fully responsible.[21] This means that, in the absence of a statute, whenever the corporation or its transfer agent knows of the existence of a trust it must ascertain whether the trustee has the power of sale.[22] As the duty to ascertain the trustee's authority is placed upon the corporation, it or its agent would be justified in declining to make transfer unless the trustee supplies the certificates for inspection or produces other evidence showing a right to make the transfer. Most states have now adopted statutes relieving corporations and their transfer agents of the duty to investigate a trustee's authority to transfer securities unless they have actual knowledge of the lack thereof.[23]

## §8.4 The Trustee's Compensation

The general rule now in the United States is that the trustee is entitled to reasonable compensation.[1] In some states the

[20] *See generally* id. §324.4.

[21] *See generally* Bogert, Trusts and Trustees §901; *see generally* §8.21 (Duty of Third Parties to Investigate Whether Trustee has Power to Act or Is Properly Exercising the Power).

[22] *See generally* Bogert, Trusts and Trustees §905.

[23] Id.

**§8.4** [1] *See generally* 3A Scott on Trusts §242; *see also* Revised Reg. 9, reprinted in Appendix II, 12 C.F.R. §9.15(a) (1997) (If the amount of a national bank's trustee's fees are set by statute,[2] and in others it is a matter of custom and practice. The prevailing practice in this country is to calculate the trustee's compensation on the basis of a fixed percentage of income and principal.[3] When the trustee is also counsel to the trust, however, the practice of charging on a time basis for the legal work and on a percentage basis for the fiduciary responsibility can give the appearance that the trust is being double-billed. In this situation, it is probably better both for the attorney-trustee and the beneficiary if all compensation is time based.[4]

When the rule is that a trustee is entitled to reasonable compensation, what is "reasonable" depends upon the facts and circumstances. Courts consider "the amount and difficulty of the services rendered by the trustee, the risks run by the trustee, and the responsibilities imposed upon him, and his skill and success in administering the trust."[5]

When there are cotrustees, some jurisdictions hold that compensation for all should not exceed an amount that would be charged if there were only one.[6] Others permit total compensation to reasonably exceed the amount a single trustee would charge, provided the trust benefits from the special skills and expertise that each cotrustee brings to the table.[7] In some states, cotrustee fees are set by statute.[8] Occasionally, a trust instrument will fix the trustee's fee at a certain percentage or amount.[9]

Table 8-1 is an analysis of the standard graduated fee schedules of corporate trustees in Boston, New York, Miami, Chicago,

---

compensation for acting in a fiduciary capacity is not set or governed by applicable law, the bank may charge a reasonable fee for its services).

[2] *See generally* Bogert, Trusts and Trustees §975.

[3] Id.

[4] *See, e.g.,* Grimes v. Perkins School for the Blind, 22 Mass. App. Ct. 439 494 N.E.2d 406 (1986); *see* §6.1.3.3 (Trustee Benefiting as Buyer and Seller); *see also,* B. Glen, Annot., Right to double compensation where some person (natural or corporate) acts as executor and trustee, 85 A.L.R.2d 537 (1962).

[5] 3A Scott on Trusts §242 at 277.

[6] Id. at §242.10.

[7] Id.

[8] Id.

[9] *See* J.P. Ludington, Annot., Limiting Effect of Provision in Contract, Will, or Trust Instrument Fixing Trustee's or Executor's Fees, 19 A.L.R.3d 520 (1968).

and Los Angeles. A review of this representative sampling should assist the trustee in formulating a fee schedule that conforms to industry standards.

**Table 8-1. Standard Charge Schedules of Corporate Trustees (June 1997)**

| *Principal* | *Boston* | *New York* | *Miami* | *Chicago* | *Los Angeles* |
|---|---|---|---|---|---|
| First $1 million | 1.05 | 1.03 | .933 | .76 | 1.01 |
| Next $2 million | .70 | .87 | .58 | .452 | .775 |
| Next $2 million | .575 | .69 | .44 | .384 | .62 |
| Next $5 million | .45 | .49 | .39 | .23 | .485 |
| Above $10 million | .40 | .40 | .39 | .23 | .40 |

The figures in Table 8-1, stated in June 1997, are percentages of principal. Many trustees charge a minimum annual fee, typically ranging from $1,500 to $7,500 per trust. One bank is charging a minimum annual fee of $20,000. Some trustee compensation schedules are calculated not only on a percentage of the value of principal but also on a percentage of the value of income earned.[10] Income charges, as with principal charges, are typically set on a sliding scale. The range of income charges is one percent at the low end and seven percent at the high end. In addition to annual charges, some trustees charge for principal distributions during the term of a trust and upon its termination. The range for principal distributions is .5 percent of principal at the low end and two percent at the high end.

For special service above and beyond the call of duty, the trustee may be entitled to extra compensation, but the matter is not without some controversy.[11] In recent years corporate fiduciaries have been the subject of class action suits for their compensation practices.[12]

Revised Reg. 9, reprinted in Appendix II, provides that a bank administering a collective investment fund may charge a reasonable fund management fee only if (1) the fee is permitted under

[10] *See generally* Bogert, Trusts and Trustees §975.
[11] *See generally* 3A Scott on Trusts §242.2.
[12] *See, e.g.,* Upp v. Mellon Bank, NA, 799 F. Supp. 540 (E.D. Pa. 1992), *reversed,* 994 F.2d 1039 (1993).

applicable law and (2) the "amount of the fee does not exceed an amount commensurate with the value of legitimate services of tangible benefit to the participating fiduciary accounts that would not have been provided to the accounts were they not invested in the fund."[13] "A bank administering a collective investment fund may charge reasonable expenses incurred in operating the collective investment fund, to the extent not prohibited by applicable law in the state in which the bank maintains the fund."[14] The bank, however, must absorb the expenses of establishing or reorganizing a collective investment fund.[15]

## §8.5 Conflict of Laws

When a trust instrument is prepared and executed in one state and the trust itself is administered in another, what is a trustee to do if the laws of the two states are in conflict? Which state's law is to be applied? Much depends upon the issue. Laws may be contradictory when it comes to the validity of the trust itself;[1] the construction of its terms;[2] rules of administration;[3] or the rights, duties, and obligations of fiduciaries, beneficiaries, creditors, and others who may come in contact with the trust.[4] One state may recognize spendthrift trusts, the other may not;[5] one may have adopted the Uniform Statutory Rule Against Perpetuities, the other may not have done so;[6] in one state, a word such as *heirs* or *issue* might encompass illegitimates; in the other state it

[13] *See* 12 C.F.R. §9.18(b)(9)(ii) (1997).
[14] *See* 12 C.F.R. §9.18(b)(10) (1997).
[15] Id.

**§8.5** [1] *See generally* J. Schoenblum, Multistate and Multinational Estate Planning §17.01 (1982).
[2] Id. at §17.02.
[3] Id. at §§17.03-17.04.
[4] Id. at §17.05.
[5] *See* §5.3.3.3(c) (The Spendthrift Trust); Schoenblum, *supra* note 1, §17.07; 5A Scott on Trusts §§625-628, 660.
[6] *See* §8.2.1.7 (Perpetuities Legislation).

might not.[7] States will have differing approaches to compensation, apportionment, revocability, disposition in default and investing. Such inconveniences are the inevitable consequence of a federal system of government.

As a general rule, the question of which law applies in a particular situation is best left in the hands of the lawyer. A review of Professor Schoenblum's treatise on multistate and multinational estate planning[8] or the conflict of laws chapter in Professor's Scott's treatise on trusts[9] will reveal to the trustee just how subtle, complicated, and unsettled — how lacking in easy answers — this area of the law is. We offer here some rough rules of thumb which the trustee may find helpful when framing requests for legal opinions. However, a detailed treatment of the subject of conflict of laws — including which court will have jurisdiction over a trust with multistate contacts — is well beyond the scope of this handbook.

First, a trust that contains a single parcel of real estate is governed by the laws of the state in which the parcel is located.[10] Unfortunately, if the trust contains real estate located in more than one state, or both real estate and movables, no similarly simple rule covers such variations on the theme.[11]

Second, a trust containing only movables is governed by the laws of the state in which the trust is being administered.[12] There are many exceptions to this rule. For example, what if a testamentary trust is being administered in a state other than the state where the will was probated? Under those circumstances, the laws of the state of probate might govern.[13] Moreover, what is the state of administration? Where the trustee resides? Where the movables are located? Which movables?

[7] *See* §5.2 (Class Designation: "Issue" and "Heirs").

[8] Schoenblum, *supra* note 1.

[9] 5A Scott on Trusts §§553-666 (ch. 14).

[10] *See generally* Schoenblum, *supra* note 1, §§17.01.1, 17.01.3, 17.02.1, 17.03.1; 5A Scott on Trusts §§648, 649, 652, 659; Restatement (Second) Conflict of Laws §§277-278 (1971).

[11] *See generally* 5A Scott on Trusts §§643-663.

[12] *See generally* Schoenblum, *supra* note 1, §§17.01.2, 17.01.4-5, 17.02.2, 17.03.2-3; 5A Scott on Trusts §§574, 592, 605-607.

[13] *See generally* Schoenblum, *supra*, §17.01.2 (1982); 5A Scott on Trusts §592.

Third, notwithstanding the first two rules, if a settlor provides that the laws of a particular state are to govern the administration of a trust and the construction of its terms, then the court will honor the provision as to moveables, except when to do so would violate the public policy of the state in which the trust is being administered.[14] A court having jurisdiction over a trust's administration, for example, would not enforce a spendthrift clause in a state which looks with disfavor on spendthrift trusts, even if the settlor's choice of law were that of some other state more favorably disposed towards such trusts.[15] In the absence of express language as to which state's laws shall apply, a court may well infer that the settlor of an inter vivos trust intended the laws of the settlor's domicile to apply, particularly if the governing instrument was prepared and signed there.[16] But what if the settlor changed domiciles after execution? Or there were more than one settlor? What if the settlor resided in one state, had the instrument prepared in another, and signed it in a third? Again, the trustee will find it difficult obtaining legal opinions free of qualification and hedging when the trust has contacts with more than one state.

We have touched briefly on the problems that arise when the settlor was domiciled in one state and the trust is administered in another. But more likely it is the *beneficiary* — not the settlor — who was domiciled in a state other than the administration state. This situation can bring with it its own set of conflict of laws issues (*e.g.*, when the settlor provides for distribution upon the death of a beneficiary to the beneficiary's "issue").[17] The word *issue* can mean one thing in the settlor's domicile and quite another thing in the beneficiary's. In the settlor's state it may include illegitimates; in the beneficiary's it may not. Which meaning applies? The better view seems to be the state where the instrument was prepared and signed, particularly if it was the settlor's domicile, unless the settlor had expressed a contrary intention in the governing instrument.[18] To some extent, it is a rule of administrative convenience: While a trust may have many beneficiaries in many

[14] *See generally* Schoenblum, *supra,* §17.01.6.
[15] *See generally* id. §17.07.
[16] *See generally* 5A Scott on Trusts §612.
[17] *See* §5.2 (Class Designation: "Issue" and "Heirs").
[18] *See generally* 5A Scott on Trusts §578.

different states, there is usually only one settlor. Moreover, it is reasonable to expect that the settlor and the drafting attorney were relying on the prevailing meaning of the word in the state of preparation and execution, particularly if it was the state of the settlor's domicile. Otherwise, the meaning of the word is held hostage to the migratory habits of the beneficiaries.

Suppose a settlor provides that upon the death of the beneficiary the trust property consisting of moveables passes outright and free of trust to the beneficiary's heirs. If the term *heirs* refers to intestate takers, which intestacy law is being referred to, that of the beneficiary's domicile or that of the settlor's? Does *heirs* cover only those persons, if any, who *actually* inherited the beneficiary's property under the laws of intestacy or those persons who *would have* inherited the property assuming the beneficiary had died intestate?[19] If the latter, then it is said the heirs take title "by purchase" from the trustee. If the term imports the indicative, then the law of the beneficiary's domicile would of course govern; if the term imports the subjunctive, then perhaps the trustee must look to the intestacy law of the settlor's domicile.[20] But to which version of the law? The one in effect when the trust was executed? The one in effect at the time of the beneficiary's death? A prospective trustee should think long and hard before accepting a trust which employs without elaboration the term *heirs*.[21]

A final word of advice: The prospective trustee should make sure that as many potential conflict of laws issues as possible are preempted in the governing instrument, and should be particularly wary of "boilerplate" language, especially if it causes unfamiliar laws to apply to the trust's administration and to the construction of its terms. The prospective trustee should know the rules of the game before the game starts.[22]

[19] *See generally* National Shawmut Bank v. Joy, 315 Mass. 457, 462-467, 53 N.E.2d 113, 117-120 (1944).

[20] 5A Scott on Trusts §578.

[21] M. Reutlinger, Wills, Trusts, and Estates: Essential Terms and Concepts 99-100 (1993); 5A Scott on Trusts §578; *see* §5.2 (Class Designation: "Issue" and "Heirs").

[22] *See generally* Rosepink, Representing Clients With Ties to Multiple States or Counties, 22 ACTEC Notes 78 (1996).

## §8.6 The Corporate Trustee

In most jurisdictions, a corporation needs governmental authority to engage in the business of acting as trustee.[1] The requirement is statutory, there being no common law impediment to a corporation per se engaging in such activity so long as it possesses the general authority to hold *property*.[2]

By statute, the Comptroller of the Currency is vested with the authority to grant a federal trust charter.[3] A corporation with federal trust powers will carry the official designation of a national bank, whether or not it is authorized to engage in commercial banking activities as well.[4] The authority to grant a state trust charter, more often than not, is vested by statute in a state's banking commissioner.[5] Corporations with state trust charters often carry the designation *trust company*. A granting authority, whether federal or state, usually is charged by statute with the responsibility of regulating how the grantee corporation then carries out its trust charter.

Whether a particular group of organizers should seek a federal or state trust charter is well beyond the scope of this handbook.[6] It will depend upon many things, including which statutory and regulatory scheme best accommodates the group's business objectives and expectations.[7] Chartering authorities, for example,

**§8.6** [1] *See generally* 2 Scott on Trusts §§96.3, 96.5; Bogert, Trusts and Trustees §131.

[2] *See generally* 2 Scott on Trusts §96.

[3] 12 U.S.C. §92a(a) (1989).

[4] *See* 12 C.F.R. §5.22(a)(2) (1992).

[5] *See generally* Bogert, Trusts and Trustees §§135, 136.

[6] For a discussion of choice of chartering authority, *see* Symons & White, Banking Law 63-69 (3d ed. 1991).

[7] *See* id. at 72-75 for a discussion of the factors which the Office of the Comptroller of the Currency considers in deciding whether to grant a federal charter.

Anyone interested in acquiring a national charter may obtain the Comptroller's Manual for Corporate Activities, a three-volume guidebook containing the policies, procedures, and forms used in the application process. The manual may be ordered by writing to the Comptroller of the Currency at the following address: Comptroller of the Currency, P.O. Box 70004, Chicago, IL 60673-0004. A ninety-dollar fee ($90), payable to the Comptroller of the Curwill differ as to capital and surplus requirements. It should be noted, however, that no federal trust charter may be issued to a national bank operating in a state whose capital and surplus requirements for banks are *below* levels set for trust institutions chartered by that state.[8]

## §8.7 Merger

The doctrine of merger is occasionally a trap for the unwary; more often it is invoked in situations where it is inapplicable. Thus the trustee needs to understand the concept if only to recognize when the doctrine is *not* a concern.

*Merger* is what happens when one person is given the entire legal interest and the entire beneficial interest in property.[1] In such a case there is no trust;[2] the person simply owns the property outright and free of trust, all interests having "merged" in that person.[3] Thus, the creditors, the spouse, and the taxing authorities might well have greater access to the property than would be the case were the property the subject of a viable trust.[4] If merger has occurred, at death the property passes in accordance with the terms of the person's will or by intestate succession, not in accordance with the terms of the instrument governing the purported trust.[5] Obviously if those who are mentioned in the trust instrument are different from those

---

rency, should accompany the written request. For a listing of state statutes relating to the chartering of bank and trust companies, *see* M. P. Malloy, The Corporate Law of Banks; appendix, chart 2.1 (State Bank Charters: Requirements) and chart 2.2 (Availability of Trust Powers: State Requirements) (1988).

[8]12 U.S.C. §92a(i) (1989).

**§8.7** [1]*See generally* 2 Scott on Trusts §99; Restatement (Second) of Trusts §99 (1959); Bogert, Trusts and Trustees §§129, 1003.

[2]2 Scott on Trusts §99.

[3]Bogert, Trusts and Trustees §129 (rev. 2d ed. 1984); *see generally* Larry D. Scheafer, Annot., Trusts: Merger of Legal and Equitable Estates Where Sole Trustees are Sole Beneficiaries, 7 A.L.R. 4th 621 (1996).

[4]*See generally* 2 Scott on Trusts §99.

[5]Id.

mentioned in the will, merger will benefit the latter. Merger may have consequences as well in the welfare eligibility and recoupment area.

But more often than not there is no merger. Let us assume a trust, *A* to *B* for *C* for life, then to *D*. If the same person is the sole trustee and the sole income beneficiary, and if upon death the property passes to the person's executor or administrator — in other words to the estate — then there is a merger. In other words, if *B, C,* and *D* are the same person, there is no trust — in fact there never was one. (Nowadays one seldom runs across instruments where an estate possesses the remainder interest, with the possible exception of nominee or realty trusts.[6] The property usually passes directly by purchase to someone's relatives.[7])

As one can see, not much need be done to prevent a merger of interests. The simple introduction of a cotrustee into the formula should avoid such a result.[8] Or if upon the death of *C* the property passes to the then-living issue of *C* rather than to *C*'s estate there is no merger, except perhaps in New York.[9] In this day and age, one has to work hard to back into a merger.

The trustee should always keep in mind that a right to revoke or the possession of a general inter vivos power of appointment is not what triggers a merger.[10] Thus if *A, B,* and *C* are the same but *D* is the *issue* of *B/C* living at the termination of the trust, then there is no merger even in the face of a reserved right of revocation or general inter vivos power of appointment in *B/C*.[11] It is when *D* is the estate of *B/C* and *B/C* are the same person that merger comes about. The existence of a reserved right of revocation or general inter vivos power of appointment does not affect the situation one way or the other. With the revocable living trust now the core of most estate plans it is important that the trustee separate issues relating to merger from issues relating

[6] *See* §9.6 (Trusts That Resemble Corporations or Agencies).

[7] *See generally* National Shawmut Bank v. Joy, 315 Mass. 457, 462-467, 53 N.E.2d 113, 117-120 (1944).

[8] *See, e.g.,* First Ala. Bank of Tuscaloosa v. Webb, 373 So. 2d 631 (Ala. 1979).

[9] *See generally* 2 Scott on Trusts §99.3; *see also,* Fratcher, Trustor as Sole Trustee and Only Ascertainable Beneficiary, 47 Mich. L. Rev. 907, 934 (1949).

[10] *See Joy,* 315 Mass. at 469-478, 53 N.E.2d at 124-126.

[11] *See* Harrison, Structuring Trusts to Permit the Donor to Act as Trustee, 22 Estate Planning 331 (No. 6-Nov./Dec. 1995).

to powers of revocation and general inter vivos powers of appointment. These powers are technically personal rights of disposition, not interests in property.[12]

## §8.8 Whom Does Counsel Represent?

The question of whether counsel represents the trustee, the beneficiaries, or both, is a difficult one[1] and depends to some extent on the facts and circumstances. The issues are subtle.[2]

If counsel is advising the *office of trustee* as it were, then the trustee is the primary client.[3] Courts have ruled, however, that counsel has certain "restrictive" duties that run to the beneficiary as well.[4] Counsel, for example, may not exploit, to the detriment of either party, confidential information acquired in the course of his or her representation.[5] Nor may counsel withhold from the beneficiary information to which the beneficiary is entitled.[6] Because

[12]*See* id., 315 Mass. at 474, 53 N.E.2d 113 at 124.

**§8.8** [1]Existing case law is confused, incomplete, and insufficient. *See* Pennell, Representations Involving Fiduciary Entities: Who Is the Client? 62 Fordham L. Rev. 1319, 1321-1326 (1994); ACTEC Commentaries on Model Rules of Professional Conduct (ACTEC Foundation 2d ed. Mar. 1995), Reporter's Note at 1-4 (hereinafter "ACTEC Commentaries")). *See generally* Reid, Mureiko, Mikeska, Privilege and Confidentiality Issues When a Lawyer Represents a Fiduciary, 30 Real Prop. Prob. & Tr. J. 541 (1996) and Johns, Fickett's Thicket: The Lawyer's Expanding Fiduciary and Ethical Boundaries When Serving Older Americans of Moderate Wealth, 32 Wake Forest L.R. 445 (1997); *see also* §5.4.1.1 (Right to Information and Confidentiality).

[2]*See generally* Frank, The Legal Ethics of Louis D. Brandeis, 17 Stan. L. Rev. 683, 694 (1965) (The Warren Matter).

[3]*See* Gadsden, Ethical Guidelines for the Fiduciary's Lawyer, 134 Tr. & Est. 8, 10 (Mar. 1995); Ross, "Particularized Guidance" for the Estate and Trust Lawyer, 133 Tr. & Est. 10, 14 (July 1994).

[4]*See* ACTEC Commentaries, *supra* note 1, at 3-4, 34 (discussing nature of duties owed to beneficiaries); Gadsden, *supra* note 2, at 10 (stating duties are restrictive in nature). *But see* Spinner v. Nutt, 417 Mass. 549, 631 N.E.2d 542 (1994) (holding no duty of reasonable care imposed with respect to beneficiaries if it would conflict with duty owed to fiduciary-client); 2A Scott on Trusts §173.

[5]*See* Gadsden, *supra* note 2, at 16 (confidentiality requirements).

[6]Id.; ACTEC Commentaries, *supra* note 1, at 5 (good faith, fairness, and impartiality.)

counsel has an obligation to advise the trustee on the nature of the trustee's fiduciary responsibilities and how best to carry them out, as well as a right to be paid from the trust, it is said that the beneficiary enjoys the status of a "derivative" or "secondary" client.[7] It is even suggested that counsel would have an affirmative duty to disclose to the beneficiary any serious wrongdoing on the part of the trustee, e.g. embezzlement.[8]

If counsel, on the other hand, has been retained by the trustee as his *personal lawyer* to advise him on matters such as how to defend an action for breach of trust, then counsel may have few, if any, duties to the beneficiary.[9]

The important thing to remember when it comes to legal representation is that the parties at all times must understand who represents whom. Or perhaps more important, who does *not* represent whom.[10] If it is reasonable for a beneficiary to assume that counsel is representing the beneficiary's interests when counsel is not, then, at minimum, counsel has a duty to communicate to the beneficiary that the beneficiary is in fact unrepresented.[11] The way around all of this is for counsel, at the time he or she is hired by the trustee, to communicate directly with the beneficiaries regarding the nature of the representation. Certainly when storm clouds are gathering on the horizon — when trouble is brewing between the

[7] *See* ACTEC Commentaries, *supra* note 1, at 3; Hazard & Hodes, The Law of Lawyering, A Handbook on the Model Rules of Professional Conduct §1.3:108 (2d ed. 1994).

[8] *See* ACTEC Commentaries, *supra* note 1, at 5, 32, 34-36 (affirmative duties to beneficiaries); Ross, *supra* note 2, at 16 (duty to disclose breach of fiduciary duty). *Cf.* Gadsden, *supra* note 2, at 41 (lawyer should first counsel fiduciary to take corrective action); *see generally* Reid, Mureiko, Mikeska, Privilege and Confidentiality Issues When a Lawyer Represents a Fiduciary, 30 Real Prop. Prob. & Tr. J. 542, 547, 552 (1996).

[9] *See* ACTEC Commentaries, *supra* note 1, at 34. *See also* Wingfield, Fiduciary Attorney-Client Communications: An Illusory Privilege? 8 Prob. & Prop. 60, 62 (1994) (protected communications); §3.5.2.3 (Rights in Equity to Exoneration and Reimbursement).

[10] *See* ACTEC Commentaries, *supra* note 1, at 29 (communications with beneficiaries); *see generally* Reid, Mureiko, Mikeska, Privilege and Confidentiality Issues When a Lawyer Represents a Fiduciary, 30 Real Prop. Prob. & Tr. J. 541, 556 (1996).

[11] *See* Gadsden, *supra* note 2, at n.17, *citing* Butler v. State Bar, 42 Cal. 3d 323, 721 P.2d 585 (1986).

trustee and the beneficiary or between the beneficiary and other beneficiaries — counsel and the trustee have an affirmative duty to advise the beneficiary in a timely fashion that the beneficiary ought to retain his or her own independent counsel. The prudent trustee sees to it that this advice is rendered in writing and that there is a record of it having been received.

In a suit by the beneficiary against the trustee, may the beneficiary compel the trustee to disclose to the beneficiary communications between the trustee and his counsel that are relevant to the matter being litigated? In other words, may the trustee successfully invoke the attorney/client privilege against the beneficiary ? As to communications uttered *after* the onset of hostilities, the answer is an unequivocal "yes".[12] As to communications uttered *before* the onset of hostilities, the answer is a hedged "no."[13] Certainly, the prudent trustee should assume that any pre-confrontation communications with counsel are discoverable and act accordingly.[14]

## §8.9 Why More Than One Trust: The Estate and Generation-Skipping Tax

Because this handbook focuses on the rights, duties, and obligations of the parties *after* the trust is established, a thorough

[12] *See generally* Gibbs and Hanson, The Fiduciary Exception to a Trustee's Attorney/Client Privilege, 21 ACTEC Notes 236 (1995).

[13] Id at 239; in New York, a trustee may only invoke the attorney/client privilege for "good cause." *See* Hoopes v. Carota, 142 A.D.2d 906, 531 N.Y.S.2d 407 (App. Div. 1988), *aff'd,* 74 N.Y.2d 716, 543 N.E.2d 73, 544 N.Y.S.2d 808 (1989). *But see,* Huie, individually and as executor and trustee, v. the Honorable Nikki De Shazo, Judge, 922 S.W.2d 920 (Tex. 1996) (suggesting there is no "fiduciary exception" to the attorney/client privilege).

[14] Gibbs and Hanson, The Fiduciary Exception to a Trustee's Attorney/Client Privilege, 21 ACTEC Notes, 236, 240 (1995) ("Assuming the inchoate existence of some fiduciary exception rule in your jurisdiction, the question for the attorney is: how do my fiduciary clients and I conduct our communications *prior* to the time a beneficiary asserts a claim . . . ? Alertly, carefully, and clearly is the certain answer."). *See generally,* Desmarais, The Fiduciary, His Counsel and the Attorney-Client Privilege, 136 Tr. & Est. 29 (no. 6 May 1997).

treatment of the tax considerations that go into the *initial design* of a trust is beyond its scope.[1] On the other hand, the trustee should have some inkling of why a trust looks the way it does. Why, for instance, did the same settlor create more than one trust for the same beneficiary? There is also the rare occasion when it falls to the trustee to act as "inadvertent executor" (for tax purposes) of the settlor's estate.[2]

Because the majority of trusts are established to minimize estate and generation-skipping taxes, that is where the author will focus and limit the discussion. There will be no discussion of the more exotic estate tax minimization vehicles, such as the GRIT, the GRAT, and the GRUT.[3] Later on, however, these are brief introductions to the QPRT (see §9.15), the CRUT (see §4.5.1.1), the CRAT (see §9.4.4.1.2), the Charitable Lead Trust (see §9.4.5.2), and the Crummey Trust (see §9.2).

### *§8.9.1 The Federal Estate Tax*

The federal estate tax is a tax on certain property transfers occasioned by the death of a beneficial owner.[4] A discussion of what property interests generate an estate tax — that is, what property interests may comprise the federal gross estate — could fill volumes.[5] Suffice it to say that in the context of trusts such prop-

**§8.9** [1]Many excellent estate planning treatises thoroughly address the role of the trust in estate planning. *See generally* Casner, Estate Planning (5th ed. 1983 & Supp. 1998); Farr & Wright, An Estate Planner's Handbook (4th ed. 1979 & Supp. 1994); Fiore et al., Modern Estate Planning (1990); Manning, Estate Planning (4th ed. 1991); Susman, Estate Planning: Forms, Practice and Tax Analysis (1989).

[2]*See generally* §8.16 (The Trustee of Revocable Trust as "Inadvertent Executor").

[3]The GRIT is a grantor-retained income trust, the GRAT is a grantor-retained annuity trust, and the GRUT is a grantor-retained unitrust. *See generally supra* note 1.

[4]I.R.C. §2001(a). *See also* Treas. Reg. §20.2033-1(a).

[5]*See generally* I.R.C. §§2031-2046; 34A Am. Jur. 2d, Federal Taxation ¶143,001 et seq.; Stephens et al., Federal Estate and Gift Taxation, ¶¶4.01-4.18 (gross estate) (6th ed. 1991).

erty is likely to include the property of a deceased settlor that was held in a revocable inter vivos trust or that became the subject of a trust upon the settlor's death.[6] A general understanding of what the tax is about and how it may have influenced the architecture of a particular trust, however, requires some familiarity with the following: (1) the unified credit, (2) the estate tax tables, and (3) the marital deduction.

#### §8.9.1.1 The Unified Credit

Under the Internal Revenue Code (the "Code"), the net taxable estate of approximately $600,000 or less for someone dying in 1997 generated no federal estate tax.[7] The number $600,000 was called the "credit equivalent," or "applicable exclusion amount" because the Code allowed a total "credit" of $192,800 against a person's *aggregate* lifetime gift and postmortem estate tax liabilities.[8] This translated into $600,000 worth of property.[9] For example, assuming no lifetime taxable transfers, the computation of a $192,800 estate tax would mean no federal estate tax due on the 1997 postmortem transfer of $600,000 to someone other than the settlor's spouse or to a charity. Again, the $600,000 figure was essentially the economic value of the "unified credit." It was an upper limit on the value of property that could pass tax-free in 1997 to someone other than the spouse or a charity.[10] The term

[6] *See* I.R.C. §§2036-2038 (discussing taxability of transfers with retained life estates, transfers taking effect at death, and revocable transfers); Stephens, *supra* note 5, at ¶4.08-4.10.

[7] *See* I.R.C. §2010; Stephens *supra* note 5, at ¶3.02 (assuming, in addition, decedent died after 1976 and there are no adjusted taxable gifts).

[8] *See* I.R.C. §2010(a). If the decedent made inter vivos gifts between September 8, 1976 and December 31, 1976, the unified credit is reduced by 20 percent of the portion of the $30,000 gift tax exclusion applicable to gifts made by the decedent during that time. I.R.C. §2010(b).

[9] *See* Stephens, *supra* note 5, at ¶3.01. A tax credit operates to reduce the tax directly on a dollar-for-dollar basis. Id. The estate tax on the first $600,000 of taxable estate is $192,800. I.R.C. §2001(c).

[10] *See supra* note 7.

"unified" is employed because it applies to both lifetime and postmortem transfers.[12]

On August 7, 1997, the President signed into law the Taxpayer Relief Act of 1997[13] which, among its many other provisions, provides for the following schedule of incremental increases in the credit equivalent (applicable exclusion amount):[14]

| In the case of estates of decedents dying, and gifts made, during: | The credit equivalent/ applicable exclusion amount shall be: |
|---|---|
| 1998 | $625,000 |
| 1999 | $650,000 |
| 2000 and 2001 | $675,000 |
| 2002 and 2003 | $700,000 |
| 2004 | $850,000 |
| 2005 | $950,000 |
| 2006 and thereafter | $1,000,000 |

### §8.9.1.2 The Estate Tax Rates

The federal estate tax rates[15] are steeply graduated. Accordingly, the federal rate schedule set forth in §2001 of the Internal Revenue Code is structured in a way that makes it difficult to tell at a glance the effective tax rate and the actual amount payable with respect to any given taxable estate. Table 8-2 depicts effective tax rates applicable to eight *arbitrarily selected* taxable estates and actual amounts payable. This should enable the reader to estimate at a glance the tax liability and effective tax rate for any taxable estate that falls between two taxable estates depicted in the chart. The percentages in the chart equal the effective rates *on the excess over the Credit Equivalent* (prior to the credit for state death taxes) as applied against the eight taxable estates. The "tentative tax" computations

[12] *See* I.R.C. §2010 (unified transfer tax). Effective for decedents dying after 1976 and gifts made after 1976, the estate and gift tax rates are combined in a single rate schedule. Id.

[13] PL 105-34, Aug. 5, 1997, 111 Stat. 788.

[14] Id. at §501; 26 S.S.C.A. §2010(c).

[15] I.R.C. §2001(c).

represent actual amounts of estate tax payable, although a portion of a particular amount may be paid to state tax authorities. When the state estate tax equals the federal credit for state death taxes, it is known as a "sponge tax." The portion of the last percentage in the table (56.54 percent) over 55 percent is due to a 5 percent surcharge. IT IS IMPORTANT TO KEEP IN MIND THAT THE ESTATE TAX REGIME (UNLIKE THE GIFT TAX REGIME) IS "TAX INCLUSIVE." THIS MEANS THAT THE AMOUNT OF THE ESTATE TAX TO BE PAID IS INCLUDED IN THE COMPUTATION OF THE "TAXABLE ESTATE." THUS IT IS SAID THAT THE ESTATE TAX IS, IN PART, A "TAX ON A TAX."[15]

**Table 8-2. Federal Estate Tax Calculations for Eight Sample Estates**

| *Taxable Estate* | *Tentative Tax* |
|---|---|
| $600,000 (Credit Equivalent) | No Tax |
| $600,000 above the CE | $235,000 (or 39.16%) |
| $1,000,000 above the CE | $408,000 (or 40.80%) |
| $2,000,000 above the CE | $886,000 (or 44.30%) |
| $2,600,000 above the CE | $1,208,000 (or 46.46%) |
| $5,000,000 above the CE | $2,528,000 (or 50.58%) |
| $10,000,000 above the CE | $5,308,000 (or 53.08%) |
| $20,000,000 above the CE | $11,308,000 (or 56.54%) |

**Warning:** This table is **not** a transcription of the rate schedule set out in §2001 of the Internal Revenue Code.

**Warning:** The Taxpayer Relief Act of 1997 provides for incremental increases in the credit equivalent beginning with $625,000 for decedents dying during 1998 and culminating with $1 million for decedents dying during 2006 and thereafter.[16]

### §8.9.1.3 The Marital Deduction

The value of property passing to the settlor's surviving spouse is not considered part of the taxable estate.[17] It is "deducted" from

[15] *See generally* Kunes, More Blessed to Give Than to Devise, 10 Prob. & Prop. 20 (Sept./Oct. 1996).

[16] *See generally* §8.9.1.1 (The Unified Credit).

[17] I.R.C. §2056(a).

the gross estate. For property to be eligible for the marital deduction, it either must pass outright to the surviving spouse or it must be transferred to a trust in such a way as to bring about the functional equivalent.[18] For example, a transfer to a trust of which the spouse is a mandatory income beneficiary and over which the spouse has a general power of appointment qualifies for the marital deduction. The theory here is that the estate of the surviving spouse will pay for the favorable tax treatment afforded the estate of the first to die. For special rules that are applicable if the surviving spouse is not a U.S. Citizen, *see* §9.14 (The Qualified Domestic Trust (QDOT)).

There is one major exception to the requirement that the surviving spouse must be given the functional equivalent of full control over the property in order that the transfer qualify for the marital deduction: When the surviving spouse is given a qualified terminable interest in the decedent's property.[19] This is what the so-called QTIP trust is all about.[20] A trust is eligible for QTIP treatment if, *during the lifetime of the surviving spouse,* (1) the surviving spouse has the right to all the net income in all events, and (2) only the surviving spouse, if anyone, would have a right to the principal.[21] If these major conditions are satisfied, then *upon the death of the surviving spouse,* the property may pass to someone designated by the settlor (often the children by a first marriage). If the trust is QTIP-eligible, then generally it is the settlor's executor who elects to have a portion or all of the property in the QTIP trust treated as marital deduction property.[22] The piper, of course, must then be paid. Upon the death of the surviving spouse, the *balance* remaining in the QTIP-elected trust must be included in the estate of the surviving spouse for tax purposes.[23]

[18] *See* id.; Stephens, *supra* note 5, at ¶5.06[2].

[19] *See* Stephens, *supra* note 5, at ¶5.06[8] (discussing terminable interests qualifying for marital deduction).

[20] Id.

[21] Id.

[22] *See* Stephens, *supra* note 5, at ¶5.06[8][d][iii]; *see generally* §8.16 (The Trustee of Revocable Trust as "Inadvertent Executor").

[23] *See supra* note 5 (gross estate).

What does all this mean when it comes to the trustee? It means that a trustee may find himself administering several trusts created by the same settlor for the same person. For example, the governing instrument may call for a "bypass" trust to administer the credit equivalent property and a QTIP trust to handle the rest, with the surviving spouse being the primary beneficiary of both. Why more than one trust? Because the settlor wants to keep the property in the credit equivalent "bypass" trust from being taxed again upon the death of the surviving spouse. If the surviving spouse has some property of his or her own, then those steeply graduated estate tax rates may well make the several-trust strategy an economically viable one. Moreover, once the trusts are up and running, the trustee with an invasion right may want to draw down the principal of the QTIP trust before tapping the principal of the "bypass" trust, and to invest the "bypass" trust more for growth and the QTIP more for income. Both strategies are designed to minimize the aggregate amount of estate tax liability resulting from the deaths of the settlor and his or her spouse.

### *§8.9.2 The Generation-Skipping Transfer Tax*

The federal generation-skipping transfer (GST) tax is imposed on transfers that skip the generation immediately below the transferor.[24] In the context of trusts, a GST event could be triggered when a settlor creates a trust for his or her grandchildren, when the trustee makes a distribution of income or principal to the grandchildren, or when the trust terminates in favor of them.[25] The GST tax rate is 55 percent.[26]

The Code allows each transferor a $1 million GST exemption, which can be "spent" by the transferor during life to exempt

[24] I.R.C. §§2601, 2611.

[25] *See generally* Stephens, *supra* note 5, at ¶¶13.01-13.03.

[26] *See* I.R.C. §2641(b) (GST tax rate equals the maximum federal estate tax rate).

lifetime GSTs or "saved" until death to exempt testamentary GSTs.[27]

It should be kept in mind that an estate (or gift) tax *and* a GST tax can be assessed simultaneously against a single transfer. Let us take a $4 million direct skip to a grandchild by a decedent who has previously exhausted his unified credit and GST exemption. Assuming a 55% estate tax rate and a 55% GST tax with respect to the transfer, can there be anything left? Yes, there can. This is because the GST percentage is applied against the $4 million *net of the estate tax* and net of the GST tax itself. In other words, the GST tax on direct skips is "tax exclusive." Thus, the total transfer tax bill on the gross $4 million is $2,838,800 or 70.97%.[28] The net amount ultimately received by the grandchild is $1,161,200.[29]

With the GST exemption in mind, settlors sometimes establish separate GSTs designed to be fully exempt, that is, to receive a full GST-exemption allocation. Along with the "bypass" trust and the QTIP trust, the trustee may find himself administering separate "exempt" and "nonexempt" GST trust, all created by the same settlor and all with more or less the same beneficiaries.

The trustee in this situation will need to take a system-wide perspective when it comes to formulating investment strategies and making principal distributions. Generation-skipping principal distributions should probably be made from an exempt trust. When principal distributions to the surviving spouse are in order, the trustee probably should draw down the nonexempt QTIP trust before looking elsewhere. The trustee should probably first exhaust the nonexempt "bypass" trust if principal distributions to the children are in order. In formulating these strategies, the trustee needs to at least understand the tax strategies that gave rise to the system of trusts that he finds himself administering. Certainly the trustee does not want to generate tax liabilities inadvertently.

[27] I.R.C. §2631. *See generally* Stephens, *supra* note 5, at ¶¶15.01-15.03 (generation-skipping transfer exemption).

[28] Harrington and Acker, 850 T.M., Generation-Skipping Tax A-58 (1996).

[29] Id.

## *§8.9.3 Tax-Sensitive Powers*

**If the settlor impresses a trust upon property but retains an income interest, or its equivalent,**[30] **the income will be taxable to the settlor; and, to the extent the reserved interest encompasses all net trust accounting income, the principal will be subject to the estate tax upon the settlor's death.**[31] But the retention of certain powers will have estate tax and income tax consequences as well. If the settlor, the beneficiary, or a third party possesses at the time of death a *general inter vivos or testamentary power of appointment,* the trust property may be subject to the estate tax.[32] In addition, if a settlor-trustee or a beneficiary-trustee possesses at the time of death certain *powers to determine who enjoys the equitable interest,* the trust property may be subject to the estate tax.[33] Similar — though not identical — rules apply in the income tax context.[34] A general inter vivos power, for example, will cause the income generated by the subject property to be taxable to the power-holder.[35] On the other hand, a general testamentary power of appointment will not.[36] Moreover, if the holder of a tax-sensitive power renounces it, then a gift tax may be due.[37] The following is a checklist of questions designed to assist the domestic trustee in identifying *a few of the more common tax-sensitive powers.* If the answer to any question is "yes," then the holder, or his or her estate, *may* have a tax liability with respect to the subject power. Further investigation is then in order. The trustee should understand that in the tax area, it is the substance of the power, not how it is packaged, that counts. The express reservation of the right to "demand" principal, for example, is a tax-sensitive power of appointment even though the term "power of appointment" is not employed.

[30] *E.g.,* if the grantor of a trust is treated as its owner and taxed on its income if the trust income is distributed actually or constructively to the grantor's spouse. I.R.C. §§671-677.

[31] I.R.C. §§671-677 (income tax); I.R.C. §2036(a) (estate tax).

[32] I.R.C. §2041(b)(1).

[33] I.R.C. §§2036, 2038.

[34] I.R.C. §674 (retained control over beneficial interests — income tax).

[35] I.R.C. §§671, 676.

[36] I.R.C. §674(b)(3).

[37] *See, e.g.,* Reg. 25.2511-2(f).

### §8.9.3.1 A Checklist For Settlors

**The Estate Tax**

At the time of the settlor's death[38] . . .

(1) Could the settlor, alone or with another person, have revoked the trust and gotten back the trust property?
(2) Could the settlor, alone or with another person, have directed the property to the settlor's creditors or to someone whom the settlor had an obligation to support?
(3) Could the settlor, alone or with another person, have directed the property by will to the settlor's estate?
(4) Could the settlor, alone or with another person, have directed the property by will to the creditors of the settlor's estate?
(5) Did the settlor's creditors have access to income or principal?
(6) Did the settlor *as trustee* have *unlimited* discretion, alone or with another person, to apply income and/or invade principal for the benefit of *persons other than the settlor?*[39]
(7) Could the settlor, alone or with another person, have amended the trust?[40]

**The Income Tax**

During the settlor's lifetime . . .

(1) Can the settlor, alone or with someone who has no interest in the trust, get back the trust property by revocation, amendment, or otherwise?
(2) Does the settlor, *as trustee,* have *sole and unlimited discretion* to apply income and/or invade principal for the benefit of a class of *persons other than the settlor*?

[38]Note an exception: certain transfers within three years of death are subject to the estate tax. *See* I.R.C. §2035(a).

[39]*See generally* Harrison, Structuring Trusts to Permit the Donor to Act as Trustee, 22 Estate Planning 331 (No. 6-Nov./Dec. 1995).

[40]Id.

#### §8.9.3.2 A Checklist For Nonsettlors

**The Estate Tax**

At the time of the nonsettlor's death . . .

(1) Could the nonsettlor, alone or with someone having no interest under the trust, have terminated the trust and gained unrestricted access to the trust property?
(2) Could the nonsettlor, alone or with someone having no interest under the trust, have directed the trust property to the nonsettlor's creditors?
(3) Could the nonsettlor have directed the property by will to the nonsettlor's estate?
(4) Could the nonsettlor have directed the property by will to the creditors of the nonsettlor's estate?
(5) Did the nonsettlor, *as trustee,* have sole discretion, *unlimited by an ascertainable standard such as health, education, support, or maintenance,* to invade principal for the nonsettlor's benefit?

**The Income Tax**

During the nonsettlor's lifetime . . .

Can the nonsettlor alone get at the income or principal at will?

## §8.10 Fiduciary Principles Applicable to the Mutual Fund

A mutual fund is essentially a trusteed portfolio of securities.[1] Legal title is either in an individual (or individuals) or in a corpo-

**§8.10** [1] *See generally* Bogert, Trusts and Trustees §248; Anderson, Rights and Obligations in the Mutual Fund: A Source of Law, 20 Vand. L. Rev. 1120 (1967); American Bar Association, A Fiduciary's Guide to Federal Securities Laws 254 (1994).

ration.[2] The investors — those who purchase shares or participations in the fund — are both settlors and the owners of fully vested (equitable) property interests.[3] Employing the formula set out in §3.5.3.2(a), one could say that each investor is simultaneously *A, C,* and *D* as to the investor's allocable share of the fund. There may also be an investment advisor in the picture. The investment advisor is an *agent* of *B,* the fiduciary. While there is much federal regulation of mutual funds,[4] the rights, duties, and obligations of the parties are first and foremost grounded in the common law principles of fiduciary law that are the subject of this handbook.

## §8.11 What Are the Duties of the Trustee of a Revocable Inter Vivos Trust?

It is now settled law that a revocable inter vivos trust legally is a trust, not an agency,[1] with the result that the trustee has all the rights, duties, and obligations that are the subject of this handbook. However, it is also settled law that the trustee, for all practical purposes, is the agent of a holder of the inter vivos right to revoke, *provided the holder is of full age and legal capacity.*[2] The consequence of this constructive agency is that the settlor of a revocable inter vivos trust (or the holder of an inter vivos power of appointment) calls the shots. The settlor (or holder) may override the expressed terms of the governing instrument. He or she may subvert the interests of the takers in default. After all, inherent in the right to revoke the trust is the lesser right to modify its terms.

Nowadays, the trustee is expected to take directions from a competent settlor who has retained a right to revoke (or from the

[2]Id.
[3]Id.
[4]Id.
**§8.11** [1]National Shawmut Bank v. Joy, 315 Mass. 457, 53 N.E.2d 113 (1944).
[2]2 Scott on Trusts §216.2. *See generally* Canter v. Commissioner, 423 Mass. 425, 668 N.E.2d 783 (1996).

third party who holds a general inter vivos power of appointment); and the trustee, in most cases,[3] will be held harmless for so doing. The prudent trustee, however, will protect himself by having a questionable direction put into the format of a written amendment (or written partial exercise of the general power). The prudent trustee also will never serve under a trust that has two or more persons simultaneously holding rights of revocation (or general inter vivos powers). Such a situation brings with it property and tax problems too intricate to be covered by a handbook of this scope and size.

## §8.12 Where the Trust Is Recognized Outside the United States

It was once thought that the trust had its origins in Roman law.[1] The currently accepted theory is that uses and trusts have their roots in ancient German law.[2] Modern Germany, however, does not recognize the trust.[3] It was in England that the use or trust evolved into the relationship that is the subject of this handbook.[4] This, in part, was because the English had separate courts of law and equity.[5]

Today, England, Northern Ireland, Wales, Australia, Canada, and "a number of former British territories in the Caribbean" recognize the type of trust that is the subject of this handbook.[6] It should be noted, however, that the law of trusts in England is not

[3]*See generally* §6.1.4 (Duty to Give Personal Attention; (Not to Delegate)).

**§8.12** [1]I Scott on Trusts §1.9.

[2]Id.; *but see generally,* Avini, The Origins of the Modern English Trust Revisted, 70 Tulane L.R. 1139 (1996) (suggesting that the Islamic "waqf" is the precursor of the modern trust, the "waqf" having been introduced into England in the thirteenth century by the Franciscan Friars returning from the crusades).

[3]Bogert, Trusts and Trustees §9.

[4]*See generally* §8.15.1 (Statute of Uses).

[5]I Scott on Trusts §1.9.

[6]Bogert, Trusts and Trustees §9; *see generally* §9.10 of this handbook (The Offshore Asset Protection Trust).

identical to the law of trusts in the United States.[7] In the United States, for example, spendthrift provisions are generally honored by the courts.[8] In England they are not.[9]

Civil law is based on Roman law. In some civil law jurisdictions, such as Scotland, Israel, Liechtenstein, South Africa, Sri Lanka, Louisiana, and the Canadian Province of Quebec, the law of trusts has been introduced by statute.[10] In other civil law jurisdictions (e.g., France, Germany, and Italy), the concept of the trust has generally made little headway.[11] Those wishing to keep abreast of initiatives in civil law jurisidictions, including Japan, to adopt by statute the law of trusts, to create trust substitutes, or to recognize foreign trusts should consult §9 of Bogert, Trusts and Trustees.

## §8.13 In Litigation Pertaining to a Trust, When Is the Beneficiary Entitled to Reimbursement from the Trust Estate for Legal Fees?

In litigation pertaining to a trust, the court has discretion to order the trustee to reimburse the beneficiary from the trust estate for the beneficiary's reasonable legal fees and other litigation costs. The litigation, however, must be indispensable to the proper administration of the trust or confirm a benefit on the beneficiary class.[1] Thus, allowance of reasonable costs[2] and attorneys' fees is

[7]Id.

[8]Id.

[9]Id.

[10]Id.

[11]Id.

**§8.13** [1]*See generally* §8.15.13 (Common Fund Doctrine).

[2]*See generally* Bogert, Trusts and Trustees §871; 76 Am. Jur. 2d *Trusts* §§731-741 (1992); Annot., Costs and Fees — Trust Litigation 9 A.L.R. 2d 1132 (1950); *see* Boeing Co. v. Van Gemert, 444 U.S. 472 (1980); *cf.* Hall v. Cole, 412 U.S. 1 (1973) (counsel fees may be awarded to plaintiff out of trust estate when litigation confers benefit on beneficiary class); *see* §8.15.13 (The Common Fund

proper if the trust instrument is sufficiently ambiguous to warrant a judicial complaint for instructions and if the beneficiary is not responsible for the ambiguity.[3] After all, the beneficiary must be a party to the proceedings if there is to be a binding resolution of the issue. Of course, when litigation involves a breach of trust, ultimate liability may well attach to the trustee himself.[4]

## §8.14 When Is a Guardian ad Litem Needed?

In matters where interests between and among beneficiaries are in substantial conflict (e.g., most suits to construe dispositive terms), or a suit against a trustee for breach of trust, all beneficiaries are necessary parties.[1] What about unborn and unascertained remaindermen, minors, and others similarly situated? Who is to represent their interests? In a few jurisdictions (e.g., Indiana and Wisconsin)[2] the doctrine of "virtual representation"[3] may offer a solution. To illustrate the doctrine, let us take a trust with the following provisions: *A* to *B* for *C* for life, then to John Jones outright and free of trust if he is then living; but if John Jones is not then living, to his then living issue from a first marriage. Let us assume that *C* wishes a distribution of principal but the governing instrument is silent on the matter. Under the doctrine of "virtual representation," the assent of John Jones to the distribution would be binding on the aforementioned issue of John Jones who are unborn and unascertained. Why? Because the economic interests of John Jones and his issue are not in conflict, at least so the argument goes. If he survives *C*, he is entitled to the remainder

Doctrine); *see* Allan E. Korpela, LL. B., Annot., Amount of attorney's compensation in matters involving guardianships and trusts, 57 A.L.R.3d 550 (1974).

[3]Id.

[4]§7.1 (Trustee's Liabilities Generally).

**§8.14** [1]Bogert, Trusts and Trustees §871.

[2]Id.; Ind. Code Ann. §30-4-6-10 (West 1994); Wis. Stat. Ann. §701.15(2) (1981).

[3]Bogert, Trusts and Trustees §871.

interest. If he does not, then they are. Of course, the argument against applying the doctrine is that John Jones may be swayed by considerations (e.g., *C* might be his second wife) that would not sway the unborn grandchildren. After all, *C* would not be their grandmother.

When the doctrine of "virtual representation" is unavailable, the services of a court-appointed guardian ad litem may be required to represent those parties not before the court. When the situation warrants, the prudent trustee will insist that a guardian ad litem be appointed so that decrees issuing from the court shall be final and binding on all beneficiaries present and future, including minors, the unborn, and the unascertained.

## §8.15 Doctrines Ancient and Modern

Sprinkled throughout the trust literature are references to doctrines, some quite ancient, some quite recent in origin. What follows are brief explanations of a few of them. The focus of this section is on what implications, if any, each may have for trustees operating in the United States today. As to the Statute of Uses, the Doctrine of Worthier Title, and the Rule in Shelley's Case, the trustee would be well advised to have near at hand Professor Moynihan's compact Introduction to the Law of Real Property.[1]

### *§8.15.1 Statute of Uses*

An important milestone on the road to the modern trust was reached in the early fifteenth century when the English courts began *enforcing* "uses."[2] A "use" was a transfer of an interest in real

**§8.15** [1]C. J. Moynihan, Introduction to the Law of Real Property (2d ed. 1988) (hereinafter "Moynihan").

[2]Moynihan, chs. 8 & 9; I Scott on Trusts §§1, 1.1-1.11; Restatement (Second) of Trusts §§67-73 (1959); IA Scott on Trusts §§67-73.

estate from *A* to *B* for the benefit of *C*. A landholder, in order to prevent the property from descending to his heirs at law[3] or to deprive an overlord of his feudal rights[4] or to avoid Crown taxes,[5] would transfer his interest in the land to a "feoffee" (a sort of paleo-trustee) for the benefit of the "cestui que use" (a sort of paleo-beneficiary).[6] Now that uses could be enforced, either the "feoffor" (*A*) or the "cestui que use" (*C*) had a cause of action against a "faithless feoffee" (*B*).[7]

In an attempt to "put a stop to the drainage of royal revenues by the evasion of feudal dues through the practice of conveying to uses," Parliament, in 1536, enacted the Statute of Uses.[8] The statute provided that title to land held upon a use would now lodge with the "cestui que use" (the beneficiary).[9] In other words, the interest of the "cestui que use" was converted into a legal estate or, as they say, "executed."[10] The intention was that the title-holding "feoffee" (trustee) would then be out of the picture.[11] Now the "cestui que use" (the beneficiary) would have *both* the legal title and the entire equitable interest.[12] Now the beneficial owner would have no "use" (trust) to hide behind for the purpose of avoiding taxes and feudal obligations. At least that was the theory behind the statute. In practice, however, the courts quickly set about defanging its provisions.

The statute was held inapplicable to trusts where the trustee had *active responsibilities*.[13] (Those responsibilities might be as minimal as collecting and disbursing rents.[14]) And of course it did not apply to *trusts of personal property*.[15] Most trusts today fall into one or both of these categories. The Statute of Uses was held not to apply

[3]I Scott on Trusts §1.5.
[4]Id.
[5]Id.
[6]Id. §1.3.
[7]Id. §1.4.
[8]Moynihan at 203.
[9]I Scott on Trusts §1.5.
[10]Moynihan at 180.
[11]Moynihan at 180; I Scott on Trusts §§1.5, 1.6.
[12]Id.
[13]I Scott on Trusts §1.6.
[14]Id.; Moynihan at 203.
[15]I Scott on Trusts §1.6; Restatement (Second) of Trusts §70 (1959).

to a so-called "*use upon a use*[16] — a concept much loved by academics[17] but beyond the scope of this handbook and of little or no practical concern for today's trustee — and not to apply to a use *raised on a terms of years.*"[18]

"Prior to the Revolution, the Statute of Uses was deemed to be in force in the American colonies and upon the formation of the states it was incorporated into their legal systems as part of the common law."[19] Today, there are remnants of the statute scattered throughout the United States.[20] What are the practical implications for the modern trustee? Simply this: In the unlikely event that a trust of real estate is truly passive, if the trustee's responsibilities are little more than to refrain from interfering with the beneficiary's enjoyment of the property,[21] then there may be no trust. The beneficiary would have the entire legal and equitable interest.

Today, however, a trustee is unlikely to find himself involved in such a "passive" arrangement. But in the rare case when the Statute of Uses is applicable, the rights of creditors, bona fide purchasers, and others may be affected, as well as the duties of the purported trustee (e.g., there may be no obligation or need to make conveyance to the remainderman upon the death of the life tenant).[22]

### *§8.15.2 Doctrine of Worthier Title*

In §5.2 we considered those trusts whose remaindermen are to be determined by reference to formulas set forth in intestacy statutes, provisions such as "upon the death of the life beneficiary, the property passes to those who *would be* the settlor's heirs," or

[16] I Scott on Trusts §1.6; Restatement (Second) of Trusts §71 (1959).
[17] Id.
[18] I Scott on Trusts §1.6; Restatement (Second) of Trusts §70, cmt. b (1959).
[19] Moynihan at 204.
[20] Id.
[21] Restatement (Second) of Trusts §69, cmt. a (1959).
[22] Id.; *see generally* §3.5.1 (Nature and Extent of the Trustees Estate), n.14 & accompanying text; *see* In re Estate of Richards, Territories Court of the Virgin Islands, St. Thomas and St. John, Probate No. 3/1979, 1996 V.I. Lexis 14 (because trust passive, executed.) by statute of uses with result that legal title in proported "Beneficiaries").

words to that effect. But what if "heirs" actually means *the estate* of the settlor? Here, the Doctrine of Worthier Title may come into play.

The Doctrine of Worthier Title, a remnant of Anglo-Norman feudal law,[23] may apply to the following type of trust: *A*(settlor) to *B* (trustee) for *A* for life, then to the "heirs of *A*." If the "heirs of *A*" actually means the *estate* of *A*, then the only beneficiary of the trust is *A*.[24] Upon the death of *A*, the property goes back to the estate of *A* upon a resulting trust.[25] *A*'s presumptive heirs *do not* take title from *B*, the trustee, as "purchasers."[26] If they take at all, they take as beneficiaries of *A*'s estate, "by descent" as it were.[27] But they may in fact not take at all because *A*, having possessed a vested reversionary interest, could have transferred out that interest to a third party before he died, or by will.[28]

Today, the Doctrine of Worthier Title has evolved into a rule of construction.[29] In other words, what did the settlor intend? Does "heirs" mean his estate or is it an abbreviated formula for ascertaining remaindermen along the lines of Professor Casner's more elaborate formula set forth in §5.2? Some states have addressed the issue by creating statutory presumptions.[30]

What is the practical concern for today's trustee? Simply this: If the Doctrine of Worthier Title is applicable to a given situation, *A* is the sole beneficiary. There are no other interests to be accommodated. Thus *A may* be able to revoke the trust, his creditors *may* be able to reach the principal, and *A* will be able to defeat the interests of his presumptive heirs at law by transferring the reversionary interest inter vivos or by will. If *A* is also the sole trustee, then there is no trust at all because all interests are "merged" in *A*.[31]

[23]Moynihan at 151-161; 2 Scott on Trusts §127.1
[24]Id.
[25]Id.
[26]Moynihan at 151, 152; 2 Scott on Trusts §127.1.
[27]Id.
[28]Id.
[29]Moynihan at 155; 2 Scott on Trusts §127.1.
[30]2 Scott on Trusts §127.1; Moynihan at 161.
[31]*See generally* §8.7 (Merger).

### §8.15.3 *Rule in Shelley's Case*

The Doctrine of Worthier Title is about the heirs of the settlor. The Rule in Shelley's Case,[32] another remnant of Anglo-Norman feudal law, is about the *heirs of someone other than the settlor* and has been limited for the most part to interests in real property.[33] Let us take the following trust: *A*(settlor) to *B* (trustee) for the benefit of *C* for life; and, upon the death of *C*, *B* shall convey the trust property to "*C*'s heirs." If the Rule is applicable, then *C* takes a fully vested equitable interest that is referred to in some places as an "equitable fee simple."[34] There are no other beneficiaries.[35] (If *C* were the sole trustee, there would be a merger.)[36] The "heirs" of *C* are cut out regardless of the intentions of the settlor.[37] In a number of states, the Rule has been abolished by statute.[38] "Where the rule has been abolished or where it is not applicable because the trust property is personalty, the inference is that the settlor intends to give the first taker only a life estate, and there is a contingent interest limited to the persons who may be his heirs or next of kin at his death."[39]

### §8.15.4 *Statute of Elizabeth (Charitable Uses)*

In §9.4.1 we discuss the Statute of Elizabeth, also known as the Statute of Charitable Uses.[40] The Statute was enacted by Parliament in 1601.[41] Its preamble catalogs those purposes that qualify as charitable and thus, by implication, are exempt from the durational constraints of the Rule Against Perpetuities.[42] In 1888 the

[32]1 Co. Rep. 93b (1581).
[33]Moynihan at 141-150; 2 Scott on Trusts §127.2.
[34]2 Scott on Trusts §127.2.
[35]Id.
[36]Moynihan at 145.
[37]2 Scott on Trusts §127.2.
[38]Id.
[39]Id. at 325-327.
[40]Stat. 43 Eliz. I, c.4 (1601).
[41]4A Scott on Trusts §368.1.
[42]4A Scott on Trusts §365.

body of the Statute itself was repealed.[43] To this day, however, courts in both England and the United States look to the preamble for guidance in determining whether or not a particular trust purpose is charitable:

> some for relief of aged, impotent and poor people, some for maintenance of sick and maimed soldiers and mariners, schools of learning, free schools, and scholars in universities, some for repair of bridges, ports, havens, causeways, churches, sea-banks and highways, some for education and preferment of orphans, some for or towards relief, stock or maintenance for houses of correction, some for marriages of poor maids, some for supportation, aid and help of young tradesmen, handicraftsmen and persons decayed, and others for relief or redemption of prisoners or captives, and for aid or ease of any poor inhabitants concerning payments of fifteens, setting out of soldiers and other taxes.[44]

### *§8.15.5 Statute of Frauds*

Parliament enacted in 1676 a statute commonly known as the Statute of Frauds.[45] Section 7 provided that "all declarations or creations of *trusts* or confidences of any *lands*, tenements, or hereditaments shall be manifested and proved by some *writing* signed by the party who is by law enabled to declare such trust, or by his last will in writing, or else they shall be utterly void and of none effect."[46] Either by case law or by statute, some form of §7 has found its way into the law of most U.S. jurisdictions.[47] As a general rule, then, with the exception of the resulting trust[48] and the constructive trust,[49] a trust concerning an interest in land requires a writing if it is to be enforceable.

[43] 4A Scott on Trusts §348.2.

[44] 4A Scott on Trusts §368.1 at 138, 139.

[45] Stat. 29 Chas. II, c.3 (1676).

[46] I Scott on Trusts §40 at 413, 414.

[47] I Scott on Trusts §§40, 40.1; Restatement (Second) of Trusts §40 (1959).

[48] Restatement (Second) of Trusts §40, cmt. d (1959); *see generally* §4.1.1.1 (The Noncharitable Trust).

[49] Restatement (Second) of Trusts §40, cmt. d (1959); *see generally* §3.3 (Involuntary Trustees).

### §8.15.6 *Parol Evidence Rule*

"Under the parol evidence rule, if the manifestation of intention of the settlor is integrated in a writing, that is, if a written instrument is adopted by him as the complete expression of his intention, extrinsic evidence, in the absence of fraud, duress, mistake, or other ground for reformation or rescission, is not admissible to contradict or vary it."[50] The Rule applies even when the law does not *require* that there be a writing.[51] Only when the trust instrument is ambiguous may extrinstic evidence be considered in ascertaining the intentions of the settlor.[52]

### §8.15.7 *The Claflin Doctrine*

Let us take the following type of trust: *A* (settlor) to *B* (trustee) for *C* for ten years, then to *C* outright and free of trust; but if *C* dies during the ten-year period, the trust property shall be distributed *to C's estate.* There is no spendthrift clause. *C* is the sole beneficiary. In other words, during the lifetime of the trust, *C* possesses a *fully vested equitable interest.*[53] In England, *C* may compel termination of the trust in his or her favor before the term of years has expired even though to do so would contravene the wishes of the settlor.[54] In the United States, most courts will look to the 1889 Massachusetts case of *Claflin v. Claflin*[55] and hold that *C* must wait out the term specified: "It cannot be said that these restrictions upon [C's] possession and control of the property are altogether useless, for there is not the same danger that he will spend the property while it is in the hands of the trustees as there would be if it were in his own."[56]

[50] I Scott on Trusts §38 at 403; Restatement (Second) of Trusts §38 (1959).
[51] I Scott on Trusts §38.
[52] Id.
[53] *See generally* §5.4.1.7 (Right to Conveyance).
[54] 4 Scott on Trusts §337.3.
[55] 149 Mass. 19, 23, 20 N.E. 454 (1889); id.
[56] Id.; *see also* Restatement (second) of Trusts §337 (1959); §5.4.1.7. (Right to Conveyance).

Note that the Claflin Doctrine would not be invoked with respect to a trust that had no purpose whatsoever. Thus it is sometimes referred to as the "Material Purpose Doctrine." Note also that the Claflin Doctrine applies notwithstanding the absence of a spendthrift clause: "It is true that [C's] interest is alienable by him, and can be taken by his creditors to pay his debts, but it does not follow that, because [the settlor] has not imposed all possible restrictions, the restrictions which he has imposed should not be carried into effect."[57] Thus it is said that the English approach the matter from the perspective of the beneficiary while the American approach, as embodied in the Claflin Doctrine, is from the perspective of the settlor.[58]

### *§8.15.8 Rule Against Accumulations*

It seems settled — at least in the United States — that if a non-charitable trust *terminates* within the period of the Rule Against Perpetuities then the income may be accumulated *for the duration of the trust.*[59] The Claflin Doctrine,[60] however, raises the question of whether income may accumulate beyond the period of the Rule in cases where remainder interests vest *but do not become possessory* within the period of the Rule.[61]

By way of illustration, let us take the following trust: *A*(settlor) to *B* (trustee) for *C1* for life, then for *C2* for life. Upon the death of *C2*, the principal shall be distributed outright and free of trust *to C2's estate. C1* is a life in being. Income shall accumulate until the death of *C2* and then be payable *to C2's estate.* As to the principal, there is no violation of the Rule Against Perpetuities. The princi-

[57]Claflin v. Claflin, 149 Mass. 19, 23, 20 N.E. 454 (1889).

[58]4 Scott on Trusts §337.3.

[59]Note, Accumulations of Income at Common Law, 54 Harv. L. Rev. 839, 840-841 (1941); IA Scott on Trusts §62.11. As to income accumulations in the context of charitable trusts, *see* Franklin Found. v. Attorney General, 416 Mass. 483, 623 N.E.2d 1109 (1993); *but see* Bogert, Trusts and Trustees §341.

[60]*See generally* §8.15.7 (The Claflin Doctrine).

[61]Note, Accumulations of Income at Common Law, 54 Harv. L. Rev. 839, 841 (1941); IA Scott on Trusts §62.11.

pal vests in *C2* upon the death of *C1*, the life in being.[62] The interest simply is not possessory during *C2*'s lifetime.[63] The income, however, could accumulate for more than 21 years after the death of *C1*, the life in being. There is a sense in some jurisdictions that this direction to accumulate violates a " 'common-law rule' limiting the permissible duration of private accumulations."[64] The matter has been the subject of some legislation.[65] As to charitable trusts, it is generally held in the United States that income may accumulate for a reasonable period beyond the period of the Rule.[66]

### *§8.15.9 Doctrine of Independent Legal Significance*

The common law Doctrine of Independent Legal Significance is a gloss on the Statute of Wills.[67] Most wills statutes provide in part that for a will to be valid it must be in writing, signed by the testator, and witnessed by third parties. What if a will contains a bequest to "those in my employ at the time of my death"? Would an employee who was hired *after* the will was signed and witnessed be entitled to take? Under the the common law Doctrine of Independent Legal Significance he would.[68] This is because the act of hiring and firing are acts whose significance are independent of the will. The preparation of a postexecution unattested *writing* outlining additional legatees, however, would *not* be such an act as its sole purpose would be to "complement" the will.[69]

The trustee needs to be concerned about the Doctrine of Independent Legal Significance primarily in the context of testa-

[62] *See generally* §§8.2.1 (The Rule Against Perpetuities) and 8.2.1.3 (The Vesting of Interests Under Trusts).

[63] Id.

[64] Note, Accumulations of Income at Common Law, 54 Harv. L. Rev. 839, 840 (1941).

[65] IA Scott on Trusts §62.11, n.10.

[66] Id.

[67] IA Scott on Trusts §54.2.

[68] Id.

[69] Id.

mentary pour-overs to *revocable* inter vivos trusts.[70] Let us take the following situation: A will provides that the residue of the testator's estate shall be distributed to the trustee of a certain revocable inter vivos trust to be held in accordance with the terms of said trust, "as from time to time amended." Would the Statute of Wills permit the residue to be administered in accordance with the terms of a trust that had been amended *by a writing* of the testator *after* the will had been signed and witnessed? Under the Doctrine of Independent Legal Significance, it would.[71] Because the revocable inter vivos trust is an arrangement of independent legal significance i.e., independent of the will), it follows that trust amendments, like hirings and firings, are the product of acts of independent legal significance.[72] In many states the Doctrine has been adopted or codified through legislation.[73]

### *§8.15.10 The Loring Exemption*

The Investment Advisers Act of 1940[74] requires that an investment advisor, as defined by the Act, register with the SEC (Form ADV), make annual reports to the SEC (Form ADV-S), and conduct his or her business activities in certain specified ways.[75] Filing with the SEC also may bring with it state filing obligations.[76] For purposes of the Act, an investment advisor is

> any person who, for compensation, engages in the business of advising others, either directly or through publication or writings, as to the value of securities or as to the advisability of investing in, purchasing, or selling securities, or who, for compensation and as

[70] IA Scott on Trusts §54.3.

[71] Id.

[72] Id.; *see generally* Second Bank-State St. v. Pinion, 341 Mass. 366, 170 N.E.2d 350 (1960).

[73] Id.; *see generally* §2.2.1 (The Pour-over Statute).

[74] *See generally* George T. Shaw, The Probate Lawyer, The Investment Process, and Selected Law Issues, 18 ACTEC Notes 91 (1992).

[75] Id.

[76] Id.

part of a regular business, issues or promulgates analysis or reports concerning securities.[77]

In 1942, Augustus P. Loring, Jr., an individual professional trustee, by SEC administrative order, was held *not* to be an investment advisor within the meaning of the Act.[78] The Loring exemption was based in part on the fact that Mr. Loring, as trustee, had legal title to trust assets and thus was acting for himself.[79] He was not "in the business of advising others."[80] A warning: One learned commentator has written that "[i]n recent years the SEC staff, in public statements and in response to requests for no-action, has distanced itself from the *Loring* decision and limited the reach of that case to its special facts and circumstances, and it probably would decide *Loring* differently today."[81]

### §8.15.11 *Rule in Clayton's Case*

The Rule in Clayton's Case[82] applies to funds that are wrongfully commingled in a bank account. It is a "first in, first out" presumption.[83] Assume that the trustee wrongfully deposits $1,000 from Trust *X*, $1,000 from Trust *Y*, and $1,000 from Trust *Z* in his own personal bank account. He then withdraws $1,000 from the account and dissipates it so that the $1,000 are untraceable. Applying the Rule in Clayton's Case, that $1,000 is presumed to have belonged to Trust *X* such that the beneficiaries of Trust *X* are now out of luck as to that account.[84] Only Trust *Y* and Trust *Z* are entitled to the remaining $2,000. The Rule as it applies to trusts has been criticized as "irrational," "arbitrary," and "unfair" by

[77]Id. at 91.

[78]In the Matter of Loring, [1942 Transfer Binder] Fed. Sec. L. Rep. (CCH) 75, 299.

[79]Id. at 887; *see generally* §3.5.1 (Nature and Extent of the Trustee's Estate).

[80]Id.

[81]George T. Shaw, The Probate Lawyer, The Investment Process, and Selected Law Issues, 18 ACTEC Notes 91, 92 (1992).

[82]1 Mer. 572 (1816).

[83]5 Scott on Trusts §519.

[84]Id.

Judge Learned Hand and Professor Scott.[85] They would have all three trusts share equally; that is, in proportion to what each, relative to one another, had contributed to the fund.[86] Numerous courts have rejected the Rule in Clayton's Case in favor of the "pro rata" approach.[87]

### *§8.15.12 Doctrine of Capture*

Let us assume that a settlor of a trust bestows on Mr. Jones a general testamentary power of appointment.[88] Let us also assume that Mr. Jones exercises the power in further trust by appointing the property to a trustee upon a trust that fails immediately or sometime thereafter. Under the Doctrine of Capture, at the time of the failure, the property reverts upon a resulting trust to *Mr. Jones' estate.*[89] In other words, it is "captured" by the donee's estate, the exercise in favor of the "new" trustee technically having been consummated. The property does not revert back to the settlor or the settlor's estate. The Doctrine would apply equally well to general inter vivos powers.[90] The Doctrine, however, is not applicable to failed efforts to exercise general powers other than in further trust (except when there has been a "blending" of the property with the property of the donee).[91] If, for example, Mr. Jones failed in an attempt to exercise the general power outright and free of

[85]Id. at 644.

[86]Id.

[87]5 Scott on Trusts §519, n.4.

[88]*See generally* §8.1 (Powers of Appointment).

[89]5 Scott on Trusts §426.

[90]Id; A failed exercise of a general *inter vivos* power of appointment in further trust could cause the property to pass to the *donee if then living,* and otherwise to the estate of the donee.

[91]Id. A "blending" could occur should the general residuary clause in the donee's will exercise the donee's general testamentary power in favor of someone who predeceases the donee. In the event of a lapse, both the trust property and the donee's estate residue would "blend" and pass by intestacy. *See, e.g.,* Old Colony Trust Co. v. Allen, 307 Mass. 40, 29 N.E.2d 310 (1940) (*Caution*: Under Massachusetts law (M.G.L c. 191, §1A), a general residue clause will no longer in and of itself exercise a general testamentary power of appointment.). *See generally* §8.1.1, n.4 (Powers of Appointment).

trust to his daughter, the Doctrine would not apply. The property would revert back to the estate *of the settlor.* The Doctrine also does not apply to limited powers of appointment.[92] The Doctrine of Capture is a default rule. If the settlor or the donee has expressed the clear intention that the Doctrine shall not apply, then it will not. The property will then revert to the settlor (or his estate) *or* pass to an alternate taker that has been designated either in the governing instrument or by the donee *or* be administered as if the power had not been exercised.[93]

### *§8.15.13 Common Fund Doctrine*

Not to be confused with the Common Trust Fund[94] or the practice of commingling in a "common fund" for investment purposes the assets of a number of trusts created under the same instrument,[95] the "common fund doctrine" relates to whether a beneficiary who brings an action involving the trust may be reimbursed from the trust estate for legal fees.[96] In other words, must those beneficiaries who did not bring the case indirectly shoulder some of the economic burden of the litigation? If the common fund doctrine is applicable, the answer is yes, provided the litigation "successfully created, increased, or preserved a fund in which the non-litigants were entitled to share." [97] Of course, the trustee, if found culpable in his individual capacity,[98] ultimately may be required to reimburse the trust for any attorneys' fees paid to the litigating beneficiary out of the trust estate.[99] It should be noted, that the common fund doctrine is an exception to the "American rule" that litigants, win or lose, absorb their own legal costs.

[92] 5 Scott on Trusts §426.

[93] Id.

[94] *See generally* §9.7.1 (The Common Trust Fund).

[95] *See generally* §3.5.3.2(d) (The power to invest in mutual funds, common trust funds, and common funds).

[96] *See generally* §8.13 (In Litigation Pertaining to a Trust, When Is the Beneficiary Entitled to Reimbursement from the Trust Estate for Legal Fees?).

[97] Feinberg v. Feinberg Hotel Trust, 922 S.W.2d 21 (Mo. App. E. Dist. 1996).

[98] *See* McNeely v. Hiatt, 138 Or App. 434 (1996).

[99] Feinberg v. Feinberg Hotel Trust, 922 S.W.2d 21 (Mo. App. E. Dist 1996).

### *§8.15.14 The Massachusetts Rule of Allocation*

The Massachusetts Rule of Allocation is a rule of convenience when it comes to the allocation of *extraordinary dividends.* Let us assume that we have a traditional trust: *A* to *B,* for *C* for life, then to *D.* Let us assume that a share of stock in a certain corporation is an asset of the trust. Upon receipt of an extraordinary dividend issued by the directors of the corporation, the trustee (*B*), pursuant to the Massachusetts Rule, merely allocates it to income (*C*) if it is a cash dividend or to principal (*D*) if it is a stock dividend.[100] The Massachusetts Rule is a reaction to the cumbersome Pennsylvania Rule of Apportionment which requires that the trustee pick apart and analyze the extraordinary dividend to determine what portion of it has been derived from income earned by the corporation during the term of the trust. That portion is then allocated to income (*C*) and the balance to principal (*D*).[101]

## §8.16 The Trustee of Revocable Trust as "Inadvertent Executor"[1]

As a general rule, the value of property in a revocable inter vivos trust will generate an estate tax upon the death of the settlor.[2] There are some exceptions. The property, for example, could be

[100] *See generally* 3A Scott on Trusts §236.3; *see also* §6.2.4.2 (What Receipts Are Entirely Allocated to Principal for Trust Accounting Purposes?).

[101] Id.

**§8.16** [1] Much of the information contained in this section is taken from Hanna, The Inadvertent Executor Under Section 2203 of the Internal Revenue Code, 22 ACTEC Notes 196 (1996). The term "inadvertent executor" was employed in the article "to refer to those persons that are treated as executors or administrators under §2203, for federal estate tax purposes, due to their actual or constructive possession of property of the decedent and the absence of a named or appointed representative of the decedent's estate." Id. at 197, n. 8.

[2] *See generally* §8.9.1 (The Federal Estate Tax).

subject to a marital[3] or charitable deduction.[4] Any tax liability could be absorbed by the unified credit.[5] The fact remains, however, that the Federal estate tax, though it is a transfer tax, cannot be avoided merely because title to the property at the time of the settlor's death is in the trustee. The settlor's executor has the responsibility for preparing the Federal estate tax return and paying the tax.[6]

What if no executor has been appointed? What if all the settlor's property, for example, had been transferred inter vivos to the trustee of a revocable trust so that there is no probate estate? In that case, the Internal Revenue Code places the responsibility for preparing and filing the Federal estate tax return on the trustee.[7] The trustee is responsible for satisfying (out of assets of the trust) the trust's tax liability.[8] The liability of the trustee as "inadvertent executor" is generally limited to the property that is the subject of the trust.[9] A warning, however: The trustee will be personally liable for any shortfall in estate taxes owed should he pay the debts of the settlor, or make distributions in accordance with the terms of the trust, and in so doing not leave enough in the trust to satisfy the trust's tax liability.[10] When in doubt, the prudent trustee will want to make written application to the IRS for a determination of the amount of the tax and for a discharge from *personal liability* therefor.[11]

The inadvertent executor's duty to *the state* is limited to filing the return, paying the tax owed and responding to any notice of deficiency. As a fiduciary, his duty to *the beneficiaries* of the trust is to see to it that only that which is lawfully owed is paid out. If there has been an estate tax overpayment, for example, the trustee must file a timely application for a refund. The trustee as inadvertent executor would also have a duty to make appropriate and timely tax

[3] *See generally* §8.9.1.3 (The Marital Deduction).
[4] *See generally* §9.4.1 (Charitable Purposes).
[5] *See generally* §8.9.1.1 (The Unified Credit).
[6] I.R.C. §2203.
[7] Id.
[8] Id.
[9] Id. *See* New York Trust Company, 26 T.C. at 262.
[10] 31 U.S.C. §3713(b).
[11] I.R.C §2204.

elections (e.g., the QTIP election and the Special Use Valuation Election).[12] The trustee should consider whether legal fees incurred by the trustee in the course of his inadvertent executorship duties, to the extent they benefit the trust estate, should be taken as a deduction for estate tax purposes.[13]

## §8.17 Trust Reformation to Remedy Faulty Tax Planning (Mistake)

As a general rule, when a settlor creates a trust in *exchange for consideration,* the fact that the settlor did so by mistake is not grounds for reformation of the terms of the trust.[1] If, however, consideration is not involved, then a mistake as to the law or the facts that induced the settlor to create the trust is grounds for reformation.[2] This would include a mistake as to the tax consequences of establishing the trust.[3] Recently, a court shifted the equitable interests under a Qualified Personal Residence Trust (QPRT) from grandchildren to children in order to avoid eventual application of a Federal generation-skipping transfer tax that would have been in the range of $1,375,000.[4] Because tax reduction was the overriding purpose in creating the QPRT, the court held that a misunderstanding of the generation-skipping tax implications of including the grandchildren was the type of mistake that warranted reformation.[5]

[12] *See* Priv. Let. Rul. 9509029 (December 2, 1994) (QTIP election) and Priv. Let. Rul. 8639022 (June 25, 1986) (§2032A — special use valuation).

[13] *See generally* Hanna, The Inadvertent Executor Under Section 2203 of the Internal Revenue Code, 22 ACTEC Notes 196, 204 (1996).

**§8.17** [1] 4 Scott on Trusts §333.4.

[2] Id.

[3] Id.

[4] Simches v. Simches, 423 Mass. 683, 671 N.E.2d 1226 (Mass. 1996).

[5] Id. at 1230.

## §8.18 Regulation 9 Revised

Regulation 9 governs *the fiduciary activities of national banks.*[1] The Office of the Comptroller of the Currency has completed the first comprehensive revision of the regulation since 1963. Regulation 9, as revised, *became effective January 29, 1997.* It is reprinted in its entirety in Appendix II of this handbook. The regulation has been "streamlined" in part to accommodate changes in the banking industry since 1963, particularly the rise of multistate fiduciary banking organizations.

It is important to understand that Reg. 9, in and of itself, is not about creating substantive fiduciary law. Nor is it about resolving conflicts among competing bodies of local law or between local law and Federal law. For the most part, it defers to the body of state law and Federal law (e.g., ERISA) that is the subject of this handbook. The regulation, for example, will not resolve a conflict between the terms of a trust instrument and a state statute or a Federal regulation. The former Reg. 9 employed the term "local law." Revised Reg. 9 instead employs the term "applicable law." The new term acknowledges that Federal law is one of many sources of law that may govern a fiduciary relationship; however, it does not preempt state law or resolve conflicts of law.

By express language, the regulation is made applicable to a national bank that is serving in certain specified capacities, e.g., trustee, executor, guardian, and compensated investment adviser.[2] Revised Reg. 9 introduces the simple test of *investment discretion*[3] for determining what other national banking "fiduciary" activities are subject to oversight by the Comptroller of the Currency.

Revised Reg. 9 requires a national bank "to establish written policies and procedures to ensure that its fiduciary practices comply with applicable law."[4] The bank's policies and procedures, "among other relevant matters,"[5] should cover:

**§8.18** [1]12 C.F.R. Part 9 (Fiduciary Activities of National Banks).
[2]12 C.F.R. §9.2(e) (Definitions).
[3]Id.
[4]12 C.F.R. §9.5 (Policies and procedures).
[5]Id.

(1) Brokerage placement practices;[6]

(2) Methods for ensuring that fiduciary officers and employees do not use material inside information in connection with any decision or recommendation to purchase or sell any security;[7]

(3) Methods for preventing self-dealing and conflicts of interest;[8]

(4) Selection and retention of legal counsel who is readily available to advise the bank and its fiduciary officers and employees on fiduciary matters;[9] and

(5) Investment of funds held as fiduciary, including short-term investments and the treatment of fiduciary funds awaiting investment or distribution.[10]

In litigation against a national bank trustee, plaintiff's counsel will want to obtain as soon as possible, through the discovery process if necessary, the bank's Reg. 9-mandated written policies and procedures. It should be noted that most of the items on the above list were derived from specific requirements in the former regulation.

The former regulation required national banks to perform two types of written reviews of their fiduciary accounts. One was an "account by account" review. The other was an "asset by asset" review to determine what assets are generally appropriate for the bank's fiduciary accounts. In a tip of the hat to modern portfolio and the prudent investor rule[11], Revised Reg. 9 has done away with the "asset by asset" review requirement. Because so much of trust operations is now automated, the "account by account" review need no longer be "written." Finally, Revised Reg. 9 has done away with the requirement that a review be conducted "within 15 months after the last review." There need only be a review of the assets of each account for which the bank has investment discre-

[6]*See generally* §6.1.3.4 (Indirect Benefit Accruing to the Trustee).

[7]Id.

[8]*See generally* §6.1.3 (Duty to Be Loyal to the Trust).

[9]*See generally* §8.8 (Whom Does Counsel Represent?).

[10]*See generally* §6.1.3.1 (Trustee Benefiting as Borrower and Lender).

[11]*See generally* §6.2.2.1 (The Harvard College Prudent Man Rule and Its Progeny).

tion once during each calendar year.[12] The purpose of the review is to "evaluate whether the assets are appropriate, individually and collectively, for the account."[13]

The former regulation had a "10% Rule" for collective investment funds: No trust or other participating account could have more than a 10% participation in a any one fund and no single asset could comprise more than 10% of the value of a fund."[14] Revised Reg. 9 does away with the "10% Rule" in both its applications on the grounds that the concerns underlying the Rule are adequately addressed by the principles of state fiduciary law that are the subject of this handbook.

## §8.19 When the Bank Trustee Merges or Consolidates

What happens when a bank that is serving as trustee of an ongoing trust merges into, or consolidates with, another bank? May the successor by merger or consolidation serve as the trustee without court appointment? Today, because of Federal and state legislation, the answer is generally yes, absent language in the governing instrument to the contrary.[1]

In the absence of legislation, one would first look to the governing instrument for guidance. It may well contain a provision for the automatic transfer of power and authority from the named trustee to its successor entity.

In the absence of legislation or express language in the governing instrument, the state of the common law is probably a presumption that the settlor intends for power and authority auto-

[12]*See* 12 C.F.R. §9.6(c) (Review of Fiduciary Accounts-Annual Review).
[13]Id.
[14]12 C.F.R. §9.18(b)(9) (**NOTE:** Superseded effective January 29, 1997).

**§8.19** [1]*See* 2 Scott on Trusts §96.7, n.3 (cataloging the federal and state statutes that authorize the automatic transmission of the fiduciary powers of named bank trustees to their successors by merger and consolidation). For related issues, *see* §3.4.4.3 (Successor Trustees).

matically to pass to the successor by merger or consolidation.[2] Ultimately, however, it would come down to the inferred or expressed intention of the settlor. One court has denied automatic transmission of power and authority because the successor institution had acquired the assets of the named trustee other than by merger or consolidation.[3]

## §8.20 Tax Apportionment Within Trust

Property in a *revocable* inter vivos trust is subject to the Federal estate tax upon the death of the settlor.[1] While the settlor may not relieve the trustee of his legal obligation to pay what taxes are owed, the settlor may specify in the governing instrument which equitable interests are to shoulder the burden of satisfying the tax obligation. The prospective trustee of a *revocable* inter vivos trust that contains charitable and noncharitable equitable interests will want to pay particular attention to the trust's "tax clause." Let us take a revocable inter vivos trust that divides into two equal shares upon the death of the settlor. One share is held for the benefit of a charity and the other for the benefit of the settlor's children. Let us also assume that the settlor intends to fund the trust with all of his or her property before death. If there is no provision in the governing instrument explaining which class of beneficiaries is to bear the burden of the estate taxes, then the trustee will have to fall back on a tax apportionment statute, if any. Such statutes are not always the model of clarity.[2] Whether or not there is an applicable statute, the question will be whether the taxes must be paid "off the top" *or* paid out of the children's share after division. The argument for charging estate taxes to the children's share is that

[2] *See generally* 2 Scott on Trusts §96.7.

[3] See In Matter of DeCoppet, 10 Misc. 2d 748, 173 N.Y.S.2d 443 (1958).

**§8.20** [1] *See generally* §8.9.1 (The Federal Estate Tax).

[2] *See, e.g.*, The First National Bank of Boston v. Judge Baker Guidance Center, 13 Mass. App. 144, 431 N.E.2d 243 (1982).

the children's share is generating the tax, the charity being entitled to a charitable deduction.[3]

On the other hand, the children are likely to put forth the argument that the governing instrument, taken in its totality, reveals an intention to put the interests of family members at least on a par with the charity. Accordingly, taxes should be paid "off the top."[4] If the taxes are paid "off the top," then the charity of course gets less than it would otherwise get if the noncharitable interests alone were to bear the tax burden. This is because the charity is sharing some of the burden of the tax. But there is an added twist: An "off the top" payment will require a circular tax computation to accommodate the corresponding reduction in the charitable deduction occasioned by the reduced amount passing to the charity. The point is that the settlor's intentions with respect to the apportionment of estate taxes between charitable and noncharitable interests should be fully and unambiguously addressed in the tax clause of the governing instrument.

Internal tax apportionment questions can arise not only when there are successive charitable and noncharitable equitable interests but also when there are classes of noncharitable interests. Let us take a funded revocable inter vivos trust that calls for the trustee, upon the death of the settlor, to carve out $1 million for the settlor's children by the first marriage and to distribute the "residue" to the children of the second marriage. Who bears the burden of the estate taxes when the governing instrument is silent on the subject? If this were a will, chances are the estate tax liability would be borne by the portion passing to the children of the second marriage, with the children of the first marriage receiving the full $1 million undiminished by estate taxes. But this is not a will. Moreover, if the "residue" were to pass to the second wife, and estate taxes were to be paid "off the top," then the marital deduction would trigger a circular tax computation. Rather than having to grapple with some tax apportionment statute after the settlor's

[3] *See, e.g.,* Estate of Boder, 850 S.W.2d 76 (Mo. 1993) (calling for taxes to be paid "off the top" before division thus causing the charitable interests to bear a portion of the tax burden).

[4] Id.

death, the prudent prospective trustee will insist that the settlor's intentions with respect to the apportionment of estate taxes are fully and unambiguously spelled out in the governing instrument.

One final note: The prudent prospective trustee will make sure that the tax clause of the revocable inter vivos trust dovetails with the tax clause of the pourover will. Under no circumstances should they be in conflict. This is because the trustee can never be sure that the trust will contain *all* the settlor's property at the time of his or her death.

## §8.21 Duty of Third Parties to Investigate Whether Trustee Has Power to Act or Is Properly Exercising the Power

Under the common law, a third party who transacted with the trustee had a duty to ascertain the trustee's authority in equity to enter into the transaction and to ascertain whether the authority was being properly exercised. As between the beneficiaries and the third party, the risk of the trustee's acting without authority fell on the third party, unless the third party were a good faith purchaser for value (i.e., a BFP).[1] And a third party who knew of the trust would not be acting in good faith if the third party failed to make reasonable investigation of the trustee's authority.[2] Thus, the third party (e.g., a prospective purchaser of trust real estate) at minimum would need to see a copy of the governing instrument to ascertain whether the trustee had authority in equity to sell the property. If the inspection raised questions regarding the trustee's authority, or the propriety of its exercise, then the third party would be obliged to expand the inquiry.

In order to facilitate the flow of commerce, the laws addressing commercial paper, investment securities and banking transac-

**§8.21** [1]*See generally* §5.4.2 (Rights of the Beneficiary Against Those Other Than the Trustee (The BFP and Others)).

[2]*See generally* 4 Scott on Trusts §297.4.

tions have downgraded somewhat the third party's duty to investigate the trustee's authority to what is essentially an "actual notice" standard.[3] Many trust instruments now contain express language relieving third parties of the duty to inquire into the trustee's actual authority to transact. The result of all of this is to shift the economic risk occasioned by a breach of the trustee's fiduciary duty from the third party to the beneficiaries (up to the value of the trust estate), to turn the trust into a quasi entity that has some of the characteristics of a corporation. Section 7 of the Uniform Trustees' Powers Act has done nothing to stem the tide. In fact, it has taken the lower "actual notice" standard of inquiry beyond the specialized world of commercial, investment and banking "paper" to encompass transactions involving tangible personal property and real estate. The reader should understand, however, that while a beneficiary's right of recourse against a third party may be eroding, these commerce-facilitating measures in no way foreclose the beneficiary from moving *against the trustee personally* for acting beyond the scope of his authority. To be sure, this may be small consolation to the beneficiary faced with an insolvent trustee.

[3]U.C.C. §§3-307(b)(1), (2) and (4) (1990) (establishing the commercial paper standard as actual notice unless the paper runs to the trustee personally); U.C.C. §§8-302, 8-304 (1990) (investment securities); Unif. Fiduciaries Act §§3-10, 7A U.L.A. 404-23 (1985) (banking transactions).

CHAPTER 9

# Special Types of Trusts

## §9.1 The Grantor Trust

The term "grantor trust" appears in the income tax sections of the Internal Revenue Code.[1] It is not a common law trust term. It simply means any trust over which someone, referred to as the "grantor," has such control that he or she is deemed to be the owner of the trust property or a portion of the trust property *for income tax purposes.*[2] When a trust qualifies as a grantor trust, any income tax liability or benefit associated with the trust property does not affix to the trust. Rather, income, deductions and credits enter into the computation of the *personal* income tax liability of the grantor.[3] This is pursuant to the Code's so-called grantor trust rules.[4]

## §9.2 The Irrevocable Life Insurance Trust

A life insurance contract (or policy) is an item of property during the lifetime of the insured. The proceeds are another form of that property interest, just as the butterfly is another form of the caterpillar. Because the estate tax system imposes a tax on property transfers occasioned by death, life insurance proceeds will generate an estate tax.[1] One way to avoid this is for the insured, during his or her lifetime, to transfer title to the contract to the trustee of an irrevocable trust. If the insured retains no beneficial interest in

**§9.1** [1]*See* I.R.C. §§671-679; Fiore, et al., Modern Estate Planning §6A.02 (1990). For a detailed analysis of the grantor rules see Zaritsky, Grantor Trusts: §§671-679, 452-2nd Tax Mngmt. (1996) And Schwartz, Grantor and Non Grantor Trusts: Asking the right questions, 11 Prac. Tax Law 31 (1997); *see also* §9.4.5 (Tax Oriented Trusts That Mix Charitable and Non-Charitable Interests (Split-Interest Trusts)) and §10.1 (Introduction to the Fiduciary Income Tax).

[2]Id.

[3]Id.

[4]Id.; For the grantor trust rules applicable to foreign trusts, *see* I.R.C. §§679 and 672; *see also* §6.3.1 (Tax Filings). And §10.1 (Introduction to the Fiduciary Income Tax).

**§9.2** [1]*See* §8.9 (Why More Than One Trust: The Estate and Generation-Skipping Tax).

the contract, then, upon death, the proceeds may not generate an estate tax liability.[2] Avoidance of estate taxes is what the irrevocable life insurance trust is all about.

In the typical irrevocable life insurance trust, the trustee pays the life insurance premium from cash contributions periodically made to the trust by someone, usually the settlor. These contributions are gifts to the trust. To ensure that the contributions qualify for the annual gift tax exclusion, the beneficiaries are given a limited withdrawal power.[3] This power gives the beneficiaries the right to withdraw the amount contributed to the trust within a specified number of days. The power lapses if it is not exercised. These limited withdrawal provisions are often referred to as "Crummey" powers and trusts containing such provisions are called "Crummey" trusts.[4] It is the trustee's responsibility to notify the beneficiaries that a contribution has been made. Failure to do so is a breach of trust.[5]

Of course, the settlor does not want a beneficiary to withdraw his or her portion of the contribution. Explaining to beneficiaries that it is not in their best interests for them to exercise their withdrawal rights will usually deter them from doing so. If the beneficiaries were to exercise their rights of withdrawal, there usually would be no money with which to pay the insurance premium and the policy would eventually lapse.

An insurance policy or contract held in a trust is an investment. Thus the Prudent Man Rule or its equivalent must guide the trustee with respect to its retention, absent language in the governing instrument to the contrary. There are unique con-

[2]It should be noted, however, that the settlor must survive for a period of three years following the transfer. I.R.C. §§2035(a), 2035(d)(2). This "three-year" rule can be avoided if the trustee purchases the policy rather than the insured. *See* Priv. Ltr. Rule 93-23002; Estate of Perry v. Commissioner, 927 F.2d 209 (5th Cir. 1991).

[3]To qualify for the annual exclusion, the transfer must be a gift of a "present" interest. I.R.C. §2503(b). A gift to a trust must be subject to withdrawal by the beneficiary in the calendar year during which the gift was made to be considered a "present" interest.

[4]Crummey v. Commissioner, 397 F.2d 82 (9th Cir. 1968); *see* 22 ACTEC Notes 216 (1996).

[5]Karpf v. Karpf, 240 Neb. 302, 309-311, 481 N.W.2d 891, 896-897 (1992); Bogert, Trusts and Trustees §961.

siderations in managing this type of financial asset. The trustee should review and monitor the financial health of the life insurance company and the policy's performance. A. M. Best, Moody's, Standard & Poor's, and Duff & Phelps are in the business of rating insurance companies.

The trustee should be familiar with the terms of the trust. The terms will usually give the trustee the power to turn in the policy for its cash surrender value, to exchange the policy for another, and to borrow against its cash value. These powers become particularly important in situations where the financial health of the insurance company is questionable, the policy itself is not performing as anticipated or the settlor has ceased making cash contributions to the trust. When considering whether or not to exercise these powers, the trustee may want to seek the advice of an insurance specialist and should keep the beneficiaries and the settlor informed.

## §9.3 The Structured Settlement Trust

A structured settlement trust is a trust established to hold a personal injury award or settlement. The corpus can take the form of a lump sum or the contractual right to receive periodic payments under an annuity issued by an insurance company. The plaintiff, often a disabled minor, is the trust beneficiary.

Notwithstanding the fact that the trust may have been established "by the court" or by the plaintiff's guardian, *the disabled plaintiff/beneficiary is the settlor of the trust.* Neither the court nor the guardian "owned" the property interest. Also, because the payments into the trust by the insurance company (periodic or lump sum) are compensation for physical injury, neither the disabled beneficiary nor the trust will be liable for income taxes on the nonpunitive component of the recovery.[1] On the other hand, because the disabled plaintiff/beneficiary is the settlor, income and princi-

**§9.3** [1]I.R.C. §104(a)(2).

pal may be reachable by the disabled beneficiary's private creditors, income subsequently generated by the trust property may be taxable to the beneficiary, and the subsequent death of the disabled beneficiary may give rise to an estate tax liability with respect to the trust property.[2]

Pursuant to OBRA-93,[3] the disabled beneficiary's *eligibility* for Medicaid will not be jeopardized by a "supplemental needs" structured settlement trust of the discretionary variety (a.k.a. "Disability Payback Trust"), provided the governing instrument requires the trustee to reimburse the state postmortem for any lifetime Medicaid assistance furnished the disabled beneficiary.[4] This obligation, however, extends only to "amounts remaining in the trust" upon the beneficiary's death.[5]

## §9.4 The Charitable Trust

A trust for a charitable purpose is exempt from the durational requirements of the Rule Against Perpetuities.[1] (The equitable interest, however, must vest in the charity within the period of the Rule.)[2] Thus contingent interests created under such trusts may remain outstanding forever. Although charitable trusts have been around for a long time, the trustee should be aware that trust law has yet to develop a workable definition of the term *charitable.*

[2]Priv. Ltr. Rul. 95-020-19 (income tax); Priv. Ltr. Rul. 95-060-04 (estate tax); Rev. Rul. 83-25, 1983-1 C.B. 116; *see also* Arrington v. United States, 76 A.F.T.R.2d (P-H) 95-6752 (Ct. Cl. 1995) (affirming estate tax liability).

[3]The Omnibus Budget Reconciliation Act of 1993.

[4]*See* 42 U.S.C. §1396p(d)-(4)(A); *see generally* Kruse, OBRA '93 Disability Trusts — A Status Report, 10 Prob. & Prop. 15 (No. 3) (1996).

[5]Id.

**§9.4** [1]Regarding income accumulation see 4A Scott on Trusts §365, §401.9; Franklin Foundation v. Attorney General, 416 Mass. 483, 623 N.E.2d 1109 (1993) (involving a 200-year accumulation trust established under the will of Benjamin Franklin); *but see* Bogert, Trusts and Trustees §341. *See generally* §8.15.8 (Rule Against Accumulations).

[2]Leach, Perpetuities in a Nutshell, 51 Harv. L. Rev. 638, 668-669 (1938).

### *§9.4.1 Charitable Purposes*

A trust involving contingent interests may continue in perpetuity for a charitable purpose but not for a private purpose or for a political purpose.[3] Unfortunately, it is not always easy to distinguish private and political trusts from charitable trusts.[4] Courts have traditionally looked to the purposes enumerated in the preamble of the English Statute of Charitable Uses (Statute of Elizabeth)[5] for examples of purposes qualifying for the charitable exemption from the time limitations of the Rule Against Perpetuities.[6] These purposes include relief for the poor, maintenance of nonprofit hospitals and schools, and repair of bridges and roads.[7] When generalizing from the preamble's list, however, one has to be careful. For example, not all trusts whose purposes are the relief of poverty or the advancement of education are charitable trusts. A trust to keep the settlor's children off the welfare rolls is a private trust, although its purpose is the relief of poverty.[8] A trust for the dissemination of literature for or against rent control is a political trust although, as far as the settlor may be concerned, its purpose is the relief of poverty and the advancement of education.[9] A trust to support a hostel for the homeless, however, would fall well within the letter and spirit of the Statute of Charitable Uses.[10] When it comes to matters charitable, trustees should seek out objective criteria: What is charity to one may be politics to another.

[3] *See generally* 4A Scott on Trusts §§368, 374.6; *see generally* J.A. Bryant, Jr., J.D., LL.M., Annot., Application of Cy Pres Doctrine to Trust for Promulgation of Particular Political or Philosophical Doctrines, 67 A.L.R.3d 417 (1975).

[4] *See generally* id.; Rounds, Social Investing, IOLTA, and the Law of Trusts, 22 Loy. U. Chi. L.J. 163, 178-181 (1990).

[5] *See generally* §8.15.4 (Statute of Elizabeth (Charitable Uses)).

[6] *See generally* 4A Scott on Trusts §368.1.

[7] Id.; Bogert, Trusts and Trustees §§321, 362.

[8] 4A Scott on Trusts §369.5; *see e.g.,* Hardage v. Hardage, 84 S.E.2d 54 (Ga. 1954).

[9] *See* Rounds, Social Investing, IOLTA, and the Law of Trusts, 22 Loy. U. Chi. L.J. 163, 179 (1990); *but see* Jackson v. Phillips, 96 Mass. (14 Allen) 539 (1867); *see also* Russell G. Donaldson, J.D., Annot., Validity, As for a Charitable Purpose, of Trust for Publication or Distribution of Particular Books or Writings, 34 A.L.R. 4th 419 (1984).

[10] See Rounds, *supra* note 9, 179 n.75 and accompanying text (1990); 4A Scott on Trusts §369.3.

A trustee who is unsure whether a particular activity is charitable should consider whether the activity is private or political before consulting the Statute of Charitable Uses. If it is neither then the chances are good that it is charitable. As a rule of thumb, a trust for the benefit of a named individual or of a class of beneficiaries ascertainable by their relationship to a named individual is a *private* trust (*e.g.*, a trust for the settlor's issue); a trust whose purpose is to influence the exercise of state power is a political trust[11] (*e.g.*, a trust for the purpose of influencing tax policy).[12] It is settled law that a trust to support a political party is noncharitable.[13] Above all the trustee should not confuse Internal Revenue Code §501(c) criteria for tax exemption[14] with the criteria that have evolved over the years in a particular state for the charitable exemption from the time limitations of the Rule Against Perpetuities. A trust may not be exempt for income tax purposes, but may still be a common law charitable trust, and a trust may be exempt from income tax but not qualify as a charitable trust.[15]

Trustees must strive in practice to maintain a clean separation between the political and the charitable. Boards of trustees of charitable trusts must resist the pressures to exploit for political purposes the enormous economic power which they control as stewards of the benefactions of others.[16]

[11]Rounds, *supra* note 9, 179-180.

[12]*But see* Register of Wills v. Cook, 216 A.2d 542 (Md. 1966) (trust to support efforts to enact an equal rights amendment deemed charitable).

[13]Restatement (second) of Trusts §374, comment K (1959).

[14]*See generally* Bogert, Trusts and Trustees §362.

[15]*See generally* Scott on Trusts §§348.4, 374.4, 374.5.

[16]The three largest charitable foundations are The Ford Foundation ($6,600,562,000); the W. K. Kellogg Foundation ($6,034,576,655), and the J. Paul Getty Trust ($6,016,488,752). Feczko, The Foundation Directory: 100 Largest Foundations by Assets (18th ed. 1996). The best endowed academic institutions are Harvard ($8,811,785,000), the University of Texas Systems ($5,697,150,000), and Yale ($4,853,010,000). Cambridge Associate's, Inc., 1996 NACUBO: Endowment Study (1996). The aggregate sum for the 470 institutions that participated in the college and university study is $88.9 billion. For further information, contact the National Association of Colleges and Universities at (202) 861-2500. The so-called Bishop Estate is the wealthiest charity in the United States with $8 billion in assets. Freedman & Cohen, Bishop's Gambit, Hawaiians Who Own Goldman Sachs Stake Play Clever Tax Game, Wall St. J., Apr. 25, 1995, at A1, col. 6.

### *§9.4.2 Standing to Enforce Charitable Trusts*

It is in the nature of the typical charitable trust that its beneficiaries are so numerous and their interests under it so contingent and tangential that, as a practical matter, no beneficiary possesses a sufficient interest to seek its enforcement.[17] While each of us, for example, is a direct and indirect contingent beneficiary of endowed medical research, in essence it is all of us *collectively* — the *public*, as it were — who is the beneficiary. Thus for hundreds of years both in the United States and in England the "duty of maintaining the rights of the public, and of a number of persons too indefinite to vindicate their own, has vested in the [state] and is exercised here, as in England through the attorney general."[18] This is a practical solution to the enforceability dilemma inherent in the charitable trust. The alternative — vesting everyone with standing to seek enforcement — would be intolerably chaotic and impractical.

But just because contingent beneficiaries of charitable trusts lack standing to seek enforcement, does it follow that others do as well? Let us assume that many years ago a number of grateful citizens contributed sums of money to a city for the purpose of erecting and maintaining a tomb and museum to house the remains and papers of a famous general. The tomb was built and the museum established. Now the tomb is in disrepair and the museum has been all but abandoned by the mayor, whose thoughts are on other matters. What about the currently living relatives of the general? Would they have standing to enjoin the city from neglecting its stewardship of the tomb and museum? Would those who contributed to the complex have standing in their capacities as settlors to seek enforcement of the trust? Must the welfare of the tomb and museum be dependent solely on the enforcement discretion of the attorney general who perhaps does not want to embarrass the mayor?[19]

According to Professor Scott, persons having a special interest in the performance of a charitable trust can maintain a suit for its

[17] *See generally* 4A Scott on Trusts §391; Bogert, Trusts and Trustees §§411-417.
[18] Jackson v. Phillips, 96 Mass. (14 Allen) 539, 579 (1867).
[19] *See generally* Hochman v. Babbitt, 94 Civ. 3000 (wk) (S.D.C.N.Y. 1994) (the "Grant's Tomb Case").

enforcement.[20] They however must show that their interest is not merely derived from their status as members of the general public. Thus the incumbent of an endowed chair at a medical research facility would have standing to seek enforcement of the endowment trust.[21] Rights of enforcement would also accrue to a minister entitled to income distributions from a clergy support trust.[22] Likewise a respectable argument could be made that the general's proximate relatives who are currently living would have an interest in the proper maintenance of their ancestor's tomb and that this interest is sufficiently "special" to vest them with standing to seek enjoinment of its neglect.

Some jurisdictions by statute allow for some settlor involvement.[23] For example, California enacted a statute granting settlors of irrevocable living trusts standing to petition for trustee removal.[24] California also provides for settlor involvement in the modification or termination of an irrevocable trust.[25] The Uniform Management of Institutional Funds Act (UMIFA) calls for donor involvement in the release of a restriction on a use or investment.[26]

In any case, public oversight of charitable trusts by multitasked, overburdened, undersupported attorneys general is generally more apparent than actual.[27] Even if, as a practical matter, there is no one looking over the trustee's shoulder, the ethical trustee conscientiously carries out the intentions of the settlor-benefactor.

### *§9.4.3 Cy Pres*

> It is . . . well settled by decisions of the highest authority, that when a gift is made to trustees for a charitable purpose, the general

[20] 4A Scott on Trusts §391.
[21] *See* id.
[22] Id.
[23] The matter of whether the settlor, in the absence of statute, has standing to enforce the trust is covered in §4.1. *See generally* Rounds, Protections Afforded to Massachusetts' Ancient Burial Grounds, 73 Mass. L. Rev. 176, 180-182 (1988).
[24] Cal. Prob. Code §15642 (West 1991).
[25] Cal. Prob. Code §15404 (West 1991).
[26] 7A U.L.A. 723, §7 (1985).
[27] *See generally* 4A Scott on Trusts §391.

> nature of which is pointed out, and which is lawful and valid at the time [the transfer is made], and no intention is expressed to limit it to a particular institution or mode of application, and afterwards, either by change of circumstances the scheme of the [settlor] becomes impracticable, or by change of law becomes illegal, the fund, having once vested in the charity, does not go to the heirs at law as a resulting trust, but is to be applied by the court of chancery, in the exercise of its jurisdiction in equity, as near the [settlor's] particular directions as possible, to carry out his general charitable intent.[28]

In the event that circumstances make it impossible or impractical to carry out the specified purpose of a charitable trust, the doctrine of *cy pres*[29] may be available as an alternative to the imposition of a resulting trust in favor of the settlor or the settlor's estate. In other words, the doctrine of cy pres may provide an alternative to the trust's termination. If the court finds that a particular trust is cy pres-eligible, it will fashion an alternative scheme of disposition that closely approximates the specified unfeasible one. For a trust to be cy pres-eligible, however, the settlor must have manifested a "general charitable intent."[30]

The concept of cy pres is not particularly esoteric or radical. It essentially involves the textual search for any generalized intent on the part of the settlor which is independent of the specific circumstances of a given moment. As many charitable trusts are designed to continue forever, specific circumstances are bound to change. Institutions come and go; what was legal becomes illegal; problems are solved and new ones surface. Even if courts had not articulated the doctrine, a trustee, in the face of changed circumstances, would always have an obligation to ascertain whether the settlor's intent was general or specific and then to act accordingly. Thus a prospective trustee of a charitable trust would do well to insist that

[28] Jackson v. Phillips, 96 Mass. (14 Allen) 539, 580 (1867); *see also* American Academy of Sciences v. Harvard College, 78 Mass. (12 Gray) 582, 596 (1832).

[29] *Cy Pres* is an Anglo-French phrase equivalent to the modern French *si près*, meaning "so near" or "as near." 4A Scott on Trusts §399. This abbreviated phrase was taken from *cy pres comme possible,* which means "as near as possible." Bogert, Trusts and Trustees §431.

[30] *See generally* 4A Scott on Trusts §399; Bogert, Trusts and Trustees §436; Restatement (Second) of Trusts §399 (1959).

the settlor-benefactor spell out unambiguously whether the charitable intent is general or specific.

An example of judicial deference to reversionary interests[31] is illustrated in the events which gave rise to the Supreme Court case of *Evans v. Abney.*[32] The Court was asked to consider the constitutional implications of the administration and termination of a trust created under the 1911 will of U.S. Senator A. O. Bacon of Georgia. Pursuant to the terms of the will, property had been transferred in trust to the Senator's home city of Macon, Georgia for the creation of a whites-only public park. Following the Court's earlier decision in *Evans v. Newton*[33] (holding that the park could not continue to be operated on a racially discriminatory basis), a state court had ruled that the Senator's intention to provide a park for whites only was not of a general charitable nature. Accordingly, it was held that the trust had failed and that the parkland and other trust property associated with it must revert upon a resulting trust[34] to the Senator's estate. If, on the other hand, there had been a finding of general charitable intent, presumably the state court, invoking the cy pres doctrine, would have ordered the continued operation of the park on an integrated basis. Such a finding would have, for all intents and purposes, voided the equitable reversionary interests of those entitled to the Senator's estate.

As to the actual holding of *Abney*, the Court found that the state court's failure to find general charitable intent in the establishment of the trust did not constitute "state action" under Fourteenth Amendment analysis. Thus no federal constitutional grounds were found for extinguishing the private reversionary interests in favor of continued public operation of the park.

In *Ebitz v. Pioneer National Bank,*[35] the Massachusetts court interpreted the concept of general charitable intent more elasti-

[31] *See, e.g.,* J. Gray, The Rule Against Perpetuities §§34, 41.1, 113, 113.1, 113.3, 327.1 (4th ed. 1942) (settlor of limited charitable purpose trust retains vested reversionary interest in trust property); National Shawmut Bank v. Joy, 315 Mass. 457, 462-469, 53 N.E.2d 113, 117-121 (1944) (failure of trust triggers resulting trust in favor of settlor or settlor's estate).

[32] 396 U.S. 435 (1970).

[33] 382 U.S. 296 (1966).

[34] *See generally* §§4.1.1, 8.2.1.5 (discussing the resulting trust).

[35] 372 Mass. 207, 361 N.E.2d 225 (1977).

cally than the Georgia court had in *Abney*. At issue was the provision of a testamentary trust established "to aid and assist worthy and ambitious young men to acquire a legal education."[36] The will was executed in 1963 and allowed in 1970. The plaintiffs were female law students who made timely applications to the trustee for assistance from the fund which were rejected on the ground that the testator had intended males, not females, to be beneficiaries of his largesse. The trial judge held that "[t]o exclude females as possible recipients of financial assistance from a trust fund established for the purpose of assisting qualified students interested in the pursuit of a legal education would constitute an unreasonable and arbitrary exclusion."[37] He then speculated that the enforcement of such a provision might be unconstitutional. With that he ruled that the term "young men" meant "young men and young women." The trustee appealed. The trial judge was upheld on appeal by the Massachusetts Supreme Judicial Court, which found the reference to "young men" ambiguous in the context of the entire instrument.

In dissent, Justice Quirico wrote: "Surely it is not the law that a testator or donor may not bestow the benefit of his own funds on a class of persons of one sex to the exclusion of persons of a similar class but of the opposite sex, if that is his stated intention."[38] Citing *Abney*, he suggested that the case was not "clouded" by any constitutional question.

The expansive approach to general charitable intent exemplified by *Ebitz* is contrasted by the approach taken by the Montana court in *In re Will of Cram.*[39] At issue was a testamentary trust that provided for cash stipends to young males certified by the Future Farmers of America of Montana and the 4-H Club of Montana to be of good character, in need of financial assistance, and interested in the sheep raising business. The two organizations had

[36]Id. at 209, 361 N.E.2d at 226; *see generally* Tracy A. Bateman, J.D., Annot., Validity of charitable gift or trust containing gender restrictions on beneficiaries, 90 A.L.R. 4th 836 (1991).

[37]Id. at 212, 361 N.E.2d at 228 (Quirico, J., dissenting) (quoting trial court's holding).

[38]Id. at 213, 361 N.E.2d at 228.

[39]606 P.2d 145 (Mont. 1980).

links to the state educational system. In response to an equal protection challenge to those provisions of the trust that were gender exclusive, the Montana lower court modified the trust to remove any state involvement in the mechanics of the grantee selection process. On appeal, the actions of the lower court were affirmed.

The settlor clearly intended to discriminate, that is, to benefit young males to the exclusion of young females. However, the trust as modified involved no state action.

> A private person has the right to dispose of his money or property as he wishes and in so doing may lawfully discriminate in regard to the beneficiaries of his largess without offending the Equal Protection Clause as long as the State and its instrumentalities are not involved, and unless the trust is unlawful, private trusts are to be encouraged.[40]

As *Abney, Ebitz,* and *Cram* suggest, there is yet no judicial consensus as to the elasticity and limits of general charitable intent. Thus the trustee, when faced with a charitable trust whose purposes cannot be carried out, is well advised to place the matter of what is to be done next in the hands of the appropriate court by way of a cy pres petition.

### §9.4.4 *May the Legislature Alter the Terms of a Charitable Trust Without Violating the Doctrine of Separation of Powers?*

With some limited exceptions, only the judiciary may apply the doctrine of cy pres to charitable trusts.[41] Application of the cy

[40] Id. at 150; *see also* In re Estate of Wilson, 452 N.E.2d 1228, 1235 (N.Y. 1983) ("The Fourteenth Amendment, however, 'erects no shield against merely private conduct, however discriminatory or wrongful.' Shelley v. Kraemer, 334 U.S. 1, 13 . . . ").

[41] *See* Opinion of the Justices to the House of Representatives, 374 Mass. 843, 371 N.E.2d 1349 (1978) (providing that the Massachusetts legislature does not have the power to alter the terms of a trust established under the will of Benjamin Franklin); *see also* Franklin Foundation v. Attorney General, 416 Mass. 483, 623

pres doctrine is not a function of the legislative branch, nor in the United States is it a function of the executive.[42]

Except pursuant to its right to take by eminent domain for just compensation, a legislature may not alter the terms of an *ongoing charitable corporation or trust with a lawful purpose that is capable of being carried out.* As to charitable corporations, the U.S. Supreme Court so held in the 1816 Dartmouth College case.[43] The New Hampshire legislature had attempted by statute to amend the charter of the charitable corporation known as Dartmouth College. The Court found that the statute violated Article I, §10, of the U.S. Constitution providing that no state shall pass any law impairing the obligations of contracts. The Court found two contracts: the implied contract between the Crown which had granted the charter and benefactors that the Crown would not alter the terms of the charter and the implied contract between the benefactors and the corporation that gifts would be administered in accordance with the terms of the charter. For a charter amendment to be effective, it must be consented to by the corporation and approved by a court in the exercise of its cy pres power.[44] The principles of the Dartmouth College case have been held applicable to charitable trusts.[45]

## *§9.4.5 Tax Oriented Trusts That Mix Charitable and Non-charitable Interests (Split-Interest Trusts)*

The equitable interests of a trust may be divided between charitable and non-charitable beneficiaries. Let us take our standard formula: *A* to *B* for *C*, then to *D*. A trust where *C* is a non-

---

N.E.2d 1109 (1993) (addressing how the Massachusetts legislature must exercise its right to dispose of a portion of the trust property upon expiration of the trust's 200 year term, Benjamin Franklin, *by express language in his will,* having given to the Commonwealth of Massachusetts a right of disposition over a portion of the trust corpus).

[42] *See generally* 4A Scott on Trusts §399.1.

[43] Trustees of Dartmouth College v. Woodward, 4 Wheat. 518, 4 L. Ed. 629 (U.S. 1819).

[44] *See generally* 4A Scott on Trusts §399.5.

[45] 4A Scott on Trusts §399.5, n. 7, and accompanying text.

charitable beneficiary (e.g., a member of the settlor's family) and *D* is a charity is a *charitable remainder* trust. A trust where *C* is a charity and *D* is a non-charitable beneficiary is a *charitable lead trust.* The incentive for establishing these split-interest arrangements is usually tax avoidance. In the case of an inter vivos charitable remainder trust, the settlor is looking for an income *and* gift tax charitable deduction at the time the *D* interest is deemed created for tax purposes (and for an estate tax deduction in the case of a revocable inter vivos trust or testamentary trust).[46] In the case of the *C* interest under a charitable lead trust, the settlor is looking for a gift or estate tax deduction,[47] and an income tax charitable deduction to the extent the lead trust qualifies as a grantor trust.[48]

### §9.4.5.1 IRS-Approved Charitable Remainder Trusts

In order for the settlor to receive a gift tax charitable deduction, or for his estate to receive an estate tax charitable deduction, the IRS requires that the remainder interest be susceptible to valuation *at the time the deduction is being taken.*[49] For a testamentary trust, that would occur when the settlor dies. For an irrevocable inter vivos trust, that would occur at the time of funding. For a revocable inter vivos trust, that would usually occur at the death of the settlor. For a charitable deduction with respect to a remainder interest to survive audit, the trust's design must conform to IRS requirements:

#### §9.4.5.1.1 Charitable Remainder Unitrust (CRUT)

The IRS has authorized a charitable deduction in connection with the creation of a charitable remainder unitrust that meets the

46 I.R.C. §170(f)(2)(A) (income tax deduction); I.R.C. §2522(c)(2)(A) (gift tax deduction); I.R.C. §2055(e)(2)(A) (estate tax deduction).

47 I.R.C. §2055(e)(2)(B) (estate tax deduction); I.R.C. §2522(c)(2)(B) (gift tax deduction).

48 I.R.C. §170(f)(2)(B); *see also,* §9.1 (The Grantor Trust).

49 I.R.C. §664(d).

following specifications:[50] Each year, 5% or more of the net fair market value of the trust property shall be distributed to the non-charitable beneficiary either for life or for a period no greater than 20 years; and upon the death of the non-charitable beneficiary, the equitable interest passes to a designated charity. *For percentage computation purposes, the trust estate is revalued each year but the percentage is fixed.* The value of the trust estate includes net income applied and principal appreciation.

The IRS also permits a so-called NIMCRUT or "Net Income With Make Up Unitrust."[51] Under a NIMCRUT, only the net income *up to the stated percentage* is paid out. Shortfalls in income distributions are made up in later years when and if net income exceeds the stated percentage. A net income *up to the stated percentage* with no make up unitrust will also pass IRS muster.

#### §9.4.5.1.2 Charitable Remainder Annuity Trust (CRAT)

The IRS has authorized a charitable deduction in connection with the creation of a charitable remainder annuity trust that meets the following specifications:[52] *A fixed sum,* which must be at least 5 percent of the initial net fair market value of the trust estate, shall be distributed yearly to the non-charitable beneficiary for not greater than 20 years or for life. The charity receives the remainder. Unlike the unitrust, there is no yearly reevaluation of the net trust estate and the value of the actual amount received each year is static.

### §9.4.5.2 IRS-Approved Charitable Lead Trust

With respect to those split-interest arrangements where *the remainder* is in a non-charity, the IRS has authorized a charitable deduction for the charitable "C" interest if the "charitable lead

[50] I.R.C. §664(d)(2).
[51] I.R.C. §664(d)(3).
[52] I.R.C. §664(d)(1).

trust" meets the following specifications:[53] the charity receives a fixed sum (that may be satisfied out of income and/or principal) for a specified period (CLAT) *or* the charity yearly receives a fixed unitrust percentage of the net fair market value of the trust estate (CLUT). The value of the net trust estate must be recomputed yearly. Unlike the charitable remainder trusts, there is no minimum percentage requirement.

## §9.5 Trusts for Deferring Taxation of Income

Employee benefit plans and IRAs essentially are arrangements for deferring the taxation of income. Many such arrangements call for the holding of assets in trust.

### *§9.5.1 The Employee Benefit Trust*

When an employer in the United States establishes a retirement "plan" for its employees it is usually of the "qualified" variety. If it is a *qualified plan,* the employer can take its contributions to the plan as a tax deduction.[1] Under certain circumstances, contributions by or on behalf of an employee are not taxed as income to the employee at the time the contributions are made.[2] Taxation on income generated by plan assets may also be deferred.[3] Plan distributions at retirement or at some other time, on the other hand, may have tax consequences.[4] The reader interested in a comprehensive and practical discussion of those consequences is referred to *Life and Death Planning for Retirement Benefits* by Natalie B. Choate.[5]

[53] I.R.C. §2055(e)(2)(B) (estate tax); I.R.C. §2522(C)(2)(B) (gift tax).
**§9.5** [1] *See generally* Bogert, Trusts and Trustees §§255, 270.20.
[2] Id.
[3] Id.
[4] *See generally* Bogert, Trusts and Trustees §264.7.
[5] Published by Ataxplan Publications, P.O. Box 1093-W, Boston, MA 02103-1093 (1996). ISBN 0-9649440-0-6.

For a plan to be qualified it must meet certain requirements set forth in the Internal Revenue Code and elsewhere.[6] Congress, by means of the Employee Retirement Income Security Act of 1974 (ERISA), articulated a comprehensive federal statutory framework for the design and administration of qualified plans.[7]

With the exception of so-called *insured plans,* for a plan to be qualified it must have associated with it a trust that serves as a receptacle for the plan's assets. While ERISA requires that the trust contain certain provisions if the plan is to be qualified, state law governs what constitutes a valid trust.[8] Thus legal issues associated with an employee benefit trust might well be brought to a state court for adjudication.[9] Unfortunately, the establishment of a plan often requires a consortium of actuaries, pension lawyers, tax lawyers, labor lawyers, human resource lawyers, and SEC lawyers in order to determine what property may enter the trust. The common law trust lawyers, that is, those who are familiar with the common law rules applicable once property finds its way into the hands of a trustee, are left out of the process altogether. Moreover, most if asked would prefer not to get involved.

When confronted with an employee benefit trust, the trustee should first assess its common law terms. Most likely it will be a trust with several trustees. Depending upon the type of plan, it could have many settlors (the employees and the employer), many beneficiaries (perhaps retirees entitled to annuitized payments) and many remaindermen (employees and retirees and the postmortem designees of employees and retirees). Some beneficiaries and remaindermen are likely to have vested interests and some to have interests that are partially vested and partially contingent upon length of time with the employer.[10] Depending upon the type of plan, some beneficiaries and remaindermen (perhaps certain retirees) may well have rights of withdrawal in the nature of general inter vivos powers of appointment. The employer may have either an equitable contingent

[6] *See generally* id. §255.
[7] Id.
[8] Id.
[9] Id.
[10] Id.

remainder or a vested reversionary interest in trust assets to the extent they are not needed to fund benefits. Each employee is probably entitled to complete the dispositive terms with respect to that employee's interest in the trust. (This is accomplished by the filling out of a beneficiary designation form supplied by the employer's human resources department.) The governing instrument is likely to provide that income generated by the trust assets be periodically added to principal.

Once the trust is looked at in common law terms (that is to say, once the governing trust document is analyzed to determine in what respects it requires a *deviation* from the common law), the trustee and trust counsel should then turn to ERISA to determine in what respects federal trust law alters and embellishes the common law trust principles discussed in this handbook.[11] They will be surprised to discover that ERISA has codified some longstanding common law trust principles; but, contrary to what they may have heard, the federal gloss has added little that would alarm the conscientious and ethical trustee of an old-fashioned private trust.

Insofar as the trustee is concerned, ERISA has codified and embellished the duty of loyalty by creating a thicket of prohibited transactions.[12] Still, it amounts to little more than an elaborate codification of the common law prohibition against self-dealing by trust fiduciaries.[13] The "Prudent Man Rule" of investment as it applies to employee benefit trusts has been altered by ERISA so that it might better be called the *Federal Prudent Expert Rule.*[14] Again, this is not a particularly radical development as it is unlikely that the common law would have long tolerated an amateur standard for investing the massive aggregation of wealth lodged in the nation's employee benefit trusts. ERISA has also limited the com-

[11]They will find, for example, that ERISA has rendered exculpatory clauses in the employee benefit context unenforceable (*see* §7.2.6 of this handbook) and that employee benefit plan and trust documents may not relieve fiduciaries of those ficuciary duties set forth, expressly or by implication, in ERISA.

[12]Id.; *see also* Wade & Loebl, Individual Prohibited Transaction Exemptions: The "Common Law," 29 Real Prop., Prob. & Tr. J. 185 (1994).

[13]Id.

[14]Id.

mon law rights of a beneficiary's creditors to reach employee benefit trust assets.[15] It has put certain nontrustees on the hot seat — particularly investment managers — by imposing on them fiduciary status. Finally, the area of allocation of fiduciary responsibilities has been elaborated and codified.[16]

Of all ERISA's codifications, the allocation of fiduciary responsibility may be perhaps the most perplexing. Many troubling common law questions lurk behind the codification. For example, if the governing instrument allocates investment responsibility to an investment manager, what common law oversight obligations remain back with trustee? To what extent have the allocation of responsibility provisions of ERISA altered the common law principles of cofiduciary liability?

The beneficiary designation form is completed by an employee usually without legal advice and usually at the human resources office. It is by means of the form that the terms of the employee benefit trust applicable to that employee are completed and that the link is made between the employee benefit trust and the employee's own estate plan. More wealth is likely to transfer pursuant to the terms of the form than pursuant to the terms of the employee's will,[17] yet much more attention and thought is likely to have gone into the drawing of the will than the filling out of the form. In any case it is in the interests of all parties that the terms of the beneficiary designation form cover all contingencies and be unambiguous.

### *§9.5.2 The IRA Trust*

An Individual Retirement Plan[18] (commonly known as an IRA) may offer some income tax deferral opportunities for indi-

[15]ERISA §1056(d)(1); I.R.C. §401(a)(13). (For an employee benefit plan to be qualified, an employee's interest in its associated trust may not be assigned or alienated.)

[16]*See generally* Bogert, Trusts and Trustees §255.

[17]*See generally* Langbein, The Nonprobate Revolution and the Future of the Law of Succession, 97 Harv. L. Rev. 1108 (1984).

[18]*See generally* I.R.C. §408.

viduals. Associated with a particular IRA may be a trust which serves as a receptacle for an individual's contributions.[19] With the possible exception of a Simplified Employee Pension (SEP) IRA,[20] the trust is essentially a common law revocable inter vivos trust.

In order for an IRA to qualify as such, the Internal Revenue Code requires that the trustee of any associated trust be a bank, a thrift institution, an insurance company, a brokerage firm, or any other person who demonstrates to the IRS that he or she will administer the account in a manner consistent with the requirements of the law.[21] It should be noted that by these provisions the Internal Revenue Code is not bestowing trust powers on such institutions or otherwise preempting state law[22] — it is merely laying down requirements that must be met if an individual is to enjoy the tax deferral advantages of an IRA.

One requirement for tax deferral is that the IRA trustee may not invest trust assets in works of art, rugs, antiques, metals, gems, stamps, coins, or other items of tangible personal property specified by the IRS.[23] Amounts invested in such "collectibles" are treated for tax purposes as distributions to the individual.[24] However, gold or silver coins issued by the U.S. government or any type of coin issued under the laws of any state will not be considered collectibles.[25] An interest in a portion of a gold coin portfolio is not considered a collectible.[26]

It is a common misconception that under federal law, an IRA trust affords the same protection from creditors as a trust associated with a qualified employee benefit plan. A qualified plan is established under §401 of the Code. To be sure, that section has an antialienation requirement which appears to preempt state property law. An IRA on the other hand is established under §408 of the Code, a section which contains no such antialienation provision.

[19]Id.

[20]In a SEP IRA, the employee establishes the arrangement and the employer participates in its funding and administration. I.R.C. §408(k).

[21]*See* I.R.C. §408(a)(2).

[22]*See* id. §408(h).

[23]*See* id. §408(m).

[24]Id.

[25]Id. §408(m)(3).

[26]Id. §408(m)(3)(A); *see also* Priv. Ltr. Rul. 89-40-067 (July 12, 1989).

Thus the trustee should first look to see if an applicable state statute speaks to the rights of creditors in the IRA context. If there is no such statute, then the assets in an IRA trust likely would be reachable by the taxpayer's creditors. This is because in an ever-increasing number of jurisdictions assets held in a common law inter vivos trust are reachable by creditors of the settlor-beneficiary.[27]

## §9.6 Trusts That Resemble Corporations or Agencies

A trust can be employed to facilitate the management of certain property and to make it readily divisible and transferable.[1] Let us assume, for example, that the owner of an apartment building wishes over a period of time to give it and the land on which it sits to his grandchildren. He might transfer the land and building to a trustee and take back 100 certificates each representing a one-percent fully vested beneficial interest in the trust. As time goes by he parcels out the certificates to his grandchildren. The nominee trust, the realty trust, the Massachusetts business trust, the voting trust[2], the investment trust (trusteed mutual fund), the Real Estate Investment Trust, and the Illinois Land Trust are variations on this theme.[3]

The key to the arrangement is that the trustee has the title and the beneficiaries have fully vested beneficial interests. Thus, in theory, the inter vivos or postmortem transfer of a certificate of beneficial interest ought not to trigger public filings at the registry of deeds or a cumbersome subdividing of the underlying asset. Thus the arrangement may offer a measure of confidentiality and convenience of management in the face of fractured ownership.

[27] *See* §5.3.3.3(d) (Trusteed employee benefit plans and IRAs).

**§9.6** [1] *See generally* Bogert, Trusts and Trustees §§247-252.

[2] *See generally* E. Le Fevre, Annot., Removal of Trustees of Voting Trust, 34 A.L.R.2d 1136 (1954).

[3] Id.; *see generally* Langbein, The Secret Life of the Trust: The Trust as an Instrument of Commerce, 107 Yale L.J. 165 (1997).

Under the governing instrument the management responsibilities of the trustee may be intense (*e.g.*, the voting trust) or virtually nonexistent (*e.g.*, the nominee trust).

Because these trusts look more like agencies[4] or corporations than trusts, the certificates of vested beneficial interests, as a matter of state property law, tend to behave like stock certificates. If a certificate holder dies, the certificate is likely to end up either in holder's estate or in a marital deduction or family trust established under an instrument that the holder executed while alive.

These corporate-like trust arrangements raise a number of tax and securities regulation issues which are well beyond the scope of this handbook.[5] There is also, however, the issue of limited liability which deserves at least a mention here. It is a matter of paramount concern to all parties, trustees and beneficiaries alike. Do the certificate owners as the equitable owners and the trustee as the legal owner of the land and building enjoy limited liability as they might if the land and building were inside a corporation?[6] What about the general rule that the beneficiary incurs no liabilities arising inherently out of his beneficial ownership, except for taxes?[7] Would such a rule apply to these corporate-like trust arrangements? Unfortunately it is impossible to generalize with respect to these issues. It depends upon the facts and circumstances and the jurisdiction.[8] Thus the first thing that the prospective trustee of a corporate-like trust arrangement should do is ascertain to what extent (if at all) the liability of the parties is limited. A

[4] *See generally* Roberts v. Roberts, 419 Mass. 685, 646 N.E.2d 1061 (1995); *see also* Moscatiello v. Board of Assessors of Boston, 36 Mass. App. Ct. 622, 626 (1994) ("We recognize that, for many purposes, nominee trusts are regarded as creating a principal-agent, rather than a true trustee-beneficiary, relationship . . . Taxing authorities sometimes disregard nominee trust arrangements altogether.").

[5] For a brief summary of the federal income tax treatment of corporate-like trusts, *see* Bogert, Trusts and Trustees §§270.30-270.40; for matters relating to securities regulation, *see generally* L. Loss & J. Seligman, Securities Regulation (3d ed. 1993). *See also* Problems of Fiduciaries Under the Securities Laws, 20 Real Prop. Prob. & Tr. J. 503 (1985).

[6] *See generally* Bogert, Trusts and Trustees §247. *See* §7.3 (Trustee's Liability as Legal Owner to Nonbeneficiaries).

[7] *See generally* Bogert, Trusts and Trustees §247; *supra* §5.6 (Liabilities of the Beneficiary).

[8] Id.

discussion of the alternatives and countermeasures available to the trustee in the face of unlimited liability however is beyond the scope of this handbook.

It should be noted that the authors over the years have encountered a number of instances where attorneys, particular conveyancers, have attempted to fashion a nominee or realty trust form into a viable private revocable inter vivos trust instrument. They do this by making the interest of beneficiaries contingent upon such events as survivorship. Usually the modified instruments are awash in ambiguities and gaps, that is to say, contingencies unprovided for. The best approach is to keep the corporate-like trust instrument separate from the private inter vivos trust instrument. It is the latter that should contain the contingent provisions, such as those which relate to generational succession and the unborn and unascertained. Moreover, there is no reason why the latter may not contain as an asset beneficial interests in the former.[9]

## §9.7 Commingled Trust Funds

As a general rule, the trustee may not commingle the assets of one trust with the assets of other trusts, absent express authority in the governing instrument. This common law prohibition generally does not apply to the common trust fund and IOLTA arrangements.

### *§9.7.1 The Common Trust Fund*

The *common trust fund* is a special type of corporate-like trust arrangement which, because of §584 of the Internal Revenue Code, is available as a practical matter only to banks and their fiduciary customers. In theory it allows for cost-efficient, diversified administration of small accounts. It works this way: The bank executes a declaration of trust or plan for the purpose of serving as trustee of a

[9]For a brief discussion of the trust issues associated with investment companies (mutual funds), *see* §8.10 (Fiduciary Principles Applicable to the Mutual Fund).

common trust fund. The specifications are set forth in a state statute[1] and in federal regulations, particularly "Regulation 9."[2] The arrangement is then available exclusively for the collective investment and reinvestment of moneys contributed to the fund by the bank in its capacity as trustee of other trusts and as executor and administrator of estates. The bank's guardianships may also participate. Essentially a participating entity, such as a trust, purchases a beneficial interest in a trusteed basket of securities — a piece of another trust. One can see the similarity between the common trust fund and the corporate-like trust arrangements mentioned in §9.6 (Trusts That Resemble Corporations or Agencies).

In the 1930s there had been concern that a common trust fund would be taxed as an association.[3] If that were the case, the common trust fund would have no economic utility, because with each participating fiduciary account being subject in any case to tax on income attributable to its participations in the fund, participation in a common trust fund would have effectively generated a double tax. Beginning in 1936 these roadblocks were removed. In that year the precursor to §584[4] was enacted into law removing the threat of federal income taxation at the fund level.

In recent years the hot issue associated with the common trust fund has been whether banks should be allowed to commingle their investment management agency accounts. This would effectively give banks the authority to market participations in their common trust funds to the public in competition with mutual fund participations. So far banks have been unsuccessful in acquiring this authority.[5]

**§9.7** [1]Thirty-four states and the District of Columbia have adopted the Uniform Common Trust Fund Act, 7 Part II U.L.A. 181 (1997). The remaining states have enacted some form of common trust fund enabling legislation. *See* 3 Scott on Trusts §227.9 n.26. *See generally* Bogert, Trusts and Trustees §677.

[2]12 C.F.R. §9.18 (1997) (where consistent with applicable law, a national bank may invest in a common trust fund that meets the requirements of §9.18); *see generally* Bogert, Trusts and Trustees §677.

[3]*See* Brooklyn Trust Co. v. Commissioner, 80 F.2d 865 (2d Cir. 1936), *cert. denied*, 298 U.S. 659 (1936) (composite fund taxable as an association); Bogert, Trusts and Trustees §677.

[4]Federal Revenue Act of 1936 §169, 26 U.S.C.A. §169 (1936). *See generally* Bogert, Trusts and Trustees §677.

[5]*See* Investment Co. Inst. v. Camp, 401 U.S. 617 (1971); *see generally* Bogert, Trusts and Trustees §677.

To reiterate, because of §584 there is no economic advantage for anyone other than a bank to operate a common trust fund. A nonbank trustee who wishes to afford his small trusts the diversification that comes with commingling must look to the mutual fund. It should be kept in mind, however, that the common law prohibits the commingling of the assets of multiple trusts and the delegation by fiduciaries of investment discretion.[6]

### *§9.7.2 IOLTA Trusts*

With the exception of Indiana, all states and the District of Columbia have adopted either by statute or judicial fiat IOLTA programs.[7] *IOLTA* stands for "Interest on Lawyers Trust Accounts." Under an IOLTA scheme, a lawyer is either authorized or compelled under threat of license suspension to commingle or pool unproductive nominal and short-term client funds that the lawyer holds in trust. The income generated by the pool is then remitted to designated charitable and professional entities. It is expected that by 1997 the aggregate amount of income generated by IOLTA nationwide since 1978 will be in the range of one billion dollars. One court has ruled that common law trust principles are not applicable to IOLTA.[8] The Federal Court of Appeal for the Fifth Circuit, however, has held that IOLTA income is the property of the Client. On appeal, the U.S. Supreme Court has affirmed holding that, "for purposes of the Takings Clause of the Fifth Amendment," IOLTA income is the property of the Client.[9]

[6] *See* §§6.1.4 (Duty to Give Personal Attention (Not to Delegate)), 6.2.1 (Duties to Take Active Control, Segregate, Earmark, and Protest Trust Property).

[7] *See* Rounds, Social Investing, IOLTA, and the Law of Trusts, 22 Loy. U. Chi. L.J. 163, 173-174 (1990).

[8] "We are not convinced that the deposit of clients' funds into IOLTA accounts transforms a lawyer's fiduciary obligation to clients into a formal trust with the reserved right to control the beneficial use of the funds as claimed by the plaintiffs." Washington Legal Found. v. Massachusetts Bar Found., 993 F.2d 962, 974 (1st Cir. 1993); *but see* Ritchie et al., Decedents' Estates and Trusts 1318 (8th ed. 1993) ("funds received by a lawyer on behalf of a client are held in trust for the client").

[9] Washington Legal Found. v. Texas Equal Access to Justice Found., 94 F.3d 996 (1996); *see* Phillips v. Washington Legal Found., U.S. Supreme Court, No. 96-1578, June 15, 1998 (1998 WL 309070 (U.S.)).

# §9.8 Quasi-trusts and Hybrids

Certain arrangements are trusts in substance but not in form. The *charitable corporation* is a classic example. Some hybrid arrangements, such as the custodial IRA, have the characteristics of both the trust and the agency. The Massachusetts Supreme Judicial Court has ruled that the Boston Common is held by the City of Boston upon a quasi-trust.[1]

## §9.8.1 *The Charitable Corporation*

Is a gift of property to a charitable corporation a transfer in trust? Is the corporation a trustee of the property such that its governing body is subject to all the common law duties and obligations of a trustee? Professor Scott, while acknowledging some technical differences between the charitable trust and the charitable corporation, on balance finds them more similar than dissimilar.[2] Certainly if the gift is restricted, the governing body should segregate the property and behave as ethical fiduciaries with respect to it. Above all they should carry out the lawful intentions of the transferor, and the attorney general and the courts should see to it that they do.

The realities of the situation are different, however, with respect to unrestricted gifts to a charitable corporation. Implicit in the gift is that the property will be used only for the legitimate expressed charitable purposes of the corporation. As a practical matter, however, the ultimate use of that particular gift may be impossible to monitor, particularly if it has been commingled with the general assets of the corporation or used for its general support. The governing body has a fiduciary duty to benefactors of unrestricted gifts to see to it that the corporation cleaves to the letter and spirit of the corporation's charitable purposes. Whether that obligation is enforceable or not is another matter.[3] If the

**§9.8** [1]Codman v. Crocker, 203 Mass. 146, 150, 89 N.E.2d 177, 178 (1909).
[2]4A Scott on Trusts §348.1.
[3]*See* Fishman, The Development of Nonprofit Corporation Law and an Agenda for Reform, 34 Emory L.J. 617, 668-671 (1985).

governing body expects to so deviate it should segregate all benefactions and conduct its deviations with other funds.

Enforceability and fiduciary obligation are key elements of the trust. With respect to an unrestricted gift to a charitable corporation, the former element may well be lacking. Thus benefactors interested in enforceability may want to shun the charitable corporation in favor of making gifts to a charitable trust where the parties are more legally defined and where their rights and obligations more legally settled.[4] It is interesting to note that the Uniform Management of Institutional Funds Act (UMIFA) generally does *not* apply to common law trusts of the type which are the subject of this handbook.[5]

While there are important similarities between the charitable trust and the charitable corporation,[6] fiduciary exculpation is one area where there is a fundamental difference. *Settlors* of charitable trusts generally control the insertion of exculpatory provisions into trust instruments, not the trustees. When it comes to charitable corporations, however, it is the *directors*, the fiduciaries themselves, who generally have statutory authority[7] to determine whether or not there is fiduciary exculpation.

Another fundamental difference between the charitable trust and charitable corporation relates to whether principal may be invaded. An unrestricted gift to a charitable corporation carries with it the presumption that principal as well as income may be devoted to its charitable purpose; a charitable trust is presumed to be income only, absent an expression of contrary intent in the governing instrument.[8]

[4] *See* Karst, The Efficiency of the Charitable Dollar: An Unfulfilled State Responsibility, 73 Harv. L. Rev. 433, 435 (1960).

[5] 7A U.L.A. 712 (West 1985).

[6] 4A Scott on Trusts §348.1 at 9 ("In both cases the Attorney General can maintain a suit to prevent a diversion of the property to purposes other than those for which it was given; and in both cases the doctrine of cy pres is applicable.").

[7] *See* Revised Model Nonprofit Corporation Act Subchapter E, comment 1 (1987); *see also* Moody, State Statutes Governing Directors of Charitable Corporations, 18 U.S.F. L. Rev. 749, 782-783 (1984) (presenting a table of state indemnification statutes applicable to nonprofit corporations).

[8] *See generally* §5.4.1.3 (Right to Income or Possession).

### *§9.8.2 The City, the States, or the United States as Trustee*

While the United States of America and the states, counties, and municipalities within it in theory may have common law or statutory authority to hold property in trust, the absence of the key element of credible enforceability makes such trusteeships something other than of the common law variety.[9] The practical, political, and legal realities are that a state attorney general, even if so inclined, would find it very difficult to effect a judicial removal of a governmental entity as trustee of a particular trust.[10] Thus to the extent political influence and press oversight[11] are the only viable means of enforcing such arrangements, a discussion of the nature of those arrangements falls outside the scope of this handbook.

### *§9.8.3 Cemeteries and Parks*

Cemetery land is usually held by a municipality or other governmental entity, a cemetery corporation, or a religious organization. Occasionally one will come across a cemetery situated within the borders of a privately owned parcel. Is a trust impressed upon such land? It would seem that some kind of trust is associated with cemetery land and there are some cases to that effect.[12] In the face of the common law rights of persons to visit, honor, and protect the

[9] *See, e.g.*, Probe Hits US Funding of Indian Trust Funds, Boston Globe, April 4, 1992, at 5 (Bureau of Indian Affairs accused of decades of mismanagement of trusts).

[10] *See* Karst, The Efficiency of the Charitable Dollar: An Unfulfilled State Responsibility, 73 Harv. L. Rev. 433, 478-479 (1960).

[11] *See, e.g.*, McGrory, Criticism Over Fund Draws Flynn Response, Boston Globe, Jan. 5, 1992, at 26 (trust administered by City of Boston becomes a center of controversy as a result of negative publicity); *see also* Chacón, City accused of mismanaging gift trusts, Boston Globe, Sept. 11, 1996, at B6 and Editorial, It's a Matter of Trust, Boston Herald, Sept. 16, 1996, pg. 20 (both regarding a draft Boston Finance Commission report that is critical of how the City of Boston manages its trusts).

[12] See Rounds, Protections Afforded to Massachusetts' Ancient Burial Grounds, 73 Mass. L. Rev. 176, 180 n.118 (1988); *see, e.g.*, Sanford v. Vinal, 28 Mass. App. Ct. 476, 552 N.E.2d 579 (1990).

graves of their deceased relatives, it is clear that those in control of cemetery land do not have untrammeled rights to exploit and alienate the land.[13] On the other hand, as a matter of classic trust law it is not always clear to whom the burden of responsibility runs. In the case of a cemetery corporation it is clear that an affirmative burden runs to the governing body; with respect to a cemetery situated on private property, the owner of the property's fiduciary responsibilities may be passive, such as merely to leave the cemetery undisturbed and to allow others onto the land at reasonable times to visit, honor, and protect the gravesites.[14] The law of trusts has been an underutilized weapon in the battle to protect cemeteries, particularly historic cemeteries.

The legal status of parkland is also somewhat ambiguous. Much depends upon how the land came to be a park. If the land was set aside pursuant to the terms of someone's will, then it may well be held upon a charitable trust,[15] although, as in the case of governmental trusts in general, the trust's enforceability may exist more in theory than in reality. If the governmental entity had carved out the parkland from public land or had taken the land by eminent domain, then the arrangement looks less like a trust. One court, however, has held that the Boston Common is held by the City of Boston upon a quasi-trust.[16] The law of trusts has been an underutilized weapon not only in historic preservation battles but also in battles for open space.

## *§9.8.4 Custodial IRAs*

In form a custodial IRA administered by a bank or mutual fund is an investment management agency relationship between the custodian and the person establishing the IRA.[17] If the arrangement were in substance a common law agency, then it would terminate upon the death of the customer. The result then would be that all funds subject to the arrangement would pass to the customer's

[13] *See* Rounds, *supra* note 12, at 180-182.
[14] Id. at 183-184, 188.
[15] *See generally* Bogert, Trusts and Trustees §322.
[16] Codman v. Crocker, 203 Mass. 146, 150, 89 N.E. 177, 178 (1909).
[17] *See* I.R.C. §408(h).

estate, notwithstanding any provisions of a beneficiary form to the contrary. Most states, however, now have statutes on their books anticipating this problem.[18] The statutes provide that the terms of custodial IRA beneficiary designation forms shall be honored notwithstanding the failure of such forms to comply with the Statute of Wills.[19] Thus by virtue of these statutes an IRA custodian begins to look very much like a common law trustee, particularly during the period between when the taxpayer dies and when the balance in the account is distributed.

### *§9.8.5 The Totten Trust*

When *A* opens a savings account in the name of *C* and retains control of the account, courts are inclined to find that the arrangement is essentially a revocable living trust with *A* being both the trustee and the holder of a reserved right of revocation.[20] Some jurisdictions require that upon the death of *A* the money be paid to *A*'s estate, unless notice of the arrangement is given to *C* during *A*'s lifetime.[21] The validity of the standard revocable inter vivos trust, however, is not contingent upon notice being given to post-mortem beneficiaries.

## §9.9 False Trusts

The public should be aware that just because an arrangement is described in trust-like terms, it does not necessarily have the requisite elements of a trust. Phrases such as *cash surrender value* or

[18] *See* Bogert, Trusts and Trustees §255 n.11 (second n.11 of section) and accompanying text.

[19] Id.

[20] *See* 1A Scott on Trusts §58.1 n.3; *see also* In re Matter of Totten, 179 N.Y. 112, 71 N.E. 748 (1904).

[21] *See* L.S. Tellier, Annot., Gift or Trust by Deposit in Bank in Another's Name or in Depositor's Own Name in Trust for Another, as Affected by Lack of Knowledge on Part of Such Other Person, 157 A.L.R. 925 (1945).

*internal build-up* do not make an insurance contract a trust. Nor is the Social Security Trust Fund a trust fund.

### §9.9.1 *Insurance*

Although many insurance products are structured or marketed to look like trusts, they are *contracts,* not trusts.[1] In spite of provisions for separate accounts and yields pegged to market performance, the insurance company does not segregate the premium as a trustee would;[2] rather the premium is commingled with the general assets of an insurance company and in exchange the insurance customer receives the company's promise to pay a certain amount, at a certain time, subject to the happening of certain events.

### §9.9.2 *Agency Arrangements*

Powers of attorney (including Durable Powers of Attorney), investment management agency accounts, and escrow agency accounts are not trusts.[3] With some common law and statutory exceptions,[4] under none of these arrangements does title to the subject property pass to the agent.[5] Upon the death of a principal, any property that is a subject of the agency must pass to the principal's estate. This of course need not happen under a trust arrangement.

**§9.9** [1]*See generally* 1 Scott on Trusts §14; *see also* Uhlman v. New York Life Ins. Co., 109 N.Y. 421, 17 N.E. 363 (1888).

[2]A trust is not to be confused with insurance company reserves, which are sums of money an insurer is required to set aside to insure the solvency of the company. Arrow Trucking Co. v. Continental Ins. Co., 465 So. 2d 691, 696 (La. 1985).

[3]1 Scott on Trusts §§8-8.1.

[4]*See* id. §8 n.6; *see also* Restatement (Second) of Agency §14B comment *e* (1957).

[5]1 Scott on Trusts §8.

### *§9.9.3 Legislative Budget Items Couched in Trust Terms*

It has become a practice of politicians to employ trust terminology to promote various governmental programs.[6] A case in point is the so-called Social Security Trust Fund, although many state legislatures are developing similar schemes for "dedicating" tax revenues. The Social Security Trust Fund is a budget item; it is not a common law trust of the type which is the subject of this handbook. A taxpayer thus could not successfully in a judicial forum invoke principles of trust law to prevent a congressional raid on the fund.[7]

### *§9.9.4 A Bank Account Is Not A Trust*

It is a popular misconception that a bank account is a trust. It is not. A bank account is a contract, the bank being the debtor and the depositor being the creditor. In other words, a debt is not a trust.[8] A debt is a personal obligation *of the debtor*. When one places money in an ATM machine, the money is commingled with the general assets of the bank. Should the bank become insolvent, the

[6] *See* I.R.C. §9501 ("Black Lung Disability Trust Fund"); §9502 ("Airport and Airway Trust Fund"); §9504 ("Aquatic Resources Trust Fund"); §9505 ("Harbor Maintenance Trust Fund"); §9506 ("Inland Waterways Trust Fund"); §9507 ("Hazardous Substance Superfund"); §9508 ("Leaking Underground Storage Tank Trust Fund"); §9509 ("Oil Spill Liability Trust Fund"); §9510 ("Vaccine Injury Compensation Trust Fund"); §9511 ("National Recreational Trails Trust Fund"); Exec. Order No. 12858 ("Deficit Reduction Fund," more commonly referred to as the Clinton Deficit Reduction Trust Fund). With respect to the Clinton Deficit Reduction Trust Fund see generally Mitchell, . . . and Marred by Trust Fund Gimmick, Wall St. J., August 5, 1993, at A12.

[7] *See generally* Flemming v. Nestor, 363 U.S. 603 (1960); Ferrara, Social Security: The Inherent Contradiction (1980); Peterson, Will America Grow Up Before It Grows Old?, 227 The Atlantic Monthly 55, 61 (No. 5-May 1996) ("It's time to face up to the fact that Social Security is in fact a pay-as-you-go system. Payroll taxes go directly to today's beneficiaries; benefits come directly from today's workers."). *See also* Miller, Uh-oh: The Social Security Mess — And How to Fix It, 214 New Republic 20, 23 (No. 6-April 15, 1996) ("Well, brace yourself for another rude awakening: the Social Security Trust Fund is an accounting fiction.").

[8] *See generally* 1 Scott on Trusts §§12, 12.9.

depositor would then be no more than a general creditor of the bank. The depositor would have no special right to a particular item of property or to a dedicated account.

If, however, the owner of the funds *intended* to *entrust* the property to the bank, as evidenced perhaps by his or her bringing the funds upstairs to the bank's trust department, then the bank would be obliged to segregate the property. The property would then be insulated from the bank's creditors in the event of insolvency to the extent the funds were not on deposit on the commercial side of the bank. Bear in mind that, as *to the depositor,* the bank account (or debt) is an item of property. As such, the contractual rights associated therewith may be made the subject of a trust. But the debt itself is not a trust.

## §9.10 The Offshore Asset Protection Trust

With the exception of Alaska and Delaware,[1] it is public policy in the United States that a settlor cannot place property in trust for the settlor's own benefit and keep it beyond the reach of creditors.[2] On the other hand, some jurisdictions outside the United States, such as the Bahamas, Barbados, Belize, Bermuda, Cayman Islands, Cook Islands, Cyprus, Gibraltar, Isle of Man, Mauritius, Turks and Caicos, Nevis, and Neue, have adopted an opposite policy.[3] This has caused U.S. citizens, concerned about exposure to attack from tort and contract creditors, to transfer their property to trustees operating in these settlor-friendly havens.[4] These

**§9.10** [1]*See generally* §5.3.3.1(c) (Reaching Settlor's Reserved Beneficial Interest: Domestic Asset Protection Havens).

[2]*See generally* §5.3.3.1 (Reaching Settlor's Reserved Beneficial Interest); *see also* Marty-Nelson, Offshore Asset Protection Trusts: Having Your Cake and Eating It Too, 47 Rutgers L. Rev. 11 (1994).

[3]Rothschild, Establishing and Drafting Offshore Asset Protection Trusts, 23 Est. Plan. 65 (Feb. 1996) n.1.

[4]Id.

trusts are known as Offshore Asset Protection Trusts.[5] Offshore trusts created by U.S. citizens are of questionable utility, however, when it comes to avoiding U.S. income and estate taxes.[6] One learned commentator offers a warning:

> A U.S. person who establishes a foreign trust is subject to the grantor trust rules if any beneficiary is a U.S. person. Such trusts may also be deemed grantor trusts by virtue of certain retained powers or interests. Furthermore, existing reporting requirements mandate filing returns upon the creation of a foreign trust or transfer of assets to such a trust. The advisor should ascertain that the client's intentions for creating a trust are not tax motivated because Sections 7206 and 7212 may provide grounds for imposing criminal liability on one who assists a taxpayer in avoiding the tax collection efforts of the Service.[7]

## §9.11 The Bankruptcy Trustee

A trustee appointed by the bankruptcy court to take title to the property of a debtor is a fiduciary.[1] He owes a primary duty to the creditors of the bankrupt and a residual duty to the bankrupt.[2] Because the trustee in bankruptcy is required by statute to "collect and reduce to money the property of the estate" his responsibilities deviate somewhat from those of the common law trustee.[3] There may be no duty to invest, for example. Unlike a common law trustee,

[5]Id.; *see also* Lorenzetti, The Offshore Trust: A Contemporary Asset Protection Scheme, 102 Commercial Law Journal 138 (1997).

[6]*But see* Marty-Nelson, Taxing Offshore Asset Protection Trusts: Icing on the Cake, 15 Va. Tax Rev. 399 (1996).

[7]Gideon Rothschild, Esq., Establishing and Drafting Offshore Asset Protection Trusts, 23 Est. Plan. 65 (1996); *see also* §9.1 (The Grantor Trust) and §6.3.1 (Tax Filings — Foreign Trusts).

**§9.11** [1]*See generally* D. B. Bogart, Liability of Directors of Chapter 11 Debtors in Possession: "Don't Look Back — Something May Be Gaining on You, 68 Am. Bankr. L.J. 155 (1994).

[2]Id. at 187.

[3]Id. at 186-212.

"[a] . . . trustee in bankruptcy . . . is not personally liable on a contract made by him in the performance of his duties . . . , even though there is no provision in the contract relieving him of personal liability."[4] A full discussion of the law of bankruptcy and the duties of the trustee in bankruptcy, however, is beyond the scope of this handbook. For that, the trustee is referred to Professor Bogart's article, Liability of Directors of Chapter 11 Debtors in Possession: "Don't Look Back — Something May be Gaining on You."[5]

## §9.12 The Condominium Trustee

The condominium is a property interest that is structured either as an interest in a corporation or as an interest in a trust. When a trust is employed, the condominium trustee takes title to the property and the "owners" of the units take the beneficial interests. Holding title to the underlying property in trust facilitates divisibility and transferability. Despite the trust form, however, the rights, duties and obligations of the condominium trustee are more corporate-like than trust-like. This is in part because much of the "default" law that forms the basis of this handbook has been preempted by condominium legislation and standardized condominium documentation that are "corporate" in orientation. But the courts also have contributed to moving things into the corporate category. Take, for example, the standard for judicial review of decisions by condominium trustees. Courts generally have found that the standard of judicial review should be along the lines of the business judgment rule, i.e., the standard courts apply when considering challenges to the actions of corporate directors.[1]

The business judgment rule would prohibit judicial inquiry

[4]3A Scott on Trusts §262 at 422; *see generally* §7.3.1 (Liability as Legal Owner in Contract to Nonbeneficiaries) and §7.3.2 (Agreements with Nonbeneficiaries to Limit Contractual Liability).

[5]68 Am. Bankr. L.J. 155 (1994).

**§9.12** [1]Levandusky v. One Fifth Avenue Apartment Corp, 75 N.Y.2d 530, 553 N.E.2d 1317, 554 N.Y.S.2d 807 (1990).

into the actions of condominium trustees that are taken in good faith and in the exercise of honest judgment in the lawful and legitimate furtherance of the purposes of the condominium enterprise.[2] The point is that the actions of the condominium trustee will not be subject to judicial sanction simply because the actions were unwise or inexpedient.[3] On the other hand, a court will review the actions of a common law trustee not only to determine whether he exercised undivided loyalty in carrying out the terms of the trust, but whether his actions were "reasonable" or "prudent."[4]

## §9.13 The Unitrust

Under traditional principles of trust law, income is segregated from principal and then distributed to someone other than the remainderman. Under a typical "unitrust," income is added to principal and the beneficiary yearly receives a fixed percentage of the net market value of the trust estate for a pre-determined term of years or for life. The distribution for a given year is typically determined by applying the percentage (usually 5%) against the value of the net trust estate computed as of the end of the preceding year. The remainderman then receives the trust estate outright and free of trust when the term of years expires or the unitrust beneficiary dies. There are many variations on the theme.

In the non-charitable context, the unitrust is considered by some to be more accommodating to total return investment strategies than the traditional "net income to *C*, remainder to *D*" format.[1] In the charitable context, a unitrust that meets rigid IRS specifications can offer the settlor tax avoidance opportunities.[2]

[2]Id.

[3]Id.

[4]*See generally* §6.1.1 (Duty to Be Generally Prudent).

**§9.13** [1]*See generally* §6.2.2.4 (The Non-Charitable Unitrust: Investment Considerations).

[2]*See generally* §9.4.5 (Tax Oriented Trusts That Mix Charitable and Non-charitable Interests (Split-Interest Trusts)).

## §9.14 The Qualified Domestic Trust (QDOT)

When a spouse dies, not all property that passes to the surviving spouse who *is* a U.S. citizen qualifies for the Federal estate tax marital deduction. To qualify, the property must pass either outright and unconditionally to the surviving spouse or to the trustee of a trust for the sole benefit of the surviving spouse. The trust, however, must meet certain design specifications if the deduction is to be allowed. The trust must be eligible for the QTIP election[1] *or* the surviving spouse must be given a general power of appointment over the property coupled with a life interest[2] *or* the property and any income not distributed to the surviving spouse must pass upon the death of the surviving spouse to the surviving spouse's estate.[3] Congress imposed these design requirements so that whatever is left over of the property that escaped the transfer tax upon the death of the first spouse to die ultimately gets taxed to the extent not consumed.

If, however, the surviving spouse is *not* a U.S citizen (or does not become one before the estate tax return of the first to die is filed[4]), the Federal estate tax marital deduction will not be available to the estate of the first to die, unless the property passes to the trustee of a trust for the benefit of the surviving spouse.[5] Furthermore, the trust must not only meet one of the marital deduction design specifications mentioned above but the trust must *also* qualify as a Qualified Domestic Trust or "QDOT," this in order to secure the ultimate payment of the deferred transfer tax. A QDOT whose assets reach a value in excess of $2 million, and each QDOT whose holdings of foreign real property reach a value that exceeds 35 percent of the value of the trust estate, must have a U.S. bank as a trustee *or* post an appropriate bond to secure at least 65 percent of the liability *or* take out a letter of credit to secure at

**§9.14** [1] *See generally* §8.9.1.3 (The Marital Deduction).
[2] I.R.C. §2056(b)(5).
[3] Rev. Rul. 68-554, 1968-2 C.B. 412.
[4] I.R.C. §2056(d)(4).
[5] I.R.C. §2056(d)(2)(A).

least 65 percent of the liability.[6] For computation purposes, indebtedness may not be taken into account; but there is a $600,000 exclusion for up to two personal residences that are used by the surviving spouse and that are assets of the QDOT.[7] For the definitive treatment of the tax implications of designating a QDOT as the recipient of distributions from qualified plans and IRA's, the reader is referred to Natalie B. Choate's *Life and Death Planning for Retirement Benefits.*[8]

As a general rule, any *principal* distributions from a QDOT to the surviving spouse (other than for hardship) will be subject to an estate tax at the marginal estate tax rate applicable to the estate of the deceased spouse whose property funded the QDOT.[9] Any property remaining in the QDOT upon the death of the surviving spouse will also be so taxed.[10] Each trustee is personally liable for payment of the tax.[11] The trustee must report a taxable QDOT distribution on IRS Form 706-QDT. The return must be filed April 15 of the year following the year in which the distribution was made.[12] Any QDOT tax owed on account of the death of the surviving spouse is owed nine months after the death of the surviving spouse.[13]

## §9.15 The Qualified Personal Residence Trust (QPRT)

The Qualified Personal Residence Trust or "QPRT" is a device for reducing estate taxes on the settlor's personal residence.[1] It works like this: The settlor transfers his or her personal resi-

[6]Treas. Reg. §20.2056A-2(d)(1).
[7]Treas. Reg. §20.2056A(d)-2(d)(1)(iv).
[8]Published by Ataxplan publications, P.O. Box 1093-W, Boston, MA 02103-1093 (1996). ISBN: 0-9649440-0-6.
[9]I.R.C. §2056A(b).
[10]Id.
[11]I.R.C. §2056A(b)(6).
[12]I.R.C. §2056A(b)(5)(A).
[13]I.R.C. §2056A(b)(5)(B).
**§9.15** [1]I.R.C. §2702(a)(3).

dence to a trustee, retaining a beneficial interest in the property for a term of years, usually ten. Upon the expiration of the term, the property passes outright and free of trust to the remaindermen, usually the settlor's children. There is no step-up in basis for capital gains tax purposes. If the settlor dies before the expiration of the term, the governing instrument might provide that the property either revert to the settlor's estate or pass to the remaindermen. Whichever is the case, if the settlor dies during the term, the full value of the property, *including any subsequent appreciation,* is included in the settlor's estate *for tax purposes.*[2] *But if* the settlor survives the term, the property is out of his or her estate for tax purposes. The price? The remaindermen may order the settlor to leave the residence. It now belongs to them.

*At the time the residence is transferred to the trustee, a gift tax will be owed.* The gift of the remainder interests is not a present interest and thus will not qualify for the annual gift tax exclusion.[3] The gift tax liability, however, will be offset by the unified credit to the extent that it has not been drawn down by other donative transfers[4] and it will *not* be computed on the then full value of the residence. This is because the value of the remainder interest is discounted for the delay in possession occasioned by the settlor's retained beneficial interest.[5] If the property is to revert to the settlor's estate in the event that he or she does not outlive the term, then the value of the gift will be further discounted to take into account that possibility.

For a personal residence trust to be "qualified," it must meet the design requirements of Treasury Regulations §25.2702-5 (c). If "qualified", the settlor is entitled to a gift tax discount and the trust may include certain features such as the conversion of the QPRT into another arrangement should the residence be liquidated in midterm.

While a QPRT may offer some potential estate tax avoidance opportunities, it does not offer much else. The prospective trustee

[2]I.R.C. §2036(a). The property will then receive a step-up in basis for capital gains income tax purposes.

[3]I.R.C. §2503(b).

[4]*See* §8.9.1.1 (The Unified Credit).

[5]I.R.C. §2702.

will want to think long and hard before getting involved in such an arrangement. The asset is illiquid. There is the matter of how taxes; insurance premiums; costs of maintenance, repairs, and renovations; counsel fees; and trustee fees are to be paid. The trustee should understand that if the settlor becomes insolvent or incapacitated before the QPRT term has expired, the trustee's responsibilities could substantially escalate in intensity and complexity.

## §9.16 Statutory Trusts

As a general rule, for a trust to arise, the owner of the property must *intend* that the property become the subject of a trust.[1] The statutory trust is an exception to this rule.[2] A legislature, by statute, may impose a trust upon someone else's property.[3] Under the Social Security Law, for example, an employee's wages for social security taxes is held in trust *for the United States.*[4]

The United States or one of its constituent states may also impose a trust upon its own property.[5] A state, for example, may take a tract of land by eminent domain for just compensation and then impress a trust on it for recreation or conservation purposes. In this case, it cannot be said that the element of intent is absent. The citizens, through their legislators, are manifesting a collective intent that an item of public property be made the subject of a trust.

**§9.16** [1]*See generally* Introduction to this handbook.

[2]*See generally* I Scott on Trusts §17.5.

[3]*See generally* Bogert, Trusts and Trustees §246.

[4]In re Carl's Estate, 94 N.E.2d 239 (Ohio 1950); *see also* §9.9.3 (social security "trust fund" *not* a trust).

[5]In 1993, for example, the Massachusetts legislature impressed a common law trust upon property over which it had a right of disposition pursuant to the terms of the will of Benjamin Franklin. *See* §127 of the Special Acts of the Massachusetts Legislature (1993 Session Laws); *see also* Franklin Foundation v. Attorney General, 416 Mass. 483, 623 N.E.2d 1109 (1993) (providing in part that the Commonwealth of Massachusetts must exercise its right of disposition *after* the trust has terminated).

CHAPTER 10

# The Income Taxation of Trusts



## §10.1 Introduction to the Fiduciary Income Tax

A trust is a fiduciary relationship with respect to property. For Federal income tax purposes, however, the trust is treated as a separate legal entity. The exception is the grantor trust. While a thorough discussion of the grantor trust rules is beyond the scope of this handbook, suffice it to say that if someone during a particular tax year possesses certain powers, the most common being a general inter vivos power of appointment (be it reserved or in the hands of someone other than the settlor), the chances are we have a grantor trust.[1] If that is the case, the property subject to the power will be treated for Federal income taxes purposes as if it were owned by the holder of the power. (Under the grantor trust rules, the settlor also will be treated as the owner of the trust property for Federal income tax purposes if he or she reserves the income interest or the settlor's spouse is the income beneficiary.[2]) If a trust is not a grantor trust, it is either a simple trust or a complex trust. This, by the way, is tax parlance. These terms do not appear anywhere else in this handbook. In either case, be it simple or complex, the trust will have to file its own Form 1041 and will be treated for tax purposes as its own entity, separate and apart from the settlor, the trustee and the beneficiaries.

A simple trust is essentially your traditional "*A* to *B* for *C* for life then to *D*" type of trust. The trustee may not invade principal or accumulate income. All net trust accounting income must be paid out to *C*.[3]

A complex trust is any trust that is not a grantor trust or a simple trust.[4] When one thinks of a complex trust one thinks of the discretionary trust.

The key thing to remember is that a simple or complex trust gets a deduction for Distributable Net Income (DNI) that is paid out to the beneficiary. DNI is discussed in the next section. The beneficiary then includes the payment on his or her own tax return. As we will see, particularly when we look at Income in Respect of a Decedent (IRD) and the "throwback rules," the past tax affairs of the beneficiary and the past tax affairs of the trust may have to be taken into account in the preparation of the various tax returns. Thanks, however, to the Taxpayer Relief Act of 1997, trustees of most domestic trusts need no longer concern themselves with the throwback rules, beginning with calendar tax year 1998.[5]

**§10.1** [1]I.R.C. §678. *See also* §9.1 (The Grantor Trust) and §8.9.3 (Tax-Sensitive Powers).

[2]I.R.C. §677(a).

[3]I.R.C. §651.

[4]I.R.C. §661(a).

[5]PL §105-34, Aug. 5, 1997, 111 Stat. 788, §507.

## §10.2 Trust Income

For Federal income tax purposes, *someone* (i.e., either the beneficiary or the trust) will have to pay an income tax on the taxable portion of trust accounting income plus capital gains, less certain deductions. We will call this the total taxable amount. To determine what is taxable to the beneficiary, we need to calculate Distributable Net Income (DNI). We start with taxable *trust accounting income* (and, in the case of a complex trust, tax-exempt income as well[1]). That is covered in §6.2.4 of the handbook where the duty to separate income from principal and the right to income is discussed. There is nothing new here. An ordinary dividend or interest on a saving account, for example, would be trust accounting income. We then add to the trust accounting income amount capital gains that are distributable to current beneficiaries[2] and, in the case of a simple trust, add back for computation purposes the trust's $300 deduction or personal exemption.[3]

If the trust is simple, the beneficiary is taxed on the DNI and the trust is taxed on the balance of the total taxable amount, usually undistributed capital gains. If the trust is complex, the beneficiary is responsible for that portion of the total taxable amount that is distributed to the beneficiary and the trust is taxed on the balance of the total undistributed taxable amount. Income, e.g., tax-exempt income or capital gains income, retains its pre-distribution character in the hands of the beneficiary.[4]

For purposes of computing the total taxable amount, one cannot forget IRD. IRD is essentially income that a decedent was entitled to receive but that was not properly includible in the decedent's final Form 1040.[5] A common example of IRD is a taxable distribution from a qualified pension or profit sharing plan. Thus, for example, IRD that enters a trust on account of the

**§10.2** [1]I.R.C. §643(a).
[2]I.R.C. §661(a).
[3]I.R.C. §642(b); I.R.C. §643(a)(1), (2).
[4]I.R.C. §652(b).
[5]I.R.C. §691.

death of the settlor may be subject in whole or in part to the Federal income tax, though it is carried on the books of the trust as accounting principal.

## §10.3 Deductions (Fiduciary Income Tax)

A simple trust is allowed a $300 deduction or personal exemption.[1] A complex trust is allowed a $100 deduction or personal exemption.[2] The total taxable amount may also be reduced by income payments made pursuant to the terms of the governing instrument to a qualified charity.[3] Deductions are allowed for costs (1) paid or incurred in connection with the administration of the trust and (2) which would not have been incurred if the property were not held in such trust or estate in arriving at adjusted gross income[4] (e.g., probate filing fees). Some deductions may be taken either on the settlor's Federal estate tax return or on the trust's Form 1041 (e.g., executor's commissions and attorneys' fees).[5] If the trust includes IRD that generated an estate tax or generation-skipping tax, then the trust is entitled to an income tax deduction for that portion of estate tax allocable to the IRD.[6]

In the case of a simple trust, the entity then gets a deduction for trust accounting income credited out to the beneficiary in a given tax year. The deduction, however, may not exceed the DNI computation[7] and does not include the tax-exempt component, if any.[8] In the case of a complex trust, the entity gets a deduction (up to its DNI ceiling)[9] for the trust accounting income required to be

**§10.3** [1]I.R.C. §642(b).
[2]Id.
[3]I.R.C. §642(c)(1).
[4]I.R.C. §67(e).
[5]I.R.C. §642(g).
[6]I.R.C. §691(c)(1).
[7]I.R.C. §651(b).
[8]Treas. Reg. §1.651(b)-1.
[9]I.R.C. §651(b) (simple trust); I.R.C. §661(a) (complex trust).

distributed currently plus other taxable amounts[10] paid out to the beneficiary, less the tax-exempt portion if any.[11] A beneficiary's share of the taxable distribution, as well as the deductions and credits allocable to it, are recorded on Schedule K-1 of Form 1041.[12] The important thing to note is that not only does the beneficiary get the income distribution, but the beneficiary also gets the benefit of the distribution's pro rata share of certain deductions and credits.

With respect to a particular tax year, the trustee of a complex trust may elect, by checking a box on the Form 1041 return for that year, to treat certain distributions made or credited within the first 65 days of the next year as having been made in the year covered by the return.[13] This "65-day rule" gives the trustee time to assess the trust's income picture for the year covered by the return and respond by making deductions that can be attributed to that year.

## §10.4 Fiduciary Income Tax and Payments

Income taxed to the trust is taxed at the following rates[1]:

1998 Tax Rate Schedule

| If Taxable Income Is: Over — | But not over — | Its tax is: | Of the amount over — |
|---|---|---|---|
| $ 0 | $1,700 | 15% | $ 0 |
| 1,700 | 4,000 | $ 255 + 28% | 1,700 |
| 4,000 | 6,100 | 899 + 31% | 4,000 |
| 6,100 | 8,350 | 1,550 + 36% | 6,100 |
| 8,350 | — | 2,360 + 39.6% | 8,350 |

[10]I.R.C. §661(a).
[11]I.R.C. §661(c).
[12]See Appendix III.
[13]I.R.C. §663(b).
**§10.4** [1]I.R.C. §1(e).

In the case of a simple trust, a distribution of current income up to the amount of its allocable DNI is taxed as if received by the beneficiary directly.

**The Taxpayer Relief Act of 1997,[2] enacted into law August 5, 1997, has done away with the throwback rules for distributions, made in any taxable year beginning after the date of enactment, from most domestic complex trusts.[3] In other words, such distributions shall be computed without regard to any undistributed net income. The following is a brief introduction to the throwback rules for those trustees who must still must deal with them:**

In the case of a complex trust subject to the throwback rules, current distributable income, known as "Tier 1" income, is taxed up to the DNI ceiling as if received directly by the beneficiary.[4] The tax rate for a distribution of DNI accumulated from prior years in a complex trust, "Tier 2" income, is determined by a complicated set of computations required by the so-called accumulation distribution and throwback rules.[5] These computations are designed to approximate the rate that a prior year's income accumulation would have been taxed had it been distributed to the beneficiary in the year of accumulation. The throwback rules are applicable in a given year only if that year's distribution of Tier 1 and Tier 2 income exceeds net trust accounting income.[6] This is because any current unexpended DNI, to the extent not used up in distributions to Tier 1 beneficiaries, gets assigned to the Tier 2 beneficiaries.[7]

To determine the tax on an accumulation distribution, one essentially computes the number of prior years in which there has been an accumulation of DNI that has not been made up by an earlier throwback. We will call these "open years." Only those

[2]PL 105-34, Aug. 5, 1997, 111 Stat. 788.

[3]Trusts still subject to the throwback rules are foreign trusts, certain domestic trusts that were once treated as foreign trusts, and any trust created before March 1, 1984, unless it is established that the trust would not be aggregated with other trusts under I.R.C. §643(f) if such section applied to such trust. *See* I.R.C. §665 (as amended).

[4]I.R.C. §662(a)(1).

[5]Treas. Reg. §1.665(a)-OA(a)(1).

[6]I.R.C. §662(a)(2).

[7]Id.

years, starting from the earliest, that can absorb the distribution are counted.[8] Years when accumulations have been "de minimis" are excluded.[9] For computation purposes, the taxes *paid by the trust* allocable to the accumulation are added to the value of the accumulation distribution.[10] The grossed up accumulation is then divided by the number of open years to arrive at an average yearly accumulation distribution.[11] An average yearly "deemed" increase in the beneficiary's tax is then computed.[12] This is done by ascertaining the beneficiary's taxable income for the five years immediately preceding the year of distribution.[13] The high year and the low year are excluded.[14] An averaged yearly accumulation is then deemed added to the taxable income of the beneficiary in each of the three middle years.[15] The deemed additional tax that would have been owed in each of the three middle years is then computed and divided by three to obtain an average yearly increase in tax that would have been owed had there been no accumulation.[16] The average yearly increase is then multiplied by the number of open years.[17] A credit is then applied for the tax that was *paid by the trust* on the accumulation.[18] A credit is also applied for any estate or generation-skipping taxes that may have been paid with respect to the accumulation.[19] *No refund, however, is available if it turns that the trust paid more in taxes on the accumulation distribution than the beneficiary would have paid had there been no accumulation.*[20]

Income accumulated before a beneficiary was born or before the beneficiary turned 21 is exempt from the throwback rules.[21]

[8]I.R.C. §666(a).
[9]I.R.C. §667(b)(3).
[10]I.R.C. §666(b), (c).
[11]I.R.C. §667(b)(1)(C).
[12]I.R.C. §667(b)(1)(D).
[13]I.R.C. 667(b)(1)(B).
[14]Id.
[15]I.R.C. §667(b)(1)(C).
[16]I.R.C. §667(b)(1)(D).
[17]I.R.C. §667(b)(1).
[18]Id.
[19]I.R.C. §667(b)(6).
[20]I.R.C. §§666(e), 667(b)(1).
[21]I.R.C. §665(b).

This exception does not apply to distributions from foreign trusts.[22]

The trustee computes the accumulation distribution on Schedule J of Form 1041.[23] The beneficiary uses Form 4970 to compute the tax he or she must pay on the distribution.

## §10.5 Practical Information Relating to the Fiduciary Income Tax

The trustee or one of the co-trustees of a domestic trust must file Form 1041 if the trust has any taxable income for the tax year or gross income of $600 (regardless of taxable income) or has a beneficiary who is a nonresident alien. Form 1041 is used to report: (1) the income, deductions, gains, and losses of the trust; (2) the income that is either accumulated or held for future distribution or distributed currently to the beneficiaries; (3) any tax liability of the trust; and (4) employment taxes on wages paid to household employees.

The trustee, or an authorized representative, must sign the Form 1041. A financial institution that submitted estimated tax payments for trusts for which it is the trustee must enter its Employer Identification Number (EIN) in the space provided for the EIN of the fiduciary. Do not enter the EIN of the trust. An attorney or other individual functioning in a fiduciary capacity should leave the space blank. That person's social security number should not be entered. Anyone who is paid to prepare the tax return must also sign it.

For calendar year trusts, the trustee files Form 1041 and Schedules K-1 for a given year on or before April 15 of the following year. (For fiscal years, it is the 15th day of the 4th month following the close of the tax year.) Trusts other than of the charitable, tax and grantor variety must use the calendar year. If the due

[22] Id.

[23] *See* Appendix III.

date falls on a Saturday, Sunday or legal holiday, then the deadline is the next business day. Form 8736 is used to apply for an automatic 3-month extension of time to file. If more time is needed, then Form 8800 must be used.

Schedule D of Form 1041 deals with capital gains and losses. The accumulation distribution for a complex trust is computed on Schedule J. The Alternative Minimum Tax (AMT) is computed on Schedule I. The trustee reports the beneficiary's share of income, deductions and credits to the IRS on Schedule K-1 and furnishes the beneficiary with a copy. The beneficiary uses the information to complete his or her own Form 1040. The beneficiary, however, does *not* file the K-1.

As to grantor trusts, Form 1041 is used only to report any income that is taxable to the trust. Income that is taxable to the "grantor" under the grantor rules is reported to the "grantor" (usually the settlor if he or she holds a reserved right of revocation *or* the holder of a general inter vivos power of appointment if it is someone other than the settlor *or* the settlor if the settlor has either reserved an income interest or a 5% reversionary interest at the trust's inception). The income taxable to the "grantor" and the deductions and credits applied to the income must be reported on the "grantor's" income tax return.

Interest is charged on taxes not paid by the due date, even if an extension of time to file is granted. Interest is also charged on the failure-to-file penalty, the accuracy-related penalty, and the fraud penalty. The interest charge is figured at a rate determined under I.R.C. §6621.

There are penalties for filing late without reasonable cause. These penalties are paid out of the trust estate. Of course, to the extent the penalties are occasioned by a breach of trust on the part of the trustee, the trustee ultimately may have to make the trust whole out of his own pocket. There are also late payment penalties. There are penalties for failure to furnish beneficiaries with K-1s. Penalties for underpaying estimated taxes are figured on Form 2210.

If Form 1041 is filed electronically or on magnetic media, Form 8453-F, U.S. Estate or Trust Income Tax Declaration and Signature for Electronic and Magnetic Media Filing, must be filed.

For more details, get IRS Pub. 1437, Procedures for Electronic and Magnetic Media Filing of U.S. Income Tax Returns for Estates and Trusts, Form 1041, and Pub. 1438, File Specifications, Validation Criteria, and Record Layouts for Electronic and Magnetic Media Filing of Estate and Trust Returns, Form 1041. To order these forms and publications, or for more information on electronic and magnetic media filing of Form 1041, call the Magnetic Media Unit at the Philadelphia Service Center at (215) 516-7533 (not a toll free number), or write to:

Internal Revenue Service Center
Attention: Magnetic Media Unit-DP 115
11601 Roosevelt Blvd.
Philadelphia, PA 19154.

Forms and publications may be obtained by personal computer. If you subscribe to an on-line service, ask if IRS information is available and, if so, how to access it. You can get information through IRIS, the Internal Revenue Information Services (IRIS), on FedWorld, a government bulletin board. Tax forms, instructions, publications, and other IRS information are available through IRIS.

IRIS is accessible directly, using your modem by calling 703-321-8020. On the Internet, telnet to iris.irs.ustreas.gov or, for file transfer protocol services, connect to ftp.irs.ustreas.gov. If you are using the World Wide Web, connect to http://www.irs.ustreas.gov. FedWorld's help desk offers technical assistance on accessing IRIS (not tax help) during regular business hours at 703-487-4608. The IRIS menus offer information on available file formats and software needed to read and print files. You must print the forms to use them; they are not designed to be filled in on-screen.

Tax forms, instructions, and publications are also available on CD-ROM, including prior-year forms starting with the 1991 tax year. For ordering information and software requirements, contact the Government Printing Office's Superintendent of Documents (202-512-1800) or Federal Bulletin Board (202-512-1387).

Forms and publications may be ordered by phone: 1-800-TAX-FORM (1-800-829-3676). You can also get most forms and publications at your local IRS office. Tax preparation software is also commercially available.

## §10.6 Final Word on the Fiduciary Income Tax

Filling out a Form 1041 can be time-consuming. By government estimates, the record-keeping alone takes over 46 hours, learning how to do it over 18 hours, preparing it takes over 34 hours, and getting it off to the IRS over 4 hours. And this does not include the time it takes to prepare Schedules D, J and K-1. Just the average recordkeeping time allocations for those three schedules are over 23 hours, over 39 hours, and over 8 hours respectively.

This chapter should be taken as nothing more than a broad brush introduction to the trustee's world of fiduciary income tax, as little more than a collection of some of the more important "red flags." When it comes to actually doing a return, the best way to start is by studying the Form 1041 itself, including the accompanying schedules and instructions. These items are reprinted in Appendix III of this handbook. Any other IRS publications on the subject, such as Publication 559, should then be perused. Finally, one should get a hold of a good treatise on the subject of fiduciary income taxation and keep that near at hand. *Federal Income Taxation of Estates, Trusts, and Beneficiaries,* by Ferguson, Freeland and Ascher comes to mind. The volume is both practical and scholarly.

The trustee cannot forget that a *state* fiduciary income tax return also may be due. The subject of the trustee's state tax filing obligations is beyond the scope of this edition of the handbook. Finally, the trustee should not fall behind when it comes to paying the trust's quarterly estimated taxes.

APPENDIX I

# Catalog of Multi-State Charts, Surveys, and String Citations

## Chapter 1. Introduction

For an alphabetical listing by jurisdiction of all uniform acts and codes adopted, see Uniform Laws Annotated (U.L.A.) Directory of Uniform Acts and Codes, Tables-Index, Master Edition Pamphlet (West 1996). The following uniform acts and codes may be of special interest to trustees and their counsel:

| | |
|---|---|
| Common Trust Fund Act | 7 U.L.A. 401 |
| Fiduciaries Act | 7A U.L.A. 391 |
| Fiduciary Security Transfers, Simplification of | 7B U.L.A. 689 |
| Intestacy, Wills and Donative Transfers Act | 8B U.L.A. 1 |
| Management of Institutional Funds Act | 7A U.L.A. 705 |
| Power of Attorney Act | 8B U.L.A. 299 |
| Revised Principal and Income Act (1964) | 7B U.L.A. 145 |
| Probate Code | 8 U.L.A. 1 |

| | |
|---|---|
| Prudent Investor Act | 7B U.L.A. Pocket Part |
| Statutory Rule Against Perpetuities Act | 8B U.L.A. 321 |
| Testamentary Additions to Trusts Act (1991) | 8B U.L.A. 451 |
| Transfers to Minors Act | 8B U.L.A. 497 |
| Trustees' Powers Act | 7B U.L.A. 741 |
| Trusts Act | 7B U.L.A. 763 |

## Chapter 2. The Property Requirement

For a catalog of states that have adopted the **Uniform Testamentary Additions to Trusts Act,** see 1A Scott on Trusts §54.3, n.47. Recent versions of the Act have expressly done away with the need for token funding in pour-over situations. (§2.2.1, n.2)

## Chapter 3. The Trustee's Office

For a catalog of state statutes dealing with the right of **out-of-state banks** and trust companies to serve as testamentary trustee, see 5A Scott on Trusts §558, n.1. (§3.1, n.17)

For a survey that summarizes statutory and case law on the authority of an agent under a **Durable Power of Attorney** to subject the principal's property to the provisions of a trust, see Van Dolson & Whitaker, Gifts by Agents Under Durable Powers of Attorney, 9 Prob. & Prop. 33, 38 (1995). (§3.4.1, n.7)

For a catalog of state statutes that deal with when and under what circumstances a trustee is required to **post bond** with the court, see Bogert, Trusts and Trustees §151, n.70. (§3.4.1, n.11)

For a catalog of state statutes that deal with the **court's authority**

**to appoint trustees,** see 2 Scott on Trusts §108.2, n.15. (§3.4.1, n.14)

For a catalog of state statutes governing the **resignation** of trustees, see 2 Scott on Trusts §106, n.4. (§3.4.3, n.54)

For a catalog of state statutes expressly providing that a person named as **trustee may disclaim,** see 2 Scott on Trusts §102, n.4. (§3.4.2, n.28)

For a catalog of state statutes providing that **fiduciaries may vote by proxy,** see 3 Scott on Trusts §193.3, nn.2-3. (§3.5.3.1, n.71)

For a catalog of state statutes enlarging the power of **trustees** to **mortgage** or **pledge** trust property, see 2A Scott on Trusts §191, n.17. (§3.5.3.2, n.93)

For a catalog of jurisdictions where the inference is that trustees do *not* have to consider **collateral sources of support,** see 2 Scott on Trusts §128.4, n.3. (§3.5.3.2, n.85)

For a catalog of state statutes authorizing **action by a majority** of a trust's cotrustees, see 3 Scott on Trusts §194, nn.21 & 22. (§3.4.4.1, n.62)

## Chapter 4. Interests Remaining with the Settlor

For statistics on **charitable foundations,** see The Foundation Directory: 100 Largest Foundations by Assets, 18th ed., compiled by The Foundation Center and edited by Margaret Mary Feczko (1996). (§§4.1, n.1, 9.4.1, n.13)

For a chart of **self-settled trusts** affected by the **welfare eligibility** provisions of Omnibus Budget Reconciliation Act of 1993 (**OBRA-93**), see Kruse, Third-Party and Self-Created Trusts: A Lawyer's Comprehensive Reference 22-25 (Chicago: American Bar Association, 1995). The chart also covers trusts created by third parties for the benefit of older persons or persons who are disabled. An earlier version of the chart may be found in the March 1995 issue of Trusts & Estates: Kruse, Self-Settled Trusts

Following OBRA 1993, 134 Tr. & Est. 66, 68 (3-1995). (§§4.1, n.26 & 5.3.5, n.113)

## Chapter 5. The Beneficiary

For a multi-jurisdictional study of statutes and cases that relate to claims against trust beneficiaries for **support and alimony,** see Dessin, Feed a Trust and Starve a Child: The Effectiveness of Trust Protective Techniques Against Claims for Support and Alimony, 10 Ga. St. L. Rev. 691 (1994). (§5.3.3.3, n.70)

For a summary of how **spendthrift trusts** are treated in the various jurisdictions, see Bogert, Trusts and Trustees §222, n.59. (§5.3.3.3, n.74)

For a catalog of state **abandoned property** statutes, see 2A Scott on Trusts §142.3, n.3. (§5.5, n.16)

For a catalog of state statutes providing for disposition of equitable interest of a **disappeared beneficiary,** see 2A Scott on Trusts §142.3, n.1. (§5.5, n.17)

For a catalog of state statutes allowing a powerholder's **creditors** access to a **naked reserved right of recovation,** see 4 Scott on Trusts §330.12, nn.7,8,9,12 & 2A Scott on Trusts §156, n.5.

For a catalog of state statutes exempting **life insurance** proceeds from the claims of **creditors** of the insured, see 4 Scott on Trusts §508.4, n.2. (§5.3.3.1, n.52)

For a catalog of jurisdictions that allow for **forfeiture** of equitable interest under certain conditions, e.g., beneficiary's **creditors** attempting to reach it by judicial process, see 2A Scott on Trusts §150, n.4. (§5.3.3.3, n.73)

For a catalog of state **disclaimer** statutes, see 1 Scott on Trusts §36.1, n.1. (§5.5, n.18)

For a catalog of jurisdictions allowing **creditors** access to **self-settled trusts,** see 2A Scott on Trusts §156, n.1. (§5.3.3.1, n.42)

For a catalog of state statutes **abolishing joint tenancy** of the equitable interest, unless there is a contrary provision in the governing instrument, see 2A Scott on Trusts §143, n.4. (§5.3.1., n.5)

For a summary of case law on the rights of **creditors** following **death of settlor-beneficiaries** of revocable trusts, see 23 ACTEC Notes 155 (1997) (§5.3.3.1(b) n.49).

## Chapter 6. The Trustee's Duties

For cases and regulations on **trustee compensation,** see Bogert, Trusts & Trustees §975, n.12. For a state-by-state list of cases addressing *whether* a trustee may be compensated from the trust for rendering legal, brokerage, or consulting services rendered to the trust, see 3A Scott on Trusts §242.2, n.1. (§6.1.3.3, nn.50-56)

For a list of state statutes authorizing trustees to **vote** corporate shares held in trust **by proxy,** see Bogert, Trusts and Trustees §556, n.98. (§6.1.4, n.103)

For a catalog of state statutes regulating the duty of the trustee to render **accountings** to the court, see 2A Scott on Trusts §172, n.10 and Bogert, Trusts and Trustees §§965-968. (§6.1.5.2, n.146)

For a list of cases and statutes from the various states addressing how and under what circumstances the trustee shall file an **inventory** with the court, see Bogert, Trusts & Trustees §597, nn.50-67. (§6.1.5.2, n.149)

For state statutes relating to the **judicial settlement of accounts,** see Bogert, Trusts and Trustees §974, n.7. (§6.1.5.2, n.155)

For a list of state statutes criminalizing the **commingling** of trust funds, see 2A Scott on Trusts §179.1, n.5. (§6.2.1.2, n.11)

For a list of state statutes governing the **investment** of trust funds, see 3 Scott on Trusts §227.13, n.1. (§6.2.2, n.59)

For a state-by-state list of cases relating to the **Massachusetts Rule of Apportionment** (stock dividends are principal and cash dividends are income), see 3A Scott on Trusts §236.3, nn.3-4. (§6.2.4.2, n.128)

For a state-by-state list of **apportionment** cases holding that estate income on **assets used to pay estate obligations** goes to the life beneficiary, see 3A Scott on Trusts §234.4, n.1. (§6.2.4.5, n.164)

For a table of jurisdictions that have adopted the **Revised Uniform Principal and Income Act-1962,** see 7B U.L.A. 1 (West Supp. 1995) or 3A Scott on Trusts §241A, n.7. (§6.2.4.6, n.177)

For a catalog of cases addressing the trustee's duty, if any, to establish a **reserve for depreciation** of a building held by a trust, see 3A Scott on Trusts §239.4, nn.2,4. (§6.2.4.3, nn.143,144)

For a catalog of **apportionment** cases involving **mining** operations, **quarries,** and **oil wells,** see 3A Scott on Trusts §239.3. (§6.2.4.3, n.136)

For a **general catalog** of state statutes applicable to the **allocation** of income and principal and the **apportionment** of expenses, see Bogert, Trusts and Trustees §816, nn.64-66. (§6.2.4, n.116)

For a table of jurisdictions that have adopted the **Uniform Management of Institutional Funds Act** ("UMIFA"), see 7A U.L.A. 712, 716 (1985). (§6.2.2.3, n.106)

For a catalog of state statutes authorizing a trustee to **compromise claims,** see 3 Scott on Trusts §192, n.14. (§6.2.1.3, n.54)

For a catalog of state statutes permitting investment of trust assets in **mutual funds,** see §6.1.3.4, n.69.

## Chapter 7. The Trustee's Liabilities

For some statutes and cases that touch on whether **punitive damages** may be assessed for breaches of fiduciary duty, see Bogert, Trusts and Trustees §862, n.34. See also Campisi et al, Emerging Damages Claims and the Right to Jury Trials in Fiduciary Litigation, 27 Real Prop. Prob. & Tr. J. 541, 542-53 (1992) for a survey of jurisdictions that allow the assessment of punitive and **appreciation** damages against fiduciaries. (§7.2.3.3, n.18)

A chart setting forth the extent to which each state will uphold **exculpatory clauses** in trust instruments may be obtained from Elizabeth A. Reece, Esq., Fleet National Bank, Boston, MA. by telephoning (617) 346-0554. (§7.2.6, n.45)

For a table of state statutes authorizing directors of **charitable corporations** to make provision for their own **indemnification,** see

Moody, State Statutes Governing Directors of Charitable Corporations, 18 U.S.F. L. Rev. 749, 782-783 (1984). (§7.2.6, n.51)

For a list of jurisdictions that permit, under certain circumstances, the **contract creditor** of a trust to proceed in equity **directly against trust assets,** see Bogert, Trusts and Trustees §712, nn.34-35. (§7.3.1, n.10)

For a catalog of state **consumer protection** statutes, see Dunbar, Comment on Consumer Protection: The Practical Effectiveness of State Deceptive Trade Practices Legislation, 59 Tul. L. Rev. 427, Table 3 at 441-448 (1984). (§7.3.3.1, n.32)

For a survey of **unauthorized practice of law** statutes and enforcement systems, see Powell, The Problem of the Parachuting Practitioner, 1992 U. Ill. L. Rev. 105, 123-124, n.97. (§7.3.4.2, n.67)

For a catalog of cases in which **trust officers** have been held **personally liable** for breaches of trust by their corporate employers, see 4 Scott on Trusts §326.3, n.2. (§7.2.9, n.58)

For a catalog of state statutes relating to the **removal of trustees,** see Bogert, Trusts and Trustees §527, nn.7,8 and 2 Scott on Trusts §107, n.22. (§7.2.3.6, n.30)

## Chapter 8. Miscellaneous Topics of General Interest to the Trustee

For a list of the jurisdictions that have adopted the **Uniform Statutory Rule Against Perpetuities** (USRAP) with 1990 amendments, see 8B U.L.A. 35 (West Supp. 1995). (§8.2.1.7, nn.27-28)

For a list of jurisdictions that have adopted the **Uniform Transfers to Minors Act-1983,** see 8B U.L.A. 47 (West Supp. 1995). (§8.2.3, n.49)

For a list of state statutes providing that the purchaser of trust property need not monitor **the application of the purchase price,** see 4 Scott on Trusts §321, nn.5-7 (§8.3.2, n.10)

For a complete catalog of state statutes that authorize the organization of **trust companies,** see 2 Scott on Trusts §96.5, n.2. (§8.6, n.1)

For a state-by-state analysis of the **Statute of Frauds** as it pertains to trusts, see Bogert, Trusts and Trustees §§62-64. (§8.15.5)

For a catalog of cases **rejecting** the **Rule in Clayton's Case,** see 5 Scott on Trusts §519, n.4. (§8.15.11, n.87)

For a catalog of state statutes imposing **restrictions** on the **accumulations of income,** see IA Scott on Trusts §62.11, n.10. (§8.15.8, n.65)

For a catalog of state **virtual representation** statutes, see Bogert, Trusts and Trustees §871, n.42. (§8.14, n.2)

For a catalog of **non-U.S. jurisdictions** that recognize the trust, see Bogert, Trusts and Trustees §9. (§8.12)

For a catalog of state statutes **abolishing** the **Rule in Shelley's Case,** see 2 Scott on Trusts §127.2, n.5. (§8.15.3, n.38)

For a catalog of state cases addressing the **duties of lawyer for fiduciary to beneficiaries,** see ACTEC Commentaries on the Model Rules of Professional Conduct, 2d ed., adopted March 1995, at 36-42. (§8.8)

For a catalog of state statutes addressing the **merger and consolidation of bank trustees,** see 2 Scott on Trusts §96.7, n.3 (§8.19).

For a catalog of state statutes addressing the **exercise of limited powers of appointment in further trust,** see 1 Scott on Trusts §17.2, n.7 (§8.1.2).

For a catalog of state statutes relieving corporations and their transfer agents of the **duty to investigate a trustee's authority to transfer securities** unless they have actual knowledge of the lack thereof, see Bogert, Trusts and Trustees §905 (§8.3.5).

For a catalog of state statutes **abolishing** in whole or in part **the Rule Against Perpetuities,** see §8.2.1.9.

## Chapter 9. Special Types of Trusts

For a complete list of state statutes authorizing trustees to invest trust assets in **common trust funds,** see 3 Scott on Trusts §227.9, n.26. (§9.7.1, n.1)

For a catalog of non-U.S. jurisdictions that welcome **Offshore Asset Protection Trusts,** see Rothschild, Establishing and Drafting Offshore Asset Protection Trusts, 23 Est. Plan. 65 (Feb. 1996) n.1. (§9.10, n.2)

For a table of state **indemnification** statutes applicable to **nonprofit corporations,** see Moody, State Statutes Governing Directors of Charitable Corporations, 18 U.S.F. L. Rev. 749, 782-783 (1984). (§9.8.1, n.7)

For a catalog of state statutes **exempting IRA beneficiary designations** from the **Statute of Wills,** see Bogert, Trusts and Trustees §255, n.11 (second footnote 11 of section). (§9.8.4, n.17)

APPENDIX II

# Regulation 9

RULES and REGULATIONS
DEPARTMENT OF THE TREASURY
Office of the Comptroller of the Currency
12 CFR Parts 9 and 19
[Docket No. 96-30]
RIN 1557-AB12
Fiduciary Activities of National Banks;
Rules of Practice and Procedure
Monday, December 30, 1996

***68543** AGENCY: Office of the Comptroller of the Currency, Treasury.

ACTION: Final rule.

SUMMARY: The Office of the Comptroller of the Currency (OCC) is revising its rules that govern the fiduciary activities of national banks. The OCC also is relocating provisions concerning disciplinary sanctions imposed by clearing agencies to its rules of practice and procedure. This final rule is another component of the OCC's Regulation Review Program, which is intended to update and streamline OCC regulations and to reduce unnecessary regulatory costs and other burdens.

EFFECTIVE DATE: January 29, 1997.

FOR FURTHER INFORMATION CONTACT: Andrew T. Gutierrez, Attorney, ***68544** Legislative and Regulatory Activities Division, (202) 874-5090; Donald N. Lamson, Assistant Director, Securities and Corporate Practices Division, (202) 874-5210; Lisa Lintecum, Director, Fiduciary Activities, (202) 874-5419; Dean Miller, Senior Advisor, Fiduciary Activities, (202) 874-4852; Aida M. Plaza, Director for Compliance, Multinational Banking, (202) 874-4610, Office of the Comptroller of the Currency, 250 E Street, SW, Washington, DC 20219.

SUPPLEMENTARY INFORMATION:

Background

The OCC is revising 12 CFR part 9, which governs the fiduciary activities of national banks, based on its authority under 12 U.S.C. 92a. This action is a component of its Regulation Review Program. One goal of the Regulation Review Program is to review all of the OCC's rules with a view toward eliminating provisions that do not contribute significantly to maintaining the safety and soundness of national banks or to accomplishing the OCC's other statutory responsibilities, including oversight of national banks' fiduciary activities. Another goal of the Program is to improve the clarity of the OCC's regulations.

This final rule is the OCC's first comprehensive revision of part 9 since 1963.[1] Much about national banks' fiduciary business

[1]National banks have been authorized to exercise fiduciary powers since 1913. In 1962, the oversight responsibility for national banks' fiduciary activities was transferred from the Board of Governors of the Federal Reserve System to the OCC. See 12 U.S.C. 92a. Following the transfer of oversight responsibility, the OCC promulgated part 9 on October 3, 1962 (27 FR 9764), and revised it soon thereafter on April 5, 1963 (28 FR 3309).

has changed since that time, including the nature and scope of the fiduciary services that banks offer and the structures and operational methods that banks use to deliver those services. The OCC's primary goal in revising part 9 is to accommodate those changes by removing unnecessary regulatory burden and facilitating the continued development of national banks' fiduciary business consistent with safe and sound banking practices and national banks' fiduciary obligations.

On December 21, 1995, the OCC published a notice of proposed rulemaking to revise part 9 (60 FR 66163) (proposal). The proposal reflected three principal themes. First, bank organizational structures — particularly with respect to the geographic structure of banking organizations — have changed significantly since Congress created the basic framework for national banks' fiduciary operations. The OCC proposed to adjust part 9 to make the requirements of the rule more workable for both large, multistate fiduciary banking organizations and small banks that conduct fiduciary activities primarily on a local basis. Second, national banks' fiduciary activities are subject to state law in many respects, though the OCC often can establish uniform Federal standards. In the proposal, the OCC attempted to strike an appropriate balance between Federal and state law. Third, over the years, the OCC has applied part 9 to a wide variety of investment advisory activities and related services, not all of which involve the bank's exercise of investment discretion. In some cases, national banks engaged in these activities operate under different standards than other financial services providers that conduct the same type of business.

Moreover, the proposal reflected an effort to update, clarify, and streamline part 9, to incorporate significant interpretive positions, and to eliminate unnecessary regulatory burden wherever possible to promote more efficient operation and supervision of national banks' fiduciary activities. The proposal added headings for ease of reference, but, for the most part, retained the numbering system used in the former regulation.

The OCC received 57 comments regarding the proposal, including letters from banks, bank trade groups, state bank supervisors, law firms, consultants, auditors and a member of Congress.

With the exception of certain aspects of the rule that concerned state bank supervisors, the commenters generally supported the proposal. However, the commenters recommended numerous modifications to the proposal. The OCC carefully considered these recommendations and incorporates many of them into this final rule.

Section-by-Section Discussion

Authority, Purpose, and Scope (§9.1)

The proposal added a new provision explicitly setting forth the statutory authority for, and the purpose and scope of, part 9. One commenter recommended that the OCC clarify that part 9 applies to national banks and their operating subsidiaries, but not to other subsidiaries or affiliates. The OCC notes that 12 CFR 5.34(d)(3), as recently revised at 61 FR 60342 (November 27, 1996), already clarifies that the OCC's regulations, including part 9, apply to national banks' operating subsidiaries unless otherwise provided by statute or regulation. Moreover, the OCC recognizes that its regulations generally do not apply to other subsidiaries or affiliates of national banks, and believes that it is unnecessary to enumerate those or other entities excluded from the coverage of its regulations. However, the OCC is amending this section to clarify that part 9 applies to Federal branches of foreign banks, which, unlike Federal agencies, may receive fiduciary powers.

Definitions (§9.2)

The proposal modified or removed some of the former regulation's definitions, and added new definitions. Moreover, the proposal relocated the definitions from former §9.1 to proposed §9.2. For the most part, the OCC is adopting the definitions contained in the proposal. The following discussion highlights the definitions that the OCC has modified significantly.

Applicable law (§9.2(b)). The former regulation used the term "local law," as defined at §9.1(g), to refer to the laws of the state or other jurisdiction governing a fiduciary relationship. The proposal replaced the term "local law" with "applicable law" in order to streamline some of the operative provisions of the regulation and to clarify that the law that governs a national bank's fiduciary relationships may include Federal law,[2] state law governing a national bank's fiduciary relationships (that is, fiduciary duties and responsibilities), the terms of the instrument governing a fiduciary relationship, and any court order pertaining to the relationship.

Some commenters supported the proposed language without reservation. Others requested that the OCC clarify what type of law takes precedence. Some believed that Federal law should override state law, while others believed that state law should override Federal law.

The OCC recognizes that the proposed definition does not provide a priority among the various bodies of authority. Thus, the definition does not resolve situations in which the terms of a trust instrument, for example, conflicts with ***68545** a state statute or a Federal regulation. Conflicts of law issues in the fiduciary area are highly fact specific and, thus, cannot be resolved by reference to a general rule of priority. The OCC does not intend the term "applicable law" to resolve conflicts of law; rather, the OCC merely intends to identify concisely the various bodies of authority that may govern national banks' fiduciary activities.

Some commenters were concerned that the OCC intended this term to effectuate a wholesale Federal preemption of conflicting state law, or otherwise to change the status quo regarding conflicts of laws. This is not the case. To clarify the OCC's intention, the OCC is modifying the definition's reference to Federal law to read "any applicable Federal law" governing a national bank's fiduciary relationships. This allows the OCC to use the concise "applicable law" term, but the definition does not presume that Federal law necessarily will apply in any particular con-

[2]The Federal law relevant to a national bank's fiduciary activities includes, for example, provisions of the Federal banking laws (12 U.S.C. 1 et seq.), the Employee Retirement Income Security Act of 1974 (29 U.S.C. 1001 et seq.) (ERISA), the Securities Act of 1933 (15 U.S.C. 77a et seq.), the Securities Exchange Act of 1934 (15 U.S.C. 78a et seq.), the Investment Company Act of 1940 (15 U.S.C. 80a-1 et seq.), the Investment Advisers Act of 1940 (15 U.S.C. 80b-1 et seq.) (Advisers Act), the Trust Indenture Act of 1939 (15 U.S.C. 77aaa et seq.) (Trust Indenture Act), the Internal Revenue Code of 1986 (26 U.S.C. 1 et seq.) (Internal Revenue Code), and the rules issued pursuant to those acts.

text. Rather, Federal law is merely one of many sources of law that may govern a fiduciary relationship.

Additionally, a few commenters noted that the proposed definition of "applicable law" did not mention foreign law, and asked the OCC to clarify the extent to which foreign law governs a national bank's fiduciary activities in foreign branches. Recognizing that the law of other jurisdictions, including foreign countries, may apply to a national bank's fiduciary activities, the OCC is modifying the definition to include the law of the state or other jurisdiction governing a national bank's fiduciary relationships. However, as with other conflicts of law, the extent to which foreign law applies to a national bank's fiduciary activities in foreign branches is a complex issue and depends on the specific factual situation. Thus, the OCC is not addressing that issue in the regulation.

Fiduciary capacity (§9.2(e)). In the proposal, the OCC attempted to establish a clearer and more objective boundary for the coverage of part 9. The proposal retained the statutory list of fiduciary capacities, but, unlike the former rule, it limited the definition of other fiduciary activities to: (1) any other capacity involving investment discretion on behalf of another; and (2) any other similar capacity that the OCC authorizes pursuant to 12 U.S.C. 92a. Thus, the proposal defined fiduciary capacity to exclude relationships (other than those listed in the statute) in which the bank does not have investment discretion. Under this approach, an investment advisory activity for which the bank does not have investment discretion generally is not a fiduciary activity subject to part 9.

The proposal also solicited comment on an alternative approach under which part 9 would apply to investment advisory and other activities if, when the same or similar activity is conducted by a competing state bank or corporation, the state regulates the activity as a fiduciary activity.

A majority of commenters who addressed this issue supported the proposed definition, which utilizes investment discretion as a test, and opposed the alternative approach on the grounds that it would lead to inconsistent treatment of accounts in a bank with multistate operations, and increase risk by creating undue complexity in fiduciary compliance. A few commenters voiced concerns with the proposed definition, and recommended that the OCC define "fiduciary capacity" to include any capacity that is fiduciary under state law.

The OCC believes that "fiduciary capacity" should be defined in a manner that fosters consistent application of part 9 throughout the national banking system. Thus, the OCC is not defining "fiduciary capacity" exclusively with reference to state law. Rather, the final rule retains the proposal's approach and defines "fiduciary capacity" by using investment discretion as a test for determining whether part 9 applies to certain activities.

With respect to non-discretionary investment advisory activities, commenters differed widely as to whether and the extent to which the OCC should treat those activities as fiduciary. After carefully considering the comment letters, the OCC has concluded that when a customer pays a national bank a fee in return for providing investment advice (whether or not the customer follows that advice), the customer has a reasonable expectation of receiving advice that is free of conflicts of interest. Additionally, other Federal statutes provide heightened fiduciary-type protection to customers of certain investment advisers who receive a fee.[3] By contrast, when a national bank does not receive a fee for investment advice (e.g., directed custodian accounts), it has no contractual or other obligation to provide investment advice. Therefore, the bank should not incur fiduciary liability for any incidental advice it offers.[4] Thus, the OCC is adding "investment adviser, if the bank receives a fee for its investment advice" to the list of fiduciary capacities. The OCC believes that this distinction between paid and unpaid investment advisers reflects the reasonable expectations of national bank customers.

Fiduciary records (proposed §9.2(g)). The proposal defined

[3]For example, under ERISA, a person is a fiduciary with respect to a plan, to the extent he renders investment advice for a fee or other compensation. 29 U.S.C. 1002(21)(A). As another example, the Advisers Act generally applies to any person who, for compensation, engages in the business of advising others (although banks are exempt). 15 U.S.C. 80b-2(a)(11).

[4]The OCC does not treat non-discretionary custodial activities as fiduciary, and the final rule continues that approach. Those activities are authorized under 12 U.S.C. 24 (Seventh).

"fiduciary records" and used that term in the record retention and separation requirement of §9.8. The final rule, however, does not use the term. Thus, the definition is eliminated in the final rule.

Fiduciary powers (§9.2(g)). The proposal provided that "fiduciary powers" means the authority the OCC permits a national bank to exercise pursuant to 12 U.S.C. 92a. Moreover, in the proposal's preamble, the OCC discussed and invited comment on the legal framework set forth in the OCC's Interpretive Letter No. 695 (December 8, 1995), in which the OCC analyzed the authority of a national bank to exercise fiduciary powers on an interstate basis under 12 U.S.C. 92a. Some commenters questioned the analysis contained in this letter. However, as stated in the letter, the effect of 12 U.S.C. 92a is that in any specific state, the extent of fiduciary powers is the same for out-of-state national banks as for in-state national banks, and that extent depends upon what powers the state grants to the fiduciaries in the state with which national banks compete. The OCC has considered the comments, but continues to believe that the legal analysis contained in Interpretive Letter No. 695 reflects a correct interpretation of the basic fiduciary powers of national banks under 12 U.S.C. 92a. The definition of fiduciary powers summarizes this basic principle. The OCC notes that neither Interpretive Letter No. 695 nor the definition of national banks' fiduciary powers in §9.2(g) addresses the applicability of particular state laws to national banks' exercise of their fiduciary powers.[5]

Investment discretion (§9.2(i)). As mentioned previously, the proposal defined the term "fiduciary capacity" to include any capacity where the bank possesses investment discretion on behalf of another, and the final rule retains this approach. The proposed term "investment discretion" includes any account for which a national bank has the authority to determine what securities or other assets to purchase or sell on behalf of the account.

Some commenters recommended that the OCC clarify that a bank has investment discretion with respect to an account whether

[5]To the extent they arise, the OCC intends to handle specific questions about the applicability of particular state laws on a case-by-case basis, which in many cases will involve preemption opinions developed with the aid of a public notice and comment process. ***68546**

or not the bank exercises that discretion. Others recommended that the OCC clarify whether a bank has investment discretion with respect to an account in which the customer or another fiduciary also has investment discretion. In response to these commenters, the OCC is modifying the proposed definition to clarify that the term does not depend on whether or not the bank exercises its authority over investments, or whether or not its authority over investments is sole or shared. Moreover, the OCC is clarifying that a bank is deemed to have investment discretion even when it delegates its authority over investments, as well as when another fiduciary delegates its authority over investments to the bank.

Several commenters asked whether the OCC considers a national bank to have investment discretion when it administers asset allocation accounts or sweep accounts. Asset allocation programs differ widely in the extent of the administering bank's discretion. In some asset allocation programs, the bank has discretion to invest initially the customer's assets among several mutual funds, and to reallocate the assets as it deems appropriate based on the customer's investment profile and the prevailing market conditions. In these programs, and in any other program in which the bank may purchase or sell an investment without the customer's approval, the OCC considers the bank to have investment discretion. In sweep programs, on the other hand, a bank typically has no investment discretion. Rather, the bank is automatically sweeping excess cash into investments pre-selected by the customer (e.g., money market funds).

Approval Requirements (§9.3)

Consistent with §9.2 of the former regulation, the proposal directed an applicant for fiduciary powers (whether the applicant is a national bank seeking approval to exercise fiduciary powers, or a person seeking approval to organize a special-purpose national bank limited to fiduciary powers) to appropriate provisions in 12 CFR part 5, which contains rules, policies, and procedures for corporate activities. This is designed as a useful reader aid. The OCC received no specific comments on this section and adopts this section as proposed.

Administration of Fiduciary Powers (§9.4)

Consistent with §9.7 of the former rule, the proposal permitted a national bank's board of directors to assign functions related to the exercise of fiduciary powers to bank directors, officers, employees, and committees thereof. The proposal also retained the requirement that all fiduciary officers and employees must be bonded adequately. Moreover, the proposal permitted a national bank to use personnel and facilities of the bank to perform services related to the exercise of its fiduciary powers, and permitted any department of the bank to use fiduciary officers and employees and facilities to perform services unrelated to the exercise of fiduciary powers, to the extent not prohibited by applicable law. Additionally, the proposal added a new provision to the section clarifying that a national bank may enter into an agency agreement with another entity to purchase or sell services related to the exercise of fiduciary powers.

Some commenters recommended that the OCC allow a national bank to use personnel and facilities of its affiliates (and not just other departments of the bank) to perform services related to its fiduciary activities, and allow affiliates to use fiduciary officers and employees and facilities to perform services unrelated to the bank's fiduciary activities, to the extent not prohibited by applicable law. The OCC believes that utilizing affiliates in this manner enhances efficiency and is consistent with safety and soundness. Moreover, this recommendation reflects the realities of modern bank organizational structures. Thus, the OCC is modifying the provision accordingly.

Policies and Procedures (§9.5)

The proposal required a national bank to establish written policies and procedures to ensure that its fiduciary practices comply with applicable law, and also provided a list of particular fiduciary practices that a bank's policies and procedures should cover. Several items on the list were derived from requirements in the former regulation, including brokerage placement practices (former §9.5); methods for ensuring that fiduciary officers and employees do not use material inside information in connection with any decision or recommendation to purchase or sell any security (former §9.7(d)); selection and retention of legal counsel readily available to advise the bank and its fiduciary officers and employees on fiduciary matters (former §9.7(c)); and investment of funds held as fiduciary, including short-term investments and the treatment of fiduciary funds awaiting investment or distribution (former §9.10(a)).

Other items on the proposed list were not based on requirements in the former regulation, including methods for preventing self-dealing and conflicts of interest, allocation to fiduciary accounts of any financial incentives the bank may receive for investing fiduciary funds in a particular investment, and disclosure to beneficiaries and other interested parties of fees and expenses charged to fiduciary accounts.

Many commenters were concerned that specific items on the list, particularly the items addressing the allocation of financial incentives and disclosures to interested parties, could be construed overbroadly (e.g., to prohibit otherwise permissible fee arrangements, or to require disclosures to creditors of settlors of revocable trusts). Some commenters suggested that the OCC not provide a list of required policies and procedures, but rather provide guidance through less formal means.

The OCC is retaining the proposal's general requirement that a national bank adopt and follow written policies and procedures adequate to maintain its fiduciary activities in compliance with applicable law. The OCC is not attempting to assemble an exhaustive list of required policies and procedures. However, the OCC believes that the regulation should provide examples of areas that a bank's policies and procedures should address. Thus, the OCC is adopting an abbreviated list of areas that a bank's policies and procedures should address. The list includes brokerage placement practices, the prevention of misuse of material inside information, the prevention of self-dealing and conflicts of interest, the selection and retention of legal counsel, and the investment of funds (including funds awaiting investment or distribution).

Review of Assets of Fiduciary Accounts (§9.6)

The proposal, like the former rule, required national banks to perform reviews with respect to fiduciary accounts at least once during each calendar year, and within 15 months of the last review. Moreover, the proposal required two distinct types of annual ***68547** written reviews: individual account reviews and reviews of assets by issuer. To contrast the two types of review, a review of assets by issuer determines what investments (e.g., common stock of Corporation X) are appropriate investments for the bank's fiduciary accounts in general. In some banks, the review of assets by issuer results in a list of permissible fiduciary investments for the bank's fiduciary accounts, and the person or committee in charge of investing for a particular fiduciary account chooses investments from this list. Under an individual account review, on the other hand, the person or committee in charge of a particular account's investments determines whether the current investments are appropriate, individually and collectively, given the objectives of the account.

Several commenters indicated that the requirement for an annual review of assets by issuer is burdensome, redundant, and may conflict with the modern portfolio theory embraced by the prudent investor rule.[6] The OCC agrees with these commenters and, thus, is eliminating the requirement for an annual review of assets by issuer.

Some commenters recommended that the OCC make the requirement for a "written" review more flexible by allowing other forms of evidence of a review (e.g., an automated screening process that screens out routine and non-complex assets and accounts), in order to allow bank personnel to conduct their reviews more efficiently. In response to this recommendation, the OCC is eliminating the requirement that the review be "written." However, if a bank adopts a review system in which reviews are not

[6]Modern portfolio theory, which underlies modern asset management practices, focuses on the reduction of specific risk through portfolio diversification. This theory, along with corresponding practice, demonstrated that "arbitrary restrictions on trust investments are unwarranted and often counterproductive." Rest. 3rd, Trusts (Prudent Investor Rule), Introduction (1992), at 4. The prudent investor rule states that the standard of prudent investment "is to be applied to investments not in isolation but in the context of the trust portfolio and as a part of an overall investment strategy, which should incorporate risk and return objectives reasonably suited to the trust." Rest. 3rd, Trusts (Prudent Investor Rule), sec. 227(a)(1992).

documented individually, the bank must be able to demonstrate that its review system is designed to perform all required reviews.

One commenter recommended that the OCC eliminate the requirement to perform a review within 15 months after the last review, and instead rely on the requirement to perform a review at least once during each calendar year. The OCC has determined that the 15-month requirement is somewhat rigid, raises timing issues (e.g., whether to measure the period from the start date to start date or end date to start date), and does not contribute significantly to safety and soundness. Consequently, the OCC is eliminating it in favor of a requirement that a national bank perform a review at least once during each calendar year.

Recordkeeping (§9.8)

Section 9.8(a) of the proposal required a national bank to document the establishment and termination of fiduciary accounts and to maintain adequate records for all fiduciary accounts. Section 9.8(b) of the proposal required a national bank to retain all "fiduciary records" for a specified period. Section 9.2(g) of the proposal defined "fiduciary records" to include all written or otherwise recorded information that a national bank creates or receives relating to a fiduciary account or the fiduciary activities of the bank.

Some commenters asserted that the proposed definition of "fiduciary records" is overly broad, and recommended that the OCC limit the record retention requirement of §9.8(b) to the records described in §9.8(a). The OCC agrees that the proposed definition of fiduciary records is overly broad and has limited the record retention requirement accordingly.

Audit of Fiduciary Activities (§9.9)

The proposal required a national bank to perform, through its fiduciary audit committee, suitable audits of its fiduciary activities annually and to report the results of the audit, including all actions taken as a result of the audit, in the minutes of the board of directors. The proposal also clarified that if a bank adopts a continuous audit system in lieu of performing annual audits, the bank may perform discrete audits of each fiduciary activity, on an activity-by-activity basis, at intervals appropriate for that activity.

For example, a bank may determine that it is appropriate to audit certain low-risk fiduciary activities every 18 months. Moreover, the proposal permitted a national bank to use an affiliate's audit committee as the bank's fiduciary audit committee.

Most commenters strongly supported allowing a continuous audit system and allowing an affiliate's audit committee to serve as a bank's fiduciary audit committee. The OCC is adopting these elements. A few commenters recommended that the OCC clarify whether a bank may use external auditors in performing the required audits. In response, the OCC is adding parentheticals to clarify that a bank may use internal or external auditors. A few commenters expressed concern that the requirement to note in the board's minutes "all" actions taken as a result of the audit could be interpreted to require a board to note excessive detail. To alleviate this concern, the OCC is modifying the provision to require the board to note "significant actions" instead of "all actions."

One commenter also noted that the proposal required a suitable audit of "all" fiduciary activities (or, for continuous audits, a discrete audit of "each" fiduciary activity), and pointed out that certain fiduciary activities at certain banks may be de minimis (e.g., a bank may have only one small account under a particular fiduciary activity, as an incidental service for a particular customer). They asserted that these de minimis fiduciary activities may not merit a full-scope audit. To provide a measure of flexibility with respect to de minimis activities, the OCC is modifying the regulation to require a suitable audit of "all significant" fiduciary activities (or, for continuous audits, a discrete audit of "each significant" fiduciary activity). The OCC intends for this standard to exclude only be minimis fiduciary activities conducted by a bank.

Moreover, as with annual reviews under §9.6, the OCC is eliminating the requirement that a national bank that performs audits annually (rather than using a continuous audit system) perform an audit not later than 15 months after the last audit. The 15-month requirement is somewhat rigid, raises timing issues, and does not contribute significantly to safety and soundness. The OCC is retaining the requirement that a national bank perform an audit at least once during each calendar year.

The proposal required that a national bank's fiduciary audit committee must not include directors who are members of a fiduciary committee of the bank. Several commenters noted that some banks would experience difficulties in complying with this restriction due to their fiduciary committee structure. To provide those banks with a reasonable degree of flexibility, the OCC is modifying this restriction to require that a national bank's fiduciary audit committee must consist of a majority of members who are not also members of any committee to which the board of directors has delegated power to manage and control the fiduciary activities of the bank. The OCC believes that this modification will not impair the safety and soundness of those banks. ***68548**

Fiduciary Funds Awaiting Investment or Distribution (§9.10)

The proposal retained the former regulation's general prohibition against allowing fiduciary funds to remain uninvested and undistributed any longer than reasonable for proper account management. One commenter pointed out that directing the treatment of fiduciary funds is appropriate only if the bank has investment discretion with respect to those funds. The OCC agrees that the duty to invest funds applies only to accounts for which a bank has investment discretion. However, the duty to distribute uninvested funds within a reasonable time may apply even in the absence of investment discretion. Thus, the OCC is limiting this prohibition to fiduciary accounts for which a bank has investment discretion or discretion over distributions.

The proposal eliminated the requirement that a bank obtain the "maximum" rate of return for fiduciary funds awaiting investment or distribution. One commenter asserted that the OCC should have some policy with respect to the rate of return for fiduciary funds awaiting investment or distribution. The OCC agrees, and is adopting a requirement that a bank obtain for such funds a rate of return consistent with applicable law. Thus, in states that require their corporate fiduciaries to obtain a market rate of return for fiduciary funds awaiting investment or distribution, a national bank must do the same. In other states, national banks are placed on a level playing field with competing corporate fiduciaries.

The proposal permitted a national bank to set aside, as collateral for self-deposits of fiduciary funds awaiting investment or distribution, any assets (including surety bonds) that qualify under state law as appropriate security. Several commenters recommended that the OCC allow a bank to collateralize self-deposits with surety bonds without regard to state law. Other commenters recommended that the OCC allow a bank to collateralize self-deposits with surety bonds only if state law permits that practice. The OCC has determined that it is consistent with national banks' fiduciary powers for banks to use surety bonds as collateral for self-deposits unless prohibited by applicable law. This standard grants national banks the ability to collateralize self-deposits with surety bonds, yet preserves for each state the ability to prohibit this practice for all fiduciaries operating in the state.

The proposal also permitted a national bank to deposit fiduciary funds awaiting investment or distribution with an affiliate and to secure a deposit of idle fiduciary funds by or with an affiliate "if consistent with applicable law". Several commenters recommended that the OCC modify the applicable law standard, though the commenters suggested various alternatives ranging from "without regard to state law" to "only if permitted by applicable law". After considering the various standards, the OCC is adopting "unless prohibited by applicable law" as the standard. This standard allows national banks to secure deposits of idle fiduciary funds by or with an affiliate, yet permits a state to preclude this practice for all fiduciaries operating in the state, if the state so chooses.

Investment of Fiduciary Funds (§9.11)

The proposal directed a national bank to invest fiduciary funds in a manner consistent with applicable law. One commenter pointed out that directing a bank how to invest fiduciary funds is appropriate only if the bank has investment discretion. This commenter's point is generally true. However, situations may arise in which a bank trustee without investment discretion receives a direction from a party with investment discretion to make an investment that violates applicable law (e.g., ERISA or the trust instrument). The bank, in these situations, should comply with applicable law notwithstanding its lack of investment discretion. Thus, the OCC is adopting the provision generally as proposed.

Self-Dealing and Conflicts of Interest (§9.12)

The proposal clarified that a bank may not lend to any of its directors, officers, or employees any funds it holds as trustee, except with respect to bank's own employee benefit plans in accordance with section 408(b)(1) of ERISA, which specifically authorizes loans to participants and beneficiaries of such plans under certain circumstances. One commenter noted that section 408(b)(1) covers plans that the bank administers for other employers, as well as the bank's own plans. The OCC agrees, and is extending the proposed exception to plans that the bank administers for other employers. Moreover, the OCC is broadening the regulation's reference to ERISA by citing to section 408 rather than section 408(b)(1), because section 408 contains several exemptions from ERISA's prohibited transaction provisions, and not just the exemption found in 408(b)(1).

The proposal authorized a national bank to make a loan between any of its fiduciary accounts if the transaction is authorized by the instrument creating the account from which the loan is made and is not prohibited by applicable law. One commenter recommended that the OCC change this standard to "if the transaction is fair to both accounts and is not prohibited by applicable law," in order to be consistent with the standard for loans to fiduciary accounts and for sales between fiduciary accounts. The OCC agrees that there is no compelling reason to have different standards for these transactions and, thus, is modifying the standard accordingly.

Finally, one commenter pointed out that these self-dealing and conflicts of interest provisions are appropriate only if the bank has investment discretion. The OCC agrees, and is limiting this provision to fiduciary accounts for which a bank has investment discretion.

Custody of Fiduciary Assets (§9.13)

The proposal allowed a national bank to maintain fiduciary assets off-premises if the bank maintains adequate safeguards and controls. However, some off-premise locations may not be appropriate for the safekeeping of fiduciary assets, depending on applicable law. Consequently, the OCC is modifying the provision to allow a bank to maintain fiduciary investments off-premises only if consistent with applicable law.

Deposit of Securities With State Authorities (§9.14)

The proposal allowed a national bank with fiduciary assets in more than one state to meet its deposit requirement in each state based on the amount of trust assets administered from offices located in that state. The OCC intended this provision to avoid duplicative securities deposits for the same trust asset.

Some commenters requested that the OCC clarify that the deposit requirement for a multistate bank depends on the amount of trust assets that the bank administers "primarily" or "principally" from offices in that state. These commenters were concerned that the proposed language still could be interpreted in a manner that results in duplicative securities deposits for the same trust asset. To ensure that the requirement is not interpreted in a manner that results in duplicative securities deposits, the OCC is clarifying that the required deposit for each state is based on the amount of trust assets that the bank administers "primarily" from offices located in that state.

***68549** Fiduciary Compensation (§9.15)

The proposal retained the substance of former §9.15, which addressed fiduciary compensation. The proposal authorized a national bank to charge a reasonable fee for its fiduciary services if the amount is not set or governed by applicable law. Moreover, the proposal prohibited an officer or an employee of a national bank from retaining any compensation for acting as a co-fiduciary, with the bank in the administration of a fiduciary account, except with the specific approval of its board of directors.

One commenter requested that the OCC provide guidance on what constitutes a reasonable fee, and that the OCC allow a bank to rely on their regularly published fee schedules to satisfy the reasonableness test. However, because reasonableness of fiduciary compensation depends heavily upon the facts of each situation, the OCC does not believe that it is possible to establish specific rules on what is and what is not reasonable. Thus, the OCC is adopting this section as proposed. The OCC points out, however, that the amount of fiduciary compensation is typically set or governed by applicable law (e.g., by the terms of the governing instrument, state fee schedules, a probate court, etc.), in which case the general reasonableness standard does not apply.

Receivership or Voluntary Liquidation of Bank (§9.16)

The proposal directed a receiver or liquidating agent for a national bank to close promptly all fiduciary accounts to the extent practicable (in accordance with OCC instructions and the orders of the court having jurisdiction) and to transfer all remaining fiduciary accounts to substitute fiduciaries. Some commenters recommended that the OCC modify this provision to reflect that a national bank's receiver or liquidating agent generally transfers fiduciary accounts to substitute fiduciaries, noting that the FDIC's usual practice is to sell a failed bank's fiduciary business. The OCC agrees that a national bank should have the option to transfer fiduciary accounts to substitute fiduciaries, regardless of whether it can practicably close those accounts. Thus, the OCC is modifying the provision accordingly.

Additionally, the OCC is clarifying that this provision does not apply to the receiver of insured national banks, which, under 12 U.S.C. 191, is the Federal Deposit Insurance Corporation.

Surrender or Revocation of Fiduciary Powers (§9.17)

The proposal retained the substance of former §9.17, which addresses surrender and revocation of fiduciary powers. The proposal set forth the standards and procedures that apply when a national bank seeks to surrender its fiduciary powers. The proposal also described the standards that apply when the OCC seeks to revoke a bank's fiduciary powers. This section provides useful guidance to banks surrendering or revoking their fiduciary powers. The OCC did not receive any comments that warranted changes to this section and, thus, the OCC is adopting it as proposed.

Collective Investment Funds (§9.18)

The proposal retained the general structure of §9.18. Paragraph (a) authorized national banks to invest fiduciary assets in two types of collective investment funds (called (a)(1) funds and (a)(2) funds, in reference to the paragraphs of §9.18 that authorize them). Paragraph (b) set forth the requirements applicable to funds authorized under paragraph (a). Paragraph (c) described other types of collective investments available to national bank fiduciaries. The OCC is adopting much of proposed §9.18, but with several significant modifications.

In General (§9.18(a))

The proposal removed a provision from former §9.18(b)(3) that specifically provided that a bank may look at a collective investment fund's portfolio in the aggregate in determining whether it may invest fiduciary assets in the collective investment fund. This treatment is consistent with the prudent investor rule.[7] One commenter noted that not all states have adopted the prudent investor rule, and recommended that the OCC retain the provision. The OCC agrees, and is retaining the provision as a footnote to §9.18(a).

Written Plan (§9.18(b)(1))

The former regulation required the full board of directors of a national bank to approve a new collective investment fund plan. The proposal provided additional management flexibility by allowing a committee of the board of directors to perform this function. Some commenters recommended that the OCC modify this requirement further by allowing a committee authorized by the board to approve a new plan. Because this modification provides banks with some flexibility in approving new plans and presents no supervisory concerns, the OCC is adopting it as recommended.

Frequency of Valuation (§9.18(b)(4)(i))

The proposal allowed a bank to value an illiquid collective investment fund (i.e., one invested primarily in real estate or other assets that are not readily marketable) at least annually rather than at least quarterly, in an effort to be consistent with the one-year

[7]See Rest. 3rd, Trusts (Prudent Investor Rule), sec. 227(a)(1992).

prior notice allowance for withdrawals from illiquid collective investment funds found at former §9.18(b)(4). Because the prior notice allowance is limited to (a)(2) funds, it is appropriate to limit the valuation exception to (a)(2) funds. The OCC is modifying the proposed valuation exception to include this limitation.

Short-term Investment Funds (§9.18(b)(4)(ii)(B))

The proposal retained the former regulation's restrictions on short-term investment funds. Several commenters noted, however, that these restrictions are more stringent than the Securities and Exchange Commission's Rule 2a-7 (17 CFR 270.2a-7), which governs money market funds. The commenters recommended that the OCC revise the restrictions to make them more consistent with Rule 2a-7. The OCC agrees that its restrictions regarding short-term investment funds should be more consistent with Rule 2a-7. Consequently, the OCC is removing (1) the requirement that a bank invest at least 80 percent of the fund's assets in instruments payable on demand or that have a maturity date not exceeding 91 days from the date of purchase, and (2) the requirement that at least 20 percent of the fund's assets must be cash, demand obligations, or assets that will mature on the fund's next business day. In their place, the OCC is adding a requirement that a bank maintain a dollar-weighted average portfolio maturity of 90 days or less, consistent with Rule 2a-7.

Method of Distributions (§9.18(b)(5)(iv))

The proposal revised substantially the former regulation's standard for distributions to an account withdrawing from a collective investment fund. Former §9.18(b)(6) required a bank to make distributions in cash, ratably in kind (i.e., a proportional share in each of the assets held by the collective investment fund), or a combination of the two. The proposal allowed a bank to make any distributions consistent with applicable law. The proposal reflected an effort to provide banks with sufficient flexibility to address complex distribution problems that may arise (particularly with respect to collective investment funds that invest primarily ***68550** in illiquid assets), while maintaining the basic protections of state fiduciary law. In the proposal's preamble, the

OCC invited comment on whether to adopt this applicable law approach in lieu of the former regulation's distribution options.

Many commenters supported replacing the former regulation's distribution options with the proposed approach. Several commenters supported the proposed approach, but only as a supplement to the former regulation's distribution options. Some commenters noted that relying wholly on applicable law, as proposed, could be unworkable for a bank whose collective investment fund includes accounts from different states.

The OCC has determined to retain the former regulation's distribution options (i.e., cash, ratably in kind, or a combination of the two) and to add, as a fourth option, "any other manner consistent with applicable law in the state in which the bank maintains the fund." The OCC believes that this approach provides ample flexibility while maintaining the basic protections of state fiduciary law. Moreover, it resolves the proposal's potential problems regarding a fund with accounts from different states by clarifying that the only state whose law applies to the fourth distribution option is the state in which the bank maintains the fund (though other forms of "applicable law," such as Federal Law, may apply).

Audits and Financial Reports (§9.18(b)(6))

Consistent with OCC precedent, the proposal clarified that a national bank must disclose in a collective investment fund's annual financial report the fees and expenses charged to the fund. One commenter recommended that the OCC further clarify that the regulation does not require per se that a national bank disclose fees and expenses on a line-item basis, or as a specific dollar amount (as opposed to a percentage of assets). The OCC affirms that the regulation does not require per se a particular form of disclosure. However, if state law (or other applicable law) governing the collective investment fund requires a particular form of disclosure, then national banks must comply with that requirement.[8] To clarify this issue, the OCC is modifying the provision to clarify that disclosures of fees and expenses are required in a

[8]See Trust Interpretive Letter #242 (January 1990).

manner consistent with applicable law in the state in which the bank maintains the fund.

Advertising Restriction (§9.18(b)(7))

The proposal retained and clarified the former regulation's restriction on advertising (a)(1) funds. In particular, the proposal prohibited a bank from advertising a common trust fund except in connection with the advertisement of the general fiduciary services of the bank.

Many commenters recommended that the OCC eliminate or at least relax the restriction on advertising past performance. Other commenters, apparently in support of the restriction, warned that if a bank markets its common trust fund to the general public, then that fund will be subject to registration and regulation under the securities laws.

The views of commenters opposed to the advertising restriction may have some merit. The OCC has carefully considered their views but has decided that, on balance, it is not appropriate to remove the advertising restriction. Therefore, the OCC is adopting the provision as proposed.

Self-Dealing and Conflicts of Interest (§9.18(b)(8))

The proposal retained the substance of former §9.18(b)(8), which addressed self-dealing and conflicts of interest specific to collective investment funds. The OCC noted in the preamble that a national bank administering a collective investment fund must comply with not only these provisions, but also the general self-dealing and conflicts of interest provisions found in §9.12. One commenter recommended that the OCC clarify this position in the regulatory text. The OCC agrees, and is amending the provision accordingly.

Elimination of Mortgage Reserve Account Provision

The proposal retained the substance of former §9.18(b)(11), which allowed a bank administering a collective investment fund to establish a mortgage reserve account for overdue interest payments on mortgages in the fund. Suspecting that this provision was outdated, the OCC invited comment on the extent to which banks use mortgage reserve accounts. The only commenter on this provision recommended that the OCC eliminate it, stating that national banks no longer maintain mortgage reserve accounts because they are unnecessary and may not be appropriate under generally accepted accounting principles. Accordingly, the OCC is eliminating this provision.

Management Fees (§9.18(b)(9))

The proposal retained the quantitative management fee limitation, found at former §9.18(b)(12), but invited comment on whether the OCC should defer to state law instead of retaining the fee limitation. Under this limitation, a bank administering a collective investment fund may charge a fund management fee only if the total fees charged to a participating account (including the fund management fee) does not exceed the total fees that the bank would have charged had it not invested assets of the fiduciary account in the fund.

Many commenters supported eliminating the management fee limitation altogether in favor of a "reasonableness" standard or a state law based approach, arguing that these alternatives would reflect modern fiduciary law standards in this area. However, some commenters supported retaining the limitation. Other commenters were concerned that a state law approach could be unworkable for a collective investment fund with participants from different states whose fee standards differ.

The OCC recognizes the desirability of providing updated operating standards for national bank fiduciary activities, but is concerned that a general "reasonableness" standard, or even a state law standard, alone, may not provide sufficient protections for banks' fiduciary customers. Accordingly, the final rule provides that a national bank may charge a fund management fee only if: (1) the fee is reasonable; (2) the fee is permitted under applicable law (and complies with fee disclosure requirements, if any) in the state in which the bank maintains the fund; and (3) the amount of the fee does not exceed an amount commensurate with the value of legitimate services of tangible benefit to the participating fiduciary accounts that would not have been provided to the accounts were they not invested in the fund.

This modification safeguards the interests of customers in several ways. First, a fund management fee is subject to an overall reasonableness standard. Second, in order to charge a fund management fee, applicable law must allow the type of fee charged. Third, the bank must justify the amount of a fund management fee based on particular services that provide a tangible benefit to participating fiduciary accounts that would not have been provided to the accounts were they not invested in the fund. Fourth, a bank that charges a fee under this approach also must comply with applicable fee disclosure ***68551** requirements. Finally, a separate provision in the final rule requires a bank to disclose a management fee, along with other fees and expenses charged to the fund, in the annual financial report in a manner consistent with applicable law in the state in which the bank maintains the fund.[9]

Additionally, this modification eliminates the possibility that multiple conflicting states' laws could apply to the same fund, and thus is responsive to commenters' concerns about administering a collective investment fund with participants from different states.

Expenses (§9.18(b)(10))

The proposal retained the requirement that the bank absorb establishment and reorganization expenses, but eliminated other provisions that specifically permitted or prohibited a bank to charge certain expenses to the fund. Rather than mandating the treatment of specific expenses (other than establishment and reorganization expenses), the proposal deferred to state law, in effect, by allowing a bank to charge reasonable expenses incurred in administering the fund to the extent not prohibited by applicable law.

Many commenters supported this approach. However, some commenters were concerned that a state law approach to permissible expenses could be unworkable for funds with participants from different states.

The OCC continues to believe that, when expenses of a fund are reasonable and permissable under state law, and are fully

[9]See §9.18(b)(6)(ii).

disclosed in appropriate documentation,[10] a bank should be allowed to charge them directly to the fund. Thus, the final rule retains the proposal's approach of allowing a bank to charge any reasonable expenses (except expenses incurred in establishing or reorganizing a collective investment fund) not prohibited by applicable law, and clarifies that the applicable law in the state in which the bank maintains the fund — including Federal law where appropriate, and excluding the law of states other than the state in which the bank maintains the fund — determines whether particular expenses are prohibited. This standard addresses commenters' concerns about funds with participants from different states.

Prohibition Against Certificates (§9.18(b)(11))

The proposal prohibited a national bank from issuing certificates of interest in a collective investment fund. One commenter recommended that the OCC provide an exception allowing a bank to issue a certificate of participation in a segregated investment to a customer withdrawing from a fund, consistent with OCC fiduciary precedents. The OCC agrees. The exception for segregated investments should not raise any of the securities-related concerns underlying the prohibition against certificates. Consequently, the OCC is adopting the exception.

Elimination of Participation, Investment, and Liquidity Requirements

The proposal eliminated the 10 percent participation limitation, the 10 percent investment limitation, and the liquidity requirement applicable to common trust funds under former §9.18(b)(9). The OCC received many comment letters on this issue. All who commented supported the proposal. These restrictions have at times interfered with optimal management of common trust funds. Moreover, the OCC believes that the protections found in state fiduciary law adequately address the concerns un-

[10]See §9.18(b)(1)(iiii) (disclosure of anticipated fees and expenses in the written plan) and §9.18(b)(6)(ii) (disclosure of fees and expenses in the annual financial report).

derlying these restrictions. Consequently, the OCC is eliminating the participation, investment, and liquidity requirements.

Other Collective Investments §9.18(c))

In addition to (a)(1) and (a)(2) funds, the proposal authorized other means by which a national bank may invest fiduciary assets collectively: (1) bank fiduciary funds, (2) single loans or obligations, (3) mini-funds (i.e., funds established for the collective investment of cash balances), (4) trust funds of corporations and closely-related settlors, and (5) special exemption funds. These other collective investments are not subject to the requirements of §9.18(b).

While the OCC did not receive any comments on the provision authorizing bank fiduciary funds, the OCC believes that banks no longer maintain this type of fund. Thus, the OCC is eliminating the provision.

With respect to single loans or obligations, the proposal eliminated the restriction that a bank invest in a variable-amount note on a short-term basis only. Those who commented on this change supported it. The change will bring that provision in conformity with §9.18(b)(4)(ii)(B), which allows a bank to invest fiduciary assets collectively in short-term investment fund composed of short-term vehicles, including variable-amount notes, but places no limitation on renewals of those investments. For this reason, the OCC is adopting the provision as proposed.

With respect to mini-funds, the proposal eliminated the requirement that no participating account's interest in the fund may exceed $10,000. Moreover, the proposal increased the total amount of assets permitted in a mini-fund to $1,000,000. Those who commented on these changes supported them. These changes remove outdated limitations on mini-funds. Consequently, the OCC is adopting the provision as proposed.

One commenter recommended that the OCC add a provision that permits a bank to use any collective investment authorized by applicable law (e.g., pre-need funeral statutes). The OCC agrees that a bank should be permitted to use any collective investment authorized by applicable law, and is adding a provision to this effect.

With respect to special exemption funds, the proposal provided an expedited procedure for their review. While most commenters supported the expedited review procedure, a few commenters strongly opposed it. Those who opposed it objected that the provision does not require notice and comment, does not distinguish between routine and novel applications, and, because approval is automatic if the OCC does not act in 30 days, could lead to inadvertent approvals of common trust funds that are exempt from the regulation's management fee and common trust fund advertising provisions. After carefully considering these concerns, the OCC has decided that it may not be appropriate to adopt the proposed expedited review precedure. Thus, the OCC is modifying the provision to eliminate the expedited review procedure.

Finally, one commenter recommended that the OCC extend the right to seek special exemptions from the OCC to state banks and other corporate fiduciaries that must comply with the OCC's collective investment fund regulation in order to receive favorable tax treatment under the Internal Revenue Code (26 U.S.C. 584). The OCC agrees that those corporate fiduciaries should have the same opportunity to establish special exemption funds as national banks. Consequently, the OCC is modifying the proposal to reflect this recommendation.

Transfer Agents (§9.20)

The proposal incorporated by means of cross-reference the Securities and Exchange Commission (SEC) rules ***68552** prescribing procedures for registration of transfer agents for which the SEC is the appropriate regulatory agency (17 CFR 240.17Ac2-1). The proposal also clarified that a national bank transfer agent must comply with rules adopted by the SEC pursuant to section 17A of the Securities Exchange Act (15 U.S.C. 78q-1), which sets forth operational and reporting requirements that apply to all transfer agents (17 CFR 240.17Ac2-2, and 240.17Ad-1 through 16).

Several commenters noted that the SEC's rules regarding transfer agents do not apply to activities in foreign countries. The OCC acknowledges that the SEC's rules regarding transfer agents apply only to domestic activities. Consequently, the OCC is clarifying this point in the regulatory text.

Waiver of Regulatory Requirements

In the preamble to the proposal, the OCC invited comment on whether the OCC should add a reservation of authority to part 9 for the purpose of setting forth standards and procedures under which a national bank may obtain a waiver from a specific provision. All but one of those who commented on this issue supported the addition of waiver standards and procedures. Upon reconsideration, the OCC has concluded that it is preferable to continue its current practice of considering any request to modify the application of any provision in part 9, and granting a request if the OCC deems it consistent with the bank's fiduciary duties and with safe and sound banking practices. The OCC expects that the additional flexibility it has incorporated into many of part 9's provisions will reduce the need for waivers and modifications. Moreover, the requests that banks are likely to file will vary significantly in subject matter and complexity, reducing the usefulness of generalized standards. Therefore, the OCC has decided not to include a specific waiver provision in part 9.

Acting as Indenture Trustee and Creditor (§9.100)

In the proposal's preamble, the OCC indicated that it was inclined to modify its restrictions on allowing an indenture trustee to act as creditor to the same debt securities issuance. In particular, the OCC suggested allowing a national bank to act both as creditor and indenture trustee until 90 days after default, consistent with the Trust Indenture Act, with the added condition that the bank maintains adequate controls to manage any potential conflicts of interest. Additionally, the OCC indicated that it would apply this policy consistently to all debt securities issuances, including issuances exempt from the Trust Indenture Act. The OCC invited comment on how banks are managing these conflicts, and on the need to address this issue in part 9.

Commenters supported a revision of the OCC's position, and indicated that bank policies and procedures effectively manage potential conflicts of interest. However, most who commented recommended that the OCC not add specific requirements to the regulation on this issue, though most of these commenters also supported less formal guidance.

Based on its experience in this area, the OCC believes that

banks generally have established adequate controls to manage those conflicts. Moreover, the OCC believes that it is important to clarify to all national banks the revised position on this issue. Consequently, the OCC is adding a short interpretive ruling to part 9 explaining that a national bank may act as creditor and indenture trustee to any debt securities issuance (whether or not covered by the Trust Indenture Act) until 90 days after default with the added condition that the bank maintains adequate controls to manage the potential conflicts of interest.

Disciplinary Sanctions Imposed by Clearing Agencies (§19.135)

The proposal eliminated much of the detail of former §§9.21 and 9.22, which concern applications by national banks for stays or reviews of disciplinary sanctions imposed by registered clearing agencies. Instead, the proposal cross-referenced the SEC's rules in this area, which are virtually identical to former §§9.21 and 9.22. The proposal also relocated the provision to 12 CFR part 19, the OCC's rules of practice and procedure, where readers are more likely to find it.

The OCC received no comments on this provision and, thus, is adopting it as proposed.

Investment Adviser to an Investment Company

Part 9 has never contained conditions applicable to national bank operating subsidiaries engaged in investment advisory activities. Instead, appropriate conditions for particular operating subsidiary activities have been dealth with by the OCC as part of the application process. However, one of the issues related to the treatment of investment advisory activities under part 9 that was raised in the proposal was whether to impose certain conditions in all situations where a national bank or its operating subsidiary acts as investment adviser to an investment company, and, if so, whether to include them in part 9.

Most who commented on this issue expressed concerns that the conditions could impose unnecessary restrictions on certain activities. After carefully considering the comments, the OCC has decided to continue its current approach of dealing with conditions imposed on national bank operating subsidiaries as part of the corporate application process. Recent amendments to 12 CFR part 5 (61 FR

60342, November 27, 1996) also provide a specific new mechanism for conditions and policies to be developed that will be applicable to operating subsidiaries engaged in particular types of activities. One of these types of activities is serving as an investment adviser to an investment company (see §5.34(e)(3)(ii)(D)). Accordingly, the OCC has concluded that it is not appropriate to deal with conditions imposed on operating subsidiaries engaged in such activities as an aspect of part 9.

Derivation Table for 12 CFR Part 9

This table directs readers to the provisions of the former 12 CFR part 9 on which the revised 12 CFR part 9 and the amended 12 CFR part 19 are based.

| *Revised provision* | *Former provision* | *Comments* |
|---|---|---|
| §9.1 | | Added. |
| §9.2(a) | | Added. |
| (b) | §9.1(g) | Significantly modified. |
| (c) | §9.1(l) | Modified. |
| (d) | §9.1(a) | Modified. |
| (e) | §9.1(b) and (h) | Significantly modified. |
| (f) | §9.1(j) | Modified. |
| (g) | §9.1(c) | Significantly modified. |
| (h) | §9.1(e) | Modified. |
| (i) | | Added. |
| §9.3 | §9.2 | Modified. |
| §9.4 | §9.7(a)(1), (b), and (d) | Significantly modified. |
| §9.5 | §§9.5, 9.7(c), 9.7(d), and 9.10(a) | Significantly modified. |
| §9.6 | §9.7(a)(2) | Significantly modified. |
| §9.8 | §§9.7(a)(2) and 9.8 | Modified. |
| §9.9 | §9.9 | Significantly modified. |
| §9.10 | §9.10 | Significantly modified. |
| §9.11 | §9.11 | Significantly modified. |
| §9.12 | §9.12 | Modified. |
| §9.13 | §9.13 | Modified. |
| §9.14 | §9.14 | Significantly modified. |
| §9.15 | §9.15 | Modified. |

| Revised provision | Former provision | Comments |
|---|---|---|
| §9.16 | §9.16 | Modified. |
| §9.17 | §9.17 | Modified. |
| §9.18(a) | §9.18(a), (b)(2), and (b)(3) | Modified. |
| (b)(1) | (b)(1) | Significantly modified. |
| (b)(2) | (b)(12) | Significantly modified. |
| (b)(3) | (b)(3) | Modified. |
| (b)(4) | (b)(1), (4), and (15) | Significantly modified. |
| (b)(5) | (b)(4), (6), and (7) | Significantly modified. |
| (b)(6) | (b)(5)(i)–(iv) | Significantly modified. |
| (b)(7) | (b)(5)(iv) and (v) | Significantly modified. |
| (b)(8) | (b)(8) | Modified. |
| (b)(9) | (b)(12) | Significantly modified. |
| (b)(10) | (b)(5)(i) and (iv), (b)(10) and (b)(12) | Significantly modified. |
| (b)(11) | (b)(13) | Modified. |
| (b)(12) | (b)(14) | Modified. |
| (c)(1) | (c)(2) | Modified. |
| (c)(2) | (c)(3) | Significantly modified. |
| (c)(3) | (c)(4) | Modified. |
| (c)(4) | | Added. |
| (c)(5) | (c)(5) | Significantly Modified. |
| §9.20 | §9.20 | Modified. |
| §9.100 | | Added. |
| §19.135 | §§9.21 and 9.22 | Modified. |

***68553** Regulatory Flexibility Act

Pursuant to section 605(b) of the Regulatory Flexibility Act, the OCC certifies that this final rule will not have a significant economic impact on a substantial number of small entities in accord with the spirit and purposes of the Regulatory Flexibility Act (5 U.S.C. 601 et seq.). Accordingly, a regulatory flexibility analysis is not required. The final rule's requirements, for the most part, are not new to the regulation. The final rule eases requirements and reduces burden for all national banks that exercise fiduciary powers, regardless of size.

**Appendix II**

Executive Order 12866

The Office of Management and Budget has concerned with the OCC's determination that this final rule is not a significant regulatory action under Executive Order 12866.

Paperwork Reduction Act of 1995

The OCC invites comment on:

(1) Whether the information collection contained in this final rule is necessary for the proper performance of the OCC's functions, including whether the information has practical utility;

(2) The accuracy of the OCC's estimate of the burden of the information collection;

(3) Ways to enhance the quality, utility, and clarity of the information to be collected;

(4) Ways to minimize the burden of the information collection on respondents, including through the use of automated collection techniques or other forms of information technology; and

(5) Estimates of capital or start-up costs and costs of operation, maintenance, and purchase of services to provide information.

The OCC asked similar questions in the proposed rule, but received no comments.

Respondents/recordkeepers are not required to respond to this collection of information unless it displays a currently valid OMB control number.

The collection of information requirements contained in this final rule have been approved by the Office of Management and Budget under Control No. 1557-0140 in accordance with the Paperwork Reduction Act of 1995 (44 U.S.C. 3507(d). Comments on the collection of information requirements should be sent to the Office of Management and Budget, Paperwork Reduction Project (1557-0140), Washington, DC 20503, with copies to the Legislative and Regulatory Activities Division (1557-0140), Office of the Comptroller of the Currency, 250 E Street, SW, Washington, DC 20219.

The collection of information requirements in this final rule are found in CFR 9.8, 9.9, 9.17, and 9.18. The OCC requires this information for the proper supervision of national banks' fiduciary activities. The likely respondents/recordkeepers are national banks.

Estimated average annual burden hours per respondent/recordkeeper: 15 hours.

Estimated number of respondents and/or recordkeepers: 1,000.

Estimated total annual reporting and recordkeeping burden: 15,010 hours.

Start-up costs to respondents: None.

Unfunded Mandates Reform Act of 1995

The OCC has determined that this final rule will not result in expenditures by state, local, and tribal governments, or by the private sector, of $100 million or more in any one year. Accordingly, a budgetary impact statement is not ***68554** required under section 202 of the Unfunded Mandates Reform Act of 1995. The final rule's requirements, for the most part, are not new to the regulation. The final rule eases requirements and reduces burden for all national banks that exercise fiduciary powers, regardless of size.

List of Subjects

12 CFR Part 9

Estates, Investments, National banks, Reporting and recordkeeping requirements, Trusts and trustees. 12 CFR Part 19

Administrative practice and procedure, Crime, Investigations, National banks, Penalties, Securities.

Authority and Issuance

For the reasons set out in the preamble, chapter I of title 12 of the Code of Federal Regulations is amended as follows:

1. Part 9 is revised to read as follows:

PART 9 — FIDUCIARY ACTIVITIES OF NATIONAL BANKS

Regulations

Sec.

9.1 Authority, purpose, and scope.

9.2 Definitions.

Authority: 12 U.S.C. 24 (Seventh), 92a, and 93a; 15 U.S.C. 78q, 78q-1, and 78w.

Regulations

## §9.1 Authority, purpose, and scope

(a) Authority. The Office of the Comptroller of the Currency (OCC) issues this part pursuant to its authority under 12 U.S.C. 24 (Seventh), 92a, and 93a, and 15 U.S.C. 78q, 78q-1, and 78w.

(b) Purpose. The purpose of this part is to set forth the standards that apply to the fiduciary activities of national banks.

(c) Scope. This part applies to all national banks that act in a fiduciary capacity, as defined in §9.2(e). This part also applies to all Federal branches of foreign banks to the same extent as it applies to national banks.

## §9.2 Definitions

For the purposes of this part, the following definitions apply:

(a) Affiliate has the same meaning as in 12 U.S.C. 221a(b).

(b) Applicable law means the law of a state or other jurisdiction governing a national bank's fiduciary relationships, any applicable Federal law governing those relationships, the terms of the instrument governing a fiduciary relationship, or any court order pertaining to the relationship.

(c) Custodian under a uniform gifts to minors act means a fiduciary relationship established pursuant to a state law substantially similar to the Uniform Gifts to Minors Act or the Uniform Transfers to Minors Act as published by the American Law Institute.

(d)Fiduciary account means an account administered by a national bank acting in a fiduciary capacity.

(e) Fiduciary capacity means: trustee, executor, administrator, registrar of stocks and bonds, transfer agent, guardian, assignee, receiver, or custodian under a uniform gifts to minors act; investment adviser, if the bank receives a fee for its investment advice; any capacity in which the bank possesses investment discretion on behalf of another; or any other similar capacity that the OCC authorizes pursuant to 12 U.S.C. 92a.

(f) Fiduciary officers and employees means all officers and employees of a national bank to whom the board of directors or its designee has assigned functions involving the exercise of the bank's fiduciary powers.

(g) Fiduciary powers means the authority the OCC permits a national bank to exercise pursuant to 12 U.S.C. 92a. The extent of fiduciary powers is the same for out-of-state national banks as for in-state national banks, and that extent depends upon what powers the state grants to the fiduciaries in the state with which national banks compete.

(h) Guardian means the guardian or conservator, by whatever name used by state law, of the estate of a minor, an incompetent person, an absent person, or a person over whose estate a court has taken jurisdiction, other than under bankruptcy or insolvency laws.

(i) Investment discretion means, with respect to an account, the sole or shared authority (whether or not that authority is exercised) to determine what securities or other assets to purchase or sell on behalf of the account. A bank that delegates its authority over investments and a bank that receives delegated authority over investments are both deemed to have investment discretion.

## §9.3 Approval requirements

(a) A national bank may not exercise fiduciary powers unless it obtains prior approval from the OCC to the extent required under 12 CFR 5.26.

(b) A person seeking approval to organize a special-purpose national bank limited to fiduciary powers shall file an application with the OCC pursuant to 12 CFR 5.20.

## §9.4 Administration of fiduciary power

(a) Responsibilities of the board of directors. A national bank's fiduciary activities shall be managed by or under the direction of its board of directors. In discharging its responsibilities, the board may assign any function related to the exercise of fiduciary powers to any director, officer, employee, or committee thereof.

(b) Use of other personnel. The national bank may use any qualified personnel and facilities of the bank or its affiliates to perform services related to the exercise of its fiduciary powers, and any department of the bank or its affiliates may use fiduciary officers, employees, and facilities to perform services unrelated to the exercise of fiduciary powers, to the extent not prohibited by applicable law.

(c) Agency agreements. Pursuant to a written agreement, a national bank exercising fiduciary powers may perform services related to the exercise of fiduciary powers for another bank or other entity, and may purchase services related to the exercise of fiduciary powers from another bank or other entity.

(d) Bond requirement. A national bank shall ensure that all fiduciary officers and employees are adequately bonded.

## §9.5 Policies and procedures

A national bank exercising fiduciary powers shall adopt and follow written policies and procedures adequate to maintain its fiduciary activities in compliance with applicable law. Among other relevant matters, the policies and procedures should address, where appropriate, the bank's:

(a) Brokerage placement practices;

(b) Methods for ensuring that fiduciary officers and employees do not use material inside information in connection with any decision or recommendation to purchase or sell any security; ***68555**

(c) Methods for preventing self-dealing and conflicts of interest;

(d) Selection and retention of legal counsel who is readily available to advise the bank and its fiduciary officers and employees on fiduciary matters; and

(e) Investment of funds held as fiduciary, including short-term investments and the treatment of fiduciary funds awaiting investment or distribution.

## §9.6 Review of fiduciary accounts

(a) Pre-acceptance review. Before accepting a fiduciary account, a national bank shall review the prospective account to determine whether it can properly administer the account.

(b) Initial post-acceptance review. Upon the acceptance of a fiduciary account for which a national bank has investment discretion, the bank shall conduct a prompt review of all assets of the account to evaluate whether they are appropriate for the account.

(c) Annual review. At least once during every calendar year, a bank shall conduct a review of all assets of each fiduciary account for which the bank has investment discretion to evaluate they are appropriate, individually and collectively, for the account.

## §9.8 Recordkeeping

(a) Documentation of accounts. A national bank shall adequately document the establishment and termination of each fiduciary account and shall maintain adequate records for all fiduciary accounts.

(b) Retention of records. A national bank shall retain records described in paragraph (a) of this section for a period of three years from the later of the termination of the account or the termination of any litigation relating to the account.

(c) Separation of records. A national bank shall ensure that records described in paragraph (a) of this section are separate and distinct from other records of the bank.

## §9.9 Audit of fiduciary activities

(a) Annual audit. At least once during each calendar year, a national bank shall arrange for a suitable audit (by internal or external auditors) of all significant fiduciary activities, under the direction of its fiduciary audit committee, unless the bank adopts a continuous audit system in accordance with paragraph (b) of this section. The bank shall note the results of the audit (including significant actions taken as a result of the audit) in the minutes of the board of directors.

(b) Continuous audit. In lieu of performing annual audits under paragraph (a) of this section, a national bank may adopt a continuous audit system under which the bank arranges for a discrete audit (by internal or external auditors) of each significant fiduciary activity (i.e., on an activity-by-activity basis), under the direction of its fiduciary audit committee, at an interval commensurate with the nature and risk of that activity. Thus, certain fiduciary activities may receive audits at intervals greater or less than one year, as appropriate. A bank that adopts a continuous audit system shall note the results of all discrete audits performed since the last audit report (including significant actions taken as a result of the audits) in the minutes of the board of directors at least once during each calendar year.

(c) Fiduciary audit committee. A national bank's fiduciary audit committee must consist of a committee of the bank's directors or an audit committee of an affiliate of the bank. However, in either case, the committee:

(1) Must not include any officers of the bank or an affiliate who participate significantly in the administration of the bank's fiduciary activities; and

(2) Must consist of a majority of members who are not also members of any committee to which the board of directors has delegated power to manage and control the fiduciary activities of the bank.

## §9.10 Fiduciary funds awaiting investment or distribution

(a) In general. With respect to a fiduciary account for which a national bank has investment discretion or discretion over distributions, the bank may not allow funds awaiting investment or distribution to remain uninvested and undistributed any longer than is reasonable for the proper management of the account and consistent with applicable law. With respect to a fiduciary account for which a national bank has investment discretion, the bank shall obtain for funds awaiting investment or distribution a rate of return that is consistent with applicable law.

(b) Self-deposits — (1) In general. A national bank may deposit funds of a fiduciary account that are awaiting investment or distribution in the commercial, savings, or another department of the bank, unless prohibited by applicable law. To the extent that the funds are not insured by the Federal Deposit Insurance Corporation, the bank shall set aside collateral as security, under the control of appropriate fiduciary officers and employees, in accordance with paragraph (b)(2) of this section. The market value of the collateral set aside must at all times equal or exceed the amount of the uninsured fiduciary funds.

(2) Acceptable collateral. A national bank may satisfy the collateral requirement of paragraph (b)(1) of this section with any of the following:

(i) Direct obligations of the United States, or other obligations fully guaranteed by the United States as to principal and interest;

(ii) Securities that qualify as eligible for investment by national banks pursuant to 12 CFR part 1;

(iii) Readily marketable securities of the classes in which state banks, trust companies, or other corporations exercising fiduciary powers are permitted to invest fiduciary funds under applicable state law;

(iv) Surety bonds, to the extent they provide adequate security, unless prohibited by applicable law; and

(v) Any other assets that qualify under applicable state law as appropriate security for deposits of fiduciary funds.

(c) Affiliate deposits. A national bank, acting in its fiduciary capacity, may deposit funds of a fiduciary account that are awaiting investment or distribution with an affiliated insured depository institution, unless prohibited by applicable law. A national bank may set aside collateral as security for a deposit by or with an affiliate of fiduciary funds awaiting investment or distribution, unless prohibited by applicable law.

## §9.11 Investment of fiduciary funds

A national bank shall invest funds of a fiduciary account in a manner consistent with applicable law.

## §9.12 Self-dealing and conflicts of interest

(a) Investments for fiduciary accounts — (1) In general. Unless authorized by applicable law, a national bank may not invest funds of a fiduciary account for which a national bank has investment discretion in the stock or obligations of, or in assets acquired from: the bank or any of its directors, officers, or employees; affiliates of the bank or any of their directors, officers, or employees; or individuals or organizations with whom there exists an interest that might affect the exercise of the best judgment of the bank.

(2) Additional securities investments. If retention of stock or obligations of the bank or its affiliates in a fiduciary account is consistent with applicable law, the bank may:

(i) Exercise rights to purchase additional stock (or securities ***68556** convertible into additional stock) when offered pro rata to stockholders, and

(ii) Purchase fractional shares to complement fractional shares acquired through the exercise of rights or the receipt of a stock dividend resulting in fractional share holdings.

(b) Loans, sales, or other transfers from fiduciary accounts — (1) In general. A national bank may not lend, sell, or otherwise transfer assets of a fiduciary account for which a national bank has investment discretion to the bank or any of its directors, officers, or employees, or to affiliates of the bank or any of their directors, officers, or employees, or to individuals or organizations with whom there exists an interest that might affect the exercise of the best judgment of the bank, unless:

(i) The transaction is authorized by applicable law;

(ii) Legal counsel advises the bank in writing that the bank has incurred, in its fiduciary capacity, a contingent or potential liability, in which case the bank, upon the sale or transfer of assets, shall reimburse the fiduciary account in cash at the greater of book or market value of the assets;

(iii) As provided in §9.18(b)(8)(iii) for defaulted investments; or

(iv) Required in writing by the OCC.

(2) Loans of funds held as trustee. Notwithstanding paragraph (b)(1) of this section, a national bank may not lend to any of its directors, officers, or employees any funds held in trust, except with respect to employee benefit plans in accordance with the exemptions found in section 408 of the Employee Retirement Income Security Act of 1974 (29 U.S.C. 1108).

(c) Loans to fiduciary accounts. A national bank may make a loan to a fiduciary account and may hold a security interest in assets of the account if the transaction is fair to the account and is not prohibited by applicable law.

(d) Sales between fiduciary accounts. A national bank may sell assets between any of its fiduciary accounts if the transaction is fair to both accounts and is not prohibited by any applicable law.

(e) Loans between fiduciary accounts. A national bank may make a loan between any of its fiduciary accounts if the transaction is fair to both accounts and is not prohibited by any applicable law.

## §9.13 Custody of fiduciary assets

(a) Control of fiduciary assets. A national bank shall place assets of fiduciary accounts in the joint custody or control of not fewer than two of the fiduciary officers or employees designated for that purpose by the board of directors. A national bank may maintain the investments of a fiduciary account off-premises, if consistent with applicable law and if the bank maintains adequate safeguards and controls.

(b) Separation of fiduciary assets. A national bank shall keep the assets of fiduciary accounts separate from the assets of the bank. A national bank shall keep the assets of each fiduciary account separate from all other accounts or shall identify the investments as the property of a particular account, except as provided in §9.18.

## §9.14. Deposit of securities with state authorities

(a) In general. If state law requires corporations acting in a fiduciary capacity to deposit securities with state authorities for the protection of private or court trusts, then before a national bank acts as a private or court-appointed trustee in that state, it shall make a similar deposit with state authorities. If the state authorities refuse to accept the deposit, the bank shall deposit the securities with the Federal Reserve Bank of the district in which the national bank is located, to be held for the protection of private or court trusts to the same extent as if the securities had been deposited with state authorities.

(b) Assets held in more than one state. If a national bank administers trust assets in more than one state, the bank may compute the amount of deposit required for each state on the basis of trust assets that the bank administers primarily from offices located in that state.

## §9.15 Fiduciary compensation

(a) Compensation of bank. If the amount of a national bank's compensation for acting in a fiduciary capacity is not set or governed by applicable law, the bank may charge a reasonable fee for its services.

(b) Compensation of co-fiduciary officers and employees. A national bank may not permit any officer or employee to retain any compensation for acting as a co-fiduciary with the bank in the administration of a fiduciary account, except with the specific approval of the bank's board of directors.

## §9.16 Receivership or voluntary liquidation of bank

If the OCC appoints a receiver for an uninsured national bank, or if a national bank places itself in voluntary liquidation, the receiver or liquidating agent shall promptly close or transfer to a substitute fiduciary all fiduciary accounts, in accordance with OCC instructions and the orders of the court having jurisdiction.

## §9.17 Surrender or revocation of fiduciary powers

(a) Surrender. In accordance with 12 U.S.C. 92 a(j), a national bank seeking to surrender its fiduciary powers shall file with the OCC a certified copy of the resolution of its board of directors evidencing that intent. If, after appropriate investigation, the OCC is satisfied that the bank has been discharged from all fiduciary duties, the OCC will provide written notice that the bank is no longer authorized to exercise fiduciary powers.

(b) Revocation. If the OCC determines that a national bank has unlawfully or unsoundly exercised, or has failed for a period of five consecutive years to exercise its fiduciary powers, the Comptroller may, in accordance with the provisions of 12 U.S.C. 92a(k), revoke the bank's fiduciary powers.

## §9.18 Collective investment funds

(a) In general. Where consistent with applicable law, a national bank may invest assets that it holds as fiduciary in the following collective investments funds:[1]

(1) A fund maintained by the bank, or by one or more affiliated banks,[2] exclusively for the collective investment and reinvestment of money contributed to the fund by the bank, or by one or more affiliated banks, in its capacity as trustee, executor, administrator, guardian, or custodian under a uniform gifts to minors act.

(2) A fund consisting solely of assets of retirement, pension, profit sharing, stock bonus or other trusts that are exempt from Federal income tax.

(i) A national bank may invest assets of retirement, pension, profit sharing, stock bonus, or other trusts exempt from Federal income tax and that the bank holds in its capacity as trustee in a collective investment fund established under paragraph (a)(1) or (a)(2) of this section.

(ii) A national bank may invest assets of retirement, pension, profit sharing, stock bonus, or other employee benefit trusts exempt from Federal income tax and that the bank holds in any capacity (including agent), in a collective investment fund established under this ***68557** paragraph (a)(2) if the fund itself qualifies for exemption from Federal income tax.

(b) Requirements. A national bank administering a collective investment fund authorized under paragraph (a) of this section shall comply with the following requirements:

(1) Written plan. The bank shall establish and maintain each collective investment fund in accordance with a written plan (Plan)

[1]In determining whether investing fiduciary assets in a collective investment fund is proper, the bank may consider the fund as a whole and, for example, shall not be prohibited from making that investment because any particular asset is nonincome producing.

[2]A fund established pursuant to this paragraph (a)(1) that includes money contributed by entities that are affiliates under 12 U.S.C. 221a(b), but are not members of the same affiliated group, as defined at 26 U.S.C. 1504, may fail to qualify for tax-exempt status under the Internal Revenue Code. See 26 U.S.C. 584.

approved by a resolution of the bank's board of directors or by a committee authorized by the board. The bank shall make a copy of the Plan available for public inspection at its main office during all banking hours, and shall provide a copy of the Plan to any person who requests it. The Plan must contain appropriate provisions, not inconsistent with this part, regarding the manner in which the bank will operate the fund, including provisions relating to:

(i) Investment powers and policies with respect to the fund;
(ii) Allocation of income, profits, and losses;
(iii) Fees and expenses that will be charged to the fund and to participating accounts;
(iv) Terms and conditions governing the admission and withdrawal of participating accounts;
(v) Audits of participating accounts;
(vi) Basis and method of valuing assets in the fund;
(vii) Expected frequency for income distribution to participating accounts;
(viii) Minimum frequency for valuation of fund assets;
(ix) Amount of time following a valuation date during which the valuation must be made:
(x) Bases upon which the bank may terminate the fund; and
(xi) Any other matters necessary to define clearly the rights of participating accounts.

(2) Fund management. A bank administering a collective investment fund shall have exclusive management thereof, except as a prudent person might delegate responsibilities to others.[3]

(3) Proportionate interests. Each participating account in a collective investment fund must have a proportionate interest in all the fund's assets.

(4) Valuation — (i) Frequency of valuation. A bank administering a collective investment fund shall determine the value of the fund's assets at least once every three months. However, in the case

[3]If a fund, the assets of which consist solely of Individual Retirement Accounts, Keogh Accounts, or other employee benefit accounts that are exempt from taxation, is registered under the Investment Company Act of 1940 (15 U.S.C. 80a-1 et seq.), the fund will not be deemed in violation of this paragraph (b)(2) as a result of its compliance with section 10(c) of the Investment Company Act of 1940 (15 U.S.C. 80a-10(c)).

of a fund described in paragraph (a) (2) of this section that is invested primarily in real estate or other assets that are not readily marketable, the bank shall determine the value of the fund's assets at least once each year.

(ii) Method of valuation — (A) In general. Except as provided in paragraph (b) (4) (ii) (B) of this section, a bank shall value each fund asset at market value as of the date set for valuation, unless the bank cannot readily ascertain market value, in which case the bank shall use a fair value determined in good faith.

(B) Short-term investment funds. A bank may value a fund's assets on a cost, rather than market value, basis for purposes of admissions and withdrawals, if the Plan requires the bank to:

(1) Maintain a dollar-weighted average portfolio maturity of 90 days or less;

(2) Accrue on a straight-line basis the difference between the cost and anticipated principal receipt on maturity; and

(3) Hold the fund's assets until maturity under usual circumstances.

(5) Admission and withdrawal of accounts — (i) In general. A bank administering a collective investment fund shall admit an account to or withdraw an account from the fund only on the basis of the valuation described in paragraph (b) (4) of this section.

(ii) Prior request or notice. A bank administering a collective investment fund may admit an account to or withdraw an account from a collective investment fund only if the bank has approved a request for or a notice of intention of taking that action on or before the valuation date on which the admission or withdrawal is based. No requests or notices may be canceled or countermanded after the valuation date.

(iii) Prior notice period for withdrawals from funds with assets not readily marketable. A bank administering a collective investment fund described in paragraph (a) (2) of this section that is invested primarily in real estate or other assets that are not readily marketable, may require a prior notice period, not to exceed one year, for withdrawals.

(iv) Method of distributions. A bank administering a collective investment fund shall make distributions to accounts withdrawing from the fund in cash, ratably in kind, a combination of cash and ratably in kind, or in any other manner consistent with applicable law in the state in which the bank maintains the fund.

(v) Segregation of investments. If an investment is withdrawn in kind from a collective investment fund for the benefit of all participants in the fund at the time of the withdrawal but the investment is not distributed ratably in kind, the bank shall segregate and administer it for the benefit ratably of all participants in the collective investment fund at the time of withdrawal.

(6) Audits and financial reports — (i) Annual audit. At least once during each 12-month period, a bank administering a collective investment fund shall arrange for an audit of the collective investment fund by auditors responsible only to the board of directors of the bank.[4]

(ii) Financial report. At least once during each 12-month period, a bank administering a collective investment fund shall prepare a financial report of the fund based on the audit required by paragraph (b)(6)(i) of this section. The report must disclose the fund's fees and expenses in a manner consistent with applicable law in the state in which the bank maintains the fund. This report must contain a list of investments in the fund showing the cost and current market value of each investment, and a statement covering the period after the previous report showing the following (organized by type of investment):

(A) A summary of purchases (with costs);

(B) A summary of sales (with profit and loss and any other investment changes);

(C) Income and disbursements; and

(D) An appropriate notation of any investments in default.

(iii) Limitation on representations. A bank may include in the financial report a description of the fund's value on previous

[4]If a fund, the assets of which consist solely of Individual Retirement Accounts, Keogh Accounts, or other employee benefit accounts that are exempt from taxation, is registered under the Investment Company Act of 1940 (15 U.S.C. 80a-1 et seq.), the fund will not be deemed in violation of this paragraph (b)(6)(i) as a result of its compliance with section 10(c) of the Investment Company Act of 1940 (15 U.S.C. 80a-10(c)), if the bank has access to the audit reports of the fund.

dates, as well as its income and disbursements during previous accounting periods. A bank may not publish in the financial report any predictions or representations as to future performance. In addition, with respect to funds described in paragraph (a)(1) of this section, a bank may not publish the performance of individual funds other than those administered by the bank or its affiliates.

(iv) Availability of the report. A bank administering a collective investment ***68558** fund shall provide a copy of the financial report, or shall provide notice that a copy of the report is available upon request without charge, to each person who ordinarily would receive a regular periodic accounting with respect to each participating account. The bank may provide a copy of the financial report to prospective customers. In addition, the bank shall provide a copy of the report upon request to any person for a reasonable charge.

(7) Advertising restriction. A bank may not advertise or publicize any fund authorized under paragraph (a)(1) of this section, except in connection with the advertisement of the general fiduciary services of the bank.

(8) Self-dealing and conflicts of interest. A national bank administering a collective investment fund must comply with the following (in addition to §9.12):

(i) Bank interests. A bank administering a collective investment fund may not have an interest in that fund other than in its fiduciary capacity. If, because of a creditor relationship or otherwise, the bank acquires an interest in a participating account, the participating account must be withdrawn on the next withdrawal date. However, a bank may invest assets that it holds as fiduciary for its own employees in a collective investment fund.

(ii) Loans to participating accounts. A bank administering a collective investment fund may not make any loan on the security of a participant's interest in the fund. An unsecured advance to a fiduciary account participating in the fund until the time of the next valuation date does not constitute the acquisition of an interest in a participating account by the bank.

(iii) Purchase of defaulted investments. A bank administering a collective investment fund may purchase for its own account any defaulted investment held by the fund (in lieu of segregating the investment in accordance with paragraph (b)(5)(v) of this section) if, in the judgement of the bank, the cost of segregating the investment is excessive in light of the market value of the investment. If a bank elects to purchase a defaulted investment, it shall do so at the greater of market value or the sum of cost and accrued unpaid interest.

(9) Management fees. A bank administering a collective investment fund may charge a reasonable fund management fee only if:

(i) The fee is permitted under applicable law (and complies with fee disclosure requirements, if any) in the state in which the bank maintains the fund; and

(ii) The amount of the fee does not exceed an amount commensurate with the value of legitimate services of tangible benefit to the participating fiduciary accounts that would not have been provided to the accounts were they not invested in the fund.

(10) Expenses. A bank administering a collective investment fund may charge reasonable expenses incurred in operating the collective investment fund, to the extent not prohibited by applicable law in the state in which the bank maintains the fund. However, a bank shall absorb the expenses of establishing or reorganizing a collective investment fund.

(11) Prohibition against certificates. A bank administering a collective investment fund may not issue any certificate or other document representing a direct or indirect interest in the fund, except to provide a withdrawing account with an interest in a segregated investment.

(12) Good faith mistakes. The OCC will not deem a bank's mistake made in good faith and in the exercise of due care in connection with the administration of a collective investment fund to be a violation of this part if, promptly after the discovery of the mistake, the bank takes whatever action is practicable under the circumstances to remedy the mistake.

(c) Other collective investments. In addition to the collective investment funds authorized under paragraph (a) of this section, a national bank may collectively invest assets that it holds as fiduciary, to the extent not prohibited by applicable law, as follows:

(1) Single loans or obligations. In the following loans or obligations, if the bank's only interest in the loans or obligations is its capacity as fiduciary:

(i) A single real estate loan, a direct obligation of the United States, or an obligation fully guaranteed by the United States, or a single fixed amount security, obligation, or other property, either real, personal, or mixed, of a single issuer; or

(ii) A variable amount note of a borrower of prime credit, if the bank uses the note solely for investment of funds held in its fiduciary accounts.

(2) Mini-funds. In a fund maintained by the bank for the collective investment of cash balances received or held by a bank in its capacity as trustee, executor, administrator, guardian, or custodian under a uniform gift to minors act, that the bank considers too small to be invested separately to advantage. The total assets in the fund must not exceed $1,000,000 and the number of participating accounts must not exceed 100.

(3) Trust funds of corporations and closely-related settlors. In any investment specifically authorized by the instrument creating the fiduciary account or a court order, in the case of trusts created by a corporation, including its affiliates and subsidiaries, or by several individual settlors who are closely related.

(4) Other authorized funds. In any collective investment authorized by applicable law, such as investments pursuant to a state pre-need funeral statute.

(5) Special exemption funds. In any other manner described by the bank in a written plan approved by the OCC.[5] In order to obtain a special exemption, a bank shall submit to the OCC a written plan that sets forth:

[5]Any institution that must comply with this section in order to receive favorable tax treatment under 26 U.S.C. 584 (namely, any corporate fiduciary) may seek OCC approval of special exemption funds in accordance with this paragraph (c)(5).

(i) The reason that the proposed fund requires a special exemption;

(ii) The provisions of the proposed fund that are inconsistent with paragraphs (a) and (b) of this section;

(iii) The provisions of paragraph (b) of this section for which the bank seeks an exemption; and

(iv) The manner in which the proposed fund addresses the rights and interests of participating accounts.

## §9.20 Transfer agents

(a) The rules adopted by the Securities and Exchange Commission (SEC) pursuant to section 17A of the Securities Exchange Act of 1934 (15 U.S.C. 78q-1) prescribing procedures for registration of transfer agents for which the SEC is the appropriate regulatory agency (17 CFR 240.17Ac2-1) apply to the domestic activities of national bank transfer agents. References to the "Commission" are deemed to refer to the "OCC."

(b) The rules adopted by the SEC pursuant to section 17A of the Securities Exchange Act of 1934 prescribing operational and reporting requirements for transfer agents (17 CFR.17Ac2-2, and 240.17Ad-1 through 240.17Ad-16) apply to the domestic activities of national bank transfer agents.

Interpretations

## §9.100 Acting as indenture trustee and creditor

With respect to a debt securities issuance, a national bank may act both as indenture trustee and as creditor ***68559** until 90 days after default, if the bank maintains adequate controls to manage the potential conflicts of interest.

PART 19 — RULES OF PRACTICE AND PROCEDURE

2. The authority citation for part 19 is revised to read as follows:

Authority: 5 U.S.C. 504, 554-557; 12 U.S.C. 93(b), 164, 505, 1817, 1818, 1820, 1831o, 1972, 3102, 3108(a), 3909 and 4717; 15 U.S.C. 78(h) and (i), 78o-4(c), 78o-5, 78q-1, 78s, 78u, 78u-2, 78u-3, and 78w; 28 U.S.C. 2461 note; 31 U.S.C. 330 and 5321; and 42 U.S.C. 4012a.

3. A new §19.135 is added to subpart E of part 19 to read as follows:

(a) Stays. The rules adopted by the Securities and Exchange Commission (SEC) pursuant to section 19 of the Securities Exchange Act of 1934 (15 U.S.C. 78s) regarding applications by persons for whom the SEC is the appropriate regulatory agency for stays of disciplinary sanctions or summary suspensions imposed by registering clearing agencies (17 CFR 240.19d-2) apply to applications by national banks. References to the "Commission" are deemed to refer to the "OCC."

(b) Reviews. The regulations adopted by the SEC pursuant to section 19 of the Securities Exchange Act of 1934 (15 U.S.C. 78s) regarding applications by persons for whom the SEC is the appropriate regulatory agency for reviews of final disciplinary sanctions, denials of participation, or prohibitions or limitations of access to services imposed by registered clearing agencies (17 CFR 240.19d-3(a)-(f)) apply to applications by national banks. References to the "Commission" are deemed to refer to the "OCC."

Dated: December 23, 1996.
Eugene A. Ludwig,
Comptroller of the Currency.
[FR Doc. 96-32943 Filed 12-27-96; 8:45 am]
BILLING CODE 4810-33-P
61 FR 68543-02, 1996 WL 738150 (F.R.)
END OF DOCUMENT

APPENDIX III

# Form 1041

Form **1041** Department of the Treasury–Internal Revenue Service
**U.S. Income Tax Return for Estates and Trusts** **1997** OMB No. 1545-0092

For calendar year 1997 or fiscal year beginning , 1997, and ending , 19

**A** Type of entity:
- ☐ Decedent's estate
- ☐ Simple trust
- ☐ Complex trust
- ☐ Grantor type trust
- ☐ Bankruptcy estate–Ch. 7
- ☐ Bankruptcy estate–Ch. 11
- ☐ Pooled income fund

**B** Number of Schedules K-1 attached (see instructions) ▶

Name of estate or trust (If a grantor type trust, see page 8 of the instructions.)

Name and title of fiduciary

Number, street, and room or suite no. (If a P.O. box, see page 8 of the instructions.)

City or town, state, and ZIP code

**C** **Employer identification number**

**D** Date entity created

**E** Nonexempt charitable and split-interest trusts, check applicable boxes (see page 10 of the instructions):
- ☐ Described in section 4947(a)(1)
- ☐ Not a private foundation
- ☐ Described in section 4947(a)(2)

**F** Check applicable boxes: ☐ Initial return ☐ Final return ☐ Amended return ☐ Change in fiduciary's name ☐ Change in fiduciary's address

**G** Pooled mortgage account (see page 10 of the instructions): ☐ Bought ☐ Sold Date:

| Section | Line | Description | Line | Amount |
|---|---|---|---|---|
| Income | 1 | Interest income | 1 | |
| | 2 | Dividends | 2 | |
| | 3 | Business income or (loss) (attach Schedule C or C-EZ (Form 1040)) | 3 | |
| | 4 | Capital gain or (loss) (attach Schedule D (Form 1041)) | 4 | |
| | 5 | Rents, royalties, partnerships, other estates and trusts, etc. (attach Schedule E (Form 1040)) | 5 | |
| | 6 | Farm income or (loss) (attach Schedule F (Form 1040)) | 6 | |
| | 7 | Ordinary gain or (loss) (attach Form 4797) | 7 | |
| | 8 | Other income. List type and amount | 8 | |
| | 9 | **Total income.** Combine lines 1 through 8 ▶ | 9 | |
| Deductions | 10 | Interest. Check if Form 4952 is attached ▶ ☐ | 10 | |
| | 11 | Taxes | 11 | |
| | 12 | Fiduciary fees | 12 | |
| | 13 | Charitable deduction (from Schedule A, line 7) | 13 | |
| | 14 | Attorney, accountant, and return preparer fees | 14 | |
| | 15a | Other deductions NOT subject to the 2% floor (attach schedule) | 15a | |
| | b | Allowable miscellaneous itemized deductions subject to the 2% floor | 15b | |
| | 16 | **Total.** Add lines 10 through 15b | 16 | |
| | 17 | Adjusted total income or (loss). Subtract line 16 from line 9. Enter here and on Schedule B, line 1 ▶ | 17 | |
| | 18 | Income distribution deduction (from Schedule B, line 15) (attach Schedules K-1 (Form 1041)) | 18 | |
| | 19 | Estate tax deduction (including certain generation-skipping taxes) (attach computation) | 19 | |
| | 20 | Reserved | 20 | |
| | 21 | Exemption | 21 | |
| | 22 | **Total deductions.** Add lines 18, 19, and 21 ▶ | 22 | |
| Tax and Payments | 23 | Taxable income. Subtract line 22 from line 17. If a loss, see page 14 of the instructions | 23 | |
| | 24 | **Total tax** (from Schedule G, line 8) | 24 | |
| | 25 | **Payments: a** 1997 estimated tax payments and amount applied from 1996 return | 25a | |
| | b | Estimated tax payments allocated to beneficiaries (from Form 1041-T) | 25b | |
| | c | Subtract line 25b from line 25a | 25c | |
| | d | Tax paid with extension of time to file: ☐ Form 2758 ☐ Form 8736 ☐ Form 8800 | 25d | |
| | e | Federal income tax withheld. If any is from Form(s) 1099, check ▶ ☐ | 25e | |
| | | Other payments: **f** Form 2439 ; **g** Form 4136 ; Total ▶ | 25h | |
| | 26 | **Total payments.** Add lines 25c through 25e, and 25h ▶ | 26 | |
| | 27 | Estimated tax penalty (see page 15 of the instructions) | 27 | |
| | 28 | **Tax due.** If line 26 is smaller than the total of lines 24 and 27, enter amount owed | 28 | |
| | 29 | **Overpayment.** If line 26 is larger than the total of lines 24 and 27, enter amount overpaid | 29 | |
| | 30 | Amount of line 29 to be: **a Credited to 1998 estimated tax** ▶ ; **b Refunded** ▶ | 30 | |

**Please Sign Here**

Under penalties of perjury, I declare that I have examined this return, including accompanying schedules and statements, and to the best of my knowledge and belief, it is true, correct, and complete. Declaration of preparer (other than fiduciary) is based on all information of which preparer has any knowledge.

▶ Signature of fiduciary or officer representing fiduciary | Date | ▶ EIN of fiduciary if a financial institution (see page 5 of the instructions)

**Paid Preparer's Use Only**

Preparer's signature ▶ | Date | Check if self-employed ▶ ☐ | **Preparer's social security no.**

Firm's name (or yours if self-employed) and address ▶ | EIN ▶ | ZIP code ▶

**For Paperwork Reduction Act Notice, see the separate instructions.** Cat. No. 11370H Form **1041** (1997)

Form 1041 (1997) Page 2

**Schedule A — Charitable Deduction.** Do not complete for a simple trust or a pooled income fund.

| | | | |
|---|---|---|---|
| 1 | Amounts paid or permanently set aside for charitable purposes from gross income (see page 15) | 1 | |
| 2 | Tax-exempt income allocable to charitable contributions (see page 16 of the instructions) | 2 | |
| 3 | Subtract line 2 from line 1 | 3 | |
| 4 | Capital gains for the tax year allocated to corpus and paid or permanently set aside for charitable purposes | 4 | |
| 5 | Add lines 3 and 4 | 5 | |
| 6 | Section 1202 exclusion allocable to capital gains paid or permanently set aside for charitable purposes (see page 16 of the instructions) | 6 | |
| 7 | **Charitable deduction.** Subtract line 6 from 5. Enter here and on page 1, line 13 | 7 | |

**Schedule B — Income Distribution Deduction**

| | | | |
|---|---|---|---|
| 1 | Adjusted total income (from page 1, line 17) (see page 16 of the instructions) | 1 | |
| 2 | Adjusted tax-exempt interest | 2 | |
| 3 | Total net gain from Schedule D (Form 1041), line 16, column (1) (see page 16 of the instructions) | 3 | |
| 4 | Enter amount from Schedule A, line 4 (reduced by any allocable section 1202 exclusion) | 4 | |
| 5 | Capital gains for the tax year included on Schedule A, line 1 (see page 16 of the instructions) | 5 | |
| 6 | Enter any gain from page 1, line 4, as a negative number. If page 1, line 4, is a loss, enter the loss as a positive number | 6 | |
| 7 | **Distributable net income (DNI).** Combine lines 1 through 6. If zero or less, enter -0- | 7 | |
| 8 | If a complex trust, enter accounting income for the tax year as determined under the governing instrument and applicable local law — 8 | | |
| 9 | Income required to be distributed currently | 9 | |
| 10 | Other amounts paid, credited, or otherwise required to be distributed | 10 | |
| 11 | Total distributions. Add lines 9 and 10. If greater than line 8, see page 17 of the instructions | 11 | |
| 12 | Enter the amount of tax-exempt income included on line 11 | 12 | |
| 13 | Tentative income distribution deduction. Subtract line 12 from line 11 | 13 | |
| 14 | Tentative income distribution deduction. Subtract line 2 from line 7. If zero or less, enter -0- | 14 | |
| 15 | **Income distribution deduction.** Enter the smaller of line 13 or line 14 here and on page 1, line 18 | 15 | |

**Schedule G — Tax Computation** (see page 17 of the instructions)

| | | | | | |
|---|---|---|---|---|---|
| 1 | **Tax:** a ☐ Tax rate schedule or ☐ Schedule D (Form 1041) | 1a | | | |
| | b Other taxes | 1b | | | |
| | c Total. Add lines 1a and 1b ▶ | | | 1c | |
| 2a | Foreign tax credit (attach Form 1116) | 2a | | | |
| b | Check: ☐ Nonconventional source fuel credit ☐ Form 8834 | 2b | | | |
| c | General business credit. Enter here and check which forms are attached: ☐ Form 3800 or ☐ Forms (specify) ▶ | 2c | | | |
| d | Credit for prior year minimum tax (attach Form 8801) | 2d | | | |
| 3 | **Total credits.** Add lines 2a through 2d ▶ | | | 3 | |
| 4 | Subtract line 3 from line 1c | | | 4 | |
| 5 | Recapture taxes. Check if from: ☐ Form 4255 ☐ Form 8611 | | | 5 | |
| 6 | Alternative minimum tax (from Schedule I, line 42) | | | 6 | |
| 7 | Household employment taxes. Attach Schedule H (Form 1040) | | | 7 | |
| 8 | **Total tax.** Add lines 4 through 7. Enter here and on page 1, line 24 ▶ | | | 8 | |

**Other Information**

| | | Yes | No |
|---|---|---|---|
| 1 | Did the estate or trust receive tax-exempt income? If "Yes," attach a computation of the allocation of expenses. Enter the amount of tax-exempt interest income and exempt-interest dividends ▶ $ | | |
| 2 | Did the estate or trust receive all or any part of the earnings (salary, wages, and other compensation) of any individual by reason of a contract assignment or similar arrangement? | | |
| 3 | At any time during calendar year 1997, did the estate or trust have an interest in or a signature or other authority over a bank, securities, or other financial account in a foreign country? See page 19 of the instructions for exceptions and filing requirements for Form TD F 90-22.1. If "Yes," enter the name of the foreign country ▶ | | |
| 4 | During the tax year, did the estate or trust receive a distribution from, or was it the grantor of, or transferor to, a foreign trust? If "Yes," the estate or trust may have to file Form 3520 or 926. See page 19 of the instructions | | |
| 5 | Did the estate or trust receive, or pay, any seller-financed mortgage interest? If "Yes," see page 19 for required attachment | | |
| 6 | If this is an estate or a complex trust making the section 663(b) election, check here (see page 19) ▶ ☐ | | |
| 7 | To make a section 643(e)(3) election, attach Schedule D (Form 1041), and check here (see page 19) ▶ ☐ | | |
| 8 | If the decedent's estate has been open for more than 2 years, check here ▶ ☐ | | |
| 9 | Are any trust beneficiaries skip persons? See page 19 of the instructions | | |

Form 1041 (1997) Page **3**

**Schedule I** **Alternative Minimum Tax** (see pages 19 through 24 of the instructions)

**Part I– Estate's or Trust's Share of Alternative Minimum Taxable Income**

| | | | | | |
|---|---|---|---|---|---|
| 1 | Adjusted total income or (loss) (from page 1, line 17) | | | 1 | |
| 2 | Net operating loss deduction. Enter as a positive amount | | | 2 | |
| 3 | Add lines 1 and 2 | | | 3 | |
| 4 | **Adjustments and tax preference items:** | | | | |
| a | Interest | 4a | | | |
| b | Taxes | 4b | | | |
| c | Miscellaneous itemized deductions (from page 1, line 15b) | 4c | | | |
| d | Refund of taxes | 4d | ( ) | | |
| e | Depreciation of property placed in service after 1986 | 4e | | | |
| f | Circulation and research and experimental expenditures | 4f | | | |
| g | Mining exploration and development costs | 4g | | | |
| h | Long-term contracts entered into after February 28, 1986 | 4h | | | |
| i | Amortization of pollution control facilities | 4i | | | |
| j | Installment sales of certain property | 4j | | | |
| k | Adjusted gain or loss (including incentive stock options) | 4k | | | |
| l | Certain loss limitations | 4l | | | |
| m | Tax shelter farm activities | 4m | | | |
| n | Passive activities | 4n | | | |
| o | Beneficiaries of other trusts or decedent's estates | 4o | | | |
| p | Tax-exempt interest from specified private activity bonds | 4p | | | |
| q | Depletion | 4q | | | |
| r | Accelerated depreciation of real property placed in service before 1987 | 4r | | | |
| s | Accelerated depreciation of leased personal property placed in service before 1987 | 4s | | | |
| t | Intangible drilling costs | 4t | | | |
| u | Other adjustments | 4u | | | |
| 5 | Combine lines 4a through 4u | | | 5 | |
| 6 | Add lines 3 and 5 | | | 6 | |
| 7 | Alternative tax net operating loss deduction (see page 23 of the instructions for limitations) | | | 7 | |
| 8 | Adjusted alternative minimum taxable income. Subtract line 7 from line 6. Enter here and on line 14<br>**Note:** *Complete Part II below before going to line 9.* | | | 8 | |
| 9 | Income distribution deduction from line 28 below | 9 | | | |
| 10 | Estate tax deduction (from page 1, line 19) | 10 | | | |
| 11 | Reserved | 11 | | | |
| 12 | Add lines 9 and 10 | | | 12 | |
| 13 | Estate's or trust's share of alternative minimum taxable income. Subtract line 12 from line 8 | | | 13 | |

If line 13 is:

- $22,500 or less, stop here and enter -0- on Schedule G, line 6. The estate or trust is not liable for the alternative minimum tax.
- Over $22,500, but less than $165,000, go to line 29.
- $165,000 or more, enter the amount from line 13 on line 35 and go to line 36.

**Part II–Income Distribution Deduction on a Minimum Tax Basis**

| | | | |
|---|---|---|---|
| 14 | Adjusted alternative minimum taxable income (from line 8) | 14 | |
| 15 | Adjusted tax-exempt interest (other than amounts included on line 4p) | 15 | |
| 16 | Total net gain from Schedule D (Form 1041), line 16, column (1). If a loss, enter -0- | 16 | |
| 17 | Capital gains for the tax year allocated to corpus and paid or permanently set aside for charitable purposes (from Schedule A, line 4) | 17 | |
| 18 | Capital gains paid or permanently set aside for charitable purposes from gross income (see page 23 of the instructions) | 18 | |
| 19 | Capital gains computed on a minimum tax basis included on line 8 | 19 | ( ) |
| 20 | Capital losses computed on a minimum tax basis included on line 8. Enter as a positive amount | 20 | |
| 21 | Distributable net alternative minimum taxable income (DNAMTI). Combine lines 14 through 20. If zero or less, enter -0- | 21 | |
| 22 | Income required to be distributed currently (from Schedule B, line 9) | 22 | |
| 23 | Other amounts paid, credited, or otherwise required to be distributed (from Schedule B, line 10) | 23 | |
| 24 | Total distributions. Add lines 22 and 23 | 24 | |
| 25 | Tax-exempt income included on line 24 (other than amounts included on line 4p) | 25 | |
| 26 | Tentative income distribution deduction on a minimum tax basis. Subtract line 25 from line 24 | 26 | |
| 27 | Tentative income distribution deduction on a minimum tax basis. Subtract line 15 from line 21. If zero or less, enter -0- | 27 | |
| 28 | **Income distribution deduction on a minimum tax basis.** Enter the smaller of line 26 or line 27. Enter here and on line 9 | 28 | |

# Appendix III

Form 1041 (1997) Page **4**

**Part III– Alternative Minimum Tax**

| Line | Description | Box | Amount | Box | Amount |
|---|---|---|---|---|---|
| 29 | Exemption amount | | | 29 | $22,500 |
| 30 | Enter the amount from line 13 | 30 | | | |
| 31 | Phase-out of exemption amount | 31 | $75,000 | | |
| 32 | Subtract line 31 from line 30. If zero or less, enter -0- | 32 | | | |
| 33 | Multiply line 32 by 25% (.25) | | | 33 | |
| 34 | Subtract line 33 from line 29. If zero or less, enter -0- | | | 34 | |
| 35 | Subtract line 34 from line 30 | | | 35 | |
| 36 | If the estate or trust completed Schedule D (Form 1041) and had an amount on line 24 or 27 (as refigured for the AMT, if necessary), go to Part IV to figure line 36. **All others:** If line 35 is–<br>• $175,000 or less, multiply line 35 by 26% (.26).<br>• Over $175,000, multiply line 35 by 28% (.28) and subtract $3,500 from the result | | | 36 | |
| 37 | Alternative minimum foreign tax credit (see page 24 of instructions) | | | 37 | |
| 38 | Tentative minimum tax. Subtract line 37 from line 36 | | | 38 | |
| 39 | Regular tax before credits (see page 24 of instructions) | 39 | | | |
| 40 | Section 644 tax included on Schedule G, line 1b | 40 | | | |
| 41 | Add lines 39 and 40 | | | 41 | |
| 42 | **Alternative minimum tax.** Subtract line 41 from line 38. If zero or less, enter -0-. Enter here and on Schedule G, line 6 | | | 42 | |

**Part IV– Line 36 Computation Using Maximum Capital Gains Rates**

| Line | Description | Box | Amount | Box | Amount |
|---|---|---|---|---|---|
| 43 | Enter the amount from line 35 | | | 43 | |
| 44 | Enter the amount from Schedule D (Form 1041), line 27 (as refigured for AMT, if necessary) | 44 | | | |
| 45 | Enter the amount from Schedule D (Form 1041), line 24 (as refigured for AMT, if necessary) | 45 | | | |
| 46 | Add lines 44 and 45. If zero or less, enter -0- | 46 | | | |
| 47 | Enter the amount from Schedule D (Form 1041), line 21 (as refigured for AMT, if necessary) | 47 | | | |
| 48 | Enter the **smaller** of line 46 or line 47 | | | 48 | |
| 49 | Subtract line 48 from line 43. If zero or less, enter -0- | | | 49 | |
| 50 | If line 49 is $175,000 or less, multiply line 49 by 26% (.26). Otherwise, multiply line 49 by 28% (.28) and subtract $3,500 from the result ▶ | | | 50 | |
| 51 | Enter the amount from Schedule D (Form 1041), line 36 (as figured for the regular tax) | | | 51 | |
| 52 | Enter the **smallest** of line 43, line 44, or line 51 | | | 52 | |
| 53 | Multiply line 52 by 10% (.10) ▶ | | | 53 | |
| 54 | Enter the **smaller** of line 43 or line 44 | | | 54 | |
| 55 | Enter the amount from line 52 | | | 55 | |
| 56 | Subtract line 55 from line 54. If zero or less, enter -0- | | | 56 | |
| 57 | Multiply line 56 by 20% (.20) ▶ | | | 57 | |
| 58 | Enter the amount from line 43 | | | 58 | |
| 59 | Add lines 49, 52, and 56 | | | 59 | |
| 60 | Subtract line 59 from line 58 | | | 60 | |
| 61 | Multiply line 60 by 25% (.25) ▶ | | | 61 | |
| 62 | Add lines 50, 53, 57, and 61 | | | 62 | |
| 63 | If line 43 is $175,000 or less, multiply line 43 by 26% (.26). Otherwise, multiply line 43 by 28% (.28) and subtract $3,500 from the result | | | 63 | |
| 64 | Enter the **smaller** of line 62 or line 63 here and on line 36 ▶ | | | 64 | |

**SCHEDULE D (Form 1041)**

Department of the Treasury
Internal Revenue Service

# Capital Gains and Losses

► Attach to Form 1041 (or Form 5227). See the separate instructions for Form 1041 (or Form 5227).

OMB No. 1545-0092

**1997**

Name of estate or trust | **Employer identification number**

**Note:** *Form 5227 filers need to complete ONLY Parts I and II.*

## Part I Short-Term Capital Gains and Losses–Assets Held One Year or Less

| (a) Description of property (Example, 100 shares 7% preferred of "Z" Co.) | (b) Date acquired (mo., day, yr.) | (c) Date sold (mo., day, yr.) | (d) Sales price | (e) Cost or other basis (see page 26) | (f) Gain or (loss) for entire year. (col. (d) less col. (e)) |
|---|---|---|---|---|---|
| 1 | | | | | |
| | | | | | |
| | | | | | |
| | | | | | |
| | | | | | |
| | | | | | |

| | | |
|---|---|---|
| 2 Short-term capital gain or (loss) from Forms 4684, 6252, 6781, and 8824 | 2 | |
| 3 Net short-term gain or (loss) from partnerships, S corporations, and other estates or trusts | 3 | |
| 4 Short-term capital loss carryover from 1996 Schedule D, line 28 | 4 | ( ) |
| 5 **Net short-term gain or (loss).** Combine lines 1 through 4 in column (f). Enter here and on line 14 below ► | 5 | |

## Part II Long-Term Capital Gains and Losses–Assets Held More Than One Year

| (a) Description of property (Example, 100 shares 7% preferred of "Z" Co.) | (b) Date acquired (mo., day, yr.) | (c) Date sold (mo., day, yr.) | (d) Sales price | (e) Cost or other basis (see page 26) | (f) Gain or (loss) for entire year. (col. (d) less col. (e)) | (g) 28% rate gain or (loss) *(see instr. below) |
|---|---|---|---|---|---|---|
| 6 | | | | | | |
| | | | | | | |
| | | | | | | |
| | | | | | | |
| | | | | | | |
| | | | | | | |

| | | | |
|---|---|---|---|
| 7 Long-term capital gain or (loss) from Forms 2439, 4684, 6252, 6781, and 8824 | 7 | | |
| 8 Net long-term gain or (loss) from partnerships, S corporations, and other estates or trusts | 8 | | |
| 9 Capital gain distributions | 9 | | |
| 10 Gain from Form 4797, Part I | 10 | | |
| 11 Long-term capital loss carryover. Enter in both columns (f) and (g) the amount, if any, from 1996 Schedule D, line 35 | 11 | ( ) | ( ) |
| 12 Combine lines 6 through 11 in column (g) | 12 | | |
| 13 **Net long-term gain or (loss).** Combine lines 6 through 11 in column (f). Enter here and on line 15 below ► | 13 | | |

***28% rate gain or (loss)** includes all gains and losses in Part II, column (f) from sales, exchanges, or conversions (including installment payments received) **either:**

- **Before** May 7, 1997, **or**
- **After** July 28, 1997, for assets held more than 1 year but **not** more than 18 months.

It also includes **ALL** "collectibles gains and losses" (as defined on page 26 of the instructions) and the taxable gain (but not more than the section 1202 exclusion) on the sale or exchange of qualified small business stock.

## Part III Summary of Parts I and II

| | | (1) Beneficiaries' (see page 27) | (2) Estate's or trust's | (3) Total |
|---|---|---|---|---|
| 14 **Net short-term gain or (loss)** (from line 5 above) | 14 | | | |
| 15 **Net long-term gain or (loss):** | | | | |
| a 28% rate gain or (loss) (from line 12 above) | 15a | | | |
| b Unrecaptured section 1250 gain (see page 27 of the instructions) | 15b | | | |
| c Total for year (from line 13 above) | 15c | | | |
| 16 **Total net gain or (loss).** Combine lines 14 and 15c ► | 16 | | | |

**Note:** *If line 16, column (3), is a net gain, enter the gain on Form 1041, line 4. If lines 15c and 16, column (2) are net gains, go to Part V, and DO NOT complete Part IV. If line 16, column (3), is a net loss, complete Part IV and the* ***Capital Loss Carryover Worksheet,*** *as necessary.*

**For Paperwork Reduction Act Notice, see the Instructions for Form 1041.** Cat. No. 11376V **Schedule D (Form 1041) 1997**

Schedule D (Form 1041) 1997 Page **2**

**Part IV** **Capital Loss Limitation**

17 Enter here and enter as a (loss) on Form 1041, line 4, the **smaller** of:
  a The loss on line 16, column (3); **or**
  b $3,000 . . . . . . . . . . . . . . . . . . . . . . . . . . . . | 17 | ( )

*If the loss on line 16, column (3) is more than $3,000, OR if Form 1041, page 1, line 23, is a loss, complete the* ***Capital Loss Carryover Worksheet*** *on page 27 of the instructions to determine your capital loss carryover.*

**Part V** **Tax Computation Using Maximum Capital Gains Rates** (Complete this part **only** if both lines 15c and 16 in column (2) are gains, and Form 1041, line 23 is more than zero.)

| | | | | |
|---|---|---|---|---|
| 18 | Enter taxable income from Form 1041, line 23. | | 18 | |
| 19 | Enter the **smaller** of line 15c or 16 in column (2). | 19 | | |
| 20 | If you are filing Form 4952, enter the amount from Form 4952, line 4e | 20 | | |
| 21 | Subtract line 20 from line 19. If zero or less, enter -0- | 21 | | |
| 22 | Combine lines 14 and 15a, column (2). If zero or less, enter -0- | 22 | | |
| 23 | Enter the **smaller** of line 15a, column (2), or line 22, but not less than zero | 23 | | |
| 24 | Enter the amount from line 15b, column (2). | 24 | | |
| 25 | Reserved | 25 | | |
| 26 | Add lines 23 and 24 | 26 | | |
| 27 | Subtract line 26 from line 21. If zero or less, enter -0- | | 27 | |
| 28 | Subtract line 27 from line 18. If zero or less, enter -0- | | 28 | |
| 29 | Enter the **smaller** of line 18 or $1,650 | | 29 | |
| 30 | Enter the **smaller** of line 28 or line 29 | | 30 | |
| 31 | Subtract line 21 from line 18. If zero or less, enter -0- | | 31 | |
| 32 | Enter the **larger** of line 30 or line 31 | | 32 | |
| 33 | Tax on amount on line 32 from the 1997 Tax Rate Schedule ► | | 33 | |
| 34 | Enter the amount from line 29 | | 34 | |
| 35 | Enter the amount from line 28 | | 35 | |
| 36 | Subtract line 35 from line 34. If zero or less, enter -0- | | 36 | |
| 37 | Multiply line 36 by 10% (.10) ► | | 37 | |
| 38 | Enter the **smaller** of line 18 or line 27 | | 38 | |
| 39 | Enter the amount from line 36. | | 39 | |
| 40 | Subtract line 39 from line 38. If zero or less, enter -0- | | 40 | |
| 41 | Multiply line 40 by 20% (.20) ► | | 41 | |
| 42 | Enter the **smaller** of line 21 or line 24 | | 42 | |
| 43 | Add lines 21 and 32 | 43 | | |
| 44 | Enter the amount from line 18 | 44 | | |
| 45 | Subtract line 44 from line 43. If zero or less, enter -0- | | 45 | |
| 46 | Subtract line 45 from line 42. If zero or less, enter -0- | | 46 | |
| 47 | Multiply line 46 by 25% (.25) ► | | 47 | |
| 48 | Enter the amount from line 18 | | 48 | |
| 49 | Add lines 32, 36, 40, and 46 | | 49 | |
| 50 | Subtract line 49 from line 48 | | 50 | |
| 51 | Multiply line 50 by 28% (.28) ► | | 51 | |
| 52 | Add lines 33, 37, 41, 47, and 51 | | 52 | |
| 53 | Tax on the amount on line 18 from the 1997 Tax Rate Schedule | | 53 | |
| 54 | **Tax.** Enter the **smaller** of line 52 or line 53 here and on line 1a of Schedule G, Form 1041. ► | | 54 | |

**SCHEDULE J (Form 1041)**

Department of the Treasury
Internal Revenue Service

# Accumulation Distribution for a Complex Trust

▶ **File with Form 1041.**

▶ **See the separate Form 1041 instructions.**

OMB No. 1545-0092

**1997**

Name of trust

**Employer identification number**

**Part I** **Accumulation Distribution in 1997**

**Note:** *See the Form 4970 instructions for certain income that minors may exclude and special rules for multiple trusts.*

| | | | | |
|---|---|---|---|---|
| 1 | Other amounts paid, credited, or otherwise required to be distributed for 1997 (from Schedule B of Form 1041, line 10) | | 1 | |
| 2 | Distributable net income for 1997 (from Schedule B of Form 1041, line 7) | 2 | | |
| 3 | Income required to be distributed currently for 1997 (from Schedule B of Form 1041, line 9) | 3 | | |
| 4 | Subtract line 3 from line 2. If zero or less, enter -0- | | 4 | |
| 5 | Accumulation distribution for 1997. Subtract line 4 from line 1 | | 5 | |

**Part II** **Ordinary Income Accumulation Distribution** (Enter the applicable throwback years below.)

| **Note:** *If the distribution is thrown back to more than five years (starting with the earliest applicable tax year beginning after 1968), attach additional schedules. (If the trust was a simple trust, see Regulations section 1.665(e)-1A(b).)* | | **Throwback year ending** 19 ----- | **Throwback year ending** 19 ----- | **Throwback year ending** 19 ----- | **Throwback year ending** 19 ----- | **Throwback year ending** 19 ----- |
|---|---|---|---|---|---|---|
| 6 Distributable net income (see page 28 of the instructions) | 6 | | | | | |
| 7 Distributions (see page 28 of the instructions) | 7 | | | | | |
| 8 Subtract line 7 from line 6 | 8 | | | | | |
| 9 Enter amount from page 2, line 25 or line 31, as applicable | 9 | | | | | |
| 10 Undistributed net income Subtract line 9 from line 8 | 10 | | | | | |
| 11 Enter amount of prior accumulation distributions thrown back to any of these years | 11 | | | | | |
| 12 Subtract line 11 from line 10 | 12 | | | | | |
| 13 Allocate the amount on line 5 to the earliest applicable year first. Do not allocate an amount greater than line 12 for the same year (see page 28 of the instructions) | 13 | | | | | |
| 14 Divide line 13 by line 10 and multiply result by amount on line 9 | 14 | | | | | |
| 15 Add lines 13 and 14 | 15 | | | | | |
| 16 Tax-exempt interest included on line 13 (see page 28 of the instructions) | 16 | | | | | |
| 17 Subtract line 16 from line 15 | 17 | | | | | |

**For Paperwork Reduction Act Notice, see page 1 of the Instructions for Form 1041.** Cat. No. 11382Z **Schedule J (Form 1041) 1997**

Schedule J (Form 1041) 1997 Page **2**

**Part III** **Taxes Imposed on Undistributed Net Income** (Enter the applicable throwback years below.) (see page 26 of the instructions)

**Note:** *If more than five throwback years are involved, attach additional schedules. If the trust received an accumulation distribution from another trust, see Regulations section 1.665(d)-1A.*

| If the trust elected the alternative tax on capital gains (repealed for tax years beginning after 1978), **SKIP** lines 18 through 25 and **COMPLETE** lines 26 through 31. | | **Throwback year ending** 19 ----- | **Throwback year ending** 19 ------ | **Throwback year ending** 19 ----- | **Throwback year ending** 19 ----- | **Throwback year ending** 19 ------ |
|---|---|---|---|---|---|---|
| **18** Regular tax | **18** | | | | | |
| **19** Trust's share of net short-term gain . . . | **19** | | | | | |
| **20** Trust's share of net long-term gain. . . . . . . | **20** | | | | | |
| **21** Add lines 19 and 20. . . | **21** | | | | | |
| **22** Taxable income . . . | **22** | | | | | |
| **23** Enter percent. Divide line 21 by line 22, but do not enter more than 100% . . . | **23** | % | % | % | % | % |
| **24** Multiply line 18 by the percentage on line 23. . | **24** | | | | | |
| **25** Tax on undistributed net income. Subtract line 24 from line 18. Enter here and on page 1, line 9. . . . | **25** | | | | | |
| **Do not** complete lines 26 through 31 unless the trust elected the alternative tax on long-term capital gain. | | | | | | |
| **26** Tax on income other than long-term capital gain . | **26** | | | | | |
| **27** Trust's share of net short-term gain . . . | **27** | | | | | |
| **28** Trust's share of taxable income less section 1202 deduction. . . . | **28** | | | | | |
| **29** Enter percent. Divide line 27 by line 28, but do not enter more than 100% . . . | **29** | % | % | % | % | % |
| **30** Multiply line 26 by the percentage on line 29. . | **30** | | | | | |
| **31** Tax on undistributed net income. Subtract line 30 from line 26. Enter here and on page 1, line 9 . . . | **31** | | | | | |

**Part IV** **Allocation to Beneficiary**

**Note:** *Be sure to complete **Form 4970,** Tax on Accumulation Distribution of Trusts.*

| Beneficiary's name | | | Identifying number | |
|---|---|---|---|---|
| Beneficiary's address (number and street including apartment number or P.O. box)<br>City, state, and ZIP code | | **(a)** This beneficiary's share of line 13 | **(b)** This beneficiary's share of line 14 | **(c)** This beneficiary's share of line 16 |
| **32** Throwback year 19 ---- . . . . . . . . . . . | **32** | | | |
| **33** Throwback year 19 ---- . . . . . . . . . . . | **33** | | | |
| **34** Throwback year 19 ---- . . . . . . . . . . . | **34** | | | |
| **35** Throwback year 19 ---- . . . . . . . . . . . | **35** | | | |
| **36** Throwback year 19 ---- . . . . . . . . . . . | **36** | | | |
| **37** Total. Add lines 32 through 36. Enter here and on the appropriate lines of Form 4970. . . . . . . . . | **37** | | | |

**SCHEDULE K-1 (Form 1041)**

Department of the Treasury
Internal Revenue Service

# Beneficiary's Share of Income, Deductions, Credits, etc.

**for the calendar year 1997, or fiscal year**

**beginning ----------, 1997, ending ----------, 19 -----**

**► Complete a separate Schedule K-1 for each beneficiary.**

OMB No. 1545-0092

**1997**

Name of trust or decedent's estate

☐ Amended K-1
☐ Final K-1

**Beneficiary's identifying number ►**

**Estate's or trust's EIN ►**

Beneficiary's name, address, and ZIP code

Fiduciary's name, address, and ZIP code

| **(a)** Allocable share item | | **(b)** Amount | **(c)** Calendar year 1997 Form 1040 filers enter the amounts in column (b) on: |
|---|---|---|---|
| 1 Interest | 1 | | Schedule B, Part I, line 1 |
| 2 Dividends | 2 | | Schedule B, Part II, line 5 |
| 3 Net short-term capital gain | 3 | | Schedule D, line 5 |
| 4 Net long-term capital gain: a 28% rate gain | 4a | | Schedule D, line 12, column (g) |
| b Unrecaptured section 1250 gain | 4b | | See the instructions for Schedule D, line 25 |
| c Total for year | 4c | | Schedule D, line 12, column (f) |
| 5a Annuities, royalties, and other nonpassive income before directly apportioned deductions | 5a | | Schedule E, Part III, column (f) |
| b Depreciation | 5b | | Include on the applicable line of the appropriate tax form |
| c Depletion | 5c | | |
| d Amortization | 5d | | |
| 6a Trade or business, rental real estate, and other rental income before directly apportioned deductions (see instructions) | 6a | | Schedule E, Part III |
| b Depreciation | 6b | | Include on the applicable line of the appropriate tax form |
| c Depletion | 6c | | |
| d Amortization | 6d | | |
| 7 Income for minimum tax purposes | 7 | | |
| 8 Income for regular tax purposes (add lines 1, 2, 3, 4c, 5a, and 6a) | 8 | | |
| 9 Adjustment for minimum tax purposes (subtract line 8 from line 7) | 9 | | Form 6251, line 12 |
| 10 Estate tax deduction (including certain generation-skipping transfer taxes) | 10 | | Schedule A, line 27 |
| 11 Foreign taxes | 11 | | Form 1116 or Schedule A (Form 1040), line 8 |
| 12 Adjustments and tax preference items (itemize): | | | |
| a Accelerated depreciation | 12a | | Include on the applicable line of Form 6251 |
| b Depletion | 12b | | |
| c Amortization | 12c | | |
| d Exclusion items | 12d | | 1998 Form 8801 |
| 13 Deductions in the final year of trust or decedent's estate: | | | |
| a Excess deductions on termination (see instructions) | 13a | | Schedule A, line 22 |
| b Short-term capital loss carryover | 13b | ( ) | Schedule D, line 5 |
| c Long-term capital loss carryover | 13c | ( ) | Schedule D, line 12, columns (f) and (g) |
| d Net operating loss (NOL) carryover for regular tax purposes | 13d | ( ) | Form 1040, line 21 |
| e NOL carryover for minimum tax purposes | 13e | | See the instructions for Form 6251, line 20 |
| f ---------------------------------------- | 13f | | Include on the applicable line of the appropriate tax form |
| g | 13g | | |
| 14 Other (itemize): | | | |
| a Payments of estimated taxes credited to you | 14a | | Form 1040, line 55 |
| b Tax-exempt interest | 14b | | Form 1040, line 8b |
| c ---------------------------------------- | 14c | | Include on the applicable line of the appropriate tax form |
| d ---------------------------------------- | 14d | | |
| e ---------------------------------------- | 14e | | |
| f ---------------------------------------- | 14f | | |
| g ---------------------------------------- | 14g | | |
| h | 14h | | |

**For Paperwork Reduction Act Notice, see the Instructions for Form 1041.** Cat. No. 11380D **Schedule K-1 (Form 1041) 1997**

# Instructions for Beneficiary Filing Form 1040

**Note:** *The fiduciary's instructions for completing Schedule K-1 are in the Instructions for Form 1041.*

## General Instructions

### Purpose of Form

The fiduciary of a trust or decedent's estate uses Schedule K-1 to report your share of the trust's or estate's income, credits, deductions, etc. **Keep it for your records. Do not file it with your tax return.** A copy has been filed with the IRS.

### Inconsistent Treatment of Items

Generally, you must report items shown on your Schedule K-1 (and any attached schedules) the same way that the estate or trust treated the items on its return.

If the treatment on your original or amended return is inconsistent with the estate's or trust's treatment, or if the estate or trust was required to but has not filed a return, you must file **Form 8082,** Notice of Inconsistent Treatment or Administrative Adjustment Request (AAR), with your original or amended return to identify and explain any inconsistency (or to note that an estate or trust return has not been filed).

If you are required to file Form 8082 but fail to do so, you may be subject to the accuracy-related penalty. This penalty is in addition to any tax that results from making your amount or treatment of the item consistent with that shown on the estate's or trust's return. Any deficiency that results from making the amounts consistent may be assessed immediately.

### Errors

If you believe the fiduciary has made an error on your Schedule K-1, notify the fiduciary and ask for an amended or a corrected Schedule K-1. **Do not** change any items on your copy. Be sure that the fiduciary sends a copy of the amended Schedule K-1 to the IRS. **If you are unable to reach agreement with the fiduciary regarding the inconsistency, you must file Form 8082.**

### Tax Shelters

If you receive a copy of **Form 8271,** Investor Reporting of Tax Shelter Registration Number, see the instructions for Form 8271 to determine your reporting requirements.

### Beneficiaries of Generation-Skipping Trusts

If you received **Form 706-GS(D-1),** Notification of Distribution From a Generation-Skipping Trust, and paid a generation-skipping transfer (GST) tax on **Form 706-GS(D),** Generation-Skipping Transfer Tax Return for Distributions, you can deduct the GST tax paid on income distributions on Schedule A (Form 1040), line 8. To figure the deduction, see the instructions for Form 706-GS(D).

## Specific Instructions

### Lines 3 and 4

If there is an attachment to this Schedule K-1 reporting a disposition of a passive activity, see the instructions for **Form 8582,** Passive Activity Loss Limitations, for information on the treatment of dispositions of interests in a passive activity.

### Lines 6b through 6d

The deductions on lines 6b through 6d may be subject to the passive loss limitations of Internal Revenue Code section 469, which generally limits deductions from passive activities to the income from those activities. The rules for applying these limitations to beneficiaries have not yet been issued. For more details, see **Pub. 925,** Passive Activity and At-Risk Rules.

### Line 12d

If you pay alternative minimum tax in 1997, the amount on line 12d will help you figure any minimum tax credit for 1998. See the 1998 **Form 8801,** Credit for Prior Year Minimum Tax–Individuals, Estates, and Trusts, for more information.

### Line 14a

To figure any underpayment and penalty on **Form 2210,** Underpayment of Estimated Tax by Individuals, Estates, and Trusts, treat the amount entered on line 14a as an estimated tax payment made on January 15, 1998.

### Lines 14c through 14h

The amount of gross farming and fishing income is included on line 6a. This income is also separately stated on line 14 to help you determine if you are subject to a penalty for underpayment of estimated tax. Report the amount of gross farming and fishing income on Schedule E (Form 1040), line 41.

# TABLE OF CASES

*References are to sections.*

## Table of Cases

# TABLE OF RESTATEMENTS

*References are to sections.*

## RESTATEMENT (THIRD) OF TRUSTS

# TABLE OF UNIFORM ACTS

*References are to sections.*

# INDEX

*References are to sections.*

# Index

# Index

## Index

## Index

# Index